Continental Divides

Continental Divides

Remapping the Cultures of North America

RACHEL ADAMS

The University of Chicago Press
Chicago and London

Rachel Adams teaches English and American Studies at Columbia University and is the author of *Sideshow U.S.A.: Freaks and the American Cultural Imagination* (2001), also published by the University of Chicago Press.

The University of Chicago Press, Chicago 60637
The University of Chicago Press, Ltd., London
© 2009 by The University of Chicago
All rights reserved. Published 2009
Printed in the United States of America

18 17 16 15 14 13 12 11 10 09   1 2 3 4 5
ISBN-13: 978-0-226-00551-5 (cloth)
ISBN-13: 978-0-226-00552-2 (paper)
ISBN-10: 0-226-00551-8 (cloth)
ISBN-10: 0-226-00552-6 (paper)

Library of Congress Cataloging-in-Publication Data

Adams, Rachel, 1968–
    Continental divides : remapping the cultures of North America / Rachel
    Adams.
        p. cm.
    Includes bibliographical references and index.
    ISBN-13: 978-0-226-00551-5 (hardcover : alk. paper)
    ISBN-13: 978-0-226-0552-2 (pbk. : alk. paper)
    ISBN-10: 0-226-00551-8 (hardcover : alk. paper)
    ISBN-10: 0-226-00552-6 (pbk. : alk. paper)   1. North America—Civiliza-
    tion. 2. Cultural geography—North America. 3. Transnationalism. I. Title.
E40.A33 2009
970—dc22

                                                              2009002364
♾ The paper used in this publication meets the minimum requirements of the American National Standard for Information Sciences—Permanence of Paper for Printed Library Materials, ANSI Z39.48-1992.

CONTENTS

ILLUSTRATIONS

ACKNOWLEDGMENTS

Anyone who knows me well is aware that I get lost easily. I have no intuitive sense of direction and am no good at reading maps. This book is an attempt to reorient myself in relation to fields that I've always found difficult to navigate. I take this opportunity to thank the many people who helped me to find my way.

My thanks begin and end with Jon Connolly, whose kindness, wisdom, and generosity made it possible for me to write this book. I've had the good fortune to find friendship and inspiration among my students and colleagues at Columbia University and Barnard College, in particular, Kelly Barry, Chris Brown, Amanda Claybaugh, Sarah Cole, Julie Crawford, Jenny Davidson, Andy Delbanco, Ann Douglas, Hilary Hallet, Jean Howard, Elizabeth Hutchinson, Nicole Marwell, Monica Miller, Ross Posnock, Martin Puchner, Sandhya Shukla, Maura Spiegel, Ezra Tawil, and Carl Wennerlind. I thank Angela Darling, Joy Hayton, and the staff of the English Department for the administrative support that allowed me to get my work done. I am also indebted to Jason Earle for help with French translations, and to my capable research assistants Bärbel Höttges, Marianna Macri, and Matia Barnett. I cannot imagine a better editor than Alan Thomas, who urged me to finish with just the right combination of severity and understanding. His associate, Randy Petilos, provided help at many stages of writing and production.

Many colleagues in American studies offered me their friendship and congenial environments for exchanging ideas, sharing work, and navigating the profession. I am especially grateful to Sara Blair, Anna Mae Duane, Paul Giles, Tim Gray, Andy Hoberek, Amy Hungerford, Valerie Karno, Jonathan Levin, Jean Lutes, Cyrus Patell, Ben Reiss, Rosemarie Garland-Thompson, and Liza Yukins. I thank colleagues in Canadian and Latin American studies for welcoming me in: Sarah Casteel, Ruth Hill, Claire Fox, Robert Irwin, Maureen Moynaugh, Heidi Tinsman, and Eric Zolov. Portions of this manuscript benefited from the thoughtful and generous feedback of Daniel Belgrad, Amanda Claybaugh, Jean-Christophe Cloutier, Wai-Chee Dimock, Shari Hundorf, Gordon Hutner, Caroline Levander, Bob Levine, Jean Lutes, John Muthyala, Claudia Sadowski-Smith, Sandhya Shukla, and Heidi Tinsman. For many years of stimulating argument and conversation, I thank the participants in the New York and Southern California Americanist groups, especially Mary Esteve, Amy Hungerford, Michael Szalay, and Sean McCann. My thinking was also enabled by opportunities to present my work at UCLA, Yale, Stanford, Columbia, Indiana, and Rice universities; the Columbia University seminar on American Studies; panels at MLA and ASA conventions; and ACLA seminars led by Nancy Ruttenberg, Pericles Lewis, and Sarah Casteel. The late stages of my work on this book benefited from the lively conversations that took place in my NEH seminar, "Toward a Hemispheric American Literature." Marissa López, Daniel Cooper Alarcon, Monika Giacoppe, and John Gruesser deserve special mention for offering advice and challenges that enhanced my thinking, as did my co-chair, Caroline Levander, and our visiting faculty, Robert Irwin, Ralph Bauer, Guillermo Verdecchia, and Michelle Stephens.

Some of this book was written during a fellowship at UCLA's International Institute, under the energetic direction of Ron Rogowski. I thank my colleagues there, and in the UCLA English Department, for their companionship that year. The costs of production were generously subsidized by contributions from Columbia's American Studies Program and University Seminars. Portions of this book have appeared elsewhere and I thank the original publishers for permission to reprint. Sections of chapter 2 were included in my essay "Blackness Goes South: Race and *mestizaje* in Our America," which appeared in *Imagining Our Americas: Toward a Transnational Frame*, edited by Sandhya Shukla and Heidi Tinsman, pp. 214–48 (Duke University Press, 2007). Copyright © 2007, Duke University Press, all rights reserved. Reprinted with permission of the publisher. Sections of chapter 4 were included in my essay "Hipsters and *jipitecas*: Literary Countercultures on Both Sides of the Border," which appeared in *American Literary History* 16, no. 1 (2004): 58–84. Copyright © 2004 by Oxford University Press. Published by Oxford University Press. All rights reserved. Sections of chapter 5 were included in my essay "Detecting the Continent: Crime Fiction from the U.S. and Mexico," which appeared in *Shades of the Planet: American Literature as World Literature*, edited by Laurence Buell and Wai-Chee Dimock (Princeton University Press, 2007), pp. 249–73. Copyright

© 2007 by Princeton University Press. Reprinted by permission of Princeton University Press. And an earlier version of chapter 6, "The Northern Borderlands and Latino Canadian Diaspora," was included in *Hemispheric American Studies*, edited by Caroline F. Levander and Robert Levine (Rutgers University Press, 2007), pp. 313–27. Copyright © 2008 by Rutgers, The State University. Reprinted by permission of Rutgers University Press.

While I was writing this book, two remarkable women passed from my life. I take this occasion to remember my dear friend Shaindy Rudoff, who dazzled me with her wit and brilliance, and my beloved godmother Diane Kovacs, who kept me anchored to family and home. I thank my family and extended family—Adams, Connolly, Kovacs, and Cray—for believing that I could get this project done, even when I didn't. My work on the book was joyfully interrupted by the arrival of my sons, Noah and Henry, who fill our days with laughter and bless us with quiet nights. I could not have finished it without the people who help me to care for them and I am deeply grateful to Angela Grullón, Peggy Sradnick, Joy Harden, and the rest of the staff at the Basic Trust. And finally, I return to Jon Connolly, my partner, collaborator, best editor, and best friend. He makes all of this worthwhile and this book is dedicated to him.

Imagining North America

Maps aren't just guides to the world as we know it; they can also be projections of the way we desire or fear it to be. Take, for instance, the map on the cover of Joel Garreau's influential 1981 bestseller *The Nine Nations of North America*, which depicts a constellation of imaginary "nations" that, he argues, more accurately represent actual economic and social conditions on the continent (fig. 0.1). Having toured North America, met with representative residents, and studied its industries and markets, Garreau believed he was witnessing the effective dissolution of vast nation-states into smaller and more cohesive regional entities. For example, he observed that affairs in the nation of "Mexamerica" were managed through collaboration between local officials from the United States and Mexico, who operated in virtual autonomy from their respective national governments. Similar cross-border relations characterized the region of "Ecotopia," where residents of the Pacific northwestern United States and Canada shared lifestyles and values that made them more like one another than fellow citizens living elsewhere on the continent. Although Garreau claims to have produced a map that better reflects existing realities, his perceptions are filtered through a wishful fantasy about the triumph of local communities over national government. Twenty-first-century readers who have witnessed the implementation of Nafta and post-9/11 debates about North American security might find such longings to be quaint and outdated. At the same time, Garreau's study continues to be a compelling reminder of the power of maps to reframe our knowledge of familiar places. Their contours orient us in space. Borders guide us in making distinctions between self and other, insiders and outsiders, the foreign and the domestic. When they are redrawn, unexpected things start to happen.

The Nine Nations of North America is part of a long tradition in which

JOEL GARREAU

The NINE NATIONS of NORTH AMERICA

0.1. The cover of Joel Garreau's 1981 bestseller, *The Nine Nations of North America*. Of particular interest are "The Empty Quarter," "Ecotopia," and "Mexamerica," which span the borders of the continent's current nation-states.

maps of the continent have reflected the hopes and anxieties of their creators. The first Europeans in the New World gave form to the contours of the terra incognita they had encountered with fantastical illustrations designed to beguile and entice their compatriots back home. Once the outlines of North America were firmly established, armchair cartographers began to play with its familiar boundaries, questioning the authority of the social and political landscapes the map so confidently represented. The production of counterfactual geographies can be a tactic for challenging received understandings of history and imagining alternative futures. In the twentieth century, we see this process at work in maps of the imaginary territories of Cascadia and Aztlán, which reflect longings for transnational communities with a shared sense of history and political purpose strong enough to override the current configuration of nation-states. Residents of Cascadia (an area roughly contiguous with Garreau's Ecotopia) imagine seceding from Canada and the United States to form an autonomous political entity (fig. 0.2). United by their disaffection with the nation-state, Cascadians run the gamut from leftists dedicated to conserving the environment and local culture, to more right-wing proponents interested in the economic benefits of an open border.[1] The map of Aztlán bespeaks similar desires for regional filiation in its depiction of a Chicano nation extending across much of the southwestern United States. Driven by the ethnic nationalisms of the 1960s and 1970s, Chicano activists appropriated the name Aztlán, which refers to the Aztecs' mythical homeland, to describe the territory ceded to the United States at the end of the Mexican-American War (fig. 0.3). Under its banner, they sought to consolidate a burgeoning sense of Chicano identity and draw attention to the longstanding presence of Mexicans within what is now the United States.[2] In the case of both Aztlán and Cascadia, the political energies of a regional constituency are galvanized by the imagination of an alternative national community.

These maps anticipate the burst of cartographic revisionism that took place in the aftermath of the 2004 U.S. presidential election. As Democrats lamented the narrow victory of George W. Bush, they used maps to try to gain an understanding of voter demographics beyond the conventional division into red and blue states. While some of these maps were quite serious, others took a more satirical bent, such as the various "Jesusland" maps that circulated among left-leaning Internet users who felt that Christian conservatives had hijacked the nation. One version divides the continent into two nations, "The United States of Canada"—encompassing Canada and the Democratic regions along the United States' Pacific Coast, northern Midwest, and Northeast—and "Jesusland"—encompassing

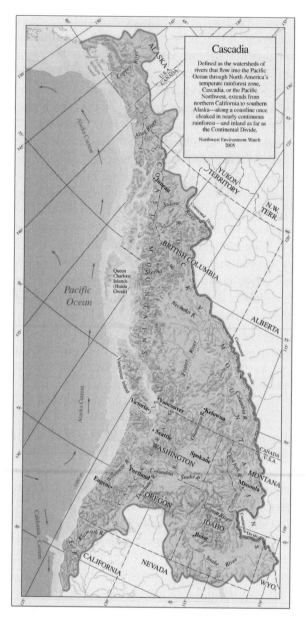

Cascadia

Defined as the watersheds of rivers that flow into the Pacific Ocean through North America's temperate rainforest zone, Cascadia, or the Pacific Northwest, extends from northern California to southern Alaska—along a coastline once cloaked in nearly continuous rainforest—and inland as far as the Continental Divide.

Northwest Environment Watch
2005

0.2. Cynthia Thomas, "Cascadia." Some residents of this region fantasize about seceding from the United States and Canada to form an independent republic. Based on data from *Costal Temperate Rain Forests of North America* (Portland: Conservation International, Ecotrust, and Pacific GIS, 1995). Reprinted by permission of the Sightline Institute.

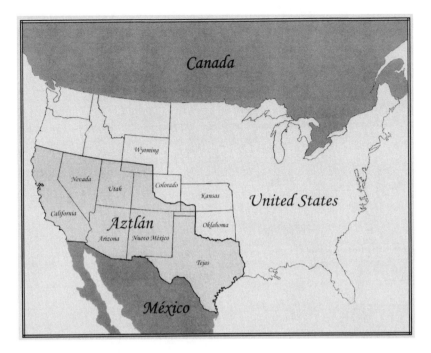

0.3. A map of Aztlán, an imagined nation comprising territory ceded by Mexico under the Treaty of Guadalupe Hidalgo. From Armando Navarro's *Mexicano Political Experience in Occupied Aztlán: Struggles and Change* (Walnut Creek, CA: Alta Mira Press, 2005). Reprinted by permission of Alta Mira Press / Rowman & Littlefield Publishing Group.

the rest of the United States to the Mexican border (fig. 0.4). Another includes a Mexico that has expanded to annex California, Nevada, Arizona, and Utah, while relegating the rest of the continent to "The United States of Jesusland." Conceiving the nation as a community of politically like-minded citizens, the images of Jesusland suggest that it makes more sense to align the Democratic areas of the country with their Canadian and Mexican neighbors than with the rest of the United States.

This discussion of maps is a point of departure for a book that seeks to rethink the geographic imaginary of American cultural study by shifting its borders and providing new frames of analysis. In the broadest sense, what revisionist maps of the continent make visible is how frequently and easily culture tends to spill across the borders of the nation-state.[3] Transnational cultural networks grant cohesion to the imagined nations of Garreau's North America, Aztlán, Cascadia, and Jesusland, where residents feel they have more in common with one another than with fellow citizens living in distant reaches of the continent. They also connect communities across

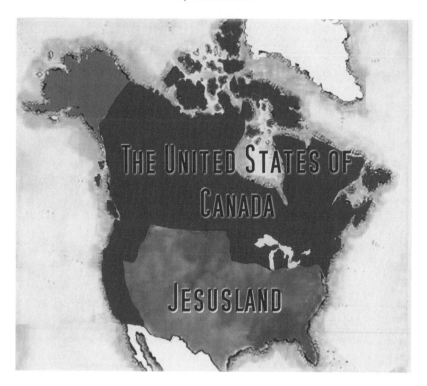

0.4. A map that circulated on the Internet following the 2004 reelection of George W. Bush depicting the absorption of the Democratic regions of the country into a nation called "The United States of Canada" while relegating the rest of the United States to the nation of "Jesusland." Reprinted by permission of CafePress.com, Inc.

great distances, linking New York to Mexico City, Quebec to San Francisco, Toronto to Virginia or the U.S.-Mexico borderlands, Nunavut to Chiapas. Messy, tangled, and provisional, these networks defy representation on a conventional map and challenge the ways scholars in the humanities have organized our knowledge of texts, periods, and authors. We do not yet have adequate vocabularies to account for their significance.

Instead, the political map of North America has long served as a template for organizing the study of culture into separate, nation-based categories. Canadian, Mexican, and U.S. American studies each evolved into a field with its own discrete histories and intellectual traditions. And much like diplomatic relations among the three nations, comparative scholarship on North America has often proceeded in terms of bilateral conversations between the United States and its neighbors, rather than an equitable dialogue involving many different parties. U.S.-based Americanists have shown considerable interest in Mexico, but typically ignore Canada or treat it as an extension of the United States, while those scholars of Mexico and Canada who have written comparatively about the United States rarely take one another as objects of critical interest. Partitioning the cultures of North America in this way has limited our reading of individual works and genres, and obscured opportunities for innovative comparative analysis. My fundamental claim is that many of the things we think we know about "American" culture appear very different when examined through transnational frames that include portions of Canada, the United States, and Mexico.

This book introduces the continent as a frame for the study of American culture. I use the term *continent* to describe the coexistence and interpenetration of diverse cultures and languages within a loosely configured territory that encompasses multiple regions and nation-states. Continents are fluid and malleable assemblages whose boundaries have shifted over time. Their number varies depending on whom you ask. Nonetheless, the concept of continents maintains a consistent investment in place, which is often lost when culture is studied through the lens of more geographically inchoate rubrics such as globalization or diaspora. So too, it offers a promising alternative to the impasse of nation-based models of cultural study. Nations are, in Benedict Anderson's influential terms, imagined communities drawn together through shared stories of origin and consolidated around a teleological sense of collective destiny.[4] But these narratives have often constrained our understanding of literature and the arts by providing a false sense of homogeneity and limiting the possibilities of comparison across time and space. Looking at culture through the lens of the continent allows us to study the nation from a critical distance by standing outside of its borders and by putting it into comparative dialogue with its closest neighbors. The continent I envision grants new centrality to people and places that have been marginalized by official histories of conquest and nation building, thus bringing a new repertoire of texts and subjects into view.

My effort to open up the repertoire of continental culture has dictated the shape and methods of my analysis. I describe my approach as a form of mapping because I am concerned with actual questions about the American geographic imaginary, which governs how and why we draw boundaries around and connect our objects of study. I also use the concept of mapping because I hope this book will become a guide for subsequent scholarship to revise and enhance the insights it offers. Given that the historical scenarios it broaches are necessarily fragmented and partial, I have deliberately avoided the creation of a singular narrative thread that would provide a false sense of cohesion to the chapters that follow. What they share is a comparative perspective on Canada, the United States, and Mexico that is intended to unsettle some of the deep-seated geographic assumptions underlying the study of American culture. For example, it has come to seem obvious that African American slaves ran north to freedom, that American modernism was oriented toward Europe, and that the American border-lands are located in the U.S. Southwest. But what if we were to redraw the map of culture to include the slaves that ran south, the modernisms orig-inating in Mexico, or the literature and art of the U.S.-Canadian border-lands? My chapters ask such questions, seeking unexpected points of con-tact and connection among genres, texts, and figures, and looking across borders that have often been seen as the final frontiers on a given subject. Read independently, they comprise a set of case studies that ask how our understanding of American literary and cultural study is deepened, and in some cases transformed, when it is reframed through a continental geo-graphic imaginary. At the same time, they can also be taken together as ep-isodes in an unfolding story about the possibilities and limits of North American community.

The Invention of North America

Continents are not discovered, they are made, as the Mexican historian Edmundo O'Gorman suggested in his classic 1961 study, *The Invention of America*.[5] *Invention* is an essential term for O'Gorman, who rejects the idea that the continent was a preexisting entity waiting to be found, emphasiz-ing instead the process whereby continents are created—and thus given material reality—by historians, educators, and other cultural authorities. Playing on the title of O'Gorman's book, my heading underscores the chain of events that brought the idea of North America into being. Continents are the building blocks of our most basic understanding of the world, a geo-graphical commonsense introduced in the early stages of elementary educa-tion that endures into the highest levels of foreign policy and international governance. The idea of continents, despite its widespread acceptance, rests on a relatively vague and shifting conception of global geography. Unlike nation-states, continents are neither sovereign political entities nor do they demarcate distinctive environmental or cultural regions. Although they are defined by the Oxford English Dictionary (OED) as "connected or contig-uous tract[s] of land," even the most cursory glance at a map of the world confirms that continents do not actually conform to any consistent geo-graphical logic. There is no obvious reason why Europe and Asia are separate continents, for example, and disagreement persists about whether the Americas are one continent or two.

However arbitrary the continental system may be, it has very real consequences for determining economic and political alignments, as well as the movement of people and goods around the globe. Geographers Martin Lewis and Kären E. Wigen note that the current scheme for dividing up the map has its basis in Eurocentric models according to which "Europe and the United States appear in swollen importance, while the rest of the world is shrunk into a distorting miniature."[6] The myth of the continents thus represents and contributes to the perpetuation of prevailing geopolitical power relations. The popular "What's Up? South!" maps produced in Australia or the well-known 1943 sketch titled "Upside-Down Map" by Uruguayan modernist Joaquín Torres-García demonstrate the deep sedimentation of our geographical assumptions by turning our sense of global order on its head (figs. 0.5, 0.6). Recent debates over membership in the European Union and the construction of a North American security perimeter are further indication of the contingent, yet materially significant, status of continents. In each case, decisions about inclusion and exclusion that are of vital importance to member nations have far more to do with politics than they do with geography.

Continents did not always seem like an obvious way to organize the map of the world. The notion of partitioning the world into seven continents has only been widely accepted since the middle of the twentieth century, although North America is a European invention that dates back to the Renaissance. Before the European discovery of the Americas, it was common cartographic practice to divide the earth into three parts: Asia, Africa, and Europe. According to Eviatar Zerubavel, so dramatic was the "cosmographic shock" of encountering the New World that it took at least three generations to register in European maps of the globe, which stubbornly clung to the belief that America was an extension of Asia before finally coming to accept that it constituted a fourth continental region.[7] Aníbal Quijano and Immanuel Wallerstein argue that the invention of the Americas in the sixteenth century had a dramatic effect on the world system, inaugurating the era of modernity and ushering in the global capitalist economy.[8] The modern notion that the world could be broken down into continents must thus be seen as a part of these larger planetary shifts and, as such, it is deeply implicated in the hierarchies of power they introduced.

Europeans were not the only ones who struggled to accept the idea of America as a continent. It would also take some time for inhabitants of the New World to develop a sense of themselves as Americans. But by the early

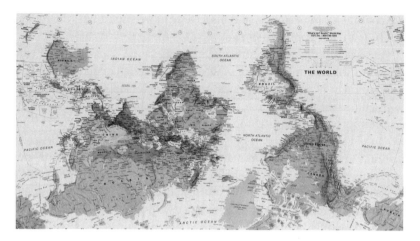

0.5. "What's Up? South!" world map, produced in Australia, intended to disorient the viewer's geographical assumptions by inverting the poles of the world. Reprinted by permission
of ODT, Inc. (ODTmaps.com).

nineteenth century, the varied populations of the hemisphere were experi-
encing a growing sense of kinship with one another.[9] Strengthened networks
of communication, travel, and commerce enabled the circulation of people,
goods, and ideas, heightening the perception of belonging to a common
geopolitical unit called America. There was a widespread belief that geography united the nations of the western hemisphere in a shared commitment to peace and democracy, and this principle would guide U.S. foreign
policy for the next hundred years. The visual instantiation of this concept
is the split-hemisphere *mappemonde* created during the Renaissance, which
depicted the Americas in a sphere of their own, isolated from the rest of the
world by the vast oceans that surrounded them (fig. 0.7).[10] With this image
in mind, Thomas Jefferson wrote to Alexander von Humboldt in 1813 that
geography would protect the Americas from foreign incursion: "The insulated state in which nature has placed the American continent, should so
far avail it that no spark of war kindled in the other quarters of the globe
should be wafted across the wide oceans which separate us from them."[11]
Ten years later, President James Monroe declared the American hemisphere
off limits for European colonization, pledging to defend the sovereignty of
fellow nations in the region against attacks from overseas.

It would soon become clear that the 1823 Monroe Doctrine was as
much an early manifestation of U.S. imperial designs as it was a blueprint
for hemispheric solidarity. It initiated a pattern in which the United States
would insist on unilaterally setting the terms for its relationships to the na-

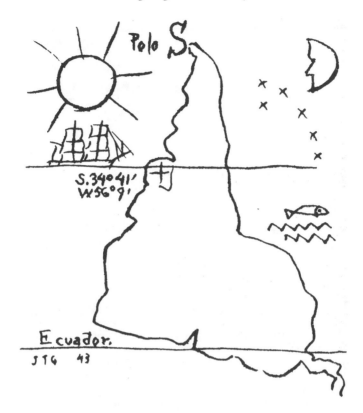

0.6. Joaquín Torres-García. *América invertida*, 1944. This sketch challenges the standard representation of South America by putting its southern pole on top. © Museo Torres García (www.torresgarcia.org.uy). Reprinted by permission of Museo Torres García.

tions of Latin America, assuming the right to intervene in their affairs while shying away from proposals for inter-American partnership generated outside its borders. However, it is also worth noting that the Monroe Doctrine represented a major shift away from the traditional isolationism of U.S. foreign policy and toward a newfound interest in understanding the nation as part of a greater hemispheric community.[12] As Anna Brickhouse has shown, this paradigm change in the domain of international relations was part of the broader emergence of what she calls a "transamerican public sphere"—the exchange of ideas, information, and visits among intellectuals in Latin America, the United States, and the Francophone Caribbean—that predominated through crucial decades of the nineteenth century and had a profound impact on literary culture of its time.[13] A belief in the geographic importance of the hemisphere would inform subsequent policies such as

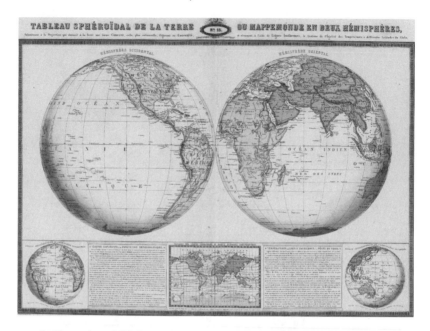

0.7. "Tableau sphéroïdal de la terre." The split-hemisphere *mappemonde* encouraged the belief that the Americas are isolated from the rest of the world by depicting them in a sphere of their own. Reprinted by permission of the David Rumsey Map Collection (www.davidrumsey.com).

the Roosevelt Corollary—which augmented the Monroe Doctrine by pledging that the United States would intervene to stabilize the economies of debt-ridden Caribbean and Central American nations—and the more idealistic era of the Good Neighbor Policy—Franklin D. Roosevelt's declaration of the United States' newfound commitment to "respect the rights" of its Latin American neighbors by not interfering in their affairs.[14] The idea of the Americas as one continent would prevail until the Second World War.[15] Indeed, many Latin Americans continue to describe *América* as one continent. So too, the five rings of the Olympic flag, which stand for the five continents participating in the games, depict America as a single unit.

The second half of the twentieth century saw the eclipse of the hemisphere as the reigning metageographic conception guiding America's relation to the rest of the world. It was replaced by other ways of partitioning the globe, including the cold war bifurcation into communist and noncommunist worlds, and a more widespread recognition of North and South America as two distinct continents.[16] These changes were anticipated in April 1941, when the economist Eugene Staley published "The Myth of the Continents," an article that attacked the notion that geographical contiguity was a sound basis for foreign policy. He challenged the logic of the Monroe Doctrine by arguing that the interests of U.S. national security were better served by concentrating on overseas alliances than on hemispheric defense. "The day of the small, completely independent, sovereign national state is past. There will be in the future—and ought to be—*larger* politico-economic units of some kind," he wrote, but then went on to ask, "is the natural progression from small, sovereign states to *continental* groupings?"[17] Against the common assumption "that the land connects, that the sea divides,"[18] Staley professed that oceans were more likely to produce circuits of trade and cultural exchange than were vast expanses of land, where contact was often obstructed by natural barriers such as "deserts, mountains, swamps, [and] jungles."[19] After noting that the distances between major U.S. and Latin American cities were often much greater than between cities in the United States and Europe, he asserted that the invasion of remote South American nations would be far less of a threat to U.S. security than the fall of Britain.

Less than a year later, Staley's propositions were born out, although the assault on the United States did not come from Europe, as he had predicted, but from Japan. The bombing of Pearl Harbor in 1941 proved the fallibility of the hemispheric worldview by showing that the United States was not insulated by oceans but vulnerable to attack from overseas. Asia and the United States, which appeared at opposite poles of the two-dimensional *mappemonde*, were in fact directly conjoined by the Pacific Ocean.[20] The United States' entry into the war constituted an undeniable recognition of its vital connections to Europe and Asia. When the conflict ended, the prospect of hemispheric unity seemed even less relevant as the United States rose to superpower status and participated in the creation of institutions like the United Nations and NATO.[21] Improved transportation and communication technologies, and the globalization of the economy, also diminished the importance of regional community. Nonetheless, invoking the Monroe Doctrine, the United States would continue to intervene in the affairs of Latin American nations throughout the cold war.[22]

During the post–World War II period the idea of North America as a continent unto itself thus came to replace the prevailing conception of America as a single metageographic unit. In the 1950s the division of the Americas into North and South became the dominant convention for maps produced in the Western world. A decade earlier, the U.S. government's Ethnogeographic Board had codified a formal system of world regions that would establish the groundwork for area studies during the cold war. It makes sense that North American studies did not evolve into its own field as did Latin

American, Middle Eastern, East Asian, or African studies, given that an important goal of area studies was to produce knowledge about other parts of the world in the service of the United States' strategic interests.[23] Nonetheless, the area studies rubric served to reinforce the sense of North America as a cohesive region distinct from its southern neighbor.[24] The rise of a unified, peaceable Europe provided a model of continental community that further enabled the incipient notion of an integrated North America.

Of course, the vision of a divided hemisphere had existed for many centuries alongside the more dominant belief in a single America. As early as 1538, Gerardus Mercator labeled North and South America as distinct entities on his map of the world.[25] Virtually from the nation's inception, U.S. Americans employed the rhetoric of continentalism not only to express the westward course of Manifest Destiny but also to articulate expansionist designs on Mexico and Canada.[26] As a result, anxieties about the unchecked spread of U.S. power in the region have periodically generated antagonism toward the notion of hemispheric community in both Latin America and Canada. Latin Americans, from Simón Bolívar to José Martí, Rubén Darío, Carlos Pereyra, Manuel Ugarte, José Vasconcelos, and José Enrique Rodó, have called for Hispanic nations to unite in their resistance to the imperial ambitions of the United States. For its part, Canada has been notably absent from the hemispheric visions of its southern neighbors, and Canadians have expressed little interest in locating themselves as part of a greater American federation. As a member of the British Commonwealth, Canada remained decisively oriented across the Atlantic until the Second World War, when it contributed for the first time to plans for joint hemispheric defense.[27] Thus, the notion of an integrated American hemisphere has a long and conflicted history in which the United States has often been out of keeping with its Latin American neighbors, and Canada has played very little role at all.

A watershed moment in the invention of North America was the signing of the North American Free Trade Agreement (Nafta) in 1993, which brought the continent into being as an economic entity and was hailed by some as a harbinger of a newfound continental sensibility. Nafta exemplifies broader shifts in the global economy as it has moved toward the formation of regional blocs such as the European Union (EU), Asia Pacific Economic Cooperation (APEC), and Mercado Común del Sur (MERCOSUR).[28] In a context where successful proposals for regional integration have almost always been initiated by the United States, it is somewhat surprising that Nafta was the brainchild of Mexican president Carlos Salinas de Gortari, who sought to relieve his nation's crippling international debt by integrat-

U.S. Protests Mexi-Canadian Overpass

WASHINGTON, DC—After nearly nine years of construction, the Mexi-Canadian Overpass, the controversial $4.3 trillion highway overpass linking Guadalupe and Winnipeg, was finally completed last week, drawing harsh criticism from U.S.

see OVERPASS page 8

Right: Chrétien and Fox at the official unveiling.

0.8. "U.S. Protests Mexi-Canadian Overpass." A story in the satirical paper, *The Onion* (vol. 38. no. 18) about plans to build a highway that would link Canada and Mexico, bypassing the United States. Reprinted with permission of *The Onion*. © 2008 by Onion, Inc. (www.theonion.com).

ing it more fully into world markets. When his advances to various European nations were rejected, Salinas turned to the United States with a proposal for economic partnership. His move was well timed, since it came at a moment when the U.S. and Canadian governments were both inclined to support closer integration, although Canada was the more reluctant participant in the trilateral accord, coming fully on board only when it perceived the inevitability of an agreement between the United States and Mexico.[29] Canada's hesitance was symptomatic of its general resistance toward entanglements with Mexico, a situation that strengthened the United States' dominance under Nafta by making it the only member nation to engage in regular dialogue with both of its trading partners. These relations were brilliantly satirized in *The Onion*, which ran a story in 2002 headlined "U.S. Protests Mexi-Canadian Overpass," about the construction of a bridge linking Guadalupe to Winnipeg (fig. 0.8).[30] Its humor derived from the unlikely prospect of an alliance between Canada and Mexico that would literally bypass the United States. It also pokes fun at conspiracy theorists who believe that plans for such a highway are secretly underway. The truth behind this joke is that Canada and Mexico have rarely dealt directly with each other unmediated by the United States, and Nafta has done little to facilitate a genuinely tripartite relationship among its signatories.

The North America created by Nafta defines the continent in very specific terms that are as meaningful for what they leave out as for what they include. Nafta's stated goals are to promote trade and investment in the region; to increase employment and improve working conditions in each country; and to enforce and augment existing laws protecting the environment and basic workers' rights.[31] Its North America is far less integrated than the EU, the entity to which it is most often compared. Whereas European unification was driven by the need to establish peace among formerly warring nations, the motivations behind Nafta were primarily economic. It made no provisions for a supranational government, a shared currency, or the movement of people across national borders.[32] Unlike the EU, which has created institutions designed to promote a common continental identity, there has been little effort to create a collective sense of North American community. As international relations scholar Robert Pastor put it in 2002, "more than four hundred million people . . . live in the United States, Mexico, and Canada, but few, if any, think of themselves as residents of 'North America.'"[33] One of the most obvious reasons for this situation is that, in contrast to an EU whose members are roughly equal, one of Nafta's signatory nations is the United States, whose economic and political power is grossly disproportionate to that of its two neighbors.[34] This makes it very difficult for Mexicans and Canadians to imagine a North American Union that is not dominated by the United States, or for U.S. Americans to see the benefits of integration with their neighbors, particularly Mexico.

Although Nafta has lived up to its promise to increase trade between its three partners, there is strong disagreement about its consequences on standards of living, employment, and productivity. Many argue that it has had a negative impact on the Canadian and Mexican economies and has widened income disparities across the continent. However, many others have questioned whether its impact can be accurately documented at all given the great number of other variables involved. What can be said reliably is that, at the time of its implementation, Nafta represented a significant acceleration of relations among the three signatory nations, reinforcing the idea of North America as a distinct region of the globe. But instead of operating in a genuinely trilateral arena, negotiations under Nafta continue to take place bilaterally between the United States and Canada *or* Mexico, and Canadians, U.S. Americans, and Mexicans seem no closer to understanding themselves as North American citizens or to developing a sense of kinship with one another than they were in the past.[35] In this sense, the North America realized by Nafta serves to underscore rather than eliminate inequities among its member nations.[36] Their differences have only been emphasized

since the events of 9/11, when Canada and Mexico were blamed for allowing terrorists onto North American soil. The ensuing discussions about constructing an impermeable "fortress continent"[37] and a North American security perimeter were initiated unilaterally by the United States rather than
through collaborative dialogue.

In short, North America is a place that few would call home, a concept
that is more the invention of politicians and economists than the product
of its inhabitants' collective imagination. History tells us that the rhetoric
of continentalism has long been deployed to serve U.S. national imperatives ranging from territorial expansion in the eighteenth and nineteenth
centuries[38] to economic dominance and national security in the twentieth and twenty-first. Given this legacy—and despite the prevailing currents
of integrationist economic policy—Canadians and Mexicans have under-
standably shied away from the prospect of a unified North America. Indeed, for many Latin Americans, the category of North America does not
include Mexico at all, but is rather a synonym for the Anglophone or Euro-
American cultures of the United States and Canada. This narrower definition is underscored in Spanish, where the term *norteamericano* refers exclusively to residents living north of the U.S.-Mexico border.[39]

These would be formidable problems if my goal were to account for a
coherent North American culture created and shared by the residents of the
continent. In such a project, the continent would be little more than a con-
siderably larger substitute for the nation, whose limitations for categoriz-
ing and delimiting the study of culture I will discuss at greater length in the
next section. The North America that is the setting for *Continental Divides* is
informed by, but cannot be reduced to, economic and political concerns.
This is a particularly important point because North America is a place that
often seems to make sense *only* as a trading bloc or a zone of military defense. Focusing on literature and the visual arts, this book documents the
uneven relations between Canadian, U.S., and Mexican cultures, which
may sometimes reflect the trajectories of national and international policy
described above, but frequently do not. Literary and visual representations
can just as easily provide a forum for resisting, deflecting, or envisioning alternatives to the more hard-edged realities of the world that produces them.
One of this book's primary agendas is to advance an alternative version of
continentalism that can serve as a flexible, dynamic model for comparative cultural study. In doing so, it tells a story that is less about the creation of a common North American identity than about the implausibility
of that project, about the disconnection between economic and political regions created by policy makers and those created by ordinary people out of

the practical imperatives of daily life, and the less material imagination of kinship and community.

The Study of North America and the "Transnational Turn" in American Studies

Continental Divides is inspired by, and seeks to contribute to, what has been called the "transnational turn" in American literary and cultural studies.[40] Over the past two decades, the field has witnessed an explosion of scholarship seeking to situate America—its vexed object of analysis—in a transnational context.[41] Many scholars have come to see the nation, which had long been the implicit organizing principle of much work in the field, as constrained by rigid borders and teleological narratives about the origin and destiny of the American people. Whereas once the "America" of American studies could be assumed to lie within the geographical borders of the United States, this is no longer the case. American studies now proceeds with an awareness of the populations outside of the United States who also lay claim to the name "American," as well as the ways that U.S. culture circulates abroad, producing "offshore Americas" in other parts of the world. Analytic frames such as the black, trans- and circum-Atlantic; the hemisphere; the Pacific Rim; the Caribbean islands; and the borderlands are attentive to the significance of geography and place while seeking to avoid the limitations of an exclusively nation-based paradigm. This work has brought new attention to such subjects as U.S. imperialism; the diasporic affiliations of U.S. immigrant groups; the transatlantic networks forged by the slave trade, abolition, and Anglo-American print culture; and cultures of the U.S.-Mexico borderlands. At its best, it does not seek to ignore borders or to bypass the nation altogether, but to situate these terms within a broader global fabric.

The recent turn to transnationalism introduces a wealth of new objects of study, including non-Anglophone texts produced in the United States and materials from abroad that illuminate our understanding of U.S. culture at home and overseas. The archive of American literary study has been further expanded through the recovery of works that would fit uneasily within the category of national literature, including the slave narratives of Olaudah Equiano and Mary Prince, Martin Delany's *Blake, or the Huts of Africa*, the romances of María Amparo Ruiz de Burton, the fiction and ethnography of Américo Paredes, and Jovita Gonzales and Eve Raleigh's *Caballero*. Figures such as José Martí, W. E. B. Du Bois, Paredes, C. L. R. James, and Edouard Glissant have found a more prominent place in the intellectual history of American studies, and more familiar authors and canons have been reinvigorated as they are resituated in comparative, transnational contexts.

The *transnational turn* refers not only to the growing interest in particular subjects but also to changing methodological commitments within the field. Whereas once foreign language training was considered a formality, Americanists have come to recognize its necessity for comparative projects that extend across national borders or that involve the multilingual cultures of the United States.[42] Americanists in the United States have acknowledged the importance of familiarity with scholarship being produced by their colleagues abroad and in languages other than English, and have sought out opportunities for collaborative teaching and research across national borders. These developments have been noted and encouraged by presidential addresses delivered to the American Studies Association;[43] the founding of the International American Studies Association in 2000; and the publication of the international journal *Comparative American Studies* in 2003.

While American studies has seen many changes take place under the rubric of transnationalism, there is a tendency to overstate the newness of these approaches and a corresponding tendency to caricature the allegedly nationalist horizons of previous scholarship within the field. Those who accuse earlier generations of Americanists of insularity have forgotten that it was Randolph Bourne who first used the term *transnationalism* in 1916 as the United States prepared to enter the First World War; that U.S.-Mexico borderlands history has been an active field since the early 1920s; that the Americanism of Popular Front intellectuals was internationalist to the core; that Henry Nash Smith's classic *Virgin Land: The American West as Symbol and Myth* is actually a critique, rather than a celebration, of American isolationism; and that the political scientist Louis Hartz was comparing U.S. and European histories in the 1940s and 1950s.[44] In each case, it is now possible to see how older internationalisms are informed by the prejudices and blind spots of their particular moment. Nonetheless, the fact remains that American studies has never been as invested in American exceptionalism, or as nationalistic, as some recent assessments of the field would suggest.[45] It is worth attending to the possibilities and limitations of this prior history as American studies' current engagement with the transnational continues to unfold.

Continental Divides draws on and combines many of the available analytic models that are emerging out of the current internationalization of American studies. Borders—metaphoric and literal; between nations, communities, and individuals—are a key location in this book, and the field of border studies has been an especially rich source of theoretical and methodological insight. At a moment when Americanists are particularly invested in identifying spaces of cultural contact, resistance, and interpenetration, borderlands are one of the field's reigning tropes. Their figurative (and sometimes literal) distance from centers of state power, association with histories of conflict, and the diverse creative expressions they inspire have made borderlands key to rethinking the place of the nation within American studies.[46] This understanding of borderlands is indebted to important work by scholars of Chicano studies. Although focused on the two-thousand-mile-long corridor where the United States and Mexico is conjoined, they have always tended to view the region as part of a broader hemispheric or global nexus. This was true of the historian Herbert Bolton, author of the influential book *The Spanish Borderlands* (1921) and president of the American Historical Association, who argued in his 1933 address for "a broader treatment of American history" that would take into account the interconnections among the many nations of the Americas.[47] So too, the folklorist, critic, and creative writer Américo Paredes's foundational work on what he called "Greater Mexico" was informed by his experiences as a journalist in occupation-era Japan, where he witnessed the realignment of global power in the wake of World War II. The broadly transnational perspectives of Bolton and Paredes have endured among subsequent generations of border scholars. Gloria Anzaldúa famously described the borderlands as "*una herida abierta* where the Third World grates against the first and bleeds," an image that aligns Mexico with the Global South.[48] The paradigmatic subject of the borderlands is mestizo, multilingual, multiracial, uneasy with fixed categories, and distrustful of centralized authority. As much as they are a geographic location, Anzaldúa's borderlands are also a metaphor for new ways of understanding culture, place, and history. "The Borderlands are physically present wherever two or more cultures edge each other," she writes, "where people of different races occupy the same territory, where under, lower, middle and upper classes touch, where the space between two individuals shrinks with intimacy."[49] It thus follows that borderlands are not found only at the literal margins of the nation-state, but rather in any place where friction among many different cultural groups produces conflict, intermixture, and heterogeneity.

Despite the portability of the borderlands concept, Americanists have paid little attention to the U.S.-Canadian border region, and have shown even less interest in comparative views of the two borders.[50] In the United States, the majority of scholarly attention has tended to focus on the border with Mexico. In Canada, scholarship comparing the United States and Canada in general is far more prevalent than examinations of the corridor where the two nations abut each other.[51] According to political scientist Roger Gibbens, this is because the region does not have a distinctive border culture comparable to that of the U.S.-Mexico borderlands. Instead, populations on both sides are "thoroughly enmeshed in a continental culture that sweeps across the border."[52] His argument suggests that populations at the U.S.-Canadian border may be less concerned with national culture and more aware of their status as North Americans than those in any other region of the continent. In this book, I consider authors and artists such as Shelley Niro, Thomas King, Lawrence Hill, Lori Lansens, John Farrow, and Guillermo Verdecchia, who explicitly foreground the U.S.-Canadian border as an arena of struggle over North American history and hope for its future.

Continental Divides aspires to a genuinely comparative view of North American borders that locates them in relation to one another and to borders in other parts of the world. Although the majority of the works it discusses were created during the twentieth century, they mine a history that extends back to the mid-nineteenth century with the consolidation of the continent's land borders, which are two of the longest in the world. As historians Samuel Truett and Elliott Young speculate, "a useful starting point for borderlands history is to ask what happened when fuzzy and mobile frontiers—first of empires then of nations—gave way to more fixed national boundaries. And no less importantly, what happened when people and places at the frontiers of state rule and power began to find themselves at a new crossroads *between* those nations that sought to contain them?"[53] Whereas answers to this question have been explored in some detail in the case of northern Mexicans, it is equally pertinent to the Native North Americans, African American slaves, and French Canadians who I discuss over the course of this book. I argue that twentieth-century literature and the arts preserve cultural memories of this shift from frontiers to boundaries, of the historical accidents that gave rise to North America's three nation-states, and of different ways the space of the continent might have been organized. While I will not make a case for anything like a coherent North American culture, literature and arts of the borderlands—in their abundant formal, linguistic, and thematic diversity—may come closest to representing the complexities of North American experience.

My initial hypothesis was that in using the rubric of continent to bypass or formulate alternatives to nation-bound categories, I could show how Canadian, U.S., and Mexican cultures influence, engage, and blend with one another. Looking across North American borders, I would encounter a rich archive of literary and visual texts that could not be adequately described in terms of national categories. I found many cases where my supposition was born out: the Native North American authors Thomas King and Leslie Marmon Silko, who write out of an awareness of, and desire to perpetuate, forms of tribal internationalism; the life and work of iconic beatnik Jack Kerouac, whose America is forged out of longstanding ties to French Canada, the United States, and Mexico; and the fictional borderlands community imagined by John Sayles's *Lone Star* or Rolando Hinojosa's Klail City cycle.

However, my work on this project has also made me aware of the crucial role of culture in *maintaining* national borders and the ongoing salience of the nation for understanding the cultures of North America. This is especially true in Canada and Mexico, where many have seen the presence of U.S. products and mass media as a threat to cultural particularity, and proximity to the United States itself as a threat to political sovereignty. As a result, Canadians and Mexicans have often imagined national borders as a crucial line of defense against the Americanization of the continent. We see this dynamic in the Quebecois and Mexican appropriations of Jack Kerouac discussed in chapter 4. For these authors, paying homage to Kerouac was a sign of their own worldliness and modernity, but it also opened them to charges of being derivative. They sought to avoid such accusations by underscoring the Canadianness and Mexicanness of their work. Chapter 5 identifies a similar tendency in contemporary Canadian and Mexican detective novels that use national borders as a setting and as a metaphor for the contradictions between the increasing integration (both criminal and lawful) of the continent and the desire to preserve the particularity of local culture, embodied in the figure of the detective. I argue that their work is marked by a desire for national distinction in the face of the worldwide popularity of crime writing from and about the United States, and the dominance of U.S. publishing houses in global markets.

The most strident attempts to maintain North America's national borders have always come from nativists within the United States who want to stem the tide of foreign-born migrants. Theirs is a familiar story. However, during times of crisis, national borders have also served as an escape hatch for many U.S. Americans, who have welcomed the firm line marking the limits of state power. Looking back to the nineteenth century, I show the importance of national borders to slaves in the United States, who (particularly in the wake of the 1850 Fugitive Slave Act) equated freedom with the ability to cross into Canada or Mexico. They were not the first to blaze a trail

to the Canadian north, which had already served as a refuge for the Empire
Loyalists during the revolutionary era. Over the next two hundred years,
their paths would be retraced by many generations of disaffected U.S. citizens, from draft dodgers, to political radicals, to contemporary gay couples
wishing to marry, and to the elderly in search of affordable prescription
drugs. In the days following the same 2004 presidential election that produced the maps of Jesusland, the Canadian immigration Web site received
record numbers of hits from Americans considering relocation north of the
border.

Continental Divides thus shows the continued significance of North
American borders at a moment when many posit that globalization is resulting in the erosion of the nation-state,[54] and where the implementation
of Nafta had promised to usher in a new era of continentalism. At the same
time that it is concerned with the flow of culture across the borders of region and nation, it also documents the extent to which North Americans
have eschewed the notion of a continental community in favor of local and
national (and in some cases, global) affiliations. In this sense, Continental
Divides is as concerned with the failures of the idea of North America in the
domain of culture—despite its robust presence in economic policy and debates over national security—as it is with the persistence or emergence of
shared cultural environments or tendencies.

Continental Divides is about the varied cultural lives of Canadians, Mexicans,
and U.S. Americans as they engage in reciprocal projects of self-examination
and reflection. But it also has a broader agenda, which is to introduce the
continent as a heuristic frame for comparative cultural study, one that can
offer valuable and specific lessons about North American cultures in all of
their geographic, linguistic, and historical diversity, and that might be pro-
ductively applied to other contexts and materials. Faced with a virtually
bottomless archive, I found it necessary to contain my investigation within
more circumscribed historical and geographic horizons. Because I am concerned with the interplay among the relatively fixed territory of nation-
states, the shifting space of the continent, and the mobility of culture, I
focus on the period from the mid-nineteenth century to the present, during which modern nations have been the dominant political presence in
North America. Although I discuss many texts that look outward to other
parts of the hemisphere and the world, I concentrate on a spatial frame that
loosely corresponds to the political map of North America, extending from
the Canadian north to Mexico's border with Guatemala. Each chapter takes

a particular cultural form—North American Indian art and fiction, slave and neo-slave narratives, American modernism, Beat culture, the detective novel, performance art—and shows how it acquires new meanings when it is reframed through the geographic imaginary of the continent.

As I have already suggested, this book begins and ends with North America's borders and with "the borderlands," a concept that is often virtually synonymous with Anglo-Mexican cultures of the U.S. Southwest. But borderlands history and culture do not belong to Anglo-Mexicans alone, nor is the U.S.-Mexico line the only border of consequence in North America. Chapters 1 and 2 bring an alternative perspective to the borderlands by examining them through the lens of Indian and black North American experiences, and by comparing the U.S.-Mexico borderlands with other North American border regions. Chapter 1 is about the first borderlanders, North American Indians whose lands were bisected during the process of colonization and nation-formation. Many of these tribes continue to maintain a sense of community across national borders in the present day, preserving cultural memories of the experience of partition in ceremonial practices; social organizations; and oral, print, and visual representations. This history is very much alive for contemporary Native authors Thomas King and Leslie Marmon Silko, whose writing is informed by an awareness of the legacy of conflict between European settlers—who were eager to divide and conquer the land—and indigenous people—who lived and worked on it for many centuries before European contact. These conflicts endure in present-day clashes between tribal nations and nation-states over questions of land, mobility, and citizenship. Locating their fiction along the U.S.-Canadian, U.S.-Mexican, and Mexican-Guatemalan border zones, King and Silko thematize the role of borders in the conquest, as well as how the transnational process of colonialism continues to shape contemporary Indian culture and politics.

What King and Silko share with Chicano/a authors is an animosity toward national borders that has its roots in a history of conquest and partition that continues to resonate in the present. Chapter 2 examines the very different place of national borders in slave and neo-slave narratives about flight to Canada and Mexico. What these narratives reveal is that for fugitives eager to escape the United States, the border is not a divisive obstacle but a welcome conduit to liberty. Historically, the study of slave narratives has emphasized the U.S.-Canadian border, locating freedom to the north and idealizing Canada as the slaves' Promised Land. In this chapter, I am concerned with how and why the north acquired its privileged, quasi-mythic status, and how this geographical convention has prevented more nuanced views of Canada's role in the history of slavery on the continent. The assumption that slaves always ran from south to north has obscured the fact that considerable numbers of slaves fled south across the U.S. border into Mexico. During the era of legalized slavery, the "other south" comprising Mexico and, in some cases, elsewhere in Latin America, was the subject of significant debate among slaveholders and abolitionists alike. It figured prominently in the fiction and political writings of Martin Delany, who called for the founding of an alternative black nation, not in Africa, but on American soil. A discussion of North and South in nineteenth-century representations of slavery provides a backdrop for my discussion of the geographic imaginary of late twentieth-century neo-slave narratives. I look at examples from Canada (Lawrence Hill and Lori Lansens), the United States (Gayl Jones and John Sayles), and Mexico (Guillermo Sánchez de Anda), in which contemporary authors draw on the slave narrative's form and contents to produce revisionist histories of blackness on the continent. Concentrating on Canada and Mexico, they attempt to unsettle the dominance of African America in accounts of North American struggles over slavery and freedom. The perspectives offered by these works expand and complicate the terrain of black diaspora and enhance our understanding of North American borders.

Quite different motivations impel the acts of border crossing at the heart of chapter 3, which is about the north-south routes of American modernism. Much of the scholarship on American modernism has been concerned with the transatlantic circuits linking the U.S. Atlantic Seaboard to European capitals such as London, Paris, and Berlin. It has focused on the cosmopolitan circles surrounding expatriate American authors like Gertrude Stein, Ezra Pound, Ernest Hemingway, and T. S. Eliot. This transatlantic bias has obscured the fact that, during the same period, Mexico City was home to its own distinctive and influential modernist movements. It too was a cosmopolitan center that attracted artists and authors who hailed from many parts of the world and whose work traveled back outward to influence the development of modernist expression elsewhere in North America and abroad. In 1920s Mexico, artists were seen as essential to the political goals of the revolution, and their modernism was politicized in a way that differed from that of their Anglo-European contemporaries. When this "Mexican renaissance" enters the story of American modernism, the focus is on the muralists Diego Rivera, David Alfaro Siqueiros, and José Clemente Orozco. This chapter seeks to reroute more familiar narratives about American modernism by focusing on three women at the heart of Mexico's transnational bohemian society—Katherine Anne Porter, Anita

Brenner, and Tina Modotti—who were themselves influential artists, but who also introduced the innovations of Mexican modernism to the rest of the world. I argue that granting their work a more central place in accounts of American modernism would revise our understanding of its key locations, cultural networks, and political projects.

Chapter 4 examines the life and work of a single author, Jack Kerouac, who crossed multiple borders of class, language, and nation. Whereas Kerouac has come to assume canonical status as a U.S. American author, I show the importance of his French Canadian background and his Mexican travels to his influential "visions of America." As much as we associate Kerouac with the Beat subcultures of New York and San Francisco, I argue that we must also recognize the profound impact of French Canadian Lowell and Mexico City on the form and content of his writing. An author whose first language was French, Kerouac wrote predominantly in English but also incorporated Spanish into his work. With this in mind, in the first part of this chapter I read Kerouac with an eye to his French Canadian and Mexican experiences, paying particular attention to his status as a theorist of language, an author concerned with the possibilities of translingual communication as well as the problem of untranslatability. The remainder of the chapter is concerned with the international circulation of Kerouac's oeuvre. Specifically, it considers his influence on French Canadian and Mexican authors who sought to build on the mystique of the American "King of the Beats" but also sought to produce distinctive forms of countercultural expression faithful to their own local contexts. Because of the more regional cast of their work and because they write in languages other than English, these authors are far less well known than Kerouac. Their geographic horizons are also narrower: Mexican writers have little to say about Canada, and Quebecois writers are equally silent about Mexico. Kerouac is thus a special figure in this book because he is one of a very select group of authors who could be described as genuinely continental in scope. Nonetheless, my hope is that the analysis of Kerouac will provide a methodological model for studying other North Americans whose life and work crossed national, linguistic, and cultural borders.

Chapter 5 takes up a set of questions about genre literature that were introduced, but not fully developed, in the discussion of slave narratives in chapter 2. Here, my subject is contemporary detective novels from Canada, the United States, and Mexico that have addressed late twentieth-century problems of crime and border security. Whereas these works have been studied almost exclusively in terms of national literature, I propose that formula fiction of this kind is particularly well-suited to comparative transnational analysis because it presupposes a multiplicity of texts, each conforming to recognizable generic conventions that have been adjusted to address the needs and concerns of a particular social context. When the detective novel crosses national borders, it becomes a telling document of the values and beliefs of a specific reading public. My subjects are the detective novels of Canadian John Farrow, U.S. Chicano Rolando Hinojosa, and Mexican Paco Ignacio Taibo II, authors who thematize the contradictions arising from the economic integration of the continent, the globalization of crime, and the continued segmentation of North American law enforcement into local and national agencies. Read together, their fiction reveals vast disparities in how Canadians, U.S. Americans, and Mexicans imagine relations with one another and among citizens and their governments. Thus, even as it narrates the criminal subversion of borders, contemporary detective fiction attests to the persistence of the regional and national differences they demarcate.

Whereas the history and culture of the United States figure prominently in each of the previous chapters, chapter 6 is concerned with the more direct link between Canada and Latin America created by the work of the Canadian Argentinean Guillermo Verdecchia. I focus on Verdecchia's acclaimed short story collection *Citizen Suarez* and his play *Fronteras Americanas/American Borders* as representations of a new North American constituency: Latin Americans in Canada. Writing about this relatively unrecognized minority, Verdecchia creates a bridge between Canada and Latin America that is mediated through the more familiar discourse of Chicanos in the United States. Framing the experiences of Latinos in Winnipeg and Toronto in terms of borderlands makes them legible to broader audiences, while also emphasizing what is particular about their Canadian locations. Reading Verdecchia's work in this way makes clear the importance of better integrating Canada into the study of the Americas, and of reorienting the field of American studies so that the United States is not always the central player.

Together, these chapters sketch out visions of many possible North Americas. They also aspire to set an agenda for future programs of study and research premised on flexible geographies that allow the questions we ask to determine the pathways of history and culture that we follow. To become a citizen of this North America does not mean echoing the economic agendas of Nafta or endorsing the scary prospect of a "fortress continent" envisioned by some national security experts. It does not require a loyalty oath or proof of residence. Instead, it means developing multiple linguistic and cultural literacies; a deep knowledge of history; and a commitment to looking across, if not necessarily eroding, national borders. In Karen Tei Yamashita's 1997 novel *Tropic of Orange*, this is a lesson learned by characters whose world is rocked when the U.S.-Mexico border literally begins to move north. The shifting border is a reminder of the finitude of maps, which are only as powerful and enduring as the cultures that create them. *Tropic of Orange* portends that the map of America will be dramatically altered by ecological and economic pressures that are bringing north and south into increasingly intimate contact with each other and with the rest of the world. But it is also making a point about the present, about how maps condition the way we see a given landscape and how familiar terrain looks strange when borders are rearranged. This is the guiding impulse of the book I have written, which crosses borders in order to approach its objects of study via uncommon routes and to observe how changed perspectives can generate unexpected meanings. The result is less a map than a set of methods, a constant redefinition of boundaries that allows me to approach well-known subjects from different angles and to seek out new interlocutors in unexpected places.

CHAPTER ONE

Before the Border: Indigenous Geographies of North America

A map of North America covers the ground in Mohawk artist Shelley Niro's 1996 installation *The Border* (fig. 1.1). Suspended above it at the 49th parallel is a steel arch in the shape of a woman's profile, a mane of hair hanging down and spreading across the continent like the roots of a tree. The location of the arch suggests that the work's title refers to the boundary between the United States and Canada. According to Niro, the piece is inspired by the life of slain activist Anna Mae Aquash. Although many suspect that the Canadian Aquash was killed by a fellow member of the American Indian Movement (AIM), who may have mistakenly believed her to be an FBI informant, a botched investigation by both Canadian and U.S. authorities failed to yield the killer.[1] "Because she was a Native American and a woman," Niro writes in her artist's statement, "her death was apparently deemed too insignificant to be worthy of a serious and persistent investigation."[2] Her words prompt the viewer to see *The Border* as a protest against the devaluation of the lives of indigenous people, particularly women. It identifies international borders as zones of particular vulnerability where marginalized populations are deprived of rights and protections as they are overlooked by government agencies on either side.

The Border also makes a more positive statement about the persistence of transnational communities and political organizations. Looking at the map again, we become aware that it has no borders, save those that divide land from sea, and that the cascade of hair falls across the map where the U.S.-Canadian border should be. The hair extends outward along all four points of the compass like the roots of a tree, evoking ties to land and people that span national borders, as did Aquash's life and political commitments. Behind the sculpture, three works of photocollage hang on the wall. The central image depicts a woman superimposed on a map of the continent, as if

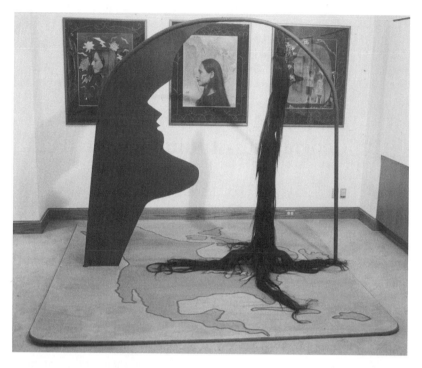

1.1. From Shelley Niro's *The Border*. This installation appeared in the Longyear Museum of Anthropology at Colgate University in 1997. Photograph by Warren Wheeler. Reprinted by permission of Longyear Museum of Anthropology.

to challenge the Indian's erasure from official versions of history by literally putting her on the map (fig. 1.2). Niro's piece thus evokes North American Indians' longstanding grievances with national borders, while affirming the strength of transnational affiliations among indigenous people on the continent.

Niro's installation is provocative in several respects. Given its title, we might expect it to take on the better-known controversies associated with the U.S.-Mexico border. Instead its subject is the United States' border with Canada. And while we might expect it to address the far more politically visible problems of Mexicans and Mexican Americans, it suggests instead that Indians in the U.S. and Canada have their own manner of border trouble. *The Border* thus invites us to look at the borderlands from the perspective of North American Indians, who bring different understandings of history, geography, citizenship, and community into view than do the Anglo-Mexican cultures typically associated with such locales.

Continental Divides begins here because Indians were the first North

1.2. Shelley Niro's *The Border* (detail). A visual metaphor for putting women "on the map" of North America, this is the central image mounted on the wall behind the arch. From the installation at Longyear Museum of Anthropology, Colgate University (1997). Photograph by Warren Wheeler. Reprinted by permission of Longyear Museum of Anthropology.

Americans, and are thus exemplary figures in my effort to imagine alternative geographies for the study of North American cultures. The struggles of Indians along the continent's national borders remind us that North America's current nation-states are not permanent or timeless, but are the product of historical forces that displaced populations already on the land.

Niro's work is one example of the way that contemporary Indian literature and visual art enjoins us to approach North American borders from
unfamiliar angles that often overlap with, but also depart in notable ways
from, more well-known narratives about the U.S.-Mexico borderlands that
privilege Anglo-Mexican perspectives. In its current form, the field of U.S.
border studies deals almost exclusively with relations between the United
States and Mexico. Although its subjects are comparative and transnational,
they are also consistently oriented toward the United States and tend to
grant priority to policies, events, values, and cultural formations emerging
from the U.S. side of the border. *The borderlands* has frequently served as a
metonym for the cultural difference of U.S. Latino/a groups, an emphasis
that risks obscuring the experiences of migrant populations in other border
regions of the Americas. At the same time that the field has concentrated
on a particular geographic region (the U.S. Southwest) and context (Anglo-
Mexican history and culture), its conceptual underpinnings are often uncritically extrapolated to apply to border cultures more generally. As John
Muthyala puts it, "while geographically the US Southwest circumscribes the
materiality of the field of border studies, sociologically the tendency has
been to view the experience of displacement and relocation of Mexicans in
the Southwest as paradigmatic of border societies."[3] This is no small matter,
since borders and borderlands have become one of the governing tropes of
American literary and cultural study, which has much to gain from untan-
gling the relationship between a specific regional locale and a set of theoretical premises it has come to associate with borders of all kinds.[4]

Niro's installation invites dialogue between borderlands and Native
American studies, a convergence that promises to enhance both areas of
scholarly inquiry. Granting North American Indians a more central role
in borderlands history and culture complicates some of the prevailing assumptions about periodization, citizenship, and geography held by the
field of U.S. border studies. The genesis of the Anglo-Mexican borderlands
is typically traced to the 1848 Treaty of Guadalupe Hidalgo, which divided
the Mexican people and diminished Mexican territory by over 50 percent.[5]
For Indians, by contrast, 1848 is not a point of origin but one instance of
a larger pattern in which European empires seized and carved up the land
with little regard for the people who already occupied it.[6] While the experience of being conquered, first by Spain and then by the United States, is
central to Chicano self-understanding, many of the Indians whose territory spans national borders insist that they are sovereign peoples, rather
than citizens of Canada, the United States, or Mexico. They often make
their demands as members of particular tribes, rather than as citizens of

nation-states, and see tribal law as the ultimate authority on legal and cultural matters. Like Mexicans and Mexican Americans, they call for less restricted international borders. However, while many Mexican migrants move north in search of economic opportunity, Indians insist on the right to move freely across what they describe as their own territory for social and ceremonial, as well as commercial, purposes. Like other border dwellers, Indians who live in the U.S. Southwest and northern Mexico decry the effects of militarization, free trade, and environmental degradation in the area. The difference is that, for Indians, these concerns are not limited to a single region, since the boundary with Canada is the source of an equivalent, if not greater, number of international disputes. These problems would have particular resonance for Niro, since Mohawk lands are bisected by the U.S.-Canadian border and, since the 1990s, have been the site of conflicts over smuggling, tariffs, and national security. However, an emphasis on indigenous experience directs us toward an even broader panorama of borderlands that would reveal how the impact of U.S. border management reverberates in Mexico, Guatemala, and other Latin American nations.

In turn, the transnational perspectives offered by Chicano/a border studies have much to contribute to the study of North American Indian history and culture. North America has been a salient concept in Native American studies for the obvious reason that indigenous histories and cultures cannot be adequately understood in terms of national categories. It has served as an organizing rubric for looking at precontact cultural and linguistic patterns, and for groups who continue to maintain cross-border social networks. But despite its transnational scope, much of the scholarship in Native American studies has focused on specific tribes. When it does approach tribalism comparatively, it tends to do so within the limits of particular nation-states. While this tendency is understandable, given the geographical and cultural disparities among North America's indigenous populations, as well as the profound influence of national laws and policies on tribal life, it obscures shared experiences of colonization and their ongoing repercussions for contemporary indigenous cultures and political agendas. As Philip Deloria explains, an exclusive emphasis on particular tribes and communities, "militate[s] against efforts to generalize or synthesize, leaving us to wonder how to do justice to the variation among hundreds of tribal and community histories while at the same time reaching for general patterns concerning such things as colonialism and empire in North America."[7] According to the historian R. David Edmunds, a more transnational perspective on indigenous cultures would complement the ways that Indians are coming to understand themselves. "The rise of transnational ties among North, Central, and South American Indians," he writes, "may constitute the foundation of the histories to be written during the coming generation, histories that will be both comparative and synthetic."[8] Edmunds contends that a comparative approach to North American Indian culture need not be concerned only with contact and colonization, but may also be guided by Indians' own perception of the circumstances that tie them together across the borders of region and nation. Border studies, with its emphasis on cultural fusion and hybridity, its investment in narrating the history of conquest from multiple viewpoints, and its concern with the current struggles of populations at the margins of the nation-state, can provide a conceptual model for the emergence of the kind of comparative, transnational history Edmunds envisions.

How that transnational sensibility is imagined by contemporary North American Indian literature is the primary concern of this chapter. It focuses on two contemporary Indian authors, Thomas King and Leslie Marmon Silko, who set their fiction in North American border zones as a way to thematize the role that borders played in the conquest, and to envision how transnational processes of colonialism continue to shape the native world. In their writing, border regions are the spatial instantiation of Indians' social and political marginality, places that cast conflicts over sovereignty, cultural survival, and territorial possession into sharp relief. Yet they also see Indians' proximity to national borders as an opportunity to affirm ties to land and people that predate the divisive experience of European contact, to identify the ways the conquest redrew the map of indigenous North America, and to project hope for a revitalized future in which transnational connections are reinforced.

While a number of critics have addressed the role of borders in King's and Silko's fiction, the two have never been examined as a pair. This is not surprising, given their significant stylistic and ideological differences, as well as their very distinct geographical orientations. Silko, by far the better known of the two, is typically treated as a U.S. Native American author, while King is claimed by critics of Canadian literature. Yet neither fits easily into such national categories, which is not surprising since both have spent their lives in proximity to and traversing borders, both literal and figurative. I bring them together in an effort to model the kind of comparative, transnational approach to indigeneity I have sketched in the preceding paragraphs. In what follows, I consider how both authors situate representations of border communities within a broader legacy of North American colonialism, recognizing how the experience of conquest has left its mark on contemporary disputes between tribes and national governments across the continent. Despite their differences, King and Silko both ultimately affirm a form of indigenous transnationalism that extends across the geographic boundaries of the nation-state, but that is nonetheless rooted in attachments to particular places. Examining these authors together thus provides a broader and more varied view of Native North American border culture than the perspectives typically generated when they are situated within more regional frameworks.

I use the term *indigenous transnationalism* to describe these authors' representation of the divisive, centrifugal forces of modernity that have dispersed North American Indians, but also of the drive to form coalitions across the boundaries of tribal nations and nation-states. In their work, such coalitions are not simply a reaction to the fractious power of the nation-state, but rather the resumption of alliances and networks of filiation that were severed by the conquest and its aftermath. Both also gesture to the limits of such transnational alliances and the vexed condition of contemporary Native American politics in which a desire for solidarity across national lines rests uneasily against the nationalist assumptions underlying tribal claims to land and sovereignty. King's and Silko's fiction thus exemplifies some fundamental contradictions that lie at the heart of the North American cultural expressions traced by this book, which cross borders of many kinds while underscoring the enduring power of the nation form.

"The border crossed us"

Thomas King and Leslie Marmon Silko take up borders as a theme at a moment of escalating conflict between North American nation-states and the Indian tribes that occupy lands at or across their boundaries. "We didn't cross the border, the border crossed us," the rallying cry of immigration rights activists, has particular resonance for tribes whose territory was bisected by North America's current national borders.[9] The first Europeans could not have explored and mapped the continent without the help of Indians, who served as guides, trading partners, and allies in combat. Despite their importance to the survival and military victories of Europeans in America, Indians were rarely included in the negotiations between colonial powers, even when their treaties established borders that cut through native lands.[10] As geographer D. W. Meinig explains, the lines on the map were "imposed upon the continent with little reference to indigenous people, and indeed in many places with little reference to the land itself. The invaders had parceled the continent among themselves in designs reflective of their own complex rivalries and relative power."[11] Of course North

American Indians were engaged in their own rivalries long before Europeans arrived. However, the newcomers often manipulated these preexisting conflicts, ultimately partitioning the land according to their own interests. As the three major North American empires gave way to nation-states, the United States, Canada, and Mexico inherited the legacies of colonial relations with Indian tribes. Each new nation developed a different system for managing its indigenous populations, and these more specific national and regional histories will provide crucial context at various points in the ensuing analysis. But these details should not obscure the fact that all three North American nations eventually took a similar course in adopting policies that led to Indian removal, enforced assimilation, and the conversion of communally held land into private property.[12]

Tribes whose members lived on both sides of a national border experienced the consolidation of North America's nation-states in especially negative ways. The Yaqui, Tohono O'odham, Kickapoo, Gila River, Yavapai-Apache, Kumeyaay, and Cocopah to the south, and the Blackfoot, Cree, Haida, and members of the Six Nations confederacy to the north, were all directly affected by the drawing of borders in the mid-nineteenth century. Routes that had traditionally been used for migration, hunting, and ceremonial purposes were disrupted. Members of the same tribe were often separated from one another and forced to declare allegiance to different nations. Those who had transient lifestyles found their numbers undercounted by government agents, diminishing their allotment of land and resources.

The fate of the Turtle Mountain Chippewa living in a region of North Dakota and Manitoba bisected by the U.S.-Canadian border provides a vivid example. In 1883, the U.S. government allocated them lands based on the recommendation of special agent Cyrus Beede, who reported that the population was significantly smaller than had been claimed in initial estimates. He based his judgment on the considerable numbers of Métis—the mixed blood descendants of French fur traders and Indians—living in the area, whom he assumed to be Canadian, despite their own claims to the contrary.[13] In Beede's eyes, the Métis could not be Americans because the United States, unlike Canada, did not acknowledge the presence of a mixed-blood population. Unable to recognize that official understandings of Indian identity were inadequate, he made sense of the evidence by deciding that the Métis must actually reside north of the border. Since allotments were determined based on band membership within the United States, his accounting diminished slated reservation lands by over 50 percent, as well as substantially shrinking band roles, leading to a corresponding loss of federal assistance. So inadequate were reservation lands that when it came time to partition them into individual allotments, there was not enough to go around. The band was scattered when some members were forced to take land in South Dakota and Montana.[14] Chippewa on the Canadian side of the border (where they are known as Ojibwa) fared no better, since they signed a treaty with the government that led to significant loss of lands and the surrender of aboriginal rights. The effects of this partition resonate in Louise Erdrich's novel *The Bingo Palace*, where the dispersal of Indian families deprives a younger generation of connections to land and community.

More recently, the Tohono O'odham, whose enrolled members live in both Arizona and Sonora, have been devastated by their proximity to the U.S.-Mexico border. In their case, the problem is not competing national understandings of indigeneity, but changing requirements for citizenship and border crossing. In 1853, tribe members living in Mexico were severed from their community by the Gadsden Purchase. For the next one hundred years, lax border regulation enabled the Tohono O'odham to move freely from one side to the other. Their situation began to deteriorate in 1952, with the passage of a U.S. Immigration and Naturalization law dictating that proper records of birth were required to claim U.S. citizenship. Significant numbers of U.S. Tohono O'odham have no birth certificates, which meant that they were cut off from government benefits and subject to detention during routine border crossings. The situation of the Sonoran Tohono O'odham is even worse, since they are not recognized by either the U.S. or Mexican governments. Despite the fact that they carry tribal enrollment cards, they receive no federal benefits and live in dire poverty. Cattle ranchers and farmers have encroached onto O'odham lands on the Mexican side, forcing many tribe members to become migrant laborers or move to nearby cities. The U.S. government has declared that it will allow enrolled members from Mexico to live and work in the United States only if it is granted greater control over border crossing on O'odham land, a solution that the tribe has deemed unacceptable.[15] In 2003, a bill was introduced to the House of Representatives affirming the sovereignty of the O'odham Nation and proposing that all enrolled tribe members be naturalized as U.S. citizens. If it had passed, it would have effectively redrawn the border to grant U.S. citizenship to a population residing in Mexico. The Tohono O'odham have also appealed to the United Nations, arguing that current border management policies are in violation of the 1997 Declaration of Rights of Indigenous People.

The Border Crossed Us, a 2005 documentary by Rachel Nez, depicts the plight of the Tohono O'odham. It begins with an epigraph that describes the place of the border in their lives. "To the United States of America and to the Republic of Mexico, the boundary is a border that separates two great nation-states," it reads. "To us O'odham their border separates our family and defiles our traditional way of life given to us by our creator I'itoi." These statements encapsulate the opposition between the indigenous view of the border as an obstacle and the nation-state's view of the border as a line that secures territory and people, conflicts that are at the heart of the representations considered in this chapter.

The Tohono O'odham are one of many North American Indian groups who argue that they should have a special relationship to a national border based on prior occupancy of the land. Issues of access came to a head in the early twenty-first century as heightened concerns about terrorism, smuggling, and undocumented migration led to the militarization of national borders. At the heart of many disputes along the U.S.-Canadian border are disagreements over interpretation of the 1794 Jay Treaty signed by the United States and Britain, which granted "the Indians dwelling on either side of the . . . boundary line . . . [the right] freely to pass and repass by land or island navigation."[16] The tribe most immediately affected by the international border is the Mohawk, whose capital, Akwesasne, extends into New York, Ontario, and Quebec. Traditionally, the Mohawk have disregarded the international border that traverses their lands, but in the late twentieth century, controversies over the transportation of cigarettes and undocumented aliens caused new tensions with the U.S. and Canadian governments. After September 11, 2001, Akwesasne became the target of further negative scrutiny as a potential gateway for terrorists seeking to enter the United States. Many Mohawk decry this unwanted attention, professing that they are a sovereign nation that never signed treaties with the United States, Britain, or Canada. They claim that the Mohawk are not citizens of the United States or Canada, and are subject instead to the law of the Haudenosaunee, a confederacy of the Mohawk, Seneca, Cayuga, Onondaga, Oneida, and Tuscarora tribes that existed in the border region for centuries before the arrival of Europeans.[17] Leaders of the Haudenosaunee argue for the right to free passage across tribal lands. According to confederacy spokesperson Richard Hill, the Haudenosaunee believe that "the land is held in common for all the people. We are meant to share the land. . . . Our people will forever see the lands now called America and Canada as part of our national cultural patrimony, essential to our survival as a people."[18] Their position is premised on belief in the sovereignty of the Haudenosaunee, whose citizens have rights that override U.S. or Canadian laws about border regulation.

While specific disputes vary from one region to another, indigenous people are increasingly coming to recognize that the challenges of cultural survival, self-determination, and preservation of ancestral lands exemplified in conflicts over national borders are common across the Americas. Indians who have been unable to find recourse at the level of the nation-state are forming transnational alliances, sometimes across vast geographical and cultural distances.[19] Whereas there had once been significant disparities in the political agendas of Indians from North and South America, shared protest against the 1992 Quincentenary, debates about the signing of Nafta, and the 1994 Zapatista uprising in Chiapas all inspired a growing sense of hemispheric solidarity. While this trans-American sensibility might be seen as an unprecedented erosion of tribalism necessitated by the crisis of modernity, participants describe it as a restoration of ancient connections. At the same time that they look to the past, activists for indigenous rights are taking advantage of modern technologies for communication and information gathering, such as Global Positioning Systems (GPS) and the Internet. As their names suggest, groups such as the International Indian Treaty Council, the South and Meso-American Indian Information Center, the World Council of Indigenous Peoples, and the Rainforest Peoples Movement include Indians from many regions of the Americas.[20] The foremost goal of these coalitions is to address immediate social and economic problems. Nonetheless, literature and the arts play a vital role in the creation and dissemination of notions of indigenous transnationalism that imbue their participants with a sense of common purpose. As we will see, King and Silko speak across the borders of tribe and region to address causes that animate indigenous people from Chiapas to Nunavut. In their work, the border is at once a specific geographical location, a historical referent, and a metaphor for the obstacles to, and possibilities of, what Silko calls a "tribal internationalism." Inherent in this term is a contradictory sense of the importance of transnational alliances and an awareness of their limitations, given the ongoing salience of more strictly bounded categories like tribe and nation.

For some, the affirmation of indigenous transnationalism found in the work of King and Silko is controversial. Critics such as Elizabeth Cook-Lynn, Robert Warrior, and Craig Womack have argued for the importance of a literature that would, in Cook-Lynn's words, "take into account the specific kind of tribal/nation status of the original occupants of this continent."[21] King and Silko violate this principle by describing the intermingling of indigenous people of different tribal origins. In this, they come closer to the position Arnold Krupat and Michael A. Elliot have described as cosmopolitan, in that they recognize "commonalities that exceed national boundaries," as well as narrow definitions of identity.[22] While advocates of tribal particularity associate localism with tradition, King and Silko believe they are giving voice to an equally lengthy tradition of pan-Indianism. They understand the contemporary assertion of transborder Indian communi- ties as a historical corrective that brings current generations closer to the ways that Indians once understood their relations to one another. Silko de- scribes a version of indigenous transnationalism that entails the recovery of affiliations that were disrupted by national borders. She claims that traces of these filiations can still be found among contemporary Indian cultures. "The Uto-Aztecan languages are spoken as far north as Taos Pueblo near the Colorado border, all the way south to Mexico City," she writes. "Before the arrival of the Europeans, the indigenous communities throughout this region not only conducted commerce; the people shared cosmologies, and oral narratives."[23] For his part, King has decried rigid notions of tribal iden- tity for dividing Indian communities that might otherwise work together. He sees the excessive attention to defining who can and cannot be counted as Indian as a dangerous by-product of federal "identity legislation" that has "had the unforgivable consequence of setting Native against Native, de- stroying our ability and desire to associate with each other. This has been the true tragedy, the creation of legal categories that have made us our own enemy."[24] In each author's fiction, borders are both a geographical refer- ent and a metaphor for the dissolution of indigenous alliances and cultural networks. Divided by the boundaries of the nation-state, Indians in their work struggle to reconceive their relations to place and community. Their difficulty in finding viable alternatives is indicative of current predicaments within Native North American culture and politics, which are often torn between the affirmation of transborder community and commitments to nationalist struggles over sovereignty and territorial rights.

Indians on the Line: Thomas King and the U.S.-Canadian Border

Referring to the U.S.-Canadian borderlands, Thomas King has written that "the border doesn't mean that much to the majority of Native people in either country. It is, after all, a figment of someone else's imagination."[25] Because borders represent the outcome of negotiations among Euro- American powers that did not take indigenous people into account, King contends that many Indians continue to think of themselves less as citizens of the United States or Canada than as members of communities whose most important cultural and familial ties extend across international bor- ders. King's transnational sensibility must be attributed in part to his own life circumstances. A person of Cherokee, Greek, and German descent, King was born, raised, and educated in the United States, but he writes fiction set in Canada from the perspective of a member of the Blackfoot Confederacy. As he explained in an interview, "I'm Cherokee from Oklahoma, but I don't think of Oklahoma as home. If I think of any place as home it's the Alberta prairies, where I spent ten years with the Blackfoot people. I'm not Blackfoot, but that feels like the place I want to go back to."[26] In King's account, identity is less a matter of tribal or national membership than of social networks and feelings of belonging.

King's identification with the Blackfoot explains his recurrent concern with the U.S.-Canadian border, which bisects lands that once belonged to the Blackfoot Confederacy. When the border was drawn, it separated one band in the United States from the remaining six bands in Canada. In spite of this division, the Blackfoot have continued to share religious ceremonies and, since the 1990s, have sought to act as a political unit in disputes over land claims, water rights, and cross-border trade.[27] According to Blackfoot spokesperson Narcisse Blood, "there are some things that transcend man-made borders. . . . Our people's relationship to the land, our spirituality and communities—that's the best defense against being divided."[28] For Blood, enduring relationships to land and community are a corrective to the divisive impact of national borders. King's view is somewhat more complicated. It is only when his Indian characters have the ability to move away that they can fully appreciate the importance of the places they call home. At their most successful, these characters pass through a variety of contexts with ease, gathering worldly knowledge and diminishing borders to "a figment of someone else's imagination." But for those who remain stuck in place, the border serves as a vivid symbol of their confinement, as well as their marginality in the eyes of the nation-state. The disparity between movement and stasis points to a contradictory impulse at the heart of King's work, which expresses wishful fantasies about the erosion of North American nation-states while at the same time condemning the state for failing to make good on its promises to its indigenous populations.

King is at his most optimistic in his short story, "Borders," which is about the importance of being able to cross national borders on one's own terms, a freedom that, as we have seen, is paramount to Native North Americans in border regions. During a driving trip, a young boy and his mother are detained at the U.S.-Canadian line after she refuses to declare herself a citizen of either nation, identifying herself simply as "Blackfoot." Her response alludes to the fact that many Blackfoot consider themselves a sovereign nation because their lands once spanned the current border, extending from the North Saskatchewan River to Yellowstone. As she presents it, being a Blackfoot is not a supplement to national citizenship but an alternative, and to identify as American or Canadian would compromise the integrity of her tribal status.

The fact that the standoff takes place between the United States and Canada is significant because it calls into question the widely shared belief that the two nations share an open border. It reveals that the border can be crossed only by those who declare their allegiance to a nation-state. The alarm of Canadian officials at the woman's refusal to identify herself as Canadian resonates with fears about national dissolution that arose around efforts to declare an independent Quebec. One consequence of the crisis triggered by the 1980 Quebec referendum was that indigenous people in Canada received constitutional recognition as First Nations, a term that underscores their status as the continent's original occupants and as sovereign entities. However, these nations within a nation have only compounded Canadian anxieties about the future cohesion of the nation-state. These sentiments are embodied by the border agent who resists the idea that Blackfoot could be a substitute for Canadian. The woman's detention has other implications on the U.S. side of the border, evoking the fact that—since the 1831 case *Cherokee Nation v. Georgia*—Indian tribes have been considered "domestic dependent nations," meaning that tribal citizenship can only be understood as a subset of national citizenship. According to U.S. law, Blackfoot cannot function as the equivalent of Canadian or U.S. American. The U.S. border agents cannot allow the woman to enter the country without a legitimate declaration of citizenship. King's story brings closure to the crisis when both U.S. and Canadian officers finally agree that the protagonist can describe herself only as Blackfoot, rather than as Canadian. If the agents are spokespersons for national policies about border crossing, their concession is freighted with symbolic import, since it suggests an official affirmation of the claim that tribal membership is the equivalent of national citizenship. The woman achieves the right to unrestricted movement that has been the goal of many tribes in the region and along the U.S.-Mexican border. Of course, the ease with which the problem is managed only serves as a reminder of fiction's capacity to grant imagined resolution to disputes that remain unsettled in reality.

Whereas "Borders" is a neat allegory for conflict between Indians and the nation state, King's *Truth and Bright Water* is a much more complicated, and less hopeful, meditation on the place of the U.S.-Canadian border in an Indian community. The novel is set in fictional towns along the Shield River, which divides Montana from Alberta. Its protagonist is the teenaged

Tecumseh, named for the famous Shawnee leader who fought to defend his people's lands. He lives with his mother in Truth, on the American side of the border, while the majority of their friends and relatives live on the other side of the river in the Bright Water Reserve. Over the course of a summer, he moves back and forth across the border as he contends with a series of difficult and confusing events. These include his apprenticeship to the zany, unpredictable Indian artist, Monroe Swimmer; his father's clumsy and often bitter attempts at parenting; and the depression and eventual suicide of his cousin Lum. Throughout much of the novel, the community is preparing for the annual Indian Days celebration, an event that brings together Indians from many tribes and regions with well-heeled tourists in search of "authentic" Indian encounters. As participants from around the world gather in Bright Water, it is temporarily transformed into a cosmopolitan hub with Indians at its center. But once the festivities are over, the visitors disperse, leaving the region's social and economic troubles unresolved. Although *Truth and Bright Water* is narrated with the humor and understatement typical of King's writing, beneath his deceptively light tone it is darker and more critical than his previous works of fiction.[29] It describes a community plagued by the fact that many of its members have forgotten their ties to land and people. Lacking a sense of their own past, they are uncertain about how to navigate the future. In this context, the border is both a literal obstacle and a figure for the impediments confronting a current generation of North American Indians.

In *Truth and Bright Water*, the international border cuts through the novel's plot and setting.[30] The problem in this sparsely populated region is not the vigorous policing of the border, but its neglect, which is emblematic of a more general attitude on the part of the Canadian government toward its First Peoples. Abandonment by the Canadian government is etched deep in the very geography of the Bright Water Reserve. The border is marked by the Shield River, which constitutes a natural boundary between the United States and Canada. There is no easy way across and a planned bridge remains perilously incomplete. Its rusting skeleton is a symbol for the destitution of the Indian community living on and around it. The bridge is all that remains of a highway designed to facilitate international commerce and bring tourists into the area. Its abandonment has left this border community isolated and almost literally immobile, due to a lack of infrastructure and the most basic public services.

Although King's novel is set in the present, it represents current relations between the Canadian government and indigenous people as the product of a long and conflicted history. In contrast to the United States, where a violent process of Indian removal coincided with the settlement of the American West, Canada's Indian populations were already decimated by starvation and epidemic disease before significant numbers of settlers arrived. Canada's frontier history is thus less bloody than that of the United States. Its Indians were typically ignored rather than relocated by force, but with equally devastating consequences for their survival. Between 1871 and 1921, the Canadian government signed eleven numbered treaties with Indians in the western interior, including the Blackfoot, resulting in a considerable diminution of tribal lands.[31] For the next fifty years, the government largely turned its back on these Indians, encouraging them to move to cities and give up their tribal affiliations, or isolating them on reserves. This position was crystallized in the infamous White Paper of 1969, which rejected Indian land claims and enjoined them to assimilate.[32] Although subsequent decades saw the increasing visibility of and public sympathy for aboriginal issues, the rhetoric of progress has often outpaced actual change.[33] A 1996 report issued by the Royal Commission on Aboriginal Peoples described the poverty and unemployment of indigenous Canadian communities and declared the need for immediate improvements in housing, education, and job training. Despite the urgent concerns it identified, budget problems in the ensuing years meant that few of the recommendations were followed.[34] *Truth and Bright Water*, which was published three years after the Royal Commission report, depicts a community plagued by poverty, unemployment, and domestic violence, where success is attainable only to those who move away.

Overlooked by the modern state, the inhabitants of Bright Water are often aware that they lack a collective sense of the past to remind them that things could be otherwise. In setting the novel along the Shield River, King ties the present-day international border to a time before the founding of the United States or Canada. The novel's opening paragraph is a single sentence, "the river begins in ice," referring to a point of origin prior to and more enduring than human history.[35] But when Tecumseh's mother tells him that the river has "been here since the beginning of time" (52), he cannot translate this information into any meaningful knowledge. The discovery of a mysterious skull near the river prompts him to speculate that it is "prehistoric," or that "maybe the bluff was once a burial ground. Maybe at one time we buried our dead there and then forgot about it" (71). This forgetting is symptomatic of a more general predicament in *Truth and Bright Water*, where native characters feel they have longstanding ties to the land, but lack concrete knowledge that could be used to translate those feelings into the more meaningful forms of action practiced by many tribes in North America's border regions. Absent any connection to their distant ancestors, the present generation struggles to establish significant relationships to place and community.

In King's novel, the consequences of such gaps in generational transmission are dire. The Shield River, which represents the tribe's ties to a precontact past, as well as the connective link between one side of the border and the other, is filled with trash. Whereas Indians are often at the forefront of protests against environmental degradation, in King's novel unemployment and financial hardship have made Indians part of the problem. Tecumseh's father actively participates in the pollution of ancestral lands by dumping medical waste illegally in the reserve landfill. Garbage, as one character puts it, is "the new buffalo" (153), an abundant resource within the prairie ecosystem as inextricably associated with the survival of modern Indians as the buffalo were for their ancestors. The trashing of the local environment is symptomatic of a more general disregard for the future among people who have little cause to be optimistic. Lum is the most tragic example of wasted resources in *Truth and Bright Water*. Repeatedly beaten and thrown out of the house by his father, Lum longs to escape the reserve but lacks the resources to do so, venting his frustrated desires for movement by running, eventually racing to his death off the unfinished bridge. Reenacting the suicidal leap taken by so many Indian characters in nineteenth-century U.S. literature, Lum's death becomes part of a self-perpetuating cycle of violence and destruction.[36] In this late twentieth-century version of the narrative, it makes sense that the search for Lum's body turns up "all sorts of junk," including "tires, car parts, a lawn mower, a mattress" and barrels of medical waste (259), since Lum—who represents a younger generation that should be the tribe's hope for the future—has been treated as refuse to be cast away. His death in the river that divides the United States from Canada turns the international border into a figure for the many obstacles that confront a young generation of Indians, who have few ties to traditions of the past, but limited opportunities to leave their past behind.

The novel's most hopeful character is the artist Monroe Swimmer, who left the reserve as a troubled young man and came back a wealthy and internationally acclaimed "Indian artist." His success at traveling the world, and irreverent, cosmopolitan sensibility, makes borders seem irrelevant. At the beginning of the novel he has returned to Bright Water, where he undertakes a series of projects that seek to restore his community's fragile relationships to their land and history. His first act is to rearrange the landscape by painting an abandoned church in such a way that it disappears and then repopulating the coulee with buffalo sculptures. Monroe's version of land art brings the church, an artifact of colonialism built by missionaries dedicated to converting the Indians, into a more felicitous relationship to its surroundings. In a reversal of the colonial process, it is the church, rather than the Indian, that vanishes. Monroe replaces it with buffalo sculptures, which recall a time when the coulee was filled with actual buffalo. The difference is that these buffalo are made of iron, and are thus emphatically a part of a modern landscape that is actually more permanent than the living animals they inspired. Monroe's other important symbolic act is to "rescue" Indian skulls by collecting them from museums around the world and laying them to rest in the Shield River. He does this not out of a nostalgic belief that he is returning them to their lost origins, but because, he claims, "this is the centre of the universe. Where else would I bring them? Where else would they want to be?" (251). His attempt to dispose of the Indian remains in a respectful manner and to fill the coulee with art bespeaks a very different relationship to the environment than the thoughtless pollution of the river. In a context where Indians have lost ancestral memories and traditions, Monroe invents ceremonies to take their place.

At one point in the novel, Monroe stands near the border, observing, "there's Canada . . . And this is the United States. . . . Ridiculous isn't it?" (131). Monroe's dismissal of the international border resonates with contemporary events, since *Truth and Bright Water* was published five years after Nafta went into effect. But the open borders King's characters envision are very different from those introduced by the free trade accords, which had been protested by Indians across North America. The most dramatic act of rebellion was the Zapatista uprising in Chiapas, Mexico; however, Indians in the United States and Canada also decried the absence of tribal governments in negotiations over Nafta, fearing its consequences for indigenous sovereignty, the environment, and local economies.[37] Given these circumstances, it is significant that Monroe's performances culminate in a potlatch, where he counters the ethos of free trade by giving extravagantly without expecting anything in return. His activities recall the fact that the potlatch was once thought to be so subversive it was outlawed by federal authorities.[38] Straddling the worlds of the Indian reserve and cosmopolitan, Euro-American culture, Monroe represents an alternative to both the economically motivated transnationalism of Nafta and the devastating immobility of many in his community. Describing his location at the margins of two nation-states as "the centre of the universe," he aspires to redraw the map so that Indian places and histories are invested with significance and value.

It is not surprising that Monroe would describe the division of land into two separate nations as "ridiculous" (131), since he has excelled at border crossing, moving easily from one country to another, from the effete world of museums and art galleries to the untutored societies of Truth and Bright Water. But however affirming Monroe's symbolic acts may be, they cannot erase the real social problems that plague the Indians on the Bright Water Reserve.[39] Monroe's heady transnationalism is not a viable option for most members of his community, whose suffering requires remedies that can only be dispensed by the state. By the novel's end, Tecumseh's father still has no gainful employment and has not managed to reconcile with his estranged wife, the Shield River continues to be awash in illegally dumped medical waste, and Lum is dead. In the final chapter, Tecumseh's mother fulfills her dream of being an actress by performing in a community theater production of *Snow White* that is actually "a political satire about the federal government and Indians" (265). This sounds like a play that King himself would write, and a more optimistic reading of the novel would find hope in the possibility that it could move its audience to take political action. But its satirical thrust strikes Tecumseh as obvious, and any pleasure in his mother's success is overshadowed by longing for his dead cousin. The Indians who perform in and watch the play are all too aware of the ways they have been mistreated by the government. What they need most is not demystification, but jobs and resources. In *Truth and Bright Water* the literal edge of the nation is the place where the failures of federal Indian policy are most glaringly evident. It thus points to the contradictions between King's claim that national borders are meaningless to Indians, and his denunciation of the nation-state for abandoning its indigenous citizens.

King's writing brings attention to the continent's northern borderlands and the histories of Indian groups and Indian-Anglo contact there. Like its southern counterpart, King's border region is home to a hybrid culture where people from many different ethnic, linguistic, and national contexts come uneasily together. And like its southern counterpart, King's region suffers from pollution and decaying infrastructure. But unlike the U.S.-Mexico borderlands, this is a place where the United States seems to offer no better opportunities than those available in Canada, their similarities registered in characters' occasional confusion about which country they are in. Indeed, it is the sameness of both sides that makes the arbitrary nature of borders so apparent and so devastating. In the U.S.-Canadian borderlands, King's characters struggle to survive and to create symbolic gestures to the Indian's persistence and future revitalization. At the same time, the unfinished bridge looms large as a sign of the nation's neglectful guardianship, as well as the limits to the kind of exuberant border crossing practiced by Monroe Swimmer. The river, with its prehistoric origins, recalls a landscape and the people who inhabited it long before the era of European contact. But its polluted waters and Lum's suicidal leap suggest that those ties to the land have become fragile. In these circumstances, we must question the victory gained by the boy and his mother in "Borders," asking whether freedom of passage is enough, given the constraints that lie on either side. Should the target of Indian protest be national borders when so many of the problems King exposes demand a stronger and more responsible federal government for their solution?

Many of the concerns about the degradation of border regions voiced in King's fiction are shared by Leslie Marmon Silko's *Almanac of the Dead*, a novel that also reflects on the long history of border trouble between Indians and North America's nation-states. However, whereas King's characters seek ways to survive within North America's current political system, Silko imagines the possibility of a revolution that would radically redraw North America's borders. To do so, she draws on a different set of regional and tribal histories, turning south to Mexico's borders with the United States and Guatemala as the epicenters of her fictive universe.

At the Southern Borders of North America: Leslie Marmon Silko's *Almanac of the Dead*

The centrality of borders to Leslie Marmon Silko's *Almanac of the Dead* is announced by its frontispiece, a map of North America centered on the U.S.-Mexico borderlands. Silko's picture of North America departs from conventional mapping techniques in significant ways. Instead of the uniform grid of Western cartography, places are sized and distances measured according to their symbolic importance. These distortions of scale evoke precontact Mesoamerican maps, which, as geographer Barbara Mundy explains, reflect a "spatial reality . . . defined and structured by social relationships."[40] Social relationships determine the significance of key locations and routes, which are labeled on the map accompanied by lists of the individuals (fictional and historical) who have been associated with them at various points in time. Places are connected by dotted lines that indicate the movement of people and things, rather than the more static landmarks that are typically indicated on a map. And whereas maps usually seek to a capture a particular moment in time, Silko depicts past, present, and future events simultaneously. This image thus serves as a fitting introduction to Silko's novel, where revisionist cartography is tied to the broader project of anticolonial critique.[41]

The prominence of the U.S.-Mexico border, which cuts across the center of Silko's "500 Year Map," is indicative of its particular importance to the novel's imagined geography. While the word MEXICO is printed beneath it in a large, dark font, the United States goes unnamed, reversing the terms of the Euro-American maps that erased the signs of an Indian presence on the continent. Yet the depiction of the U.S.-Mexico border as a dark, seemingly fixed straight line seems out of keeping with the map's otherwise dynamic view of time and space. It is of the same shade and thickness as the lines dividing land from sea, as if to suggest that it is equally permanent and natural. This initial impression of an impassable, permanent border will be eroded by the narrative, which relates events that promise to bring about the profound reconfiguration of North America's national boundaries. However, the contradictions encoded in the map also represent the ongoing struggle between those who insist on the fixity of borders and those who aspire to subvert them.

Almanac of the Dead is Silko's most ambitious literary project to date. The scope of her first novel, *Ceremony*, and the autobiographical *Storyteller* are far more local, concentrating on the Laguna Pueblo Reservation in New Mexico where she was born and raised. With *Almanac*, Silko expands her fictional geography beyond the borders of the United States to the Americas, Europe, and other parts of the globe.[42] This is a novel of epic proportions, divided into five parts that are labeled according to ascending models of geographic scale, moving from countries ("The United States of America" and "Mexico") to a continent ("Africa"), a hemisphere ("The Americas"), and worlds ("The Fifth World," and "One World, Many Tribes"). Its plotlines are numerous, tangled, and diffuse. Unlike King's *Truth and Bright Water*, *Almanac* is not a novel about individuals but about groups and sweeping historical events. No one protagonist emerges amidst the many characters who are introduced and then sidelined, sometimes for hundreds of pages, only to reemerge just as they seem to have disappeared altogether. It depicts a world on the edge of anarchy, inhabited by such cartoonishly unsavory characters as the greedy, dishonest Judge Arne, who has furtive sex with his pet basset hound; David, a photographer who heartlessly captures scenes of brutal violence on film; Beaufrey, who makes and sells snuff films; Serlo, a white supremacist who conspires to rid the world of inferior races; and Max Blue, the ruthless patriarch of a family crime ring. Against the corrupt and unjust society these characters represent, pockets of resistance are amassing in the United States and Mexico. Key figures in this incipient revolution include, in the South, the twin prophets Tacho and El Feo, and Angelita La Escapia, leader of the People's Army of Justice and Retribution; and in the North, a black veteran and radio broadcaster named Clinton, who imagines himself the leader of an army of the homeless, a political organizer who calls himself the Barefoot Hopi, and the lawyer-poet, Wilson Weasel Tail. While many of the insurgents are Indians whose ultimate goal is the reclamation of stolen land, they are joined by fellow travelers of many different races and nationalities, who have had enough of the violence, environmental degradation, and economic inequities plaguing North America. These alliances among indigenous and nonindigenous people confound any notion of tribal purity. Moreover, the novel's account of the ongoing, violent rivalries among precontact Amerindian people makes it impossible to draw simple oppositions between indigenous and Euro-American conceptions of power and sovereignty. It depicts an unstoppable north-south migration that promises to bring North and South together to fulfill the map's foreboding legend: "Ancient prophecies foretold the arrival of Europeans in the Americas. The ancient prophecies also foretell the disappearance of all things European." The signs of this coming revolution are most evident at Mexico's borders with the United States and Guatemala. There, conflict between indigenous people and the nation-state has led to conditions of near anarchy, which portend further bloodshed and destruction but also enable the imagination of a postnational future to emerge from the chaos.

The longitudinal organization of Silko's novel is central to its effort to transform the American geographic imaginary. As Arnold Krupat has observed, *Almanac* rewrites the westward course of Manifest Destiny by making "a north-south/south-north directionality . . . central to the narrative of 'Our America.'" This is a subversive gesture, he claims, because it undermines "the hegemonic Euramerican narrative, whose geographical imperative presumes an irresistible ('destined') movement from east to west."[43] However, neither Krupat nor any other critic has adequately explained why Silko, an author whose previous work was set within the borders of the United States, would locate a significant portion of her novel in Mexico. While, in many ways, *Almanac* presumes to be a novel about the Americas and even the world, the action takes place almost exclusively in the United States and Mexico. Its literary geography does more than simply reverse the east-west terms of Manifest Destiny. Rather, it seeks to imagine the reconciliation of the Americas that were divided by the conquest, turning to the indigenous histories of present-day Mexico as a vital source of inspiration for future revolutionary activity. These histories are contained in the eponymous Almanacs, based on the Mayan codices, which tie together the lives of many characters across vast temporal and geographical distances. Ultimately, the novel predicts, national borders will be powerless to stop the inexorable movement of populations that have been sundered and the formation of new alliances that span the boundaries of tribe and nation.

Silko's essays "Fences against Freedom" and "The Border Patrol State" provide a context for interpreting the representation of national borders in *Almanac of the Dead*. At the center of each piece is an anecdote about being detained by the U.S. Border Patrol while driving from Albuquerque to Tucson. This scary and humiliating experience leads Silko to reflect on the practice of racial profiling, and the injustice of policies that seek to facilitate trade while impeding human movement across national borders. Over the course of the essays, her perspective shifts from a critique of U.S. border management to a more expansive view of migration and the struggles of border communities throughout the Americas. Silko begins "The Border Patrol State" by speaking as a U.S. citizen. She describes the inhabitants of the Laguna Pueblo Reservation where she was raised as patriotic Americans who taught their children to believe that "the freedom to travel was our inalienable right."[44] Having been taught that mobility is "an integral part of the American identity," she condemns the restrictive policies of the U.S. government and institutions such as the Immigration and Naturalization Service (INS) and Border Patrol.[45] However, as her argument unfolds, her targets become geographically and historically broader and she begins to make connections between the border troubles faced by Indians in the United States and in other parts of the Americas. "The so-called Indian Wars from the days of Sitting Bull and Red Cloud have never really ended in the Americas," she writes. "The Indian people of southern Mexico, of Guatemala, and those left in El Salvador, too, are still fighting for their lives and for their land against the cavalry patrols sent out by the governments of those lands. The Americas are Indian country, and the 'Indian problem' is not about to go away."[46] She recognizes that national borders have divided Indians from one another not only in the United States and Mexico but also in many other parts of the Americas. Despite the dire circumstances it describes, "The Border Patrol State" ends with Silko's defiant claim that national borders are powerless to stop the inexorable alliance of indigenous people: "It is no use; borders haven't worked, and they won't work, not now, as the indigenous people of the Americas reassert their kinship and solidarity with one another. A mass migration is already under way."[47] These words are lifted nearly verbatim from the pages of *Almanac*, where Silko sees the erosion of national borders as the first step toward the reclamation of Indian lands and the realization of her prophetic vision of "the disappearance of all things European."

Almanac is an opportunity for Silko to work through, in fictive terms, the anger toward the militarization of national borders expressed in her essays. In the novel, North America's borders are failing as nation-states lose their ability to control the transnational circulation of people and goods. Whereas King's Monroe Swimmer imagines a forgotten place along the U.S.-Canadian border as "the centre of the universe," Silko turns south to Mexico's borders as places where the future transformation of North America's sociopolitical landscape is already in evidence. In an interview, she explains that the Mexican portions of the novel were inspired by the passage of English-only legislation in Arizona. Outraged at U.S. voters' rejection of the Mexican elements in their midst, she determined to write about the inextricable mixture of U.S. and Mexican cultures in North America.[48]

The Mexicanization of the United States is vividly apparent in Silko's hometown of Tucson, described on the map as "home to an assortment of speculators, confidence men, embezzlers, lawyers, judges, police and other criminals, as well as addicts and pushers, since the 1880s and the Apache Wars." Although it is seventy miles from the actual border with Mexico, Silko represents Tucson as plagued by unrest coming up from the south. Although significant numbers of undocumented Mexicans are a relatively recent phenomenon in Tucson, her reference to the Apache Wars links Arizona's current border troubles to an ongoing history of conflict between Indians and the nation-state. In the novel's present, violence in the region is driving wealthy Mexican consumers away, with dire effects on local economies. As one character reflects, "Tucson was too close to Mexico. Tucson *was* Mexico, only no one in the United States had realized it yet."[49] His observations are apt, coming at the end of a novel that has illustrated the interdependence of the two national economies, the multidirectional movement of populations, and the rapid spread of conflict across national borders. They provide an ironic commentary on the thick and seemingly permanent border depicted by the "Five Hundred Year Map." If Tucson *is* Mexico by the novel's end, then the narrative has undermined the solidity and permanence of the border depicted on the map, which, in retrospect, looks more like the compensatory fantasy of those in power than a representation of current realities.

Despite the centrality of the U.S.-Mexico borderlands to the "Five Hundred Year Map," this region is not the exclusive focus of *Almanac of the Dead*. Instead it takes a broader view of the continent by looking to Mexico's southern border, which shares many of the problems that plague its counterpart to the north. Without erasing the differences between the two regions, *Almanac* identifies their historical and cultural similarities, providing a comparative perspective that is often missing from literature and criticism about the U.S.-Mexico border. The novel shows that concern about proximity to a poorer nation is not exclusive to the United States, since the Mexican government is equally worried that Guatemala's social and political problems will seep across their shared border. In both cases, the border bisects land that has been inhabited by Indians since long before the era of European contact, and the transborder movement of Indians is perceived as a growing threat. And in both cases, ever since there has been a border, indigenous people have been finding ways to circumvent it.

The Mexican portions of the novel are set primarily in Chiapas, a region that has a history of Indian rebellions extending back to the sixteenth century. As a result of its geographic and administrative distance from centers of federal government, Chiapas has never been effectively assimilated into the Mexican national community.[50] The linguistic and cultural similarities of populations on either side of the border mean that they have more in common with one another than with fellow citizens.[51] As Menardo, a wealthy Mexican businessman, reflects (sounding much like his counterparts in Arizona and Texas), "Chiapas had the misfortune of being too close to the border, which leaked rabble rousers and thieves like a sewage pipe" (261). His comment alludes to the fact that, since the 1970s, Mexico's southern border has served as a gateway for migrants seeking refuge from poverty and political repression in Central and South America. In the 1970s and 1980s, large numbers of Mayans from the Guatemalan side of the border fled into Mexico in an effort to escape assaults by the government, which believed them to be associated with forces of political insurgency.[52] Menardo seeks to capitalize on this instability by selling his clients insurance "against all losses, no matter what the cause, including acts of God, mutinies, war, and revolution." His argument is convincing to many Chiapan elites, who believe that the government will be powerless to protect them against the "great storm [that] is gathering on the southern horizon" (293). Echoing the xenophobic sentiments of some U.S. citizens, their words point to the ripple effect of the United States' punitive immigration policies, as wealthier Latin American nations seek to reinforce their borders against incursion from their poorer neighbors. Here *Almanac* anticipates Mexico's Plan Sur, a policy of stringent border management instituted in 2000 under the presidency of Vicente Fox that was supported by, and modeled on, the United States' efforts to secure its own borders.[53] Mexico's actions reverberated farther south in Guatemala, which inaugurated the Venceremos 2001 program one year later, intending to flush out its own population of undocumented migrants. The more general effect of comparisons between the United States and Mexico is thus to portray the continent, and the hemisphere, as an integrated system in which local events often have far broader regional, or even global, consequences.

In the novel, the strenuous efforts of nation-states to police their southern borders are doomed to failure. One problem with the excessive anxiety about incursion from the south is that flows of illicit goods and people are actually multidirectional. Another is that the incendiary juxtaposition of extreme wealth and poverty associated with border regions exists in many different places. This means there is as much political instability within North America's nation-states as there is at their borders, so that conflict cannot always be attributed to external antagonists. Indians in *Almanac* have an exceptionally keen understanding of North America's current political crisis because they can situate it within a deep historical perspective that extends back before the birth of the nation-state. This knowledge enables them to recognize the impermanence and fallibility of borders, and to play an instrumental role in their erosion. For example, the Tohono O'odham Reservation is depicted as the location of "secret border-crossing routes" (201) used by the smugglers Root and Calabazas. As Calabazas explains:

> We don't believe in boundaries. Borders. Nothing like that. We are here thousands of years before the first whites. We are here before maps or quit claims. We know where we belong on this earth. We have always moved freely. North-south. East-west. We pay no attention to what isn't real. Imaginary lines. Imaginary minutes and hours. Written law. We recognize none of that. And we carry a great many things back and forth. We don't see any border. We have been here and this has continued thousands of years. We don't stop. No one stops us. (216)

It is not surprising that these words are spoken by Calabazas, a Yaqui Indian whose ancestors fiercely defended their autonomy from both the U.S. and Mexican governments.[54] Dispersed on either side of the border, today Yaqui in the United States and Mexico continue to maintain a sense of common identity and shared religious practices.[55] As a smuggler, Calabazas represents the outgrowth of many generations that have defied the existence of the border, based on claims to the land that precede the era of European contact. The novel imagines a future in which illicit activity such as smuggling becomes so pervasive that national borders break down altogether.

It is significant that Calabazas comes from south of the U.S. border, since Mexico and Mexicans are crucial to the novel's depiction of indigenous history in the Americas, as well as its vision of a "tribal internationalism" that would unite Indians from North and South. Mexico is the origin of the most important cultural artifacts in the novel, the eponymous Almanacs containing the history of an unnamed tribe that was driven north during the conquest. As they fall into the hands of the Yaqui, who revise and append their contents, they become a collective story of Indians in the Americas. According to Yoeme, the Yaqui woman who bequeaths the notebooks to her granddaughters Lecha and Zeta, the Almanacs' records of the past constitute a "living power," since they are also prophecies for a future "that would bring all the tribal people of the Americas together to retake the land" (569). In a context where history is said to move in cycles, it is crucial for Indians in the present to know about their Mexican ancestors, since such information can form the basis for decisions about future action.

Mexico is also at the epicenter of a revisionist history of European conquest. In this version, "the so-called conquerors merely aligned themselves with forces already in power or forces already gathered to strip power from rivals. The tribes in Mexico had been drifting toward political disaster for hundreds of years before the Europeans ever appeared" (220). *Almanac* emphasizes violent rivalries among indigenous people, refusing to romanticize the precontact past. It diminishes the conquerors by representing them as parasites who, through an accident of good timing, were able to take advantage of preexisting political instabilities among the great Indian civilizations of southern Mexico. According to this indigenous view of history, New Spain (and then Mexico) is also the location of numerous subsequent and ongoing acts of resistance against European colonialism. The notion of tribal internationalism articulated by the novel would require indigenous people to overcome historical animosities in order to marshal their collective insurrectionary power. When Angelita La Escapia, leader of the Indigenous People's Army, recounts a chronology of Indian rebellion in the Americas, she lists many events that occurred on Spanish or Mexican soil (528–30). Her catalogue reflects the particularly brutal nature of Spanish colonialism, as well as the fierce defiance of groups such as the Maya of the Chiapas region, and the more dispersed Indian populations in the north.[56] Taken together with the description of uprisings in other parts of the Americas, these events play a vital role in La Escapia's account of an unbroken history of indigenous resistance. Thus, as the narrative spreads across the U.S. border, Mexico and other Latin American nations provide an essential link to indigenous cultural ancestry and an inspiration for future revolutionary activity.

This point is reconfirmed in the final chapter, which is about the home-coming of Sterling, a young Laguna Indian who was banished by his tribe early in the novel after failing to stop a Hollywood movie crew from film-ing their sacred idol, a stone snake. As he moves toward home, he recalls a legend about his ancestors, who lived in what is now Mexico. They were forced to flee north when the land was taken over by a tribe of evil sorcer-ers, who shared the European conquerors' penchant for violence and de-struction. Sterling gains a new appreciation for this story when he makes a pilgrimage to the stone snake and discovers that it is "looking south in the direction from which the twin brothers and the people would come" (763). The "twin brothers" Tacho and El Feo are Mexican prophets who have been instrumental in amassing support for an indigenous movement to reclaim lost lands. By the novel's end, Sterling has learned to see the snake as a mes-senger whose orientation toward Mexico portends the reconciliation of in-digenous people from North and South, and the fulfillment of the proph-ecy that together they will repossess the Americas. Southern Mexico, where the twin brothers reside, is thus figured as a point of origin for Indians who were dispersed across the continent, and one important source of the revolutionary energies that are amassing in many different regions in the novel's present.

In a fascinating convergence of fiction and history, Silko's representa-tion of the incendiary climate among the indigenous people of southern Mexico would have a real-life analogue in the Zapatista uprising, which took place less than three years after the publication of her novel. What made *Almanac* seem so prescient is that it identified Chiapas as the source of a coming indigenous revolution that would sweep across the Ameri-cas. Indeed, some have claimed that the novel was a catalyst for the revolt, noting the writerly nature of the Zapatistas' communiqués and the more concrete fact that a number of the Zapatista Army of National Liberation (EZLN [Ejército Zapatista de Liberación]) insurgents were known to have read it during the summer of 1993. Regardless of whether the novel has any causal connection to the events in Chiapas, the region's association with ancient Mayan culture, its history of indigenous rebellions, and contempo-rary problems of poverty and resource depletion explain why it became one of the epicenters of Silko's imagined revolution.[57] Although the Zap-atistas articulated the goals of the rebellion in nationalist terms—claiming their rights as citizens of the Mexican state—Silko, and many other Native North Americans, believed that it had broader implications.[58] She took it as evidence for the prophetic claims she had made many times in *Almanac* that European power in the Americas was beginning to erode and that its decline would begin at the borders of the nation, far from centers of state power.

With *Almanac*, Leslie Marmon Silko provides a view of the borderlands that is quite different from more conventional accounts coming from the United States, which tend to be focused predominantly on Anglo-Mexican relations. Like Thomas King, she insists that Indians are important participants in the story of North America's borderlands and shows how attention to indigenous history can change the questions we ask about these regions. In Silko's case, the turn to Mexico's borders with the United States and Guatemala reorients the east-west geography of Manifest Destiny toward an emphasis on movement between north and south. By situating her novel along both borders, she introduces a comparative perspective that is rare in representations of the U.S.-Mexico borderlands, drawing parallels between different national policies of immigration and border management, as well as transborder indigenous cultures such as the Maya to the south and the Yaqui and Tohono O'odham to the north. By placing Indian people and concerns at the heart of the novel, she draws on a historical archive that extends back before European contact. From this perspective, the borders of North America's current nation-states seem far less stable and permanent than their representation on the map would suggest, and this deep view of history is the basis for the novel's claim that eventually things European will vanish from the Americas. It is not clear that a superior form of political organization has been developed to take their place, since indigenous people have their own history of violent rivalry, as well as their own attachments to land and nation. Nonetheless, the novel holds out some hope that tribal internationalism—forged of prolonged and fruitful interchange between North and South—is a form that would simultaneously maintain the specificity of local attachments and recognize solidarities that extend across national borders.

This chapter ends with one more look at the map of North America, this time through the eyes of the Oglala-Sicangu/Lakota artist Colleen Cutschall. Her 1994 painting *Beads and Boat People* depicts the American continent(s) surrounded by ships approaching from all sides. In Cutschall's rendition, North America is distorted and diminished, as if to challenge the position of grandiose centrality it occupies on a conventional political map (fig. 1.3). Both continents are outlined in blood red and labeled, respectively, ARTIFACT #1 and ARTIFACT #2, playing on the ethnographic impulse to objectify and order the world, and suggesting that they are relics of the past

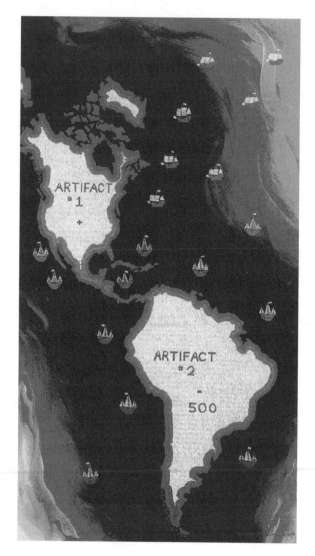

1.3. Colleen Cutschall, "Beads and Boat People" (1994). Reprinted by permission of the artist.

with little contemporary relevance. The signs "+" and "- 500" allude to the five hundred indigenous nations as well as the process of colonization that began five centuries ago, giving rise to the map as it exists today. Cutschall shows us that the map is not timeless and permanent, but rather a product of the historical forces involved in what historian Edmundo O'Gorman called "the invention of America."[59] But there is more here than what im-

mediately meets the eye. These Americas have no borders, save the outlines
that divide land from sea. It is unclear whether the boats that surround
them are coming or going. The arithmetic signs make the map's historical
location ambiguous: is this a picture of the continents after they have been
claimed and colonized by Europeans? Or are these the Americas that belonged to indigenous people for thousands of years before the first European arrivals? Are they marked as "artifacts" because the colonizers have reduced them to objects to be studied and classified? Or is the map itself an
artifact appropriated by the Indian artist in a reversal of the colonial process? Does the fact that there are no nations identified by this map suggest
the all-encompassing nature of European colonialism? Nostalgia for precontact America? The potential for indigenous people to form alliances that
transcend current national borders?

The power of Cutschall's work lies in its refusal to answer these questions, while confronting us with the defamiliarizing spectacle of a borderless America. While neither King nor Silko goes to quite this extreme, each
contends, in no uncertain terms, that North America's current national borders pose an affront to indigenous people, who have made every effort to
challenge and thwart their legitimacy. In doing so, these authors tap into
histories of North America's borderlands that are often overlooked in the
emphasis on Mexican-Anglo cultures along the U.S.-Mexico border. And
in the process, they rely on cultural geographies that exceed the boundaries of the nation-state, geographies defined not by the borders of the
United States, Canada, or Mexico, but by the routes and roots established
by people who inhabited the land long before the first European arrivals,
and whose lifeways were profoundly reconfigured by the conquest. As their
work remaps the continent, it poses a challenge to dominant understandings of North American borderlands' theoretical and material significance.
The distinctive contribution of this indigenous perspective comes more
clearly into focus when these authors are examined together, lifted out of
the more narrowly regional and/or national frames in which they are often
discussed. The next chapter provides further context for these views by examining the significance of national borders to former slaves and their descendants, who see them not as divisive obstacles, but as pathways to liberty
that distinguish property from personhood, enslavement from freedom.

CHAPTER TWO

Fugitive Geographies: Rerouting the Stories of North American Slavery

In Alice Walker's 1998 novel *By the Light of My Father's Smile*, a husband-and-wife team of anthropologists and their daughters spend several life-changing years among the Mundo, descendants of black and indigenous ancestors who fled the United States during the Civil War and settled in Veracruz, Mexico.[1] The primary narrative function of Walker's invented Afro-Mexican culture is to provide an idealized alternative to her troubled African American protagonists. In this sense, *By the Light of My Father's Smile* is not really about the Afro-Mexicans, but about an African American family plagued by alienation and conflict. Yet Walker's Mundo are not simply a foil for her more well-rounded African American characters, since they also have their basis in an unfamiliar chapter of North American history: the fugitive slaves who ran *south* from the United States to Mexico in significant numbers and whose descendants, as well as those of Africans brought to Mexico by the Spanish slave trade, are concentrated along the Mexican coasts of Veracruz and Costa Chica. In the meeting of these two very different cultures, Walker's novel thus embeds tangled and overlapping stories about blackness in the Americas, some of which are familiar and others so obscure they are almost lost to history.

The latter category must include the nineteenth-century slaves who sought freedom in Mexico. In slave narratives and other well-known documents of North American slavery, it is axiomatic that *north* is the direction of liberty and enlightenment. Fugitive slaves who crossed U.S. borders went to Canada, not to Mexico, the story goes. Familiar images of the Underground Railroad, the North Star, and the Canadian Promised Land have obscured the fact that slaves from the United States actually traveled in many directions in search of freedom. Those who ran across national boundaries not only went north to Canada, but also farther south into Spanish Florida and Mexico. The reason is clear if we turn to a map of U.S. slave territory, which reveals how many slaves lived far from free territory to the north and how close they were to the nation's southern borders (fig. 2.1). Given the great difficulties and perils of northern flight, it makes little sense to assume that the desire for freedom always led in one direction. But because these southern fugitives left no written archive, their stories have nearly vanished from the historical record. In contrast to former slaves in the North, who were encouraged to contribute to the abolitionist cause by writing about their experiences, those who went south often found themselves in communities that were nonliterate or lacked the resources for translating oral narratives into print. Their history must thus be gleaned from documentary evidence left by slaveholders and abolitionists, as well as from what Diana Taylor calls the "embodied memor[ies]" that persist among their descendants. According to Taylor, the repertoire of "performances, gestures, orality, movement, dance, singing—in short, all those acts usually thought of as ephemeral, nonreproducible knowledge" enacted by minority populations can serve as a rich repository of alternative historical insight about the Americas.[2] The performative repertoire of the Afro-Mexicans bears traces of their otherwise forgotten African ancestry and thus, by extension, their unacknowledged place within the black diaspora.[3]

In the late twentieth century, authors and artists began to follow out such traces in an effort to translate the repertoire of fugitive experience into narrative. As Walker's example attests, fiction is particularly adept at the kind of historical recovery that is the subject of this chapter, since it can fill gaps in the evidentiary record that cannot be addressed by conventional histories. Innovative uses of narrative form can foreground fragments, inconsistencies, and silences that might confound the historian's task. My encounter with representations of black North America in the work of authors from Canada (Lawrence Hill and Lori Lansens), the United States (Walker, Gayl Jones, and John Sayles), and Mexico (Guillermo Sánchez de Anda) first inspired me to wonder about the stories left out of U.S. slave narratives. From a variety of different perspectives and narrative strategies, their work depicts a longstanding black presence in Mexico and Canada. Some draw on the abundant, if scattered, historical evidence about slaves who went north to Canada and stayed there, defying stereotypes about the whiteness and homogeneity of Canadian culture, while others attempt to recapture the fainter traces left by those who crossed U.S. borders into Mexico, confounding a geographic imaginary that equates freedom with flight to the north.

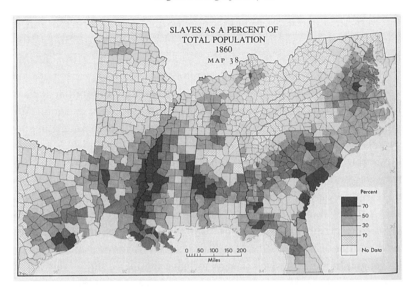

2.1. "Slaves as a Percent of Total Population" (map 38, p. 34). A map depicting slaves in proportion to the total population of the United States in 1860. Reprinted by permission of Louisiana State University Press from *Atlas of Antebellum Southern Agriculture* by Sam Bowers Hilliard. Copyright © 1984 by Louisiana State University Press.

The kind of historical revisionism exemplified by these authors has become increasingly common in North American fiction of the late twentieth and early twenty-first centuries. As Kathleen Brogan explains, "we see in literature by minority authors, particularly in the descendants of enslaved or colonized peoples, a heightened awareness of the disjunction between official history and the lived experience of minority groups. This awareness leads to an emphasis on multiple viewpoints, the fictionality of any reconstruction of the past, and the creation of alternative histories through the telling of unheard or suppressed stories."[4] While Brogan's study focuses exclusively on the United States, I find these tendencies heightened in authors whose work is set in multiple national contexts, where fiction provides a license to bypass the obstacles created by entrenched national histories. Following the lead of North American fiction and film, this chapter begins by reconsidering what we know about fugitives from U.S. slavery, exploring how and why the North became a synonym for freedom and juxtaposing the more familiar stories of slaves who fled to Canada with those of flight south to Mexico. It then turns to contemporary works of fiction and film, which seek to recover stories of transnational flight that could not be told by slave narratives and other nineteenth-century precursors and, in doing so, to revise dominant understandings of black history and culture in North America.

These contemporary works of literature and film, together with the nineteenth-century history they summon up, provide unfamiliar ways of thinking about the fugitive slaves and the culture of black diaspora. African Americans have long dominated the history of North American slavery and its aftermath. Turning to black experience beyond U.S. borders brings much-needed perspective to our understanding of race on the continent. Descendants of fugitive slaves living north of the U.S. border unsettle the common view of Canada as a nation of white European settlers whose black citizens always come from elsewhere. Their struggles with prejudice and inequality show that Canadian culture is often no more racially tolerant than that of the United States. To the south, Afro-Mexicans confound the geographic imaginary of slavery and give the lie to official versions of *mestizaje*, which describe the Mexican population as made up exclusively of indigenous and Spanish ancestors.

Attending to this history allows me to link two strands of scholarship that have become central to the field of American studies: Paul Gilroy's concept of the Black Atlantic, which recognizes how the transnational slave trade inextricably conjoined the cultures of Africa, Europe, and North America; and Chicano/a studies' figuration of the borderlands as a contact zone between the United States and Latin America. This chapter connects the borderlands to the Black Atlantic by demonstrating the unacknowledged importance of Mexico to the history of U.S. slavery and black diaspora. It also expands the boundaries of Gilroy's Black Atlantic by inserting black Canadians more prominently into the history and legacy of the transatlantic slave trade. Whereas Gilroy associated the Black Atlantic with maritime tropes such as the ship and the ocean, land-bound images of the Underground Railroad are central to the literature of black North America, where walking, running, and riding are often seen as the precondition of freedom.

So too, stories of the fugitive slaves complicate Chicano/a studies' focus on the U.S.-Mexico borderlands by emphasizing the importance of the U.S.-Canadian border to nineteenth-century debates about slavery and freedom. For escaping slaves, borders were not a divisive intrusion, as they were for northern Mexicans displaced by the Treaty of Guadalupe Hidalgo or North American Indians whose lands and people were divided by European colonialism. Instead, they found that U.S. borders, particularly in the wake of the Fugitive Slave Act, marked the line between freedom and bondage. They were a welcome conduit to liberty and personhood, rather than an obstacle, a longed-for destination rather than a target of animosity. Thus, the history and culture of black North America points us toward a very different understanding of national borders than the one developed in the previous chapter, where they represent the loss of territory, breakup of kinship networks, and sundering of cultural traditions. Following the footsteps of the runaway slaves as they cross national lines, traveling in multiple directions, is the work of this chapter.

Nineteenth-Century Routes to Freedom

Of all the routes taken by runaway slaves in the nineteenth century, the flight to Canada was by far the most legendary. Because most former slaves of necessity kept their whereabouts and means of escape shrouded in secrecy, their numbers are difficult to ascertain. However, historian Robin Winks speculates that thirty thousand fugitives made their way across the Canadian border, while many more settled in the northeastern United States.[5] By the 1830s, Canada looked like an ideal location for resettlement to black leaders determined that freed slaves should remain on North American soil rather than returning to Africa.[6] They were home to Wilberforce, Dawn, the Refugee Home Society, and Elgin, black colonies that Winks calls "Canadian Canaans," a moniker that underscores their identification with the biblical Promised Land. British Canada was the terminus of the fabled Underground Railroad because it was governed by a legal system that recognized blacks as equals, allowing them to vote and own property. It was home to abolitionist societies that provided help to the fugitive slaves, fought against racial prejudice in the provinces, and aided the efforts of antislavery groups in the United States.[7] Canada became an especially important destination after the passage of the U.S. Fugitive Slave Act of 1850, which required authorities in Northern states to return runaway slaves to their owners. In a number of Canadian court cases, judges determined that British extradition treaties with the United States did not apply to fugitive slaves, thus leaving slave owners without legal recourse for recovering their property north of the border.[8] As the abolitionist George Brown stated in 1851, Canadians felt themselves to be charged with the "duty of preserving the honour of the continent" from slavery.[9]

These circumstances helped to elevate flight to the north to mythic status among nineteenth-century slaves and abolitionists. Indeed, subsequent generations of black North Americans would allude to this history in representing Canada as a symbol of freedom itself. For example, in a

1967 speech delivered on Canadian public radio, Martin Luther King Jr. declared,

> Canada's not merely a neighbor to the Negroes. Deep in our history of struggle for freedom Canada was the north star. The Negro slave, denied education, dehumanized, and imprisoned on cruel plantations, knew that far to the north a land existed where a fugitive slave, if he survived the horrors of the journey, could find freedom. The legendary Underground Railroad started in the south and ended in Canada.[10]

Here, King reinforces the binary opposition between north and south, equating Canada with freedom from bondage and the realization of the former slaves' humanity. Ishmael Reed drew on the same myth to describe the black artist's struggle for autonomy when he remarked in an interview, "we are going to get our aesthetic Canada, no matter how many dogs they send after us."[11] Reed parodies this symbolic geography in his 1976 neo-slave narrative, *Flight to Canada*, about a slave-poet who escapes from a Virginia plantation to find freedom in the north. As intimated by its title, Reed's novel has much more to say about the significance of Canada as the imagined endpoint of the slave's flight than about Canada itself. This sentiment is aptly expressed by Reed's hero, the fugitive slave-poet Raven Quickskill, when he proclaims, "he preferred Canada to slavery, whether Canada was exile, death, art, liberation, or a woman. Each man to his own Canada."[12] In Quickskill's formulation, Canada is slavery's idealized antithesis, whatever that may be.

Reed's novel is an early example of the genre Ashraf Rushdy calls the "neo-slave narrative," which emerged in the 1960s as an outgrowth of the civil rights movement and changing perspectives on the history of American slavery.[13] Borrowing, in highly parodic fashion, the conventions of its nineteenth-century precursors, *Flight to Canada* attests to the way that slave narratives helped to crystallize the mythic equation of the north with freedom. Strikingly similar in content and structure, slave narratives chart the movement from southern oppression to northern freedom. These works follow strict generic conventions, beginning with the narrator's birth, the burgeoning of his (or occasionally her) resourcefulness and intelligence, vivid description of the horrors of the slavery, the cruelty of an exceptionally unfeeling master or mistress, a carefully plotted and executed escape, and the harrowing journey north. More often than not, the fabled north was associated with Canada. "In the thirty most widely known fugitive slave accounts published between 1836 and 1859," Winks writes, "British North America is mentioned in all but four."[14] Since these narratives typically focus on the atrocities of slavery and the perils of escape, Canada tends to surface primarily through anticipatory references to freedom rather than as a concrete and fully developed place. For instance, in *Incidents in the Life of a Slave Girl* Harriet Jacobs observes that in the wake of the Fugitive Slave Act, "many a poor washerwoman, who, by hard labor, had made herself a comfortable home, was obliged to sacrifice her furniture, bid a hurried farewell to friends, and seek her fortune among strangers in Canada."[15] In his narrative, the former slave Reverend J. W. Loguen describes how, having escaped into Ohio, he learned that "there is no place in the States where you can be safe. To be safe, you must get into Canada." To do so, he is instructed to "follow the North Star."[16] And in *Narrative of William Wells Brown*, the author writes that during his life as a slave he imagined "escape to Canada, which I had heard so much about as a place where the slave might live, be free, and be protected."[17] In an 1856 letter, the poet Frances E. W. Harper wrote, "I have just returned from Canada. / I have gazed for the first time upon / Free land, and, would you believe it, / tears sprang to my eyes and I wept."[18] The formula is echoed in contemporaneous novels of slavery. Most famously, in *Uncle Tom's Cabin* George and his family reach the "blessed English shores" of Canada, where they are "charmed by a mighty spell,—with one touch to dissolve every incantation of slavery, no matter in what language pronounced, or by what national power confirmed."[19] George eventually leaves Canada for France, with the ultimate goal of making his way to Africa. However, the autobiographical *Life of Josiah Henson*, on which Stowe's novel is based, never leaves North American soil, concluding instead with Henson's efforts to settle in Canada.

In each case, whether autobiographical or fictional, the narrators emphasize the unacceptable condition of human bondage, turning Canada into a metaphor for the frightening but necessary quest for liberty. One consequence of Canada's elevation was the concentration of racial animus in the South. Locating evil in a single geographic region, slave narratives confirmed the northern reader's moral superiority and absolved the North of blame for the institution of slavery and its attendant racial logic. To be sure, not all slave narratives framed the issue in such simple terms: Josiah Henson and J. W. Loguen describe the hardships of Canada, and Jacobs details Yankee racism. But many others conclude with the joyous arrival or the unqualified celebration of life beyond slavery, never considering the challenges of life on free soil.

Indeed, relatively little attention has been paid to the fate of the former slaves who settled in Canada.[20] Canadian author George Elliott Clarke attributes this neglect to the dominance of African American culture in Canada, a situation that has obscured a more developed understanding of Canada's own black cultures. Clarke writes, "the flight of slaves to Canada is hymned, but those who chose to live out their fates north of the 49th Parallel, rather than return to the United States, have been excised from African-American consciousness."[21] Similarly, Rinaldo Walcott remarks on the absence of Canada and its black populations from Paul Gilroy's influential account of the Black Atlantic. He takes this oversight by one of the foremost scholars of the black diaspora as indicative of a more general neglect of black Canadian history and culture.[22] Canadian treatments of the history of slavery and black culture are often little better, since they tend to be limited by a compulsion to affirm the nation's role as a harbor for fugitives from the United States.

What gets left out of these accounts is the century and a half during which British Canada participated in the slave trade, until it was abolished by the Imperial Act of 1834. Canadians' vaunted opposition to slavery was, for some, a question of morality. But in French Canada, there was no official system of slavery simply because it was deemed unprofitable, and the abolitionist stance of many British Canadians was motivated less by altruism than by anti-Americanism. As Winks argues, "much of Canada's participation in the abolition movement resulted from geographical proximity rather than from ideological affinity."[23] Fugitives who made their way to Canada enjoyed freedom, but also encountered substantial hardships. Although equal under the law, black people tended to be shut out of opportunities for land and employment, and as a result endured levels of poverty and racial prejudice very similar to what they would have found south of the border. Antiblack sentiment heightened with the large influx of runaways following the passage of the Fugitive Slave Act. These racial antipathies would become all the more pronounced with the conclusion of the U.S. Civil War. Once legalized slavery ceased to be a factor that could distinguish the United States from Canada, Canadians could no longer claim that providing a home for black Americans was a badge of honor.

The nineteenth-century author and activist Martin Delany offered one of the most comprehensive evaluations of Canada's potential as a harbor for fugitive slaves in his novel *Blake*, which he wrote while living in Chatham, Ontario.[24] *Blake* is Delany's response to Stowe's *Uncle Tom's Cabin*. Not only does he replace the passive, humble Uncle Tom with the fiery revolutionary leader Henry Blake, but he also rewrites Stowe's geography of freedom, transplanting the ideal locations for black resettlement from Canada and Africa to Latin America. In *Blake* Delany recognizes, but ultimately rejects, Canada as a place of refuge, a position Robert Levine has attributed to the author's experiences in Chatham.[25] The novel begins by following the conventions of slave narrative, its first part culminating with flight to Canada, which its eponymous hero Henry Blake calls "a free country."[26] Along the way, the fugitives sing in anticipation of "that cold and dreary land . . . where fugitives are free."[27] Modeled after one of Harriet Tubman's own songs, their words at once give voice to the myth of northern freedom and enact the process of oral transmission whereby it was passed from one group of enslaved people to another. Upon their arrival, a humble and un-tutored member of their party named Andy kisses the earth and gives ex-travagant thanks to God, a convention lifted directly from slave narrative. But having made Canada his characters' destination, the author somewhat unexpectedly turns from Andy with a skeptical narrative aside: "Poor fel-low! he little knew the unnatural feelings and course pursued toward his race by many Canadians."[28] Delany underscores the gap between his autho-rial knowledge and Andy's ignorance by elaborating the many injustices committed against black people by Canadians, who he accuses of failing to uphold the principles of equality set forth by British law. Having articulated the shortcomings of Canada, Henry then departs for Cuba. This moment, which occurs almost exactly halfway through the novel, constitutes an im-portant turning point, for it is here that the text veers away from the con-ventional routes of slave narrative and into an understanding of American geography coincident with its assumption of a more radical revolutionary program.

Blake's critique of Canadian justice sets the stage for Henry's departure to the south. His geographical trajectory corresponds to sentiments expressed in Delany's 1852 study The Condition, Elevation, Emigration, and Destiny of the Colored People of the United States and Official Report of the Niger Valley Ex-ploring Party, and reiterated in his 1854 pamphlet, "Political Destiny of the Colored Race on the American Continent," which lists Canada as one of several "places of temporary relief, especially to the fleeing fugitive—which, like a palliative, soothes for the time being the misery" only to reject it as a "permanent [place] upon which to fix our destiny, and that of our chil-dren, who shall come after us."[29] In addition to the accusations of racism elaborated in Blake, Delany had other reasons for opposing long-term col-onization in Canada. One is that he predicted its imminent annexation by the United States. Another is that it did not fit his vision of a new home-land dominated by blacks. As Gregg Crane has argued, Delany's revolution-ary agenda relies on black possession of the political power of the majority, since he is unable to imagine a society in which the dominant group can be trusted to protect the rights of minorities.[30] Thus Henry must leave Canada for Cuba, whose racial demographics make it a more appropriate place to plot his unrealized rebellion.

Henry's journey reflects the views Delany laid out in *Condition* and "Political Destiny," which discuss possible sites for black colonization, strongly advocating immigration south of the U.S. border. In *Condition*, Delany asserts that Central and South America "are evidently the ultimate destination and future home of the colored race on this continent."[31] Accordingly, potential runaways who know there is freedom in Canada are in need of geographic reeducation to teach them the benefits of flight to the south: "They already find their way in large companies to the Canadas," he writes in "Political Destiny,"

> and they have only to be made sensible that there is as much freedom for them South, as there is North; as much protection in Mexico as in Canada; and the fugitive slave will find it a much pleasanter journey and more easy of access, to wend his way from Louisiana and Arkansas to Mexico, than the thousands of miles through the slave-holders of the South and slave-catchers of the North, to Canada. Once in Mexico, and his farther exit to Central and South America and the West Indies, would be certain.[32]

Not only does Delany favor the greater accessibility and temperate climate of the south, but he also asserts the right of former slaves to remain on the American continent because it was "designed by Providence as a reserved asylum for the various oppressed people of the earth, of all races."[33] Delany claims that black people belong in America by virtue of their oppression, but, more significantly, because they in fact "discovered" it long before the Europeans, having arrived as a part of the ancient "Carthaginian expedition." According to his revisionist history, black people are a longstanding presence in the New World, rather than the unwelcome newcomers they are often mistaken for. Thus, he insists, "Upon the American continent . . . we are determined to remain, despite every opposition that may be urged against us."[34] Although his plan for actual black resettlement was interrupted by the Civil War, Delany significantly revised the geographic imaginary of the slave narrative by representing Mexico and Central America as alternatives to Canada.

Other opponents of slavery would attempt to put the alternatives envisioned by Delany into practice. When Philadelphia abolitionist Samuel Webb inquired about the relocation of former slaves, the Mexican government expressed its willingness to accept new immigrants. Vice President Valentín Gómez Farías responded to Webb's letter: "If they [the former slaves] would like to come, we will offer them land for cultivation, plots for houses where they can establish towns, and tools for work, under the obligation [that they will] obey the laws of the country and the authorities already established by the Supreme Government of the Federation."[35] Responding to a similar invitation, the Black Seminoles—former slaves of the Seminole tribe—traveled to Mexico in 1849. Initially, the arrangement promised to be mutually advantageous. In crossing the border, the Black Seminoles hoped to evade the white slave owners who threatened their freedom in Florida. For its part, the Mexican government sought to populate the sparsely inhabited border region with settlers who might help to fight off hostile Indian tribes and invaders from the United States.[36] Although the relocation ended in disappointment on both sides, the Black Seminoles remained in Mexico until after the Civil War.

Other migrants, including a free black named Luis N. Fouché, and a group of ex-slaves who traveled from New Orleans to Veracruz, successfully petitioned for land to establish colonies in Mexico.[37] But the most ambitious plan for resettlement was devised by Benjamin Lundy, a Quaker and publisher of the first abolitionist periodical, the *Genius of Universal Emancipation*. Like Delany, Lundy thought comparatively about Canada and Texas (then a part of Mexico) as potential homes for a black colony and concluded in favor of Texas.[38] At considerable cost to his health and finances, Lundy traveled to Mexico in search of available land and permission to establish a colony. His journals document encounters with a number of black people who expressed enthusiasm about joining the new settlement, as well as others who were already comfortably relocated in Mexico, several in mixed marriages to Anglos or Mexicans. Interrupted by the Texas uprising, Lundy's project remained unrealized.

Black resettlement south of the border was also an attractive prospect for more ambivalent opponents of slavery who worried about the presence of a free black population in the United States.[39] They saw an opportunity in the annexation of Texas, which could serve as a safety valve to siphon off unwanted elements from the continent. In 1844 Senator Robert J. Walker of Mississippi argued that as slave labor used up land in the U.S. south, planters and slaves would migrate into Texas. Finding the land beyond the Texas border inadequate for new plantations, they would be forced to free their slaves, who would continue to move south, where "the sparse population occupying the land would welcome the Negroes and treat them as equals."[40] A similar case was made in the late 1850s when one Frank P. Blair Jr. of Missouri proposed a "drainage system" whereby the U.S. government would buy large blocks of land south of the border for the resettlement of freed blacks. He argued that, as they vacated more desirable regions, the former slaves "would be succeeded by the most useful of all the tillers of the earth, small freeholders and an independent tenantry. The influx of immigrants from Europe and the North, with moderate capital, already running into Maryland and Virginia, would, as these States sloughed the black skin, fill up the rich region round the Chesapeake Bay."[41]

In arguing for population drift to the south, Walker claimed that, unlike the United States, where freed blacks would never be treated as equals, Latin Americans "cherish no race prejudice against Negroes."[42] While this was not entirely true, it is the case that Mexico refused to sign any treaty requiring the extradition of fugitive slaves to the United States and that Mexicans regularly helped slaves to escape.[43] Even before Mexican independence, the Spanish—who were slave owners themselves—had a history of encouraging British and American slaves to escape by promising freedom in exchange for military service and conversion to Catholicism.[44] With independence from Spain, Mexico turned the strategic objection to slavery into official policy. The Federal Act of July 13, 1824 abolished the slave trade and declared that any slave introduced to Mexican territory would be free.[45] Mexican assistance to fugitives was due in part to genuine abhorrence to slavery.[46] Mexico inherited New Spain's legacy of liberalism on matters of race, an attitude that grew from the high degree of racial mixture among its population combined with recognition of the fundamental equality of all human beings by both the government and the Catholic Church.[47] But Mexicans also helped the fugitive slaves out of a desire to discourage Anglo-American settlers along the northwestern border by establishing obstacles to slaveholding in the region.[48] Like British Canadians, Mexicans were often motivated to undermine slaveholding interests on the basis of anti-American, rather than moral, grounds. Threatened by an aggressive northern neighbor, they reasoned that the more difficult it became to keep slaves in proximity to Mexican territory, the less incentive there would be for slave owners from the United States to take up residence in the region.

Evidence of the large number of U.S slaves who did escape into Mexico must be found in the words of outraged slave owners and observers, since the slaves left no written record themselves. Absent the culture of abolitionism that flourished in the northern United States and British Canada, there was little motivation for those who fled south to set their stories to paper. There was no archive of earlier slave narratives to draw from, as there would be for aspiring fugitive authors in Canada. There was neither an audience nor a marketplace to make such a product financially viable. Coming from the Anglophone United States, former slaves south of the border confronted the additional challenge of linguistic difference as they encountered populations who spoke only Spanish or indigenous languages. Since the communities they entered were often nonliterate, there was little incentive or opportunity to learn to write or to document their stories in print.

The circumstances of fugitive slaves in Mexico pose an interesting challenge to the logic of the slave narrative, which assumes that the desire for freedom was necessarily coupled with the desire to be literate and to record one's experiences on paper. As Frances Smith Foster puts it, "slave narrators had great respect for literacy, and it is axiomatic in slave narratives that a literate slave is incapable of accepting the legitimacy of his bondage."[49] While it may be true that literacy often inspired the quest for liberation, the slaves who ran south were no less determined to escape their bondage, although they lacked the cultural contexts that would encourage them to read and write, ultimately producing slave narratives. However, conditions of illiteracy, linguistic differences, and extreme poverty did not prevent the fugitive slaves from telling their stories: in the mid-twentieth century, historians and anthropologists began to collect the remarkable oral narratives generated by those who escaped to freedom and passed down over the generations.[50] Absent the strict generic formulas of slave narrative, these stories are often partial, fragmented, and varied in form and content. What they tell us is that slaves escaped in many directions and that freedom was not always connected to literacy in the slave's mind. Rather, the details of this murky and piecemeal southern history have been obscured by the more well documented stories of slaves who escaped to the north.

Some slaves who fled south, particularly from Georgia, Alabama, Louisiana, and other states in the vicinity, joined the Florida Seminoles. Settled in Spanish territory, the Seminoles were slaveholders themselves, but were known to be far more lenient than white masters. Their twentieth-century descendants claimed that "[the Seminole slaves'] everyday life was idyllic compared to that of plantation slaves."[51] According to historian Kenneth W. Porter, many slaves in the region were motivated to escape from their white owners by the promise of a better life under the Seminoles. Often the Seminoles and their slaves were enlisted to help the Spanish in military conflict against the United States. During the siege of St. Augustine in 1812, Colonel Thomas A. Smith wrote that the Seminoles had "several hundred fugative [sic] slaves from the Carolinas & Georgia at present in their Towns & unless they are checked soon they will be so strengthened by [more] desertions from Georgia & Florida . . . It will be found troublesome to reduce them."[52] His words provide evidence that the region was unsettled by large numbers of fugitives, who were often willing to fight against their former masters. The vaunted military prowess of the Black Seminoles distinguishes them from their writerly northern counterparts.

Texas was an even greater source of conflict between slaveholders and their opponents. When slavery was abolished in Mexico in 1829, a large and influential population of slaveholding colonists from the United States ensured that Texas would be exempt from the new legislation. Mexico saw this arrangement as a means of keeping peace in the region by recognizing already-existing slavery and deterring further Anglo colonization by prohibiting the introduction of new slaves. Nevertheless, proximity to free territory enticed many slaves in Texas to escape to the south, often with the help of local Mexicans.[53] In planning his assault on the Alamo, General Antonio López de Santa Anna, president of Mexico and commander of the Mexican Army, promised to free the Texas slaves.[54] During the Texas War of Independence, many slaves either joined the Mexican forces or took advantage of the confusion to flee across the border. Following annexation by the United States, the chaos increased as more slave owners arrived and their chattel attempted flight across the border in large numbers. According to historians John Hope Franklin and Loren Schweninger, "During the 1840s and 1850s, southern Texas became a thoroughfare for slaves crossing the border to freedom in Mexico."[55] In a complaint made before the General Assembly in Austin, a delegation of slave owners stated, "You are well aware of the insecurity of Slave Property in this County . . . and will at once perceive the necessity of enacting an appropriate remedy."[56] A resident of San Antonio wrote in 1855 of the difficulty of keeping slaves in border regions: "the number of negroes in the city and indeed in all this part of the state is comparatively small. . . . They cannot be kept here without great risk to their running away . . . [There are] always Mexicans who are ready and willing to help the slaves off."[57]

The vigor of Texan demands for help with the return of fugitive slaves attests to the significance of the problem. Although there are no print autobiographies about escape from Texas, oral histories of former slaves corroborate the accounts of slaveholders. One Walter Rimm recalled a runaway he had encountered in the woods and speculated that "maybe he got clear to Mexico, where a lot of slaves ran to."[58] Another named Felix Haywood compared the prospects of escape, north and south:

> Sometimes someone would come along and try to get us to run up North and be free. We used to laugh at that. There was no reason to *run* up North. All we had to do was to walk, but walk *south*, and we'd be free as soon as we crossed

the Rio Grande. In Mexico you could be free. They didn't care what color you were, black, white, yellow, or blue. Hundreds of slaves did go to Mexico and got on all right. We would hear about them and how they were going to be Mexicans. They brought up their children to speak only Mexican.[59]

From the standpoint of a slave in Texas, it is easy to see why flight to the south seemed like a much better proposition than flight to the north. The fact that Haywood, who claimed to like his life as a slave and never attempted to escape, was well acquainted with the adventures of those who had fled, illustrates the ubiquity of such stories.

The most detailed contemporary description of slavery in Texas comes from Frederick Law Olmsted, who published an account of his travels there in 1860. *Journey through Texas* confirms the frequency with which slaves fled to Mexico and Mexican objections to slavery, concluding, "No country could be selected better adapted to a fugitive and clandestine life, and no people among whom it would be more difficult to enforce the regulations vital to slavery."[60] While journeying through Mexico, Olmsted encountered a number of former slaves who had relocated south of the border, such as a man living in Piedras Negras who explained that "runaways were constantly arriving here." Olmsted continues, "two had got over, as I had previously been informed, the night before. He could not guess how many came in a year, but he could count forty, that he had known of, in the last three months. At other points, further down the river, a great many more came than here."[61] He claimed that "the Mexican Government was very just to them, they could always have their rights as fully protected as if they were Mexican born." Olmsted validates his informant's account by noting that it was corroborated by other stories he had heard: "I believe these statements to have been pretty nearly true; he had no object, that I could discover, to exaggerate the facts either way . . . They were confirmed, also, in all essential particulars, by every foreigner I saw, who had lived or traveled in this part of Mexico, as well as by Mexicans themselves, with whom I was able to converse on the subject."[62] Of the fugitives' fates, Olmsted observes that those living closer to the border suffered far more than those who moved deeper into Mexican territory. "The runaways are generally reported to be very poor and miserable, which, it is natural to suppose, they must be," he writes. "Yet there is something a little strange about this. It is those that remain near the frontier that suffer most; they who have got far into the interior are said to be almost invariably doing passably well."[63] Since life was hard for blacks in northernmost Mexico, many returned to the United States following the Civil War. This was the case with the Black Seminoles, some of whom went on to become Indian fighters for the U.S. Army. But those who penetrated farther south became absorbed into the Mexican population. With time, they would come to identify as Mexican and, to this day, few Afro-Mexicans would describe themselves as members of the black diaspora, although traces of an unrecognized African heritage can still be found in their music, performances, and customs.[64] Because the fugitives typically settled in rural, nonliterate communities, their stories remain unrecorded and the reconstruction of their history must necessarily be partial and fragmentary. The problem is compounded by Mexico's official racial ideology, which describes the nation's *mestizo* population as a hybrid mixture of Spanish and Indian, effectively denying the existence of black populations.

In truth, the U.S. slaves who escaped into Mexico were but a small part of an already significant black presence south of the border.[65] In the sixteenth and early seventeenth centuries, Mexico was an important location for the Spanish slave trade. The dwindling of the native population as a result of disease and overwork required the Spanish to introduce African slaves into colonial industries such as mining, sugar culture, and urban textiles.[66] At least two hundred thousand Africans were brought to Mexico as slaves, so that by 1810 they made up more than 10 percent of the population, at times outnumbering the indigenous inhabitants.[67] During the War of Independence, Mexicans promised the abolition of slavery and equality for all citizens. In contrast to the United States, where miscegenation has been discouraged, many African slaves and their descendants were assimilated into the population, so that instead of distinct groupings of black and white, a large percentage of Mexicans could claim at least some African heritage. Demographers estimate that much of this amalgamatory process had taken place by 1900.[68] Thus, by the time the slaves fleeing the United States entered Mexico, there would have been very few Mexicans of purely African descent, but many with one or more black ancestors. However, the most significant numbers of Afro-Mexicans lived in the north and thus would have been among the first Mexicans encountered by fugitives from U.S. slavery.[69]

Contemporary Mexico is also home to the more isolated black communities in Costa Chica and Veracruz that are the model for Walker's Mundo. Although Afro-Mexicans have tended to identify as Mexican rather than black, they are starting to become more aware of their African ancestry, and scholars and artists have recently recognized their experience as an overlooked element of the black diaspora. The growing visibility of Afro-Mexicans serves as a corrective to Mexican versions of *mestizaje* that recognize only European and indigenous ancestry, while suppressing the African heritage that is so pervasive among the populace that it has been described as a "third root."

Taking a comparative view of the fugitive slaves and the diasporic cultures left in their wake complicates prevailing understandings of black North America that are centered on the United States and its African American population. Missing from this U.S.-centered history are the stories of individuals who fled across the U.S.-Mexico and Canadian borders, and their experiences of resettlement in a new country. Their absence cannot be filled by documentary evidence alone, as there is no southern equivalent to the abundant archive created by runaway African Americans and their abolitionist supporters in the United States and Canada. But in the late twentieth century, fictional narrative has turned to these more unfamiliar stories, using imagination to supply details missing from the historical record. The works I discuss not only thematize the work of recovering the past, but also attempt to make it manifest at the level of form by simultaneously evoking and rupturing the techniques of nineteenth-century slave narrative. Inevitably, representations of the nineteenth-century past are driven by the needs and desires of the present and informed by the particular contexts out of which they emerge. Twentieth-century narratives thus reflect how understandings of slavery and blackness have differed from one national context to another, as well as how the greater story of African diaspora in the Americas is altered by the recovery of fugitive voices otherwise lost to history.

North to Canada

Given the popularity of neo-slave narratives since the 1960s, it is surprising how rarely flight to Canada appears in recent U.S. fiction about the era of slavery. Fueled by the civil rights and black power movements, the neo-slave narrative emerged as a new mode of African American self-expression that challenged the romantic views of slavery dominating historiographic thought in the United States at the time. It did so by recovering the form that had first provided African Americans with a writerly voice and an avenue for the expression of political subjectivity.[70] Yet, despite African American writers' embrace of a genre in which Canada plays such a central role, with the exception of Ishmael Reed's *Flight to Canada*, there is no major fictional work about slavery that crosses the United States' northern border. Widely read novels such as William Styron's *The Confessions of Nat Turner*, Ernest J. Gaines's *The Autobiography of Miss Jane Pittman*, David Bradley's *The Chaneysville Incident*, and Sherley Anne Williams's *Dessa Rose* are set within the boundaries of the United States, and identify freedom with the Northern states. Perhaps the most well known example is Toni Morrison's Pulitzer Prize–winning novel *Beloved*, in which the slaves of the Sweet Home Plantation run from Virginia to Ohio. Despite the fact that they are pursued by a cruel slave driver, they never mention Canada as a more secure alternative. This is not to say that Morrison's treatment of slavery is exclusively national, since her characters evoke—through dreams and ghostly apparitions—the specter of the Middle Passage and an African past. However, like other works of its kind, *Beloved* implies that slavery *within North America* is a concern exclusive to the United States.

The limitations of the neo-slave narrative's imagined geography would be recognized by Canadian authors at the end of the twentieth century. Their insights arise in part out of Canadians' increasing desire to claim their historic role in the fight against slavery. They have long cherished the legend that escaped slave Josiah Henson, one of the founders of the black settlement Dawn and author of the autobiographical *The Life of Josiah Henson*, was a model for Harriet Beecher Stowe's Uncle Tom. As Robin Winks describes it, despite the tenuous connection between the real and fictional slaves:

> Over the years, the link between Uncle Tom and Josiah Henson grew stronger, and whether thrust upon him by Mrs. Stowe's need or grasped by his own showmanship, to the general public the identification was complete. His cabin and grave became tourist attractions, and Dresden, the center of Ontario's most openly practiced color bar, advertised itself as the Home of Uncle Tom. The grave became the scene of Negro Masonic pilgrimages. Henson's house—for years used as a chicken coop—was opened as a museum in 1948, and the cemetery of The British-American Institute was restored by the Ontario Historic Sites Board, which gave the considerable force of its approval to the Henson saga by placing a plaque near the home to honor the man "whose early life provided much of the material for . . . 'Uncle Tom's Cabin.'"[71]

The Henson legend evolved into a thriving industry marketed to tourists from abroad, as well as Canadians eager to claim an affirming chapter in their own history. In the 1990s, Henson was joined by growing lists of figures, monuments, and sites associated with the Underground Railroad that were selected as "designations of historic significance."[72] This approach to recovering Canada's antislavery past is not without controversy. Winks complains that Canadians' affection for the legends of the Underground Railroad, Josiah Henson, and abolitionist history has "reinforce[d] their self-congratulatory attitudes toward their position on the Negro."[73] He argues that the emphasis on Canada's reputation for racial equality distracts attention from the persistent realities of race-based economic and social injustice that plague actual black Canadians. George Elliott Clarke concurs, accusing Canadian authors and intellectuals of using the African American experience as a negative example that allows them "to paint Canada as a tolerant 'peaceable kingdom' in contrast to the blood-spattered, gun-slinging, lynch-'em-high Republic."[74] The problem with such representations, for Clarke and Winks, is that they obstruct a more nuanced understanding of black Canadian history and culture. Both critics contend that, absent the frisson of black-white relations in the United States, Canadians have largely neglected to consider the Africanist presence within their own history and culture.

Growing numbers of Canadian authors have challenged such sanitized views by drawing attention to black Canadians' experiences of racism, poverty, and social isolation; their struggle to identify a distinctive group identity; and their contribution to a multiracial Canadian culture. The writing of Austin Clarke, George Elliott Clarke, Dionne Brand, Dany Laferrière, Andre Alexis, and Rinaldo Walcott provides diverse perspectives on the black presence in Canada. I focus here on two works of contemporary fiction, Lawrence Hill's *Any Known Blood* (1997) and Lori Lansens's *Rush Home Road* (2002), which more directly address histories of slavery that span the U.S.-Canadian border and their legacy for subsequent generations of black Canadians. While neither could be described as a neo-slave narrative, each alludes to the genre by depicting Afro-Canadian experiences that can be traced back to the era of slavery, when significant numbers of fugitives escaped to Canada and settled there. Both were picked up by major U.S.-based publishing houses, which recognized the market potential of Canadian materials that had been largely overlooked by U.S. authors. Hill's novel, about the descendants of an escaped slave who fled to Canada, was published by HarperCollins Canada and then in the United States by Morrow. First-time novelist Lori Lansens made news with a $500,000 advance from Little, Brown for *Rush Home Road*, which tells the story of a relationship between an abandoned girl and an old woman whose ancestors were fugitive slaves in southern Ontario and the northern United States. Both novels weave their protagonists' experiences into a larger historical fabric that locates Canadian people, events, and locations prominently within the narrative of escape from U.S. slavery. Using fiction to fill absences in the historical record, they thematize the mechanisms—repressed memories, oral narratives, archives, monuments, photographs, documents—whereby fragmented subaltern histories disrupt the coherence of official narratives about the past. Both novels depict success-ful communities of black people as a permanent part of the Canadian pop-ulace, rather than as temporary residents in an otherwise homogenous na-tional scene. They refuse simplistic oppositions between the United States and Canada by portraying the complexities of racial politics on both sides of the border. As their protagonists retrace the paths of the fugitive slaves, they disclose the contradictions between Canada's official language of tolerance and its long history of racist practice. The recovery of lost stories makes these contradictions visible and subject to debate.

Lawrence Hill has grappled with the subject of black Canadian his-tory over several volumes, including the critically acclaimed novels *Some-one Knows My Name* (2007), *Some Great Thing* (1992), and three nonfiction studies. He is also author of *Black Berry, Sweet Juice* (2001), about children of mixed-race parents in Canada. Hill writes frankly about Canadian rac-ism and racial segregation, while also seeking to make black Canadians aware of their distinctive heritage. He understands his work as a correc-tive to African American racial narratives, which have so dominated Cana-dian understandings of race that they have caused "Canadians [to] develop a second-hand, borrowed impression about what it means to be black in Canada from the American experience."[75] While calling for a specifically black *Canadian* history, Hill is well aware of the prominent role that both Africa and the United States will play in it.[76] The history that black Canadi-ans must reclaim is thus inherently transnational. This is illustrated by *Any Known Blood*, the story of a thirtysomething Canadian professional named Langston Cane V, who embarks on a quest to learn more about his ances-tors. Their story begins with his earliest namesake, Langston Cane I, who was born a slave in Virginia and fled to Oakville in Canada in 1850. Five subsequent generations of Langston Canes have spread their lifelines across the northeastern United States and southern Canada, from Oakville and Winnipeg to Baltimore and Washington DC. Reversing his predecessor's northward journey, the protagonist (whom I refer to as Langston) drives from his home in Toronto to Baltimore in an attempt to reconstruct his family's history. Cutting between past and present, the novel moves back and forth across the U.S.-Canadian border, following the Cane family as they travel by foot, car, and train. Langston's movement is propelled by a series of archival clues discovered in diaries, letters, photographs, and oral histories, which will ultimately provide him with both a felt connection to his ancestors and documentary corroboration of partial and fragmented family mythologies.

Any Known Blood is a neo-slave narrative insofar as it is at least partially concerned with the story of flight from slavery, and with the development of a literary voice to express its protagonist's personal and political subjectivity. As we have seen, nineteenth-century slave narratives emphasized the importance of literacy to the slave's assertion of humanity. As Charles T. Davis and Henry Louis Gates Jr. put it, "the slave narrative represents the attempts of blacks to *write themselves into being*," an aspiration that is often explicitly thematized when the protagonist learns to read and write.[77] Typically the arduous journey to freedom is inaugurated by the discovery of a personal voice. This scenario is evoked at the beginning of *Any Known Blood*, where Langston's absence of voice is tied to an acute crisis of identity. He is employed as a speechwriter for the Ontario Ministry of Wellness, where his job is literally to put words in the mouths of others. He obtained the job under false pretenses, having applied for the position—reserved for "racial minorities"—as a person of Algerian descent. Quite literally, then, while at work he labors under a fabricated identity and an assumed voice. His own voice returns when he inserts a statement of support for some controversial human rights legislation into a highly publicized speech, leading to his immediate dismissal. On the same afternoon that Langston effectively discovers his voice, his identity is also disclosed when his father—not an Algerian immigrant, but a prominent black civil rights activist—pays him a surprise visit at work. The recovery of voice and heritage in a single day prompts Langston's quest to probe the depths of his family history, an endeavor the novel equates with his quest to write himself back into being. Investigating the past requires him to travel south across the U.S. border, retracing the migration of ancestors who fled from slavery four generations before.

The climactic stage in Langston's journey involves accessing the story of his original namesake, who is said to have participated in the raid on Harper's Ferry before he disappeared from the historical record. As he participates in the work of archival recovery, Langston feels an increasingly intimate sense of connection to his ancestor. During the final and most important stage of the journey he finds Cane I's long-lost autobiography in the Harper's Ferry Museum in West Virginia. Hill uses the autobiography as a vehicle for historical and generic commentary. Cane I's story, which is written in the form of a slave narrative, challenges the values and assumptions of this seminal African American genre. It revises mainstream views of American history by inserting Canadian settings and people into well-known episodes in the fight against slavery, and it corrects Langston's sanitized understanding of the past by revealing the flaws in his ancestor's character.

Like Martin Delany's *Blake*, Cane I's story initially conforms to the conventions of slave narrative, then casts them aside once it crosses the U.S. border. Like most slave narrators, Cane I possesses unusual talents and ingenuity. His quick intelligence is ideally suited to enable his escape. "In Maryland, I . . . became handy with horses," he writes, "I learned all the routes around town. I learned which way was North. Passing through Petersville and talking quick to Negroes—free and captive—I learned that to the north, in a land called Canaan, all men were free."[78] To this point, his story draws on familiar tropes that equate the North with freedom and Canada with the Promised Land. But from the moment Cane I attains his freedom, the autobiography veers away from generic expectations. In contrast to Henry Blake, who confounds the geographical trajectory of slave autobiography by traveling to Africa and Cuba to plot an international rebellion, Cane I breaks with generic type in his unconventional behavior and attitude. Where the classic slave narrator's rhetoric is pious and uplifting, Cane I is blunt and cynical. In candid terms, he writes of the numerous personal imperfections that disqualify him from attaining the heroic stature of the great men who cross his path, including Frederick Douglass and John Brown. He can do so because his autobiography is written as a private document, meaning that he is unconstrained by the expectations of a white reading public or by the obligation to serve as representative of his race.

For Cane I, Canada, which seemed a haven from south of the border, is the place where reality sets in and freedom becomes a series of disappointing compromises. On his arrival, Cane I avoids the conventional gestures of thanksgiving typically described by slave narrators. In a moment reminiscent of *Blake*, he distances himself from his companion Paul Williams, whose religious fervor caused him to make "a sight of himself" (447). Cane I shares Delany's skepticism about a god that lulls slaves into complacency and encourages fugitives not to question the circumstances of their freedom. Once settled in Oakville, he refuses to comply with the community's strict moral codes. In contrast to the sober tone of nineteenth-century slave narrators, Cane I is outspoken about his penchant for women and drink. A character with all-too-human flaws, Cane I perceives family and work as encumbrances akin to slavery. He objects to the notion of an exclusively black settlement, such as the one he finds in Chatham, where "there were too many colored folks, too close together, each one making sure the other was praying enough" (463). He is also resistant to manual labor, explaining, "I didn't care for farming. I didn't like the idea of bending down over growing plants and breaking my back to pick them. The whole thing made me think of the Virginia plantation where I was born" (463). The hardships and restrictions Cane I encounters remind him of his life under slavery, his narrative undermining the strict opposition between the freedom of Canada and bondage in the U.S. South.

A wanderer averse to commitment and prone to drunkenness, Cane I is not the monumental figure his profile as an escaped slave and participant in the raid at Harper's Ferry might suggest. He moves constantly out of an instinctive aversion to all responsibilities and attachments, his meandering path a contrast to the purposeful journey from slavery to freedom around which the classic slave narrative is structured. In Canada, his intelligence and pluck put him in proximity to revolutionary activities even as his less laudable qualities prevent him from becoming a hero. When John Brown speaks in Chatham in 1858, Cane I is impressed by his vision and oratorical skill.[79] While it is known that Brown visited Canada for an abolitionist meeting in May 1858, there is considerable disagreement among historians about whether he involved his Canadian comrades in his plans for the rebellion.[80] *Any Known Blood* upholds the view that he plotted his raid in Canada, putting Cane I in the room with Brown so that he becomes a witness to conversations that have otherwise been lost to history. This could be an opportunity for Hill to romanticize Cane I for his participation in the ill-fated rebellion. Instead, he sullies Cane I's motivations and subsequent behavior by having him confess that he joined Brown's mission to escape punishment for being a polygamist with wives in two different Canadian towns. His legacy is further deflated by the quality of his participation in the raid. Instead of fighting to the death, he abandons his companions to run away with Brown's daughter Diana. His story thus ruptures the idealized vision of Canada promulgated among slaves and abolitionists during the nineteenth century, while insisting that this more nuanced and heterogeneous Canada is a significant location for black North American history. In this sense, his autobiography is very much a story for the present, reflecting Hill's conviction that black Canadians must learn more about their distinctive past in all of its complexity.

However, Hill's project is compromised by an insistence on biological continuity at the expense of other models of historical transmission. In *Any Known Blood*, an unbroken chain of male descendants (all named Langston Cane) is necessary to the dissemination of familial histories that are figured as representative of a broader Afro-Canadian experience. One of the reasons for Langston's lack of direction at the beginning of the novel is a literal breakdown in the process of generational transfer: his wife Ellen has had a miscarriage, leading to the dissolution of their marriage. In the novel's logic, the relationship cannot last because it failed to produce the next Langston Cane. The fetus, which Langston identifies as male, is the casualty of an inhospitable union that leads to death rather than continuity. This unhappy event might have prompted Langston to imagine carrying on his legacy through other means that are less reliant on the reproduction of his patriarchal lineage. Instead, it leads him to a new partner who may be more capable of giving birth to the next Langston Cane. *Any Known Blood* uncritically portrays this turn of affairs as the hopeful conclusion to Langston's quest. Emphasizing the stories of the five Langston Canes, the novel thus suggests that biological continuity is essential to the recovery and preservation of historical knowledge about North American slavery and black culture. Women are important conduits to that knowledge because they bear children and often serve as key participants in consequential events, but they cannot be the primary subjects of history, a position reserved exclusively for men.

The emphasis placed on kinship in *Any Known Blood* comes into sharper relief when it is read alongside Lori Lansens's *Rush Home Road*, another recent work of Canadian fiction that seeks to restore the submerged stories of runaway slaves and their descendants. *Rush Home Road* employs a very similar cross-border setting and plot in which present-day characters retrace the routes of fugitive ancestors who moved between Detroit and the historic black Canadian settlements of Chatham, Dresden, and Buxton. Like *Any Known Blood*, *Rush Home Road* aspires to educate its readers about the history of blacks in Canada. It does so by alluding to such familiar transnational events as the arrival of fugitive slaves in Canada via the Underground Railroad, the founding of a black community in Chatham, John Brown's historic visit, and the relationship between Josiah Henson and Harriet Beecher Stowe, in each case underscoring the significance of Canadian places and participants. However, Lansens's novel differs from Hill's in its reliance on personal memory as the source of historical lessons and on women as the bearers of history. Whereas Hill's protagonist seeks documentation to corroborate the fallible work of memory and oral transmission provided by his relatives, Lansens's suggests that memory is a valid form of evidence in its own right, whether or not it is substantiated by archival documents. And whereas Hill traces out a continuous line of masculine descent, Lansens portrays a more fragmented history involving broken families, unsympathetic or abusive mothers, and the nonbiological forms of kinship that arise in their absence. Her protagonist is the elderly Addie Shadd, a surname that recalls the influential black abolitionist Mary Ann Shadd, who argued in favor of black immigration to Canada and who serves as a reminder of the prominent role women played in the abolitionist movement.[81] After Addie takes in Sharla, a five-year-old who has been abandoned by her mother, the novel cuts between the story of their developing relationship and Addie's memories of her own youth among a generation with living connections to the era of slavery.

Place is the most potent trigger for memory in *Rush Home Road*, although ultimately it proves an inadequate vehicle for conveying the transnational history of slavery and blackness. In a manner akin to Toni Morrison's concept of "rememory,"[82] Lansens depicts charged objects and places where the past accumulates so thickly that Addie literally stumbles across it. The novel validates these unpredictable, visceral encounters over more conventional methods of communicating historical knowledge that have left people like Addie out of the story. For example, when Sharla and her classmates take a field trip to the Chatham Museum, they are bored by the curator's account of Canadian military accomplishments. Addie steals the show by sharing her memories of how the various implements of daily life displayed in the museum were used during her youth. In contrast to the curator, who sees the objects as historical artifacts, Addie relates to them by explaining their utility. Overcome by memories, she realizes that the museum was once an apartment building where she lived as a young woman. Addie is thus figured as a living connection to the past, preserving knowledge of the building and the ordinary people who inhabited it and who would otherwise be unremembered.

The problem is that only a limited number of North Americans live in proximity to such vivid reminders of black Canadian history. Lansens's novel questions how the past can be meaningful to those who don't have access to the places where important events transpired. The extent of this dilemma becomes clear when Addie leaves behind the insular Canadian community where she was born and raised. Living with an African American family in Detroit, she is startled to find that they are ignorant about black Canadians. Absent immediate reminders, Canada's black history is in danger of being forgotten or subsumed by the more well known details of African American history. One provisional solution proposed by the novel is that individuals carry knowledge and experience with them as they travel. Addie educates her African American hosts by claiming her own place in black Canadian history through a direct link to the Reverend Josiah Henson. "My Daddy sat on Reverend Henson's knee when he was a boy," she declares. "His Daddy played trumpet in the band that saw the Reverend to his grave."[83] In contrast to Langston, whose contact with slavery is five generations removed, Addie provides an immediate connection to one of its most legendary figures. Her upbringing in the prosperous black community of Rusholme—which was once a black settlement at an endpoint of the Underground Railroad—is a reminder of the success of black people in Canada. However, Addie's experiences also complicate the myth of Canada as the Promised Land. Self-sufficient and respectable as her community may be, it is also rigid and provincial, casting her out after she is raped and impregnated by a family friend. The racism she encounters on a segregated train undermines any sense that Canada is a place free of the restrictions and prejudices found south of its border. The train must recall the Underground Railroad, casting its heroic function in an ironic light by suggesting the limits to the freedom found in Canada. As she moves across the border, Addie serves as a conduit to the complexities of black Canadian experience.

Ultimately, the question that remains unanswered by the novel is what happens to the knowledge Addie bears when she is no longer there to communicate it. Just before her death, Addie travels by car down the eponymous road to Rusholme. The town's history—passed down through the generations of black inhabitants—has finally been recognized by the government, which will designate it as a historical site and establish a museum there (376). But such recognition is fairly unsatisfying, given the description of the visit to the Chatham Museum by Sharla and her classmates, who are unimpressed by its relics minus the living connection Addie provides. The breakdown in the chain of historical transmission caused by Addie's death contrasts with the potential for continuity at the end of *Any Known Blood*. Once Langston has retraced the path traveled by his ancestors, he feels ready to contribute to the Cane genealogy by starting a family of his own. *Rush Home Road* is more skeptical about the communicability of its historical narratives. It is also less hopeful about the possibilities of biological continuity, since its protagonist does not leave a blood relative behind when she dies. Descended from a father who sat on Josiah Henson's knee, Addie is the last of her family line. Her legacy is that she gave the abused Sharla a better home and left her in the care of her biological father. Whereas the direct chain of patriarchal descent is crucial to the history portrayed by Hill's novel, Lansens's narrative is filled with missing, weak, or abusive mothers. In the absence of familial continuity, it leaves open the question of what will be lost once Addie—with her vivid memories of the past and stories of a community only a few decades out of slavery—is gone. But in raising these questions, it also implicitly bequeaths that history to its readers. The knowledge it buries with its characters is not lost, since it is preserved in the pages of Lansens's book.

Read together, these two Canadian novels participate in a larger project aimed at recovering the history of fugitive slaves and commemorating lives that books, school curricula, museums, and other repositories of national history have overlooked. Although they disagree over how that history should best be preserved, their underlying goals are similar. They seek to overturn the assumption that blackness is always a foreign presence within the Canadian populace by telling stories about black people who have called Canada home for many generations, and have made signal contributions to Canadian culture and politics. At the same time, these novels are not simply mouthpieces for an uplifting national history, since they confront problems of segregation, poverty, and racial discrimination that Canada shares with its southern neighbor. Nor can they be described exclusively as Canadian literature, since they are published by major U.S.-based houses and their historical lessons and cross-border settings address an implicitly transnational community of readers. They thus seek to give voice to unfamiliar stories of Canadian abolitionism and black Canadians and, in doing so, to change their readers' understanding of the history of slavery and its legacy. These novels at once erode distinctions between the United States and Canada by showing both to be key locations in the experience of black diaspora on the continent, and they reinforce the border between them by asserting the importance of a black Canadian experience that is distinct from that of African Americans to the south.

South to Mexico

When Canadian novelists fictionalize the stories of fugitives who crossed the northern border, they do so in the context of a culture committed to recovering the histories of black slaves and their ancestors. When they establish Canada as the destination for escaped slaves, they draw on the words of slave narrators and abolitionists, as well as an oral tradition that equated Canada with freedom. Mexicans, by contrast, are far less interested in acknowledging their ties to black North America, and contemporary narratives of southward flight have no literary antecedents akin to the slave narrative. They thus conjure up a history that—at least from the perspective of the enslaved—existed *only* through oral transmission until the mid-twentieth century. In addition to the challenge of representing activities that were necessarily shrouded in secrecy, something they share with their Canadian counterparts, these works seek to represent events that were never recorded at all, surviving only through repertoires of myths, songs, and performances. This silence presents both difficulties and opportunities for imaginative expression. The work of the artists I consider here—the filmmaker John Sayles, and novelists Gayl Jones and Guillermo Sánchez de

Anda—is part of a marked surge of interest in the submerged histories of blacks in the southwestern United States and Mexico. Although much of our current knowledge about Afro-Mexicans comes from historians and anthropologists, creative writers from the United States and Mexico are starting to take an interest in these cultures as well. Sayles, Jones, and Sánchez de Anda each thematize the struggle to represent lives and experiences that have been virtually lost to the historical record, while also seeking to make these representational challenges visible at the level of form. And although each situates their portrait of black fugitives in a transnational context, ultimately I will argue that there are significant differences between Sayles and Jones, who come from the United States, and Sánchez de Anda, their Mexican counterpart. While the former seek to expand the terrain of transnational African diaspora, the latter attempts to shore up Mexican nationalism by excavating a little-known revolutionary past.

The 1996 film *Lone Star*, written and directed by John Sayles, is set in the U.S.-Mexico borderlands, where black people are a small minority amid the more familiar mix of Anglos, Mexicans, and Native Americans. As Sayles describes it, the film is "very much about the specifics of a very particular place and history—the Texas-Mexican border with its baggage of wars and racial politics."[84] What interested him about this area is its diverse population and conflicted relationship to local history. In Frontera, a fictional town where high-school teachers and parents argue about the meaning of the Alamo, and illegal immigrants run through homeowners' backyards, history is a matter of considerable urgency. Each of the film's central characters is drawn into a quest for knowledge about his or her own past, which becomes entwined with the collective histories of the region. These thematic interests are echoed at the level of form, as Sayles uses the camera to illustrate the enduring impact of the past on the present. When someone begins to remember, a point-of-view shot pans slowly across space, its movement a metaphor for the journey backward in time. When the camera comes to rest, we have entered the space of memory. This visual motif illustrates the power of memory to resurrect important past events as vividly as if they were occurring in the present. It also emphasizes how particular spaces become so laden with history that they function as portals into the past.

African Americans in *Lone Star* have an especially conflicted relationship to the local history of Frontera. Flashbacks depict the more vibrant black community of a generation ago. In the film's present, it is largely associated with the local army base, which is scheduled to close in two years. The popular hangout Big O's Roadhouse seems to be patronized primarily by black servicemen and women who will soon be relocated. As its owner

Otis Payne describes their dwindling numbers, "there's not enough of us to run anything in this town" (168). Overlooked by the town's political leadership, African Americans find their primary occupation in the Army, a national, rather than a local, institution. The film is ambivalent in its depiction of the military, which is a source of pride and professional success for African American men like Otis's son, Colonel Del Payne, but also has a long history of exclusion and violence against nonwhite Americans. As one black private justifies her situation, "it's their country. This is one of the best deals they offer" (217). Her comment underscores the uneasy position occupied by black people in *Lone Star*. Their fraught relationship to both local and national culture crystallizes in Otis's identification with the migratory, multiracial Black Seminoles, former slaves whose history traverses the U.S.-Mexico border.

Given the importance of the military in *Lone Star*, it is fitting that the Black Seminoles—whose best fighters joined the U.S. Army when they returned from Mexico after the Civil War—are central to a series of encounters among three generations of Paynes, the film's African American family. Colonel Del Payne has been sent back to his hometown to oversee the closure of the military base. An incident of violence involving an enlisted man requires Del to visit his father's bar (Big O's) to investigate. There, he finds a sign posted outside that reads: BLACK SEMINOLE EXHIBIT—REAR ENTRANCE (166). Del, who has long been estranged from his father, shows no interest in the collection of artifacts and documents that comprise the exhibit, which Otis describes as his "hobby." Like other former slaves who took unconventional routes to freedom, the Black Seminoles did not leave written records of their experiences, which have largely survived through oral history. In the film, their past is not related as a coherent narrative, but through the fragmentary collection of documents, photographs, and other visual artifacts assembled in Otis's exhibit. Although the Black Seminoles appear inconsequential to this initial encounter, they will be evoked later when Del visits Otis's home. There, he discovers news clippings and photographs chronicling his military career hanging on the wall next to more of Otis's Black Seminole collection. Since Otis claims to be a proud descendant of the Black Seminoles, the juxtaposition of the two displays constitutes an unspoken acknowledgement of his son's accomplishments. Otis compensates for his failures as a father by creating an archive devoted to the success Del achieved on his own. In this, Otis resembles many other characters in *Lone Star*, who shrink from difficult interpersonal situations in the present by turning to stories about the past. To be sure, there is far less at stake in claiming the Black Seminoles as his kin than seeking reconciliation with his living son. However, the film insistently links past and present, suggesting the impossibility of either retreating into the past or attempting to escape it altogether. Thus, at the same time that Otis announces his connection to the Black Seminoles, he concludes that "blood only means what you let it" (216), a statement that has as much significance for his relationship to Del as it does to his more distant ancestors. Like other characters in the film, he will need to find that meaning by coming to terms with past mistakes in order to reorient himself toward the future. At this point in the narrative, it remains an open question whether Otis will allow their blood connection to become as meaningful as his tie to the Black Seminoles, or whether he will continue to deny its significance.

Another scene of encounter mediated through the Black Seminoles occurs when Del's son Chet, who has never met his grandfather, visits Big O's. Although he recognizes Chet immediately, Otis's first words to his grandson (spoken as he gestures to a portrait on the wall) are "that's John Horse" (212). Instead of awkwardly introducing himself, Otis introduces Chet to the Black Seminoles and begins to relay their history. Chet's genuine surprise and curiosity stands in marked contrast to his father's lack of interest. Prompted by his grandson's questions, Otis tells him of the Black Seminoles' migration to Mexico and their return after the Civil War, when some of the bravest warriors were organized into a celebrated regiment of the U.S. Army called the Seminole Negro Indian Scouts. When Chet expresses incredulity at the prospect of Indians fighting against Indians, Otis responds, "they were in the Army. Like your father" (214). This is the first time Otis intimates that he knows Chet's identity. The distant history of the Black Seminoles serves to deflect the more difficult problem of Otis's strained relationship to Del. Having made his connection with Chet, Otis explains that he is interested in the Black Seminoles because "these are our people" (215), a veiled suggestion of belated interest in his own family. Otis's efforts to forge a relationship with Chet are also the first step toward reconciliation with his son. Through their meeting, Chet gains a connection with his grandfather, as well as with a heroic and little-known strand of black North American history. This pedagogical exchange between grandfather and grandson expands the terrain of black diaspora, connecting the histories of Native America, African America, and the U.S.-Mexico borderlands.

By embedding the story of the Black Seminoles within a contemporary story about the struggles of Mexican Americans, the film also suggests a parallel between the two groups, both of which traversed the U.S.-Mexico border (albeit in different directions) in search of better lives. It shows Mexicans employing desperate measures to cross the border, only to find that the United States is hardly the Promised Land they had imagined. The new immigrants face prejudice, corruption, difficult working conditions, and the constant threat of repatriation. The haunting presence of the Black Seminoles recalls the historical injustice of slavery that stains the American past, as well as the ways the histories of blacks and Native Americans have been conjoined in the U.S. Southwest. Their work as Indian fighters with the U.S. Army is one instance of how minority groups have often been thrown into combat against one another in the service of national interests. Over the course of the film, ongoing arguments over the Alamo evoke Texas's own conflicted past. Although only Anglos and Chicanos participate in the debate over the high-school curriculum, the presence of African Americans in the region is a reminder that black people have been a longstanding presence along the U.S.-Mexico border, and that slavery was a crucial motivating factor in the annexation of Texas. As framed by *Lone Star*, the history of the southwestern borderlands is incomplete without an understanding of the black populations who either passed through or put down roots in the region.

Gayl Jones's massive, sprawling novel *Mosquito* (1999) shares many of Sayles's concerns with history, place, and collective memory. It too takes the occluded histories of migrants and fugitives who have crossed the U.S.-Mexico border as a recurring theme. And like *Lone Star*, the novel also moves back and forth between historical periods, but it does so within a geographical setting that extends from the U.S. Southwest to the entire hemisphere and beyond. *Mosquito* is a logical outgrowth of Jones's previous writing, which has frequently examined slavery and the black diaspora from an inter-American perspective. In a 1977 interview, she attributed her innovative narrative style to the influence of Latin American authors such as Carlos Fuentes and Gabriel García Márquez, whom she admired because their experiments in literary form were always accompanied by an awareness of "the moral/social implications" of their subjects.[85] Jones would subsequently chafe at the notion of being described as an author of U.S. literature, claiming: "I'd like to be able to deal with the whole American continent in my fiction—the whole Americas—and to write imaginatively of blacks anywhere/everywhere."[86] However, this capacious sensibility is informed, at least in part, by her location in the United States, where African Americans have found inspiration and strength in imagining their connections to blacks in many parts of the Americas.

Early in her career, Jones was especially concerned with Brazil's participation in the transatlantic slave trade. Her first novel, *Corregidora*, is named for a brutal Brazilian slave owner who "fucked his own whores and fathered his own breed," a line of scarred, mixed-race female descendants.[87] As one of the characters tells Ursa, the novel's protagonist, "you seem like you got a little bit of everything in you."[88] In *Corregidora*, containing "a little bit of everything" means carrying the weight of the collective oppression experienced by people of the New World. A blues singer, Ursa seeks an appropriate expression for the burden of ancestral possession: "I wanted a song that would touch me, touch my life *and* theirs. A Portuguese song, but not a Portuguese song. A new world song. A song branded with the new world. I thought of the girl who had to sleep with her master and mistress. Her father, the master. Her daughter's father. The father of her daughter's daughter. How many generations?"[89] Ursa's "new world song" would connect singer and listener with the violence of a brand, an image that evokes the brutality of American slavery. In connecting the song to generations of daughters, she also emphasizes the particular hardships endured by women under slavery and its aftermath.

Although New World slavery is a similarly vivid presence in *Mosquito*, its protagonist is less damaged by her connection to it. The idiosyncratic Sojourner Nadine Jane Johnson (a.k.a. the eponymous Mosquito) is a truck driver who lives and works in the U.S. Southwest. Much of the novel is set in the U.S.-Mexico borderlands, which also becomes a backdrop against which Nadine unearths the history of black people in the region. When she finds a Mexican dissident named Maria hidden in the back of her truck, she is introduced to the covert world of Sanctuary, a movement to assist political refugees. Jones's fictional underground has its basis in the real-life Sanctuary movement initiated in the 1960s by U.S. religious communities who sought to shelter victims of political oppression from El Salvador, Honduras, and Nicaragua. In *Mosquito*, Sanctuary is described as a present-day Underground Railroad, a term that implicitly connects past and present, but also links the paths to freedom across the United States' northern and southern borders. Spanning the geography of North America, *Mosquito* uncovers the repressed legacy of blacks in Mexico and Central America by way of comparison with their African American and African Canadian counterparts.

Because *Mosquito* connects the history of fugitive slaves to that of others who have fled across national borders, Sarika Chandra has described it as a cross-ethnic neo-slave narrative.[90] However, despite the fact that it takes up some of the slave narrative's themes, the novel bears very little formal resemblance to the earlier genre. The story of Nadine's involvement with the Sanctuary movement provides a framework for the lengthy digressions that constitute most of the novel's bulk. In contrast to the nineteenth-century slave narrator, whose tale was delivered in an impeccable, elevated diction, Nadine speaks in the rambling, folksy vernacular of a storyteller. Many of the initial reviewers found her excessive, redundant narrative voice maddening, and dismissed the novel as virtually unreadable.[91] But what these readers see as Jones's failure might also be understood as her attempt to represent voices and experiences that have been all but lost to history, drawing attention to the difficulties of historical recovery in the absence of a recognizable archive. Like many of the subaltern histories it excavates, orality is key to what Nadine calls a "true jazz story," for her voice is more evocative of the spoken word than of print literature.[92] As she travels around North America, she accumulates the stories of people she meets along the way. Because of her uncanny talent for recall, she believes she is possessed by "auditory memory obligations" (615) that require her to share the stories she has collected, lest they be forgotten.[93] They spew forth in a collaborative, improvisational form well suited to the novel's subject, the secret (and often unwritten) history of flight from injustice. As Nadine observes, "I knows if the colored peoples of the world writes they view of history it is a different history" (137). And the fragmented, redundant, and excessive novel that results is evidence that this history must be different in form as well as content. Digression, repetition, and circularity are thus elements of, rather than distractions from, the novel's meaning. Jones's protagonist functions as both a character and a channel for more collective, accumulated wisdom. Her friend Delgadina likens her speech to the way "those old slave women might sound, if you hear them talking" (135). Their own words unrecorded, the slave women—and a myriad of others—are given voice through the mouth of Nadine. Delgadina claims she can "hear them talking" because Nadine is, in a sense, resurrecting them (as opposed to simply representing them) through free association. The result is "a true jazz story," in which Nadine's experiences constitute the central motif that is then supplemented, revised, and expanded by the contributions of multiple characters and subjects.

Nadine's own family history spans the continent. Like many black Americans, the Johnsons locate U.S. slavery at the root of their family tree, attributing their surname to a "John" who fought for the Union during the Civil War. Although "somebody told me that Johnson were my slave name," Nadine insists, "We changed us name after Emancipation to the name of John, so's it wasn't a slave name, it were a Emancipation name" (322). The distinction is significant. Unlike Ursa Corregidora, who is damaged by knowing she bears the name (and bloodline) of a cruel slave owner, the

Johnsons are proud of a genealogy rooted in freedom. They trace another early North American relative to the black regiment that fought for the English "up in Canada" (351) during the Revolutionary War. This branch of the family tree is connected to the longstanding communities of black Canadians who antedate the arrival of the fugitive slaves in the mid-nineteenth century. Yet a third set of Johnson roots extends to the south, giving Nadine a familial link to the region where she lives and works. She explains: "Us family history say that some of us Johnsons originated in Mexico, that we was originally Mexican Africans, then if that is true history then maybe that's why I's never had the typical American attitude towards Mexicans. I know I don't look like no Mexican, but family history say there's a little Mexican in me" (317). These Latin American origins, which she recalls numerous times during the course of the novel, are central to the recovery of a history even more submerged than that of the Underground Railroad to Canada: the blacks in Mexico.

The Afro-Mexicans are one of the underrepresented minorities that are given voice by Nadine's monologues. She attributes her affinity for the Southwest and its inhabitants to traces of Mexican blood in her own ancestry, easily associating with the Chicanos and Mexicans she meets during her travels.[94] By contrast, her Chicana friend Delgadina is decidedly reticent on the subject of black Mexican history. Delgadina is representative of a collective resistance among Mexicans and Mexican Americans to acknowledging black ancestry. As Nadine puts it, "ain't never heard nobody talk about African Mexicans" (189). Alluding to José Vasconcelos's famous 1925 description of Mexico as "la raza cósmica," Nadine observes, "Mexicans they's supposed to be the cosmic race. . . . 'Cept nobody wants to identify with the African in the cosmos" (27). Her own circuitous narrative detours break the silence surrounding Mexico's African heritage. Nadine gives credence to her musings by reference to more legitimate archival sources, such as a book called *A Natural History of Afro-Mexico*, "which deals with the African presence in Mexico, from the slaves who jumped slave ships to seek refuge in Mexico to others who traveled south to Mexico rather than north to Canada" (362). Her description links Mexico to Canada as a destination for fugitives from the United States and a place of freedom for black North Americans.

By designating Sanctuary an Underground Railroad, the novel invites the kinds of comparisons between north and south that are the subject of this chapter. Indeed, the Sanctuary movement spans the hemisphere, since the majority of the victims it assists come from Central and South America, and it often identifies Canada as a potential harbor for Latin American dissidents threatened with deportation from the United States. Like Martin Delany a hundred years before, the participants in Sanctuary are constantly reevaluating the viability of North American places of refuge. Having driven transcontinental routes into Canada as well as Mexico, Nadine has considerable experience with the very different personalities of the United States' two border regions. She refers to the border between the United States and Canada as "the free border" (131, 239). While this description is more an ideal than a reality, it underscores the contrast with its heavily policed Mexican counterpart. The characters in *Mosquito* are well aware of the power of the nation-state to control the movement of people and goods at its borders. As a truck driver, Nadine regularly experiences the impact of restrictive state power when she is stopped, searched, or interrogated by border patrols. She remarks of the INS: "I guess a lot of them immigration agents acting on what they believe. But then they got what you call the state behind them. The state be saying, I got your back, so it pretty easy for them to act on what they believe, I mean, when they believe the same thing the state believe" (313). In contrast with the immigration agents, members of the Sanctuary movement describe themselves as working in favor of a higher international or human law, which often directly contradicts the interests of nation-states. From their perspective, states are responsible for the injustice of national borders, which are open to commerce and the right kinds of travelers (Nadine remarks, "the rich don't have borders" 297), and closed to those who may need to cross them most.

Mosquito illustrates that the conditions of any one border are best understood comparatively and in deep historical perspective. Taking a more geographically capacious view of North America than does *Lone Star*, the novel suggests that the comprehensive perspective required to combat the injustices of U.S. immigration policy can be attained only by considering circumstances at *both* of North America's land borders, by approaching the continent as a unit rather than treating each nation separately, or in relation only to its closest neighbor. Nadine's rambling monologues do this and more, weaving connections among blacks in North America, as well as in the Caribbean, South America, and Africa. The narratives she summons forth redraw the map of black history and culture on the continent by emphasizing the importance of the U.S.-Mexico borderlands to the fugitive slaves. The difficulty of following her relentless and annoyingly circuitous voice emulates for the reader the painstaking and often tedious work of recovering the stories of those who sought to obscure their own tracks or were deliberately erased from national consciousness. In contrast with the popularity of *Lone Star* among both audiences and critics, few readers have understood the nature of Jones's experiment with narrative voice or found it compelling enough to make it to the end of this massive novel. As a result, Jones's novel may not perform the work to which its protagonist aspires, failing to make Afro-Mexican history a part of collective North American consciousness. But for those willing to accept its challenges, *Mosquito* provides one of the most geographically and culturally expansive views of slavery and black diaspora in recent North American literature.

Mosquito and *Lone Star* seek to recover the suppressed histories of African Americans with the goal of creating a more diverse portrait of the contemporary southwestern United States and northern Mexico. Both complicate conventional views of the region, which tend to focus on Anglo-Mexican relations, by connecting the current struggles of Mexican *indocumentados* to the history of slave resistance. They emphasize the northern side of the U.S.-Mexico border by demonstrating how the recovery of suppressed histories and drawing of unfamiliar historical parallels challenges dominant narratives about race and nation in the United States. But they leave open the question of those fugitive slaves and other black migrants who chose not to return and instead put down roots in Mexico. Concentrating exclusively on the black populations along the U.S.-Mexico border, *Lone Star* is completely silent on the subject of New Spain's participation in the slave trade and the people of African descent who remained in Mexico as a result. This history surfaces only obliquely in *Mosquito*, where Nadine reports that she has "heard tales of Africans jumping off the slave ships headed for the United States and swimming to Mexico, 'cause they abolished that slavery in Mexico earlier than in the States" (190). What became of those Africans and their descendants may be the most deeply buried history of all, one that is still relatively untouched by artists and historians alike.

There is no obvious Mexican counterpart to Gayl Jones and John Sayles, someone using fiction to tell the stories of fugitive slaves who settled in Mexico and linking them to the larger story of North American slavery.[95] Guillermo Sánchez de Anda's 1998 *Yanga*, a rare work of contemporary Mexican literature that takes up the question of black Mexicans, does so in order to buttress Mexican nationalism, rather than to expand the terrain of black diaspora in the Americas. Sánchez de Anda's novel tells the story of Silverio, a journalist on assignment to write about an uprising of the neo-Zapatistas in southern Mexico, who stumbles onto the history of Yanga, the Nigerian slave who led a thirty-eight-year revolt against the Mexican crown in the late sixteenth and early seventeenth centuries. As he becomes increasingly absorbed in uncovering these events, Silverio shows more interest in connecting his discoveries to other revolutionary moments in Mexico's past than in the transnational history of slave rebellion. As he explains, the recovery of Yanga's radical legacy can serve as a corrective to the corruption and indifference plaguing "el México de hoy con sus carencias y limitaciones, con el abuso de autoridades y caciques y la inconciencia e indolencia de sus habitantes, los cuales no están dispuestos a realizar sacrifico alguno en aras del bienestar colectivo" [contemporary Mexico, with its deficiencies and limitations, with the abuses of authorities and political bosses and the thoughtlessness and indolence of its inhabitants, who aren't disposed to make the slightest sacrifice on the altar of the collective good].[96] Sánchez de Anda thus differs from his U.S. American counterparts because his purpose in relating the history of slave rebellion is to redeem Mexico from its current political malaise, shoring up, rather than destabilizing, a sense of national coherence and purpose.

However, the novel also emphasizes the ways that Yanga's revolt is different from other revolutionary moments in Mexico's past in that it is linked to the unacknowledged history of the Afro-Mexicans. In order to understand it, Silverio must first "reconocer la importancia de la 'negritud' en la historia de México" [recognize the importance of 'negritude' in the history of Mexico].[97] The difficulty and significance of this task is underscored by his local informant, Don Tiburcio, who tells him: "tienes la gran oportunidad de escudriñar en un episodio trascendente de nuestra historia patria y de América, muy poco conocido, tal vez ignorado, quizá repudiado" [you have the great opportunity to examine a transcendent episode in our nation's history and that of America, one that is very little known, perhaps ignored, perhaps repudiated].[98] As he pursues the story of Yanga's victorious struggle against the Mexican military, Silverio undertakes the larger project of uncovering Mexico's forgotten black roots.

In representing and enacting the task of historical recovery, *Yanga* is less formally inventive than the work of Jones and Sayles. When Sánchez de Anda, who is a professional journalist, writes of a journalist on assignment, it reads like thinly veiled autobiography. The story of Silverio's quest provides a rather clumsy narrative frame, designed to create obvious parallels between the present situation of the EZLN and that of the rebellious slaves. Yet Sánchez de Anda's realism might also be seen as an aesthetic decision in keeping with the intended goals of his novel. As Amanda Claybaugh has argued, the realist novel has close connections to the literature of social reform.[99] More than other authors, Sánchez de Anda conceives his novel as a direct agent of social change, whose purpose is to revise dominant understandings of Mexican history in the hope that it would have an immediate effect on contemporary Mexican politics.

Unlike Jones or Sayles, Sánchez de Anda is uninterested in building bridges between Mexico and other parts of the Americas. Instead, he sees the recovery of Afro-Mexican history as a means of consolidating Mexican national community against the threat of Americanization. He shares the skepticism of many Latin American intellectuals about the role of the United States in the region. This is evident when Silverio orders a Coke during his meeting with Don Tiburcio and is told "es mejor que tome un café, pues sólo los negros americanos abreban de las aguas negras del imperialismo yanqui" [better to drink a coffee, since only the corrupt Americans imbibe the black waters of Yankee imperialism].[100] However, Silverio is equally critical of the Mexican state. Later, he warns that if Mexico fails to recognize its own constitutional principles of universal equality, "dentro de unos años nos invadirán los gringos aduciendo que los mexicanos somos el pueblo 'del mañana'" [within a few years the gringos will invade us, predicting that Mexicans are the people of the future].[101] Sánchez de Anda criticizes the state for its authoritarianism and neglect of its own people, cautioning that a weakened Mexico is vulnerable to U.S. imperialism. His goal in reclaiming the history of Afro-Mexicans is thus to awaken the Mexican nation's slumbering revolutionary energies so that it can defend its autonomy against the encroachment of its northern neighbor.

Reading Sánchez de Anda's novel in relation to Jones and Sayles underscores significant differences between Mexican and Anglo-American views of blackness. Since at least the mid-twentieth century the experiences of African Americans have been seen as an integral part of the culture of the United States, whereas Mexicans are generally reticent to lay claim to their black heritage. Canada presents yet a third alternative, a context where black Canadians have often been lumped together with African Americans, but have recently sought to assert the distinctive features of their past and current situation. Many black people in the United States embrace their African heritage and identify with black diasporic cultures in the Americas and across the globe. We see this perspective reflected in Jones's desire "to write imaginatively of blacks anywhere/everywhere" and in the Payne family's association with the Black Seminoles. A similar impulse underpins the work of Canadian Lawrence Hill, whose *Any Known Blood* brings the Cane family—with its longstanding North American roots—into contact with a recently arrived Cameroonian immigrant, their relationship symbolically instantiating ties between blacks in North America and Africa. By contrast, people of African descent in Mexico do not tend to identify with the history of slavery or the black diaspora, and often do not even see themselves as black. Conducting research among relatively isolated populations of Afro-

Mexicans, anthropologist Bobby Vaughn found that his informants in Costa Chica lacked a consciousness of slave ancestry and often claimed to be descended from the survivors of shipwrecks.[102] What we must conclude from the works examined in this chapter is that the desire for a transnational view of slavery and black diaspora in the Americas is more germane to U.S. and Canadian authors than it is to Mexican. While some Mexicanist scholars and critics may be drawn to such comparative perspectives, they do not have the same appeal among ordinary Mexicans as they do among black people in the United States or Canada. If the transnational sensibility that undergirds the works in this chapter is itself a manifestation of national situatedness, then it must follow that the experience of blacks in North America has been shaped not only by the legacy of slavery, but also by significant cultural differences regarding how that legacy is to be remembered.

The works of literature and film I have considered gesture back to forgotten or misunderstood episodes in this history of black North America. In doing so, they use fiction to revise dominant understandings of the history of slavery and blackness on the continent. By drawing attention to Canada and Mexico, they remind us that North American slavery was not exclusive to the United States and that abolition was often fueled as much by anti-Americanism as by moral objections. In contrast with the slave narrative, which typically ended with the achievement of freedom (often by crossing the U.S. border into Canada), these contemporary works tell stories of freed blacks' experiences in Canada and Mexico. And perhaps most strikingly, they complicate the geography of freedom with narratives of slaves who ran south, as well as north. Such texts lead us to the realization that freedom took quite different forms depending on where it was found. Examining them comparatively allows us to make often-overlooked connections between the transatlantic slave trade and North America's borderlands, linking the black diaspora to border cultures in Canada, the United States, and Mexico. It is no accident that these connections have been most compellingly expressed in fiction, which recognizes the crucial role of the imagination in filling gaps left by an absence of historical data, and solidifying local, national, and diasporic sensibilities. Listening to the voices contained in these representations can thus guide us to a more varied and multidirectional understanding of American routes to freedom.

CHAPTER THREE

Women of the South Bank: The Mexican Routes of American Modernism

In a well-known series of photographs by Edward Weston, a female nude is pictured against a black background, her body filling the frame (figs. 3.1– 3.3). These photographs subvert the norms of classic portraiture by deemphasizing the face and approaching the subject from behind. In two of them, Weston's framing decapitates the woman; in the third her head is relegated to a small corner, her gaze turned to the side and slightly downward. Abstracted into an alabaster pear, her figure becomes a testament to the camera's capacity to produce art. Shorn of context, the female subject is mute and unrevealing, even as her body is exposed for the camera. While she remains silent, these images speak volumes about the photographer's modernist obsession with objects distilled to their purest and most basic forms. Weston described them as "my finest set of nudes, —that is, in their approach to aesthetically stimulating form. Most of the series are entirely impersonal, lacking in any human interest which might call attention to a living, palpitating body."[1] With these photographs, Weston believed he had achieved mastery over his subject, shearing away all signs of contextual detail and human sentience, leaving only form itself.

Reading Weston's photographs against the grain, this chapter begins by asking: Who is this anonymous woman with the smooth ivory back? And where were these photographs taken? I will argue that the answer to these questions opens up unrecognized circuits of modernist contact, introducing new personalities and texts, and providing opportunities to remap better-known geographies of modernism. Weston produced his "finest set of nudes" in 1925, during the period when he lived and worked in Mexico. His subject is Anita Brenner, a journalist, scholar, and patron of the arts who was at the center of a powerful modernist cohort in Mexico City that rivals the artistic communities that flourished in New York, London,

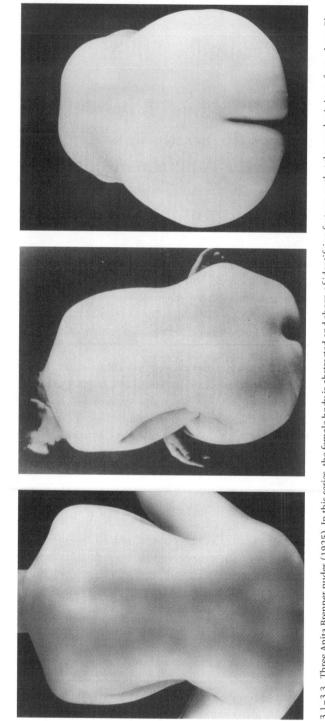

3.1–3.3. Three Anita Brenner nudes (1925). In this series, the female body is abstracted and shorn of identifying features so that the emphasis is on form alone. Photographs by Edward Weston. © 1981 Arizona Board of Regents. Used by permission of Collection Center for Creative Photography, University of Arizona.

and Paris during the same period. Scholars have long recognized Euro-American modernism as a transnational phenomenon. In the first decades of the twentieth century, aesthetic innovation traveled along the transatlantic routes that connected major European cities to the eastern United States. While many of the era's most prominent creative figures were mobile cosmopolitans, some of the most interesting research on modernism has explored the emergence of its bohemian subcultures within particular places.[2] However, Mexico has been largely absent from the map of significant Euro-American modernist locales, despite the fact that, as Peter Wollen has argued, "the Mexican Renaissance is the one recent Third World art movement that has had a significant impact on the metropolis."[3]

More commonly, critics recognize Mexico's importance to Latin American *modernismo*—the late nineteenth-century movement associated with Chilean poet Rubén Darío and his contemporaries—and its successor, *vanguardismo*. Latin Americanists have been critical of the way that *modernism* has become synonymous with European cultural developments, effectively eclipsing modernist production in other parts of the world. While more work remains to be done to create a dialogue between Latin American and Anglo-European modernisms, the focus of this chapter is on modernist cultures of North America that have relatively little to do with *modernismo*. Although both movements can be loosely described as reactions to the circumstances of modernity, cosmopolitan in sensibility and invested in formal innovation, they differ in significant ways. Whereas *modernismo* was predominantly literary, the American modernism coming out of Mexico embraced many different mediums, particularly the visual arts. Indeed, the emphasis on nonliterary forms during the period known as the "Mexican renaissance" (roughly 1920–35) was conceived as a reaction against the elitism and europhilia of the *modernistas*.[4] Whereas the previous generation had sought self-realization and transcendence through art, postrevolutionary Mexicans proclaimed their commitment to a modernist expression that was collectively produced and politically dedicated to the masses.

When Mexico enters the conversation about North American modernism, it is typically through the towering figures of *los tres grandes*, the muralists José Clemente Orozco, David Alfaro Siqueiros, and Diego Rivera, whose international training and reputations brought them into the circles of their Anglo-American and European counterparts. But the modernist community in Mexico was far broader and more heterogeneous, and the aesthetics of Mexican modernism more diverse, than is implied by this trinity. Viewing Weston's photographs in context serves as a reminder that women were not only artistic subjects, but were also producers and promoters of culture.

Women such as Frida Kahlo, Tina Modotti, Alma Reed, Frances Toor, María Izquierdo, Antonieta Rivas Mercado, Nahui Olín, Lola Alvarez Bravo, Lupe Marín, and Katherine Anne Porter played an integral role in creating and sustaining the Mexican renaissance, a term coined by Brenner herself. Many were important artists in their own right, while others curated exhibits, arranged contacts, published articles, organized salons, and provided other occasions for informal gathering. Their accomplishments are a testament to the expansion of personal and professional opportunities for women in Mexico City of the 1920s. As Carlos Monsiváis describes it, "in an unequal fashion, amongst pressures and scandals, that which had been previously unthinkable for women in certain circles emerged: free love, independent criteria, creativity, flights of imagination, political commitment, freedom of movement, and even bisexuality."[5] Monsiváis's description is appropriately qualified in its acknowledgment that these opportunities were available primarily in the progressive climate of "certain circles." As Jean Franco notes, postrevolutionary Mexico was characterized by a "discourse that associated virility with social transformation in a way that marginalized women at the very moment when they were, supposedly, liberated."[6] The predominance of this masculinist discourse has obscured the centrality of women to Mexican cultural history of the time.

The goal of this chapter is to restore these women to visibility and to show how attention to their lives and work adds new dimensions to current understandings of North American modernism. Because they were promoters, as well as producers, of culture, they help us to better grasp how creative partnerships emerge and how the influences of those collaborations are disseminated. By charting their journeys to and from Mexico, we can track the spread of a Mexican element in international modernism. Not only did Mexican influences travel to the United States, as the careers of *los tres grandes* would suggest, but significant numbers of Americans traveled south, leading to sustained cultural cross-pollination. Finally, because they were women, my subjects are attentive to the gendering of *mexicanidad* in ways that elude their male counterparts. My title plays on Shari Benstock's influential study of female modernists in Paris, *Women of the Left Bank*. Like Benstock, I seek to understand how a particular space—Mexico City and its environs—enabled the self-discovery and professional development of women artists and intellectuals. However, whereas Benstock treats space as a static backdrop for social relations, I will argue that these women engaged dynamically with their environment; they did not simply participate in the Mexican renaissance, but they also had a hand in creating it as a national and international phenomenon. Their work contributed to the rise of an

American modernism that was specifically oriented toward Mexico but also traveled outward to the continent and the world.

These topics point toward a rather different set of concerns than the previous two chapters, which focused on literary and visual expression inspired by some of the most devastating events in North American history: the dispossession and genocide of indigenous people and the enslavement of Africans and their descendants. In both cases, the impulse to cross national borders and/or erode political boundaries arises out of a struggle for survival and, among subsequent generations, an imperative to ensure that crimes of the past are not lost to collective memory. This chapter turns to a more privileged group of North Americans, many of whom traveled voluntarily rather than under duress, but who did so out of similarly deep convictions that could not be addressed within the confines of regional and national boundaries. Their movements span the continent, from the northeastern United States to Mexico City, tracing an aesthetic and political project that involved participants from many different areas of the world and that sought to cross divides of gender, class, and culture.

More specifically, this chapter focuses on the intersecting lives and careers of Katherine Anne Porter, Anita Brenner, and Tina Modotti. While each is from a different part of the world and skilled in a different genre, their creative output is indebted to time spent in Mexico. They are representative of the broader social milieu in which they moved, but the quality and significance of their accomplishments is exceptional. The literary and visual texts they produced are an integral part of the aesthetic and political accomplishments of the Mexican renaissance. Of the three, the Texan Katherine Anne Porter spent the shortest time in Mexico, but she would later hail her Mexican experiences as the impetus for her career as an author. What she sought and ultimately failed to find there was an alternative to the social inequities and spiritual alienation of modern life in the United States. In contrast to the primitivism of her Euro-American modernist contemporaries, Porter's quest for authentic indigenous forms of expression grew out of her exposure to the politics of *indigenismo* at the heart of Mexico's revolutionary nationalism. Anita Brenner, who was born in Mexico, returned there in the 1920s and devoted her career to educating foreign readers about her homeland. Fashioning herself as an unofficial cultural ambassador, Brenner shaped her representation of Mexico to emphasize its relevance to Anglo-American audiences. Although her work seems less evidently modernist, it shares the Mexican modernists' preoccupation with the import of their own historical moment, their progressive political views, and some of their formal strategies. The Italian-born photographer Tina Modotti also arrived in Mexico in the early 1920s, after having lived for ten years in the United States. It was in Mexico that she embarked on her short career as a photographer and developed her lifelong commitment to communism, which would lead to her deportation in 1930. Modotti rearranged the terms of modernist politics with an art that situated the portable values and icons of international socialism within a specifically Mexican context.

Although I have identified each of these women by the location of her birth, national affiliation proves not to be an especially meaningful way of describing peripatetic lives that spanned the U.S.-Mexican border and the Atlantic Ocean. Rather, they are part of a modernist cohort that is best labeled as "trans-American," in that its themes and circuits of travel were continental in scope. Their work belongs to a modernism that is both local, in that it could not have emerged anywhere but postrevolutionary Mexico, and global, in that it was attuned to events and cultural developments in many parts of the world. Filling in the picture of modernist activity in Mexico, this chapter focuses on what these women tell us about why foreigners were drawn there in the 1920s and 1930s, how the Mexican renaissance circulated abroad, and how women negotiated its contradictory sexual politics.

From *Insurgent Mexico* to Modernist Mexico

The story of Mexico's trans-American modernist cohort begins in the aftermath of the Mexican Revolution, a ten-year conflict that devastated the nation but set the stage for the cultural reforms of the 1920s. Under the twenty-four-year dictatorship of Porfirio Díaz, Mexico had seen a period of rapid modernization and political stability that came at the cost of extreme disparities between rich and poor and heavy indebtedness to foreign interests. The revolution arose out of demands for democratic leadership, redistribution of land, labor reform, and national self-determination. By the time it was over, Mexico was bankrupt, its infrastructure had been destroyed, and years of famine, epidemic, and migration had reduced the population by 800,000.[7] Although Mexico was embroiled in a civil war, the conflict was of grave concern to U.S. and European powers, which repeatedly intervened in an effort to manipulate its course. Historian Friedrich Schuler writes that by the eve of the Great War, "the domestic Mexican conflict over national development had become a bilateral U.S.-Mexican issue, a Latin American concern, and an increasingly important sideshow for European and U.S. military strategists."[8] For the United States, the shared border with Mexico was cause for particular alarm. During the First World

War, Americans worried that their German enemies would infiltrate Mexican revolutionary factions. Residents of the U.S. Southwest regularly gathered along the Mexican border to watch the conflict unfolding just across the Rio Grande. In 1916, the proximity of the revolution was driven home when Pancho Villa—angered by President Wilson's support for the faction of Venustiano Carranza—crossed the border into Columbus, New Mexico, and killed eighteen citizens.

Although the raid on Columbus prompted a punitive military response, the United States more consistently applied diplomatic and economic pressures to its affairs with Mexico. During the Porfiriato, Mexico had provided a welcoming climate for foreign investors, and American money had poured into its oil, mining, and sugar industries. As Anita Brenner described it, "for Americans, the invasion dreams of the 19th century were no longer necessary, for American industrial and agricultural enterprises were spread peacefully over the whole north and ran deep southward along both coasts."[9] During the revolution, those investments were threatened by Mexico's political instability and the strongly nationalistic bent of its revolutionary leaders. Of particular concern were articles 27 and 123 of the new constitution, which established the state's right to nationalize foreign-owned property and shifted the balance of power from employers to labor and government.

With a reputation for violence and corruption, Mexico was known to most North Americans only through stereotypes. It was certainly not a place to visit: in 1923, a mere 4.6 percent of U.S. travel expenditures went to Mexico, compared to 36.9 percent to Canada.[10] This situation would change significantly during the next decade. Military conflicts between revolutionary factions had subsided by 1920 and in 1923 the United States granted official recognition to the administration of President Alvaro Obregón. While diplomatic relations with the United States would not solidify until Mexico joined the Allies during World War II, affairs between the two nations improved enough to support a thriving cultural exchange. Its high point was the period from 1920 to the mid-1930s, which saw what Helen Delpar describes as "the enormous vogue of all things Mexican" spread across North America.[11] Reflecting immodestly on this development in 1932, Edward Weston considered publishing his diaries, since "I am in the limelight as a photographer—and Mexico is on everyone's lips—Mexico and her artists."[12]

The war in Mexico, which caused such alarm among conservative and mainstream U.S. citizens, was a magnet for North American political radicals, who saw it as an opportunity to witness the first revolution of the twentieth century. From the beginning, the Mexican Revolution was covered by radical English-language periodicals like *Appeal to Reason*, *Mother Earth*, *The Nation*, *New Republic*, and *The Masses*. John Reed, John Kenneth Turner, Robert Dunn, Frederick Palmer, Lincoln Steffens, Linn Gale, and Richard Harding Davis were the century's first embedded journalists, reporting from the front lines on the conditions of Mexico's poor, combat between rival factions, and the strategies of their leaders. In 1914, Reed published *Insurgent Mexico*, an account of the months he spent with Pancho Villa, while Turner traveled the countryside in disguise in order to observe the plight of workers in the Yucatán and Oaxaca.[13] For radical leftists, Mexico provided the hope of realizing revolutionary dreams that had failed to materialize in the U.S.

In the early 1920s, the journalists were followed by leftist scholars and artists (among them Robert Haberman, Frank Tannenbaum, John Dewey, Ernest Gruening, Carleton Beals, Alma Reed, Bertram Wolfe, Frances Toor, and John Dos Passos), who were attracted to the prospect of the new social order that promised to emerge in postrevolutionary Mexico.[14] Helen Delpar and John Britton have described these visitors as "political pilgrims," a term coined by the sociologist Paul Hollander to characterize twentieth-century intellectuals who traveled to witness incipient revolutionary societies.[15] According to Delpar, these observers helped to modulate understandings of the revolution for U.S. audiences: "in this period of strained relations between the governments of Mexico and the United States, political pilgrims provided an interpretation of Mexico that represented an alternative to the critical view espoused by many American diplomats, members of Congress, businessmen, and religious leaders."[16] Of particular interest to the political pilgrims were the radical social experiments taking place in provinces like Tabasco, Veracruz, Campeche, and Yucatán, where activist governors attempted to implement programs of land reform, unionization, and women's suffrage.[17] However, the exchange of ideas did not take place in only one direction, as the term *political pilgrim* might misleadingly imply. As radical Americans traveled to Mexico, Mexican artists and intellectuals made their way to the United States. Mexican visitors and émigrés such as the author Maria Christina Mena, composers "Tata Nacho" and Silvestre Revueltas, the artists Adolfo Best Maugard, Miguel Covarrubias, José Clemente Orozco, and Marius de Zayas, movie stars Dolores del Río and Ramón Novarro, and scholars Miguel Gamio and Moisés Sáenz influenced U.S. cultural life and brought new ideas to leftist political circles.

Contact with Mexican émigrés, the favorable reports of political observers, and thawing relations between the United States and Mexico made the prospect of cultural exchange increasingly viable. Growing numbers of artists, authors, and intellectuals were drawn to postrevolutionary Mexico, where culture was a key element in plans for social reform. Rejecting the europhilia of the Porfirian era, Mexicans embraced their history and culture with a nationalist fervor akin to that of the postcolonial societies of the later twentieth century. This sentiment was enforced from above as the postrevolutionary state sought to confer a sense of unified national identity on a dispersed and fractured polity. Secretary of Education José Vasconcelos was instrumental in implementing programs for social uplift, which were seen as an important component of national consolidation. He launched a massive effort to train new teachers to bring literacy to rural communities. Through common standards of knowledge, hygiene, exercise, and work, Vasconcelos believed that local populations would be brought under the umbrella of *mexicanidad*. The arts were central to his vision of cultural reform, and he summoned a core group of Mexican artists back from Europe, awarding them commissions to decorate the walls of public buildings with murals celebrating national history and traditions.

At the heart of this burgeoning *mexicanidad* was a new appreciation for indigenous cultures. In 1922, the muralists organized the Syndicate of Technical Workers, Painters, and Sculptors, which issued a manifesto proclaiming their collective dedication to the portrayal of Mexico's indigenous past. The artistic validation of native culture was seen as a constituent element of postrevolutionary social reform. "The creators of beauty must put forth their utmost efforts to make their production of ideological value to the people," the syndicate's manifesto declared, "and the ideal goal of art . . . should be one of beauty for all, of education and of battle."[18] Yet although the syndicate and other proponents of *indigenismo* professed their dedication to the native, they were relatively unsuccessful at collaborating with actual Indian people or significantly improving their lives. Indeed, there was no such thing as a coherent "Indian tradition"; *indigenismo* was an invented concept designed to consolidate Mexico's diverse native populations into a coherent whole. Under the auspices of the postrevolutionary government, it became a tool of national unification: behind the state's embrace of *mestizaje* was a desire to eliminate racial differences, replacing them with a uniform hybridity. Programs for social uplift, like their counterparts in the United States, were motivated by racial and class prejudices that went hand in hand with the project of strengthening national identity. As the Mexican renaissance traveled, it would often carry these biases along with a more celebratory invocation of *mexicanidad*.

And travel it did. The strongly nationalistic bent of the Mexican artists did not make them provincial. Not only was the Mexican renaissance engaged with cultural developments in other parts of the world, but its participants also were seasoned cosmopolitans themselves. The rising fame of the Mexican muralists brought them lucrative commissions in the United States. During the 1920s, they were welcomed in the artistic circles of Greenwich Village, San Francisco, and Los Angeles, and U.S. Americans were struck by a growing interest in all things Mexican. But by the 1930s the muralists had become more controversial, as dwindling resources led to the allegation that they were taking jobs from U.S.-born artists. In a more conservative political climate, they were also accused of promoting radicalism, most famously evidenced by the scandal surrounding Diego Rivera's mural in the Rockefeller RCA Center building. When Rivera refused to remove a prominent portrait of Lenin, his work was whitewashed and painted over by another artist. These controversies did nothing to diminish the muralists' impact on art in the United States, however. They influenced not only the architects of the WPA public art projects, but also painters of the Harlem Renaissance and others like muralist Philip Guston and a young Jackson Pollock.[19]

While the muralists' escapades in the United States are familiar, less is known about the trans-American bohemia that flourished in Mexico at the same time, which John Britton has compared to the Greenwich Village of 1912–17. He writes, "the visitors from the US were fascinated by the prospect of the creation of a new world in old Mexico by means of processes that operated outside the realm of bourgeois values."[20] Although Britton notes that the Mexico City group was more geographically dispersed than its New York counterpart, it was intimate enough that its participants were well acquainted with one another. As Olivier Debroise describes it, "to live in the city's colonial heart at this time was to be truly at the center of everything. The extent of the city in 1920 was such that one could walk almost anywhere."[21] Susannah Glusker, Anita Brenner's daughter and biographer, writes that her mother's social circle "was small. . . . They socialized regularly and, thanks to the manageable size of Mexico City at that time, bumped into one another on the street, at Sanborns [a popular café], or at the movies."[22] Recalling his trip to Mexico in 1925, Kenneth Rexroth wrote, "it was all very free and open, even riotous. Nobody had become so famous as to be inaccessible."[23] In 1934, Langston Hughes described a "bohemian community" in Mexico City. Of his months there, he reflected, "I have never lived in Greenwich Village in New York, so its bohemian life . . . was outside my orbit. Although once I lived for a year in Montmartre in Paris, I lived there as a worker, not an artist. So the nearest I've ever come to *la vie de boheme* was my winter in Mexico when my friends were almost all writers and artists."[24]

Despite comparisons to London, Paris, or New York, there were also significant disparities between the Mexican and European or U.S. bohemias. Although Mexico City was a cosmopolitan metropolis, much of the country remained untouched by industrialization and ravaged by the effects of a ten-year civil war. If modernist expression arises in response to the conditions of modernity, these were different in Europe or the United States than they were in Mexico, which had only very partially entered the industrial age. In the Mexican context, the distance between tradition and modernity, "primitive" and contemporary, felt greater but also more proximate. As Peter Wollen and Laura Mulvey argue, compared to European modernism, "'ancient' history was chronologically much closer and also in many ways culturally closer" in Mexico. Because "in the Mexican revolution, appeals to the pre-Conquest Indian past still had a political value . . . it was possible for political and artistic avant-gardes to overlap in Mexico in way that they never could in Europe."[25] The politics, content, and form of Mexican-inspired modernism were different because it grew out of a largely agricultural national setting, one with a significant indigenous population that still spoke the languages and maintained the culture of its ancient precursors.

As was the case in the modernist bohemias of Paris or New York, women were important participants in the Mexican cohort, whose antibourgeois values meant they enjoyed a degree of social and sexual liberation far greater than that of ordinary Mexican women. While none of the women discussed in this chapter would have identified herself as a feminist, all were touched by the political activism of Mexican women in the surrounding culture. Under Vasconcelos, large numbers of women were employed as teachers. Professor Elena Torres—co-organizer of the Consejo Feminista Mexicana—was appointed as head of the Bureau of Cultural Missions,[26] and girls, who had always been educated at home, were invited to attend rural schools for the first time. Through organizations like the Union of American Women (UMA), the Pan American League for the Advancement of Women, and the Women's Society, Mexican women sought alliances with their sisters across the Americas.[27] Of course, progress for Mexican women took place in the context of the strongly masculinist legacy of the revolution. All of the members of the artists' syndicate were men, and the lion's share of critical acclaim went to the male muralists. A Mexican woman would not receive a government commission to paint a mural until 1936, when an assignment went to the artist Aurora Reyes.[28] Despite their demands for suffrage, women did not receive the vote until 1946. Porter, Brenner, and Modotti were participants in this contradictory climate, where their own circumstances granted them considerable social and professional freedom, and progressive women's organizations agitated for equal treatment, but the broader social order continued to relegate women to secondary status.

Bohemias are defined by their ephemerality, and Mexico City is no exception. Although Hughes found bohemia in the Mexico of the 1930s, many things had already begun to change by then. Artists who arrived from the United States after the economic crash tended to be driven by financial troubles rather than the desire to participate in a social experiment. In Mexico, the worldwide economic downturn caused the collapse of many of the programs instituted after the revolution. By 1930, the key revolutionary leaders were dead. Their radical initiatives had been diluted as the power of unions was absorbed by the state and efforts at land reform stalled. The government had paid lip service to women's suffrage without granting them the right to vote. An atmosphere of rising political conservatism led to the persecution of communists, leftists, and even liberals. Under Article 33 of the new constitution, the government could deport foreigners for political insurgency, and as a result, Tina Modotti and other leftists were sent into exile following the assassination of the new president, Ortiz Rubio, in 1930. Many Mexican artists left the country in search of better financial opportunities in the United States or Europe. Yet despite the disbanding and dispersal of Mexico's bohemian community, its impact would endure. Although hope for political and social transformation was short lived, the cultural work it inspired would resonate throughout the twentieth century, and it would no longer be possible to see Mexico as a blank space on the map of North American culture.

Three Lives

Katherine Anne Porter

While most American participants in the high modernist culture of the 1920s recognized travel to Europe as a requisite experience, Katherine Anne Porter went to some lengths to distance herself from those circles. In 1965, she told an interviewer, "I was brought up in the generation that Miss Stein described as 'lost,' but I'll be damned if ever I was lost."[29] Although as a young woman she had wished to visit Europe, she did not make it there until 1931, when she sailed by an unconventional route that departed from the Mexican port of Veracruz. In Europe, she moved among the literary giants of her time and came away unimpressed. In her *Notebooks*, she recalled one such encounter:

One evening a crowd gathered in Sylvia's bookshop to hear T. S. Eliot read some of his own poems. Joyce sat near Eliot, his eyes concealed under his dark glasses, silent, motionless, head bowed a little, eyes closed most of the time, as I could see plainly from my chair a few feet away in the same row, as far removed from human reach as if he were already dead. Eliot, in a dry but strong voice, read some of his early poems, turning the pages now and again with a look very near to distaste, as if he did not like the sound of what he was reading.[30]

Porter's tableau of a moribund Joyce and a self-hating Eliot captures the end of an era. Decades later, she would express gratitude for having avoided the movement at its apogee. Her years in Mexico meant that she "missed more than half of the 'twenties in Greenwich Village; I missed the Hemingway epoch in Paris; and I think these are two of the luckiest misses I ever made. . . . I have never been drawn into a group; I cannot join a circle, a crowd, the thing I call a 'huddle.'"[31] Proudly claiming her artistic autonomy, Porter rejects the transatlantic modernist community as an insular clique.[32]

While these memories are colored by the compensatory embellishment that often characterized Porter's self-representation, they nonetheless represent an effort to map her career differently from many members of her generation. Mexico occupies an important place on that map. Although Porter's feelings about it would vacillate widely depending on her state of mind, both she and her biographers seem to agree that the time she spent in Mexico on and off between 1920 and 1931 left an indelible mark on her writing, her understandings of art and politics, and the subsequent course of her life. Although she is often identified as a writer of the American South, on the map of American modernism Porter asserts herself as a different kind of southern writer, one who connects Mexico to Greenwich Village, the European cities of Berlin and Paris, and the U.S. Southwest that was her birthplace and frequent literary subject. As Malcolm Cowley would write, equating Porter's Mexico with the Europe of the high modernist cohort, "Mexico City was her Paris and Taxco was her south of France."[33] So strong was this southern orientation that when she visited New England for the first time, Porter wrote that "it had all the strangeness of a foreign country. Mexico seems a simple, natural place to me, I can live there almost without adjustment, but the air of New England put the fear of God in me. It seems to me that the dry rot of America began there, it is a dead body that breathes out a plague on all life in this country."[34] It therefore makes sense that Porter struggled for many years to complete the biography of Cotton Mather for which she had been awarded a Guggenheim fellowship, while producing numerous literary portraits of the people she knew in Mexico, including the artists Pablo O'Higgins, Diego Rivera and his wife Lupe Marín, the labor leader Luis Morones, filmmaker Sergei Eisenstein, the activist Mary Doherty, author Carleton Beals, and President Alvaro Obregón. Thus, turning our attention to Porter—the only major U.S. American author of her generation to spend a significant part of her literary career south of the U.S. border[35]—helps to situate Mexico more prominently on the map of modernist geography. The fact that she came and went without settling permanently makes her a model participant in the Mexican bohemia of the 1920s. In contrast to the transatlantic modernists who Porter describes as a "huddle," she recalled the loose organization of her Mexican connections: "Mexico was wonderful—a crowd of us were there, perfectly free of each other, yet happily knit together by our interest in Mexican art."[36]

Porter was instrumental in introducing Mexican arts and letters to audiences in the United States at a time of widespread ignorance about Latin America. She began her literary career as a journalist, and her first Mexican writings were articles for such English-language periodicals as the *New York Call*, the *Christian Science Monitor*, *New Republic*, and the *New York Evening Post*. She published numerous reviews of books on Mexico in the *New York Herald Tribune*, translated essays by Diego Rivera and the poetry of Sor Juana Inez de la Cruz, and worked with her first husband Eugene Pressley on the translation of José Joaquín Fernández de Lizardi's early nineteenth-century novel, *El periquillo sarmiento* (*The Itching Parrot*), to which she wrote a lengthy introductory essay hailing it as "without dispute The Novel of the past century, not only for Mexico but for all Spanish-speaking countries."[37] These articles, reviews, and translations were at the forefront of a rising tide of interest in Mexico among North Americans.

Initially drawn to Mexico by the revolution's promise of social reform, Porter quickly became disillusioned with Mexican politics. Her desire to travel south was ignited by her acquaintance with the Mexican musician "Tata Nacho" (Ignacio Fernández Esperón) and painter Adolfo Best Maugard when all three lived in Greenwich Village in 1919. An assignment to write a series of Mexican "sketches" for the *Christian Science Monitor* meant that she would have an income while living abroad.[38] Porter was primed to embrace the ideals of the Mexican Revolution, given that she came to them as a socialist with an antipathy toward organized religion, and as someone who had long been concerned with the plight of tenant farmers in Texas. She believed that Mexico would provide the opportunity to witness a political experiment aimed at solving the problems that had preoccupied her since her youth. Soon after her arrival, she coauthored her most politically optimistic article, "Striking the Lyric Note in Mexico" (1921), with socialist Robert Haberman. In celebratory language, it describes how the government came to the aid of Mexican workers on strike against a foreign-owned lumber company. Porter would soon grow more cynical about Mexico's leadership, condemning the greed and hypocrisy of Mexican politicians and foreign investors. As she lost faith in Mexican politics, however, she maintained her belief in the virtues of cultural reform. Her article "Where Presidents Have No Friends" (1922) describes the impossibility of political alliances in a nation riven by competing factions. Amid the widespread corruption, she noted the efforts of a few who genuinely believed in the ideals of the revolution and sought to promote them through "an esthetic appreciation of the necessity of beauty in the national life, the cultivation of racial forms of art, and the creation of substantial and lasting unity in national politics."[39] Significantly, Porter found hope for political stability in postrevolutionary leaders' appreciation of native aesthetics.

Porter celebrates Mexico's cultural revolution in her *Outline of Mexican Popular Arts*, the catalogue for a major exhibit of Mexican folk art that was slated to travel to the United States in 1922. The show was intended to promote positive images of Mexico abroad by expanding a collection curated by Roberto Montenegro and Jorge Enciso that had been part of the centenary celebration of Mexican independence.[40] In a short piece in the *Christian Science Monitor*, Porter described her excitement at receiving the commission, promising her American readers, "there are new currents stirring. Perhaps the art world is beginning to break away from the traditions of Greece and Rome."[41] The notion of an artistic reorientation away from classical European models toward indigenous American roots was key to Porter's framing of her catalogue essay.

The ideas expressed in Porter's *Outline* are not unique, but they synthesize the indigenist philosophy of Mexican intellectuals for an Anglo-American audience that knew virtually nothing about Mexico or the Mexican arts. Anticipating the ignorance of her readers, Porter framed the essay as "an introduction to the arts of the Mexican people, on the occasion when they are sending for the first time an exhibition of their work to a foreign country."[42] She presented her *Outline* as a corrective to the reigning understanding of Mexican arts in the Anglophone world. Porter criticized those who believed that the recent rejection of European models signaled a fall into the degeneracy of "a mere meaningless peasant art."[43] Instead, "the alien, aristocratic influence [had been] a catastrophe that threatened the vitals of the Mexican race."[44] She found hope in a generation of contemporary artists who were united in purpose with the Mexican folk, "direct and savage, beautiful and terrible, full of harshness and love, divinely gentle, appallingly honest."[45] In her 1922 "Letter from Mexico," she held up Diego Rivera as a model. After inaccurately describing Rivera as the founder of cubism, she reported that he had recovered from his misguided affair with Europe: "now he is simple and splendid and paints like a god in a mood of repentance for the hurts he has given his creatures."[46] Incorrect as an account of cubism's origins, Porter's story performs a geographic realignment of modernism from Europe to the Americas, as well as a temporal revision in which Europe is no longer the home of the avant-garde, but a repository of spent forms.

Inspired as she found contemporary Mexicanist artists to be, Mexican Indians themselves were the primary focus of Porter's attention. When writing the *Outline* she still supported the Mexican modernists' claim to speak on behalf of the Indian, but by the time she reviewed Anita Brenner's history of Mexican art seven years later, Porter would write critically that "the great renascence of Indian art was a movement of mestizos and foreigners. . . . They respected the fruitful silence of the Indian and they shouted for this silence at the top of their lungs."[47] Because none of the muralists could claim pure indigenous ancestry, Porter came to feel they were incapable of representing the essential qualities of an Indian art that emerged naturally out of the timeless and uncomplicated patterns of native life. In Porter's idealized view, "all [Indians] share ideas, intuitions, and human habits; they understand each other. There is no groping for motives, no divided faith."[48] Porter held up the artifacts in the exhibit as examples of unalienated labor, since they had not been designed for show but "gathered from the little country villages, from the common shops and street markets, where the native brings his goods to sell them to his own people. They are personal, authentic creations."[49] Given that Porter's description relies so much on the objects' original use, it is ironic that the catalogue photos pose them against blank backgrounds that provide no sense of context. Absent any visual identification of their function or the circumstances of their production, they appear no different from more traditional works of art or ethnographic specimens, a tendency Tina Modotti later resisted by photographing native artifacts as a part of everyday life.

Dividing the history of Mexican popular art into three periods, the *Outline* reserves special praise for the pre-Hispanic civilizations of the Otomí, the Maya, and the Nahoa. One telling sign of the Nahoas' enlightenment was their treatment of women. "The position of women was that of a completely civilized race," Porter writes. "The legal or religious bondage of women was unknown. They served with honor as priestesses, and had a responsible share in the education of the children. Every evidence is that they enjoyed a cleanly human equality in society utterly foreign to the ideals that governed the relations between men and women of the European and Asiatic races."[50] It is not surprising that Porter confirmed the Nahoas' superiority by reference to their egalitarian view of gender, since women's struggle for autonomy is a consistent theme in her writing. But it is telling that she finds her model for gender relations in indigenous, not Anglo-American, sources. At her most hopeful, she would idealize Indian women for possessing an equanimity unavailable to their modern American counterparts.

Porter's most romantic treatment of the Mexican Indian is a draft of an essay called "Xochimilco," which appeared, in edited form, in the *Christian Science Monitor* in 1921. Xochimilco, a village on the southern outskirts of Mexico City, was a frequent weekend destination for Porter and her friends.[51] Although it was a target of the rural education campaign instituted by José Vasconcelos (Laura, the protagonist of Porter's short story "Flowering Judas," is a teacher there), Porter describes Xochimilco as a place untouched by modernity. Like the popular art praised by the *Outline*, the natives of Xochimilco are far removed from Mexico's tumultuous political scene; indeed, they have been bypassed by history altogether. They "seem a natural and gracious part of the earth they live in such close communion with, entirely removed from contact with the artificial world."[52] In a passage eliminated from the published version, Porter develops her views on gender, explaining that the village is named for Xochitl, "the legendary Aztec goddess of the earth, of fruit, of abundance."[53] She attributes the goddess's power to the matriarchal society of the Xochimilcanos: "In a race where the women sowed and reaped, wove and span and cooked and brewed, it was natural that a goddess should be fruitful and strong."[54] According to Porter, this full but uncomplicated lifestyle had an especially salutary effect on women, as "there are no neurotics among them. No strained lines of sleeplessness or worry mar their faces."[55] Porter, who frequently complained of nervous illnesses, idealized the native, a figure she believed to be free of the afflictions that plagued her contemporaries. Further evidence of these views is found in a portrait of Porter dressed as an Indian woman, her head swathed in a rebozo, a basket of fruit at her hip (fig. 3.4). If she was unable to share the Indian's untroubled state of mind, she could appropriate her garb and, upon her return to New York, would attempt to write from her point of view.

Porter's indigenism landed her in a contradictory position. On the one hand, she recognized that the renaissance was responsible for introducing

3.4. Katherine Anne Porter in the dress of a city Indian woman, Mexico City, 1930. (Series XII, Box 3, item 1035.) Papers of Katherine Anne Porter, Special Collections, University of Maryland Libraries. Reprinted by permission of the University of Maryland Libraries.

the best of Mexico's popular culture to the world; on the other, she believed that such attention exerted a corrosive effect on the pristine folk she so admired. The revolution, which claimed to represent the Mexican people, left many of them in a worse place than where they had started. She found justice and contentment only in ancient precontact societies like the Nahoa or those she imagined to be outside of modernity, like the Xochimilcanos.

Porter's bleak and contradictory views are most apparent in her first short story set in Mexico, "María Concepción" (1922). Because she wrote it just after returning from Mexico to New York City, it can be seen as an initial attempt to make sense of her experiences there. "María Concepción" has been praised for being one of the few literary works of its time to grant subjectivity to an Indian woman. José Limón reads it as evidence for Porter's identification with "oppressed, marginalized, or subordinate groups such as Mexico's Indians."[56] Alluding to the portrait of Porter wearing an Indian costume, Thomas Walsh concurs, writing that in some respects "María Concepción is Porter dressed in Indian garb. . . . Porter attempted to get inside her skin and feel the suffering of the Indian."[57] Whether or not Porter identified with her protagonist, my reading of the story is more cynical. While she recognizes the oppression of the indigenous woman, Porter grants her agency only in order to kill off the transformative possibilities of the revolution. Critics are able to cast a positive light on her eventual triumph only by forgetting that Porter builds the story around two Marías, one of whom must die for the other to find satisfaction.

"María Concepción" illustrates the corrosive impact of the revolution and the impossibility of preserving native culture from the encroachments of modernity. That the story is intended to have larger symbolic import is indicated by the fact that its two central female characters are both named María: one is the protagonist, a pregnant peasant woman who is abandoned by her husband, Juan; the other is María Rosa, the object of Juan's affections, who also gives birth to his child. At the beginning of the story, Porter indulges in a romanticism similar to that of "Xochimilco" when she describes María Concepción as "walk[ing] with the free, natural, guarded ease of the primitive woman carrying an unborn child."[58] But María does not exist in a state of nature, nor is she a primitive. Henchmen of the local revolutionary faction police her village, and most of its population is employed on an excavation project run by an American archaeologist. Although the purpose of the dig is "to uncover the lost city of their ancestors," the villagers are uninterested in the work of historical recovery.[59] They cannot understand why their boss, Givens, puts such stock in the broken and dirty artifacts they are exhuming. Whereas Givens values the objects for their age and historical value, the villagers dig for a living.

The story details the impact of the revolution on the *campesinos*, especially the village women. It touches María Concepción's life directly when Juan abandons his tedious job on the archaeological site to join the army. He is accompanied by his new mistress, María Rosa, who becomes a *soldadera*, one of the many rural women who followed male relatives into the war. Porter's description echoes eyewitness accounts of the hardships of the *soldaderas*:

> Juan had a rifle at his shoulder and two pistols at his belt. María Rosa wore a rifle also, slung on her back along with the blankets and cooking pots. They joined the nearest detachment of troops in the field, and María Rosa marched ahead with the battalion of experienced women of war, which went over the crops like locusts, gathering provisions for the army. She cooked with them, and ate with them what was left after the men had eaten. After battles she went out on the field with the others to salvage clothing and ammunition and guns from the slain before they should begin to swell in the heat. Sometimes they would encounter the women from the other army, and a second battle as grim as the first would take place.[60]

This passage reveals the life of the *soldadera* to be even more grueling than that of her male companions. Each obstacle faced by the male troops is amplified for the women who follow behind. Their work involves scavenging, nursing, caretaking, and, sometimes, armed combat. Glorified by the muralists and popular *corridos*, the *soldadera* was essential to the victory of revolutionary forces. However, Porter represents this iconic Mexican figure as an adulteress who must die so that social order can be reestablished.

The story's political message rests on the contrast between the two Marías. María Rosa is brave and tenacious. She defies tradition by leaving home and bearing Juan's child out of wedlock. Her baby is healthy, despite the hardships she has endured. By contrast, María Concepción is more closely tied to various forms of tradition. At a time when the Church was associated with the antirevolutionary values of the Porfiriato, she is deeply religious and proud to have been married by a priest. The silent and long-suffering María Concepción remains rooted in place while Juan and María Rosa travel the countryside. When Juan deserts the army and returns home he beats María Concepción and orders her to cook for him, which she does without complaining. As if to embody her own deadly stasis, María Concepción's child is stillborn.

Critics have tended to treat María Concepción's revenge as a feminist victory, if an ambivalent one. Ostracized from her community and eaten away by rage at Juan's betrayal, she brutally murders María Rosa. When the corrupt local gendarmes attempt to charge her with the murder, Juan and the other villagers come to her defense by refusing to cooperate with the investigation and justifying María Rosa's death as punishment for her immorality. The exonerated María Concepción assumes responsibility for

María Rosa's newborn son and returns home with Juan. At the story's end, Juan contemplates his future with despair: "tomorrow he would go back to dull and endless labor, he must descend into the trenches of the buried city as María Rosa must go into her grave."[61] With the death of María Rosa, his hope for change is extinguished. By contrast, María Concepción is satisfied by this return to the status quo, even though it means living with a faithless, abusive husband. In the final lines of the story, her breathing is attuned to the rhythms of her surroundings, suggesting that the restoration of order is sanctioned by a natural world larger and more permanent than any human conflict.

If there is a victory at the end of this story, it goes to the woman who embodies antirevolutionary values over the woman who fights for a different world. While it is impossible to take any one piece as representative of Porter's views about the revolution, "María Concepción" condenses many of her most pessimistic reactions. Drawn to the promise that unionization and land redistribution were the first steps toward the creation of a more just society, she came to believe that the *campesinos* were incapable of fighting for their own rights. She idealized precontact rural folk, but wrote them into an impossible position whereby they were corrupted as soon as they encountered the forces of cultural or political modernization.

The combination of idealization and despair that characterized Porter's responses to the Indian sounds much like modernist primitivism. To what extent, then, does it matter that her writing is set in Mexico rather than Africa, Asia, or the Caribbean? The difference is that Porter's version of primitivism is a direct outgrowth of her exposure to the Mexican indigenists, who saw the turn to folk aesthetics as a political gesture in keeping with the populist goals of the revolution. While she shares their blind spots, she also participates in their political project. "Xochimilco" is not simply a romantic celebration of the primitive, but part of a more general elevation of indigenous folkways taking place in Mexico, which was closely tied to agendas for social reform. "María Concepción" is not only about the conflict between tradition and modernity, but also about the ways the Mexican Revolution has failed the populations it claimed to represent. Porter anchors recognizably modernist concerns in a Mexican setting that is not simply a backdrop but a constituent feature of her literary project. Her life suggests alternative routes for a modernism that is oriented south toward Mexico, as well as toward Europe and the eastern United States. Looking back on the period of her Mexican sojourns in 1965, Porter would make the case for a modernism that embraced, rather than fled from, its North American roots. She ridiculed her generation for "all this going into exile and being so romantic about it and turning their backs on this 'crass American civiliza-tion' and so on." Against the modernist europhilia, Porter claimed, "I am an old North American. . . . Our foreign travel was Mexico, which we loved, and so when the time came for me to travel and get out in the great world a bit, I just came back to Mexico."[62] Identifying herself as "an old North American," Porter includes Mexico as a part of the world she got out in, a place that would forever change the course of her life and her art.

Anita Brenner

Porter reserved some of her harshest criticism for authors who represented Mexico through the scrim of their own fantasies rather than attempting to understand its history and people. Her negative reviews of D. H. Lawrence's *The Plumed Serpent*, the letters of Rosalie Evans, Vicente Blasco Ibáñez's *Mexico in Revolution*, Harry L. Forester's *A Gringo in Mañanaland*, Vernon Quinn's *Beautiful Mexico*, and Stuart Chase's *Mexico: A Study of Two Americas* accused these writers of ignorance and prejudice. Porter was much kinder about Anita Brenner's *Idols behind Altars* (1929). Her review began by calling it "a really beautiful book" and concluded that it was "not to be missed— a stimulating record of a vital period in the history of American art told by a contemporary eyewitness."[63] While slightly less enthusiastic about Brenner's study of the revolution, *The Wind That Swept Mexico* (1943), Por-ter praised its skillful condensation of a complex history and acknowledged the difficulty of publishing controversial material in the sensitive political climate of wartime. These reviews create a concrete link between Porter, the native Texan who went to Mexico, and Brenner, who was born in Mexico and who migrated to Texas with her family when she was eleven. Like Por-ter, Brenner traveled to Mexico as a young woman because she was attracted to the political and cultural promises of the postrevolutionary moment and eager to escape the conservative atmosphere of San Antonio, where she faced anti-Semitism and xenophobia. Both women drew lifelong in-spiration from their Mexican experiences, although Brenner would eventu-ally settle there permanently, spending the last thirty years of her life at her ranch in Aguascalientes. Both opened up lines of contact between Mexico and the United States, as well as between North America and more distant parts of the world. Brenner accepted this role more permanently and en-thusiastically than Porter, fashioning herself as a cultural ambassador who championed Mexican artists and Mexican political causes abroad through-out her adult life. Whereas Porter sought purity in indigenous people and arts, Brenner affirmed *mestizaje* as Mexico's richest cultural resource. Without denying the brutality of Spanish conquest, she found strength in the fusion of European and indigenous elements within the modern Mexican populace. And whereas Porter saw the corruption of the Mexican state as a reason to repudiate the revolution, Brenner sought to recuperate its legacy as a way of managing strained relations between the United States and Mexico.

Brenner dedicated her career to introducing Mexico to English-speaking audiences and facilitating cultural exchange between Mexico and the United States. Over the course of fifty years as a journalist, she published hundreds of articles on the history and culture of Mexico in periodicals like the *New York Times*, *The Nation*, *ARTnews*, *Atlantic Monthly*, *Harper's*, and *Saturday Review*. She worked as a translator and edited the successful tourist magazine *Mexico This Month* from 1955 to 1972. In addition to her two major historical studies, she wrote several children's books and a travel book called *Your Mexican Holiday*. *Idols behind Altars*, her first book, was illustrated by the photographs of Tina Modotti and Edward Weston, who Brenner commissioned after receiving government funding to conduct research on Mexican decorative arts. Having provided Weston with a list of objects and necessary letters of introduction, she sent him on a photographic tour of the country. She is thus not only a model for Weston's famous series of nudes, but the force behind many of his Mexican photographs.

The map of Brenner's life repeatedly traverses the U.S.-Mexico border, from her family's initial flight to Texas in 1912, to her assumption of more permanent residence in Aguascalientes in 1944. In 1923, Brenner moved from Texas to Mexico City to attend the National University. Four years later, she relocated to New York to study at Columbia. Under the tutelage of Franz Boas, she received a PhD in anthropology just three years later. Boas was an ideal advisor for Brenner. He had conducted his own fieldwork in Mexico, where he established the International School of American Archaeology and Ethnology, and he had trained its foremost anthropologist, Miguel Gamio (who employed Brenner before her move to New York). By the time she met Boas, Brenner was already an accomplished journalist and author of the forthcoming *Idols behind Altars*, a study of Mexican art that combined history, ethnography, and memoir. In New York, she became part of a circle of Mexican artists and intellectuals she dubbed the *Mexicanada*.[64] She was also friendly with the group of Jewish intellectuals affiliated with the *Menorah Journal*. From her first published article, Brenner wrote consistently about Jewish cultural identity and anti-Semitism. She attributed her identification with the plight of Indians, workers, and other oppressed groups to her Jewish and Mexican ancestry.

During her years in Mexico, Brenner was at the hub of an inter-American artistic community. She formed close ties with some of the era's most important women artists and intellectuals. Among her friends were the anthropologist Lucy Parry Knox, Lupe Marín, painter and poet Nahui Olín, composer Concha Michel, Tina Modotti, the author Frances Toor, and journalist Ella Goldberg. As Glusker describes them, "this community of women shared concerns and interests similar to those expressed by women in the [nineteen] sixties and the nineties. Their style, however, was different. Anita and her sisters were de facto feminists. They didn't form or join feminist organizations, nor did they demonstrate with suffragettes active in Mexico. Most were independent in their creative and intellectual lives but highly dependent in their relationships with men."[65] Brenner never identified with any particular feminist cause, nor did she write about women or gender issues, as Porter did. Nonetheless, she took advantage of a climate in which women enjoyed expanding professional opportunities and where men and women often engaged in collaborative working relationships. Mexico was thus not just the subject that earned Brenner her professional stature; it was a place that gave her the combination of intellectual camaraderie and independence required to develop her career as an acknowledged expert on its arts and politics.

Written for a foreign audience, *Idols behind Altars* is an ambitious overview of Mexican art from precontact indigenous civilizations to the present. Its title, an allusion to the persistence of pantheistic beliefs despite the imposition of Christianity, is a metaphor for Brenner's understanding of the Mexican people, whose mestizo vitality comes from the mingled cultures of colonizer and colonized. While Porter's *Outline* introduced American audiences to Mexico's artistic renaissance, Brenner made a more sustained case for its importance to the continent and the world. Brenner's argument was heard. Published in 1929, *Idols* received over sixty reviews, most of them positive.[66] It influenced the conceptualization of public art projects in the United States over the next decade. George Biddle, head of the WPA's Federal Arts Program, wrote that his understanding of the Mexican muralists was indebted to "the wisdom and scholarship" of *Idols*.[67] So too, Sergei Eisenstein, director of the unfinished film *Viva Mexico!*, credited Brenner's book with inspiring his interest in Mexico. *Idols* is still cited today in discussions of Mexican arts. It is not just a source of historical information, however; it is also a representation shaped by Brenner's agenda of conferring on contemporary Mexico a coherent national past and communicating its importance to the rest of the continent.

Idols behind Altars puts Mexico at the center of the history of American art. In an article for the *New York World*, Brenner described a renaissance that had begun south of the U.S. border, but would come to represent all of North America: "Mexico, so long camouflaged in bandits, oil, and revolution, emerges with an art which is not only a significant expression of itself, but a rebirth of genuine American art, representative ultimately, not only of the purple-mountained home of artists south of the Rio Grande, but of the entire Western continent."[68] Brenner argued that, in contrast to a moribund Europe, Mexico was witnessing a creative resurgence akin to the artistic awakening that had taken place across the Atlantic five centuries earlier. As Mexican artists returned home from Europe to recover their native American traditions, they were shifting the history of art itself from established centers in Paris, Italy, and Spain to Mexico and the Americas.

Whereas Porter was drawn to the uncorrupted culture of the Mexican Indian, Brenner saw no possibility for such an escape from modernity. She recognized indigenism as a distinctively modern formation that entailed a recovery of the "folk" in response to contemporary aesthetic and political needs. As she put it, "the return to native values, spiritual and artistic . . . often occurred by way of modern European art" (231). Rather than fleeing from modernity, these artists had been prompted by their encounters with modernism to reconsider the themes and traditions of their own American culture. As they translated modernism into a New World context, they infused it with a different understanding of the relationship between politics and art. "Brush and gun are . . . not alternatives to any Mexican artist," she wrote, emphasizing the necessary conjunction of cultural and political revolution (243). In her view, the Mexican artists were, at least in theory, at one with the people, rather than being elevated above them like their European counterparts: "since the [Mexican] artist is as a rule economically one of the masses, his work should be directed toward their enjoyment, instruction, and benefit. This implies a repudiation of the intellectual and social snobbery that determines much of the appearance and character of 'modernist' work."[69] For Brenner, the Mexican renaissance thus introduced an alternative modernism, one that was politically engaged and attuned to the needs and values of a mass public. Its antecedents were not only ancient indigenous art but also the popular forms of the *corrido* and *pulqueria* murals, which had long been a means of self-expression for ordinary Mexicans. In the spirit of these popular forms, the new artists aspired to work collectively and anonymously in media that did not require literacy for their meanings to be understood.

While the artist might share an economic position with the people, Brenner acknowledged that "racially, few of the revolutionary Mexican artists are pure Indian. In colour they deepen from indoor white to the richest sunned tinge. . . . They are typically a Mexican troop" (232). But whereas Porter saw this racial impurity as a sign of hypocrisy, Brenner believed that race was less important than populist commitment, the fact that "nowhere as in Mexico has art so intimately been linked to the fate of its people" (244). Indeed, Brenner's position is consistent with the Mexican understanding of race, which has more to do with class position than blood. As Alan Knight describes, "slices [of the population] are socially, not racially, determined; even in respect to inherited somatic features 'Indian' and 'Mestizo' people may be indistinguishable, individually or collectively."[70] Origins or physical features are less meaningful than racial self-identification, which is closely tied to economic class. Eschewing the Poundian dictum of "art for art's sake," the Mexican artists understood themselves as workers, and they aspired to represent the interests and values of working-class and rural audiences. Brenner took them at their word, elevating their dedication to indigenous traditions over their privileged backgrounds.

Although *Idols* endorsed the values of the revolution, Brenner was not blind to its contradictions. She describes how the political foundations of the Mexican renaissance were shaken by the withdrawal of government support for the muralists and the disbanding of the syndicate. The structure of her book reflects the dissolution of the ideal of art as a collective enterprise, the chapter on the syndicate giving way to chapters on individual artists. After citing the manifesto's claim that "our fundamental aesthetic goal is to socialize artistic expression, and tend to obliterate totally, individualism, which is bourgeois" (254–55), *Idols* devotes chapters to Siqueiros, Orozco, Rivera, Goitia, and Charlot, a choice that reflects the return of an understanding of the artist as an exceptional figure rather than a worker for the public good. Like Porter, Brenner also recognized that the revolution had failed to improve the lives of the very people who were glorified by the new artists. To a fault, Mexicans privileged art above all other social institutions: "It is a nation which establishes a school for sculpture before thinking of a Juvenile Court, and which paints the walls of its buildings much sooner than it organizes a Federal Bank. Sanitation, jobs, and reliably workable laws are attended to literally as a by-product of art" (314). Where Porter finds hope only in retreat from modernity, Brenner calls for an infrastructure of modern institutions to better realize the new social order envisioned by Mexican artists.

Idols ends somewhat surprisingly by turning from the attractions of Mexican art to Mexico's strategic position in the hemisphere. In the last pages, Brenner introduces two themes that would be central to her most important book, *The Wind That Swept Mexico*, the first English-language account of the Mexican Revolution. On the one hand, she notes the strained but mutually dependent relationship between Mexico and the United States, which has consistently intervened in Mexican affairs to the point that "there is a saying in Mexico that revolutions are made in the United States" (328). On the other, she observes that Mexico's resistance to the United States has made it a model for other Latin American nations. These points expand the book's diplomatic mission, which is not only to promote the accomplishments of the Mexican modernists but also to remind American readers of the interdependence of the renaissance and the revolution that preceded it. As Brenner describes it, the Mexican renaissance was not merely an explosion of artistic creativity; it was the outgrowth of a violent social and political upheaval that had enduring consequences for the entire region. Brenner understood culture and foreign policy as inextricably entwined, implying that English-language readers should know about Mexican art not only because of its aesthetic appeal but also because it testified to the delicate balance of power on the continent and in the hemisphere.

Brenner would bring these issues of foreign policy to the fore fourteen years later in *The Wind That Swept Mexico*. Published as the United States was entering the Second World War, *Wind* seeks once again to bring Mexico into the sightlines of American readers as their attention turned toward Europe. It begins by cautioning that Americans ignore Mexico at their peril: "We are not safe in the United States, now and henceforth, without taking Mexico into account; nor is Mexico safe disregarding us. This is something that Mexicans have long known, with dread, but that few Americans have had to look at" (1). Whereas the Brenner of *Idols* emphasized her Mexican roots, the Brenner of *Wind* speaks from a position of dual subjectivity that comes from her long-term status as a commuter between the two nations. She includes herself in the "we" of U.S. residents, but she also writes as a Mexican. In her short catalogue of sources, she lists herself as an eyewitness to the revolution and an authority who "later knew many of its important participants and learned something about the way it looked to each of them" (298). Brenner thus identifies herself as an advocate of both Mexican and U.S. interests who seeks common ground while recognizing a long history of conflict and animosity between the two nations.

The Wind That Swept Mexico is formally interesting because of the uneven relationship between the print narrative of the revolution that comprises its first half and a visual essay—made up of 184 captioned photographs—that retells the same story with a difference in the second half. The inconsistencies between print and visual materials that may seem like flaws effectively underscore the book's double (and often contradictory) mission of easing U.S.-Mexican relations and speaking on behalf of Mexican interests. The contrast between the two conclusions highlights these tensions. Brenner's written account of the revolution ends by urging collaboration between the United States and Mexico based on the fact that "independence, complete isolation of any country's affairs from all others, is now recognizably everywhere a fiction" (100). She is referring to the onset of the Second World War, which drove home the need for regional alliances and the global interconnection of nations. The United States and Mexico could no longer afford to ignore each other. The photo essay ends quite differently, with a plea for Mexican autonomy. Beneath a portrait of an anonymous *campesino* staring out at the viewer, the caption asks whether his generation will lose the accomplishments of the revolution, "or [whether] the prospect [is] still fair and bright . . . would Mexico someday belong to Mexicans?" (184) (fig. 3.5). The written text's call for partnership is undercut by the photo essay's suggestion that the Mexican people still hope to expel foreign influences and attain national autonomy. While this representation of Mexican desire might on its own be too controversial for U.S. audiences during wartime, it is muted by the message of interdependence presented in the prose essay that preceded it.

Subtly undercutting the print narrative, the photo essay employs a number of other modernist strategies to destabilize the relationship between written and visual texts. Its contents are gleaned from archives of newspaper and magazine photographs, which were substantial because the Mexican Revolution had been the subject of such extensive visual documentation. Circulated to domestic and foreign audiences via periodicals, postcards, and film, visual representations played a decisive role in shaping public opinion about the war.[71] Lifted from their original contexts and adorned with captions that are often caustic or unrevealing, the images become an ironic commentary on North American history. In some cases, the photographs undermine the captions. For example, illustrations of daily life in Porfirian-era Mexico are accompanied by the sarcastic description: "everywhere peace reigned and . . . for 90% of the population . . . the blessings of poverty also. It was Mexico's misfortune, said Limantour and the *Científicos* [Díaz's Secretary of Treasury and his inner circle], to try to progress with such a burden upon it: more than three-fourths of the population nearly pure Indian . . . irresponsible . . . lazy. Such beings could never perform, surely could not claim, participation in the acts of government. Let them work and keep the peace" (15–17). Photographs of these allegedly irresponsible and lazy people at work and play reveal their abject poverty and abandonment

3.5. Portrait of a *campesino* from Anita Brenner's *The Wind That Swept Mexico* (1943). Black Star (Calleja). Reprinted by permission of Black Star.

by the state. These sentiments set the stage for subsequent images showing the same populations rising up in armed rebellion. In other cases, the captions tell a story that cannot be conveyed through visual images, suggesting the communicative limits of documentary photography. The caption to a photograph of a scarred landscape reads: "There were other capitalists who owned the Ojuela mine in Durango. Other foreigners owned other mines, smelters and metals . . . gold, silver, lead, copper . . . in Guanajuato, the

3.6–3.7. *U.S. News* photographs from Anita Brenner's *The Wind That Swept Mexico* (1943). On the left-hand page, ambassador to Mexico Dwight W. Morrow addresses a formal banquet, while on right we see the bloody corpse of a *soldadero*. The juxtaposition of the two images is intended to create an ironic contrast between Mexico's public facade and the devastating consequences of the revolution.

Silver City of the World, in Pachuca, in a score of towns . . ." (27). The fact that the landscape in the photograph is unidentified subverts the explanatory function of captioning. The implication is that the particular mine in the photograph is just one instance of a larger problem; its precise name and location are less important than its symbolic status. A third strategy employed by the essay is a form of photomontage, where irony is produced through the strategic juxtaposition of images: social elites in a horse-drawn carriage are pictured on a page facing a pair of *peones* on horseback; a portrait of Porfirio Díaz and his wife is paired with a picture of rebels amassing ominously in the countryside; the U.S. American Ambassador Morrow speaking of reconciliation at a Mexican banquet is paired with the bloody corpse of a *soldadero*, indicating that the conflict remains unresolved (figs. 3.6–3.7). Whereas the manifest project of *Wind* is to strengthen relations between the United States and Mexico by educating Americans about Mexico's recent history, the print and visual narratives together tell a story of

mutual distrust, corruption, and abuse of power. In her review of the book, Porter accused Brenner of glossing over the worst of that history. She wrote, "the whole story of the relations of [Mexico] with the United States . . . is ugly, grim, bitter beyond words, and so scandalous I suppose the whole truth, or even the greater part of the simple facts, can never be published: it might blow the roof off this continent."[72] As Porter recognized, Brenner's goal was not to "blow the roof off this continent," particularly as world war drew the United States and Mexico together. Instead she called for partnership, but, as I have attempted to show, her advocacy of cross-border collaboration was strategic. A close reading of the text yields a more critical perspective than its cautious presentation might suggest. While announcing the necessity of an alliance between the United States and Mexico, Brenner also made her U.S. readers aware of the violence in Mexico's recent past, the devastating impact of foreign intervention, and the lingering anti-Americanism of the Mexican people. Unlike Porter, who swung from extremes of enthusiasm to condemnation depending on her mood, Brenner consistently worked to strengthen cultural ties between the two nations in the hope that they would lead to improved political relations. Under Brenner's pen, the history of Mexican art and its revolution are motivated by similar goals. In both stories, Mexico is a pivot for inter-American affairs: it is the source of a vibrant and politically committed American modernism and a conduit between the United States and Latin America, a connective link that has the potential to confer or destroy the hemispheric balance of power.

Tina Modotti

Brenner and Porter both recognized the power of visual images to communicate the excitement of Mexico's cultural renaissance to foreign audiences. But no matter how vivid their prose, these authors could not adequately describe the work of Mexican artists in words alone, and the murals, their most celebrated accomplishments, could not travel at all. It was through photography that the muralists' work became known in the United States, enabling them to receive lucrative commissions and international acclaim. Projects that incorporated written and photographic matter brought Brenner and Porter into contact with Tina Modotti, the Italian-born photographer whose artistic career was concentrated almost exclusively in Mexico. Noting that Modotti contributed to Porter's *Outline of Mexican Popular Arts*, her biographer Letizia Argenteri claims that "it was after this overwhelming show that Tina developed a taste for Mexican art and *lo mexicano* in general."[73] The two women became friends and in 1930, when Modotti was forced to dispose of her belongings after being sentenced to deportation, she left behind a camera that made its way into Porter's hands by way of the Mexican photographers Lola and Manuel Alvarez Bravo.[74] Modotti's acquaintance with Brenner began with their collaboration on *Idols behind Altars*. When Brenner hired Edward Weston—Modotti's partner and lover at the time—to illustrate her study, Modotti accompanied him on his tour of the country. She helped to mediate his otherwise hapless encounters with rural Mexicans and shot some of the photographs herself, leading to an ongoing critical debate about their attribution.[75] Although their collaboration on *Idols* was a success, social interactions between Brenner and Modotti were strained. Brenner, who sensed that Modotti lacked respect for her accomplishments, recorded in her journal that the photographer had called her "a vulgar scheming adventuress."[76] Eventually the relationship would thaw, and Modotti would photograph Brenner and several members of her family. During the difficult period when Modotti was accused of murdering her lover, the Cuban communist Julio Antonio Mella, Brenner wrote, "Tina behaved with great poise and dignity throughout" her ordeal.[77] Brenner's ambivalence toward Modotti is perhaps best summarized by a journal entry in which she drew up a list of people who were "Actively Friends; Actively Enemies; and Actively Both." Modotti was included in the last category.[78]

Unlike Brenner, whose life and work has received very little attention, Modotti's career has assumed legendary proportions that have as much to do with her notorious life as with the work itself.[79] When Kenneth Rexroth recalled his visit to Mexico in his 1964 *Autobiographical Novel*, he wrote, "the most spectacular person of all was a photographer, artist, model, high-class courtesan, and Mata Hari for the Comintern, Tina Modotti. She was the heroine of a lurid political assassination and was what I guess is called an international beauty."[80] Rexroth's unflattering description synthesizes the competing myths that surround Modotti, who has been claimed as a feminist heroine, a promiscuous seductress, and a hardened Stalinist. Her best-known photographs have been turned into icons that are even more familiar than the artist herself: after a bidding war with rock star Madonna, *Roses* was bought by fashion mogul Susie Tompkins, who converted it into a label for her Esprit clothing line; *Woman with Flag* inspired a 1993 sculpture by the artist María Grazia Collini and a well-known fashion shoot by photographer Christophe Kutner. The mythologization of Modotti and her work has obstructed a more complex understanding of her accomplishments.[81] Here, I attempt to produce an alternative view by situating Modotti in the trans-American community that inspired her most creative period and her photography in the context of a new map of American modernism.

The two interrelated strands of Modotti's biography are her political radicalism and her participation in American bohemias in San Francisco, Los Angeles, and Mexico City. As a young woman, she was a model and actress on stage and in silent films. Her first "husband" (they were never officially married, although some of her biographers claim otherwise) was the romantic Robaix ("Robo") de l'Abrie Richey, a native of Oregon who exoticized himself by claiming French Canadian ancestry. In 1922, Robo died suddenly of smallpox just as Modotti was planning to join him in Mexico. She moved there a year later to establish a photographic studio with her lover, Edward Weston. Modotti's beauty and vibrant personality made her the center of social gatherings and the inspiration for many in Mexico's artistic community. Like Brenner, she was the subject of Weston's nude photography, a fact that has obscured serious attention to her own career. Whether focused on the striking beauty of her face, artfully fragmented body parts, or her naked body in toto, Weston's portraits of Modotti bespeak his quest for aesthetic perfection via the female form (fig. 3.8). One of his nude photographs of Modotti would be the inspiration for a figure in Diego Rivera's mural *Life and Earth* at the National School of Agriculture in Chapingo (fig. 3.9). Depicted by such giants as Weston and Rivera, Modotti can seem more like muse than agent, making it difficult to see this gorgeous, prone body as that of an artist in her own right.

A very different Modotti appears in Rivera's mural *Del corrido de la revolución* (Ballad of the Revolution), which decorates the walls of Mexico's Ministry of Education. Here she is pictured as a comrade alongside other figures associated with the Mexican Revolution. Clothed conservatively in a sweater and dark skirt, Modotti stands at the edge of the composition offering an ammunition belt to her armed compatriots (fig. 3.10). Rivera's mural gives some intimation of Modotti's longstanding socialist filiations. Born into a socialist family in Udine, Italy, her political education began at a young age. Her first job after immigrating to the United States in 1913 was as a seamstress, and her working-class origins are often cited as the impetus for her later political career. The increasing radicalism of Modotti's beliefs reverses the political journey of Porter and, to a lesser extent, Brenner. Whereas Porter's leftist commitments first drew her to Mexico, Modotti moved there because of her romantic and professional partnership with the apolitical Weston. Her growing politicization caused them to grow apart as she increasingly dedicated her art to politics, joining the Communist Party in 1927. In a letter to Anita Brenner, she wrote that she aspired to photograph with "a class eye": "I look upon people now not in terms of race [or] types but in terms of *classes.*"[82] Her subsequent photography fused the iconography of socialism and the formal concerns of Euro-American modernism, situating these international movements in a Mexican setting. Modotti's political activities made her a repeated target of criminal investigation. She stood trial for Mella's murder amid newspaper coverage that condemned her as a woman of loose morals. The nude portraits taken by Weston were held up as evidence of her degeneracy, sparking heated public debates about art versus documentary photography. In his memoirs, José Vasconcelos wrote cruelly, "[Modotti] practiced the profession of vampire . . . She was seeking, perhaps notoriety, but not money. We all knew her body because she served as a gratuitous model for the photographer [Weston] and her bewitching nudes were fought over. Her legend was a dark one."[83] In 1930 she was deported from Mexico, after being accused of plotting the murder of Mexican president Ortiz Rubio. She traveled through Europe as an agent for the Soviet Comintern and a member

3.8. Tina Modotti as *Half-Nude in Kimono* (1924).
Photograph by Edward Weston. © 1981 Arizona Board
of Regents. Used by permission of Collection Center
for Creative Photography, University of Arizona.

of International Red Aid, returning to Mexico under an assumed identity
in 1939.

Like Porter, Modotti was not a native Mexican, but Mexico was the location for her most important work. As one curator puts it, "her photographs
and Mexico were inextricable."[84] She can be identified as an American modernist because her formal experimentation and political commitments are

3.9. A figure inspired by Tina Modotti, from Diego Rivera's *Life and Earth* (1924–27) mural at the National School of Agriculture, Chapingo, Mexico. Photograph by Bob Schalkwijk. © 2008 Banco de México Diego Rivera and Frida Kahlo Museums Trust. Reprinted by permission of Bob Schalkwijk.

3.10. Diego Rivera, *Del corrido de la revolución* (1928). A more serious, politically engaged Tina Modotti is pictured on the far right holding an ammunition belt. Courtesy of Throckmorton Fine Art.

grounded in New World settings. Many of Modotti's later photographs are explicitly ideological. Some are manifestly political in content, whereas others are given a political cast through their publication in socialist or communist periodicals. But she also documented Mexico's artistic scene with a less overt ideological agenda. Modotti was particularly instrumental in promoting the art of the muralists for viewers abroad. Her photographs of the work of Diego Rivera, José Clemente Orozco, and Máximo Pacheco made Mexico's cultural renaissance visible to the world.[85] Her portraits of Edward Weston, Anita Brenner, Jean Charlot, Dolores del Río, Federico Marín, Carleton Beals, Moisés Sáenz, Julio Antonio Mella, Antonieta Rivas Mercado, Vittorio Vidali, and many others leave a visual record of key participants in Mexican cultural life of the 1920s.

Modotti's portrait of Brenner illustrates her stylistic differences from Weston (fig. 3.11). Whereas Weston depicts the pristine surfaces of Brenner's naked body, Modotti concentrates on her face. In Modotti's version, Brenner is dressed in a mannish suit, her eyes enigmatically shadowed by the brim of a large hat. In the former, Brenner's body becomes a work of art that Weston described as "lacking any human interest;"[86] in the latter, it expresses the distinctive facets of her personality. Resisting her mentor's commitment to form at the expense of social context, Modotti more effectively captures the scenes, personalities, and political concerns of her trans-American community.[87] Whereas Weston could not have been less interested in the events unfolding around him, Modotti was immediately caught up in the social and political foment of post-Revolutionary Mexico. Her images attest to, rather than resist, a relationship between photographer and subject. The camera is a device for intervening in, rather than mastering, the surrounding world.

Modotti's Americanist themes are evident even in her still-life photographs. Although they share Weston's formal preoccupations, they are far less insistently decontextualized, and they often portray objects native to a New World landscape: the *flor de manita* reaching up like a gnarled, grasping hand; the asymmetrical, stunted geranium struggling to grow from a cracked pot; nopal cactus; stalks of sugar cane; corn; and the calla lily that became a signature of Diego Rivera. Shot against a blank background or close up in the style of Weston, these objects are nonetheless highly expressive. The deepening of Modotti's political commitments is evident in a series that combines the international socialist icons of hammer and sickle with the specifically Mexican symbols of petate, bandolier, guitar, and sombrero (fig. 3.12). Here, a modernist precision and simplicity of form is applied to manifestly political content that is at once local and international.

3.11. Tina Modotti's portrait of Anita Brenner attempts to capture the unique character of her subject. From *Anita Brenner: A Mind of Her Own*, by Susannah Joel Glusker (Austin: University of Texas Press, 1998), 65. Courtesy of Susannah Joel Glusker and Peter Glusker.

Modotti also shared the indigenists' interest in native people and cultures. Her photographs of popular arts and crafts illustrate Brenner's *Idols behind Altars*, as well as appearing in the Mexican journals *Forma* and *Mexican Folkways*, the American *Creative Arts*, and the French *L'Art Vivant*. While some of these images picture artifacts in isolation, others show them in use, evidence of Modotti's concern with placing her subjects in a social setting. Her photographs of Mexican Indians complement the themes of the muralists' paintings while placing particular emphasis on the activities of indigenous women. Just after her release from prison, she traveled to Juchitán, a traditionally matriarchal society on the Isthmus of Tehuantepec. Modotti's photographs suggest a world apart from the difficulties she had recently

3.12. Tina Modotti, *Guitar, Bandolier, and Sickle* (1927).

faced. These could be illustrations for Porter's essay "Xochimilco," for they offer a similar commentary on the harmonious simplicity of native society (fig. 3.13). In a fictional rendition of this episode from Modotti's life, the Mexican author Elena Poniatowska describes the setting in idealizing terms very similar to those of Porter's essay: "In Juchitán, people go freely in and out of houses that are always open. The children play in the mud along with the chickens and the pigs. A kind of Dionysian effervescence permeates the public spaces. Juchitán is one big public space—market, cantina, plaza—full of people of all ages, peasants from outlying areas, everything bursting with exuberance, like the painted gourds, the iguanas, and especially the women, who carry earthenware trays overflowing with fruits on their heads."[88] In Modotti's photographs, women engage in daily tasks of marketing, washing, and caring for children. They appear calm and untroubled, the visual instantiation of Porter's claim that the native woman is free of modern neuroses. The women of Juchitán are directly connected to the products of their work, seeming to live out the socialist ideal of unalienated labor. Indeed, in some of these photographs, implements such as bowls, baskets, and jars appear as extensions of the human subject, their rounded surfaces echoing the contours of the female body.

3.13. Tina Modotti, *Woman from Tehuantepec Carrying Yecapixtle* (ca. 1929). Gelatin silver print. 83/8 × 73/8" (21.3 × 18.7 cm). (Acc. No. 1968-162-40.) Courtesy Department of Rights and Reproductions, Philadelphia Museum of Art. Gift of Mr. and Mrs. Carl Zigrosser, 1968. Photograph by Lynn Rosenthal. Reprinted by permission of Philadelphia Museum of Art.

As her political commitments deepened, Modotti documented the radi-calization of the Mexican people in the years following the revolution. Her photographs of workers meeting, parading, and reading communist pub-lications suggests their awakening connection to socialist struggles around the world. Modotti's iconic postrevolutionary subject is a politically con-scious *mestiza*. One of her most famous photographs depicts a woman carrying an enormous red flag of communist solidarity (fig. 3.14). Her dark hair and skin bespeak indigenous ancestry, while her actions iden-

3.14. Tina Modotti, *Woman with Flag* (1928). Palladium print by Richard Benson (1976). 913/16 × 73/4″ (24.9 × 19.7 cm). Courtesy of Isabel Carbajal Bolandi. (SC1976.257) The Museum of Modern Art, New York. Digital Image © The Museum of Modern Art / Licensed by SCALA / Art Resource, NY. Reprinted by permission of Art Resource, NY.

3.15. Tina Modotti, *Workers' Parade* (1926). Courtesy Susie Tompkins Buell.

tify her as a political comrade. Another, called *Workers' Parade*, shows Mexicans participating in a ritual of class identification. Shot from above, the workers are concealed beneath their sombreros, which form a random pattern of circles that identifies them as Mexican (fig. 3.15). As Andrea Noble explains, "within the context of 1920s Mexican cultural politics, the sombrero was heavily invested with revolutionary connotations. Indeed, the sombrero achieved iconic status during the armed struggle when unprecedented mass mobilization was photographically documented and widely disseminated."[89] Modotti's photograph alludes to this earlier history, suggesting that the violence of armed combat has given way to the performative ceremony of the parade. It depicts the emergence of two kinds of collective identification: the sombrero attests to the consolidation of *mexicanidad* out of diverse regional identities, while the category of worker signifies the marchers' class affiliation across national boundaries.

Modotti's photographs of *campesinos* reading the communist paper *El Machete* testify to the power of literacy to instill national and transnational political consciousness (fig. 3.16). The paper's headlines, which are clearly legible, address a combination of Mexican concerns (land redistribution) and international socialist causes (the war against Russia). The camera looks down from above as if to include the viewer in the circle of readers. These photographs are laden with irony, for they evoke the literacy campaigns of José Vasconcelos, which were designed to empower workers and *campesinos*. But by the late 1920s when Modotti's photos were shot, the Mexican government had begun to persecute communists, and it would declare *El Machete* illegal in late 1929. The ability to read, so recently championed by the postrevolutionary regime, had made *campesinos* conscious of their oppression and critical of state authority. Published in *El Machete*, these photographs create a mirror effect in which the viewer finds himself reflected back in photographs of workers reading the paper.

Alluding to the device of photomontage, the images of workers reading *El Machete* derive their meaning from a combination of print and visual forms. Modotti conducted a number of other experiments that incorporated writing into her photographs. These include the bluntly political *Elegance and Poverty*, where a man dressed in filthy, ragged clothing appears to sit beneath a billboard advertising an elegant clothier, although the two scenes actually come from different photographs artfully fused together (fig. 3.17). Another is her famous symbolic portrait of Mella's typewriter containing a sheet of paper on which a quote from Trotsky is clearly visible (fig. 3.18). These images suggest that, for Modotti, photography was not simply illustration for written texts, as in the work of Porter and, in some cases, Brenner. The relationship could also be reversed so that words become a supplement to the photographic image. Words appear in Modotti's photographs in the form of slogans and headlines, which lack complexity but are capable of immediate and dramatic communication. Her work with photomontage responds to the problem of widespread illiteracy, which compelled socially conscious Mexican artists to seek forms that could best

3.16. Tina Modotti, *Peasant Reading "El Machete"* (1927).

reach untutored audiences. More than Porter or Brenner, Modotti aspired not only to represent the Mexican people but also to find ways to address them directly.

When Tina Modotti was deported from Mexico, she left behind not only her camera, but also her passion for photography. Although she would attempt to work in Germany, the photographs she took during that period

3.17. Tina Modotti, *Elegance and Poverty* (1928). Gelatin silver print by Richard Benson (1976). 9 15/16 × 6 1/2″ (25.2 × 16.5 cm). Courtesy of Isabel Carbajal Bolandi. (SC1976.280) The Museum of Modern Art, New York. Digital Image © The Museum of Modern Art / Licensed by SCALA / Art Resource, NY. Reprinted by permission of Art Resource, NY.

3.18. Tina Modotti, *Mella's Typewriter; or, La Técnica* (1928). Gelatin silver print. 93/8 × 71/2″. Anonymous gift. (353.1965) The Museum of Modern Art, New York. Digital Image © The Museum of Modern Art / Licensed by SCALA / Art Resource, NY. Reprinted by permission of Art Resource, NY.

reflect the lack of inspiration and opportunities that she found there. Her rapid and involuntary exile, and the precipitous decline of her work, reveal her creative reliance on the American setting. Absent the crucible of history, culture, and politics that had informed her American photographs, Modotti abandoned art, devoting her life exclusively to politics. Her image—as the beauty of Weston's Mexican photographs and the comrade of Rivera's mural—and her photographs would remain, becoming an important part of the legacy of the Mexican renaissance. With her camera, she found innovative ways to combine aesthetic and political commitment, locating them in a Mexican setting that shared the convictions and showed the failures of the postrevolutionary moment.

Modotti's departure from Mexico is a fitting end to this chapter because it coincided with the growing conservatism of the government under President Portes Gil, the abandonment or dilution of revolutionary commitments, and the departure of many of Mexico's leading artists and intellectuals. But as Michael Denning argues in *The Cultural Front*, political defeat is not an effective gauge for the cultural consequences of a revolution.[90] Like the U.S. Popular Front that is Denning's subject, the Mexican Revolution, whatever its many political failures, left an indelible imprint on North American modernist culture. For a brief period it gave rise to a Mexican bohemia, where artistic creativity flourished amid hopes for a new, more egalitarian social order. The benefits of this heady moment were particularly significant for women, who found unprecedented opportunities for financial independence and professional advancement in Mexico. Due in large part to their efforts, it would subsequently be much more difficult for foreigners to view Mexico as a place devoid of culture. And Mexican culture would continue to exert a formative, if often unacknowledged, influence on the arts across North America.

Until now, the Mexicanist presence in American modernism has been recognized primarily through the towering reputations of the muralists. While we know a great deal about them, far less has been written about the Mexican context that gave rise to their art and about how their achievements were communicated to international audiences. Focusing on how modernism traveled, particularly along less well-illuminated routes, inevitably points the way to women like Porter, Brenner, and Modotti, who were conduits and producers of an American modernism anchored in Mexico. As they promoted Mexico's renaissance, they also represented its accomplishments as uniquely American and as bearing a significance that extended well beyond Mexico to the continent, the hemisphere, and the world.

The three women who are my focus are not unique, but they are exceptional representatives of a group whose Mexican experiences had a formative impact on their creative output, and who used their experience to convey the significance of Mexico to populations in North America and beyond. Unlike equally accomplished women in their circles, such as Frida Kahlo, Nahui Olín, or Lola Alvarez Bravo; Porter, Brenner, and Modotti traveled broadly, identifying themselves less as Mexican than as members of a greater North American or global community. The fact that none of them came of age in Mexico, arriving there as adults with a strong sense of themselves and their place in a wider world, probably has much to do with their uncommon independence and mobility. Bringing their work together and putting it in the context of a Euro-American artistic scene draws attention to the importance of Mexico on the map of international modernism. Not only does this altered perspective feature new personalities, but it also brings into view a different set of aesthetic and political commitments than those associated with the more familiar transatlantic modernist cohorts. Sharing an interest in formal innovation and the adoption of new or hybrid media, the Mexican modernists aspired to produce an art that addressed the politics of revolution. Not only did they seek to represent the concerns of indigenous and working people, but they also hoped that their art might communicate with those audiences. And having been exposed to the aesthetic experiments of their Anglo-European counterparts, they dedicated themselves to an art that was specific to the New World context. An awareness of their aspirations, as well as their failures, should be part of an evolving understanding of an American modernism oriented as much to the south as to Europe.

CHAPTER FOUR

Jack Kerouac's North America

HERE DOWN ON DARK EARTH

    before we all go to Heaven

VISIONS OF AMERICA

All that hitchhikin

All that railroadin

All that comin back

    to America

Via Mexican & Canadian borders

—JACK KEROUAC, "Piers of the Homeless Night," *Lonesome Traveler* (1960)

Jack Kerouac's *Lonesome Traveler* begins with these verses, a reminder that he came to know America by crossing national borders. Raised in the Franco-American community of Lowell, Massachusetts, Kerouac did not learn English until he entered elementary school, and he would continue to identify as Franco-American even as he was being hailed as a great American author and moving into the more worldly, bohemian environs of New York, San Francisco, and Mexico City. Lowell is a frequent setting for his writings, and many of his protagonists are Franco-Americans who lapse into the French language at moments of particular tension or longing. Although Kerouac did not visit Mexico until he was an adult, it occupied an equally important place in his life and work. Following in the footsteps of the modernists discussed in the previous chapter, Kerouac belonged to a generation of Americans who sought escape and artistic inspiration by traveling south. His classic travel narrative *On the Road* culminates with a fictionalized account of his first road trip to Mexico, which would become a meaningful location in a number of his subsequent works, and references to Mexico, Mexicans, and the Spanish language would surface recurrently throughout his oeuvre. French and Spanish inspired his experiments with sound and his thinking about the challenges of communication in multiple tongues. Since Kerouac's life is one of the most chronicled of any twentieth-century author, the biographical details of his border crossings into Mexico and Francophone Canada are well known.[1] However, critics have not convincingly addressed the significance of these experiences to his writing, or to his afterlife as a transnational American icon whose influence extends far beyond the borders of the United States. Those who have noted Kerouac's affiliations with either Canada or Mexico have not considered them together as elements of the same creative endeavor. Taking the Canadian and Mexican dimensions of his writing seriously allows us to see how Kerouac's understanding of himself (his most important character), his innovative use of sonic imagery, and his beliefs about culture and history relied on visions of an America that was more a continent than a nation.

This chapter reads Kerouac, an author whose work is most commonly situated in the context of U.S. literary history, as a *North American* whose connections to Mexico and Canada were essential to his artistic vision. On the surface, the Mexican and Canadian elements of Kerouac's work appear quite different, even antithetical. His French Canada is tinged by nostalgia for childhood, home, and his beloved *Mémère*, while Mexico is a place of alluring alterity, where the profoundest forms of intimacy, love, and inspiration are found and lost. French is his native language, belonging to the realm of dreams and truthfulness, while Spanish is the more exotic, foreign tongue that teases Kerouac with the limits of comprehension. What is more interesting, however, are the subtler affinities between Kerouac's representations of Mexico and Canada, locations that are crucial to his conception of American, and indeed human history, and—as the sources of his exposure to Spanish and French—contributed an auditory dimension to his most innovative poetry and prose. Approaching Kerouac as a North American author, one who took the continent rather than the nation as his stage, adds new perspective to current understandings of his work, but it also draws attention to far less familiar literary projects that he inspired just beyond the borders of the United States.

If travel was essential to Kerouac's creative life, his writing enjoyed a similar transnational mobility, gathering momentum and significance in the decades after his death. The emergence of post-Kerouac literary cultures among Mexican and Canadian authors is the subject of the second and third parts of this chapter. Their imagined America is narrower than Kerouac's, since their work marries Beat aesthetics and values to more regionally specific concerns. Nonetheless, they see themselves as participants in an unfolding continental, or even global, dialogue growing out of the political and social upheavals of the 1960s. In Canada, during the climactic years of Quebec's Quiet Revolution, a younger generation of authors and critics turned Kerouac into a symbol of French-Canadian nationalism. They appropriated Kerouac as a means of expressing pride in a distinctive French Canadian culture, and a sign of their commitment to expanding the terrain of Quebecois literature beyond its traditional geographic borders. From among this cohort, I concentrate on Victor-Lèvy Beaulieu and Jacques Poulin, authors whose identification with Kerouac grows out of a climate in which Quebecois nationalists sought to reclaim a distinctively Franco-American history and culture. At the same time, their work marks the emergence of an unprecedented internationalist perspective in French Canadian literature as it moves away from a more traditional focus on *québécitude* and toward the broader exploration of *l'américanité*.

To the south, the atmosphere of youthful rebellion fomenting in the United States and Europe inspired the emergence of La Onda, the name for Mexico's own countercultural movement and the literary cohort that accompanied it. Eschewing foreign perceptions of Mexico as a land of untainted, primitive charm, Mexican teenagers gravitated toward a modernity introduced from abroad, a move epitomized in their enthusiasm for Anglo-American literature, music, and other forms of popular culture. The authors who captured this sensibility were less directly concerned with Kerouac's work and persona than their Franco-American counterparts, instead seeking to incorporate Beat values and aesthetics into a youthful, cosmopolitan Mexican literary scene. Fusing Anglo and Latin American influences, La Onda was a crucible where transnational popular culture met uneasily with the politics and aesthetics of Mexican nationalism.

This chapter tells the story of tangled and multidirectional flows of literary influence. Kerouac is a particularly important figure in this book because he is one of the very few North American authors for whom Canada, the United States, and Mexico were equally meaningful. By locating him exclusively within the canon of U.S. literature, we lose sight of the multilingual and transnational dimensions of his work and foreshorten our understanding of his influential "visions of America." The readings that follow aim to contribute to critical conversations about Jack Kerouac, but also to present Kerouac as a case study, an opportunity to better understand how literature circulating outside of national boundaries acquires unexpected meanings when it is taken up by new communities of readers and writers. Kerouac, who identified as French Canadian (despite his U.S. citizenship), and whose creative impulses were fueled by the experience of travel, exemplifies the need for more flexible understandings of national literature. As Kerouac's work and image moved abroad, they exerted a formative impact on literary countercultures in Canada, Mexico, and beyond. Of course, the degree of reciprocity among groups marked by significant disparities in power and resources should not be overstated: Kerouac's work has been translated into numerous languages and read by audiences around the world, whereas his Quebecois and Mexican descendants are known to a far more circumscribed readership. Nonetheless, we diminish our understanding of the circulation and reception of culture if we imagine that processes of imaginative cross-pollination stop at the borders of language or nation. The continental Kerouac and his Quebecois and Mexican successors thus provide a revealing look at the possibilities and limits of the cultural traffic across North American borders that is the broader subject of this book.

Continental Kerouac

During an extended stay in Mexico in 1950, Jack Kerouac wrote a letter to Yvonne Maitre, who had recently reviewed his first novel, *The Town and the City*. Amid her general praise for the book, Maitre expressed regret that Kerouac had not done more to represent his French Canadian background. Kerouac responded that he was deeply touched by the review, explaining that he had given his fictional family the surname Martin because it could "also be a French name. . . . It was one of the few personal clues I wanted to establish. Because I wanted a universal American story, I could not make the whole family Catholic. It was an American story. As I say, the French-Canadian story I've yet to attempt."[2] Kerouac promised that he would never again hide his identity by "Englishizing" himself or his characters. True to his word, much of his subsequent writing would make the veiled "French-Canadian story" told by *The Town and the City* explicit. The Franco-American community of Lowell, Massachusetts, where Kerouac was born and raised, is the setting for his novels *Doctor Sax, Maggie Cassidy*, and *Visions of Gerard*; at the time of his death, he left behind an unfinished novel about his Canadian ancestors[3]; and French words and references surfaced as "personal clues" in nearly everything he wrote for the rest of his life. Yet the ambivalence evident in Kerouac's statements to Maitre would persist throughout his career, as he found himself torn between the desire to write "a universal American story" and the story of his own people. He understood his oeuvre as an interconnected series of autobiographical works, and he spent a lifetime revising and reinventing the self he presented through his literary personae. What remains consistent is that Kerouac's protagonists inhabit a capacious America, whose population comes from many different racial, ethnic, and class backgrounds, an America that extends into Canada and Mexico rather than fitting neatly within U.S. geographical borders.

From childhood, Kerouac was socialized to assume that local and transnational affiliations ran deeper than ties to the nation-state. Born Jean-Louis de Kerouac, he grew up in the Pawtuckettville neighborhood of Lowell, where "commuting immigrants" continued to identify more deeply with Montreal than with Boston.[4] His parents, Leo and Gabrielle, were part of a wave of French Canadians who moved from Quebec to the manufacturing cities of New England in search of work during the late nineteenth and early twentieth centuries.[5] Although Gabrielle and Leo were immigrants to the United States, the Kerouac family had longstanding roots in the New World, which they traced back to an ancestor who emigrated from Brittany in 1720.[6] Over the course of his life, Kerouac often made unsubstantiated claims that he was the descendant of French aristocracy. As he wrote in the publisher's questionnaire for *Lonesome Traveler*, "My people go back to Breton, France, first North American ancestor Baron Alexandre Louis Lebris de Kérouac of Cornwall, Brittany, 1750 or so, was granted land along the Rivière du Loup after victory of Wolfe over Montcalm."[7] Whether or not the first American Kerouac was a baron, Kerouac's response bespeaks a longstanding interest in his family's French genealogy. Kerouac also identified another set of roots that were deeply implanted in American soil, since his maternal great-grandmother was half Iroquois. Often his protagonists describe themselves as hyphenated subjects who personify the mingling of French and indigenous America: a "Canuck Fellaheen Indian" in *Maggie Cassidy* or "Jack Iroquois" in *Book of Sketches*. Thus Kerouac, who in 1950 had written ruefully that his ethnic identity had to be subordinated in order for him to create "a universal American story," would go on to author works in which to be American is to embody racial mixture and to trace one's tangled roots across multiple borders.

Kerouac views Lowell through a wash of nostalgia for the people and scenes of childhood. At times it is a place of darkness and mystery, where connections to a distant past are palpable. These atmospherics are most evident in *Doctor Sax*, where the landscape bears traces of indigenous ancestors who once lived there. "My Lowell," the narrator recalls, "had the great trees of antiquity in the rocky north wavering over lost arrowhead and Indian scalps, the pebbles on the slatecliff beach are full of hidden beads and were stepped on barefoot by Indians."[8] Similarly, in *Visions of Gerard*,

Kerouac writes, "our shadows in the brown frozen grass are like remembrances of what must have happened a million aeons of aeons ago in the Same and blazing Nirvana-Samsara Blown-Out-Turned-On light."[9] At times, the aura of antiquity is more specifically connected to a French Canadian community that has preserved the beliefs and lifeways of the Old World. Indeed, Kerouac describes the Centralville neighborhood of his youth as closer to premodern Europe than its contemporary French counterparts, "a close knit truly French community such as you might not find any more (with the peculiar Medieval Gaulic closed-in flavor) in modern long-eared France."[10] Although Kerouac's protagonists are Franco-American, his Lowell is by no means homogenous, since it is also home to an assortment of other immigrant groups, including Greeks, Poles, Italians, Russians, and Irish, who give voice to "the great raving *patois* of Lowell on all sides."[11] Kerouac's appreciation for the vibrant cacophony of boyhood anticipates his interest in the many dialects and languages he would encounter during his travels as an adult. As he saw America moving into a fast-paced, impersonal, and culturally homogenous modernity, the sounds and images of Lowell would be associated with an unrecoverable past.

Kerouac's understanding of himself as French Canadian made him uneasy with the categories of identity available in his time. "I, poor French Canadian Ti Jean become / a big sophisticated hipster esthete in / the homosexual arts," he wrote in *Book of Sketches*, attentive to the wide gulf between the Lowell of his past and the bohemian circles of his present, as well as the fact that—on some level—he would always be "poor French Canadian Ti Jean."[12] He often described himself as an outsider within the privileged worlds of the Horace Mann School, Columbia University, and the New York literary scene. Surrounded by groups of rebellious male associates, his protagonists are plagued by the sense that they don't quite belong. In *Vanity of Duluoz*, Jack is the working-class Canuck newly arrived into the posh, rarified circles of wealthy prep school Jews and the rougher, but no less alien, culture of all-American athletes. In *The Subterraneans*, Leo Percepied calls himself a "wily Canuck" and confesses that he spoke English "with a halting accent" even in high school.[13] And in *Desolation Angels*, "a French Canadian Iroquois American aristocrat Breton Cornish democrat" Jack is estranged from the refined sociability of an ocean liner dining room.[14] Yet despite barriers of language and economic class, Kerouac was attuned to the privileges of being ethnically white. He knew that his whiteness allowed him to at least partially assimilate into alien environments, but he also came to understand it as an impediment to accessing what he saw as the more vital, authentic experiences of people of color. Outsiders themselves, his protagonists persistently identify with nonwhite people and others on the social margins, such as addicts, migrant laborers, vagrants, and prostitutes.[15]

Kerouac's sense of alienation from the Anglophone world that granted him success and notoriety was compounded by the fact that he did not learn English until he entered elementary school.[16] "I am a Canuck," announces Leo Percepied in *The Subterraneans*. "I could not speak English till I was 5 or 6."[17] Kerouac recognized his late arrival to the English language as a source of creative potential. As a linguistic outsider, he claimed to be aware of rhythms and cadences that were imperceptible to a native speaker. "The English language is a tool lately found," he wrote to Maitre. "The reason I handle English words so easily is because it is not my own language. I refashion it to fit French images."[18] Professing that he continued to think in French, Kerouac hovered at a remove from the English he used in all of his written work. According to Tim Hunt, he associated French with "sound and gesture but also the language of family, storytelling, and a child's sense of neighborhood community. English was not only the language of reading and writing but also the language of success beyond the community, of serious literature and career."[19] Although born in the United States, Kerouac thus had the divided sensibility of an immigrant who associated one language with the intimacy of home and the other with public life and accomplishments.

Even more significant was the fact that the Kerouac family communicated in *joual*, an idiosyncratic, vernacular language that exists *only* in speech, which Kerouac described as "Frenchy slang."[20] That Kerouac's first encounter with language was in a tongue that had no written analogue must have influenced his later interest in the spoken word and the use of sonic imagery. Kerouac's *joual* and what he called his family's "semi-Iroquoian French-Canadian accent" also contributed to his sense that he was different from his peers.[21] In *Vanity of Duluoz* he writes of the anxiety-inducing experience of studying French in school, where he had to "read all those funny French words we never speak in Canadian French, I have to consult and look them up in the glossary in back, I think with anticipation how Professor Carton of French class will laugh at my accent this morning as he asks me to get up and read a spate of prose."[22] Here, Kerouac describes his first language as impure and illegitimate, so different from the textbook French that he requires a dictionary to understand it. Throughout his life, Kerouac identified *joual* with his Franco-American childhood, although it is also the language he continued to speak with his mother even as an adult. In the same 1950 letter to Maitre, he associated his inability to write in *joual* with a perennial feeling of exile: "Because I cannot write in my native language and have no native home anymore, I am amazed by that horrible homelessness all French-Canadians abroad in America have."[23] Here, language and home are closely entwined in their association with lost origins.

Given these sentiments, the French words and phrases that surface in nearly all of Kerouac's work must be read as expressions of longing and recognitions of loss. *Visions of Gerard* may be the work that is most attuned to the sounds of French, which are closely tied to the death of Jack's saintly older brother at the novel's climax. Having died at the age of nine, Gerard speaks only French and his language is bound up with connotations of innocence and purity, since he escapes the fall into English required of his living brother. French is the language of comfort in the face of abandonment and failure in *The Subterraneans*. When Leo Percepied wanders through the night weeping over his lost love, Mardou, he has a vision of being consoled by his mother, who tells him in *joual*, "Pauvre Ti Leo, pauvre Ti Leo, tu souffri, les homes souffri tant, y'ainque toi dans le monde j'va't predre soin, j'aim'ra beaucoup t'prendre soin tous tes jours mon ange" [Poor Leo, poor Leo, you suffer, men suffer so much, and I will take care of only you in the whole world, I would like to take care of you all of your days, my angel].[24] Unable to sustain an adult relationship, Leo looks for comfort by imagining an infinitely compassionate maternal figure who acknowledges his suffering and absolves him of blame. Although Kerouac does not provide a gloss on this passage, his French is usually followed by an English paraphrase. These moments position the author as translator, attesting to his ability to move comfortably from one language to another. Indeed, given Kerouac's claim that he would "refashion [the English language] to fit French images," these translations might provide glimpses into an otherwise invisible cognitive process.[25] They also assume a monolingual Anglophone audience, becoming yet another sign of the author's "horrible homelessness" as they underscore his distance from readers unable to understand his "native language." Occasionally, the strain of code-switching shows through, as in a scene in *Maggie Cassidy*, when Jack Duluoz abandons himself to a wild, impressionistic flood of emotion, followed by the explanation that his feelings "were all in French, almost untranslatable."[26] Here, Kerouac creates multiple layers of estrangement as the narrator distinguishes himself from the reader (who requires the act of translation) as well as his younger self (whose French thoughts are virtually untranslatable). This passage encapsulates many of the meanings that French Canada and the French language assumed in Kerouac's work, where they were associated with home and boyhood, with strong emotions that could not be adequately translated into an adopted tongue, and with the author's perpetual sense of himself as an outsider. Incorporated into the Anglophone text, French represents an embrace of that difference, a refusal to assimilate coupled with nostalgia for lost origins.

While French Canada was one important pole of Kerouac's transnational "visions of America," Mexico was the other, the place he went to escape the obligations of family and society, and to seek contact with an Other he believed to be more spontaneous, free, inventive.[27] As he describes it in *Desolation Angels*, Mexico was "a great city for the artist—where he can get cheap lodgings, good food, lots of fun on Saturday nights (including girls for hire)—Where he can stroll streets and boulevards unimpeded and for that matter at all hours of the night while sweet little policemen look away minding their own business which is crime detection and prevention."[28] This passage provides a sense of what attracted Kerouac to Mexico during the 1950s and 1960s, when the promise of good times, tolerance for vice, and affordable accommodations made it an ideal destination for an aspiring writer from the United States. Whereas Franco-American Lowell represented the irretrievable experiences of childhood, Mexico was a place Kerouac visited repeatedly during his adult life and occasionally fantasized about making his home. It was there that he wrote his novels *Doctor Sax*, *Desolation Angels*, and half of *Tristessa*; completed revisions to *Visions of Cody*; and composed his long poem *Mexico City Blues*.

Kerouac was not the only member of his circle who took refuge in Mexico. Like the artists, authors, and intellectuals described in chapter 3, the Beats traveled abroad in search of antidotes to their disillusionment with U.S. culture and politics of their time. As Daniel Belgrad explains, the Beats entertained "a vision of Mexico as a locus of opposition to the corporate-liberal culture that had developed in the United States in the 1920s and was spreading in the post-war era to other parts of the world."[29] Where the Beats differed from their modernist precursors is that they were relatively uninterested in the specific details of Mexican politics or history; its primary attraction was the cheap and permissive climate it offered for writing and recreation. The first to arrive was William Burroughs, who fled south to escape charges for possession of marijuana. In his novel *Queer*—composed while living in Mexico City—he wrote, "In 1949, it was a cheap place to live, with a large foreign colony, fabulous whorehouses and restaurants, cockfights and bullfights, and every conceivable diversion. A single man could live well there for two dollars a day."[30] In 1952, Burroughs played host to Kerouac for a time, growing increasingly indignant as the money ran out and his guest—whose already healthy appetite was stimulated by heavy use of marijuana—ate more than his share of their meager supply of food.[31] Allen Ginsberg visited Mexico in 1954, describing it as a "naked hipster labyrinth" in his poem "Ready to Roll."[32] He toured the Mayan ruins of Yucatán and recorded his experiences in "Siesta in Xbalba." Gregory Corso, Lawrence Ferlinghetti, and Neal Cassady were also an essential part of this mobile expatriate cohort. At times, the lawlessness and hedonism the Beats associated with Mexico looked more tragic than enticing. In *Desolation Angels*, Ralph Urso (Kerouac's fictionalized Corso) observes that "there's *death* in Mexico—I saw a windmill turning death this way—I dont [*sic*] *like* it here."[33] These intimations of mortality would come to pass for some: in 1951, a drunken Burroughs aimed a gun at a glass perched on his wife's head and accidentally shot her to death, and in 1968 Neal Cassady was found dead beside the railroad tracks outside of Celaya. The passing of Cassady—followed later the same year by Kerouac—signaled the end of an era in which Mexico served as a gathering place for an American cohort that viewed the encounter with foreignness as essential to the form and content of their work.

Of all the members of this group, Kerouac would be the most enduringly affected by his Mexican travels and his encounters with the Spanish language, which had a vital impact on his thinking about sound. In contrast to French, which was the familiar language of family and home, Spanish was an exotic tongue associated with travel and adult encounters with alterity. Kerouac never learned Spanish well and rarely uses it properly in his writing. In "Mexico Fellahin," he puts a garbled mixture of French and Spanish into the mouth of a former revolutionary, who tells him "La Tierra esta la notre"; he calls Tristessa, "'Mi gloria angela' or 'Mi whichever is'"; and in *Mexico City Blues* children yell in the streets "Mo perro / Mo perro, mo perro."[34] Conceiving of himself as a lingual musician, Kerouac sought to reproduce the improvisational, spontaneous qualities of jazz in the written word. As Ann Charters describes it, Kerouac "made his poems out of what he heard, not necessarily what was said, and what he associated in memory with what he had heard."[35] The fragmented, agrammatical sounds of Spanish were an essential ingredient in these experiments, since they provided a wealth of new auditory sensations, such as the Mexican radio he overhears in Tristessa, "the high whiney violins and the deberratarra-rabaratarara of the Indian Spanish announcer."[36] His interest in the sounds of Spanish is most vividly illustrated in his long poem, *Mexico City Blues*, where words are sometimes used purely for their sonic qualities, without regard for rules of grammar or syntax.[37] His 5th Chorus ends with the couplet "If you know what I / p a l a b r a." The Spanish *palabra* [word] has no grammatical relation to the sentence, its symmetrical, rounded intonation leaving the stanza invitingly open. At the same time, the unusual decision to put an extra space between each letter suggests that it is almost more meaningful as a visual image than as a word.

Mexico was not only the source of linguistic inspiration; it was also the setting of some of Kerouac's most important work. *On the Road* provides an extended fictionalized account of his first trip south of the U.S. border in the company of Neal Cassady (Dean Moriarty) and Frank Jeffries (Stan Shepard). Although they comprise only a few chapters, the Mexican sequences of *On the Road* are crucial both to an understanding of the novel's meaning and to establishing the terms Kerouac would use to write about Mexico over the course of his career. As with subsequent works, the treatment of Mexico in *On the Road* vacillates between a naive primitivism and a more genuine attempt to probe the difficulties of communication across borders of language and nation. Repeatedly, Kerouac's characters glimpse the possibilities of transformative dialogue with a foreign Other, only to veer back into the more solipsistic pleasures of self-exploration.

Mexico is essential to *On the Road* because it is there that his characters break out of the impasse created by their earlier travels, finding a route that is "no longer east-west, but magic *south*."[38] Whereas previously they had followed the route of American Manifest Destiny, Mexico changes the course of their movement and, in doing so, how they envision their place within American history. Plotting their route on a map leads to flights of fancy as they imagine "flying down the curve of the world into other tropics and other worlds" (265–66). In this episode, Kerouac's characters retrace a route taken by past generations of North American radicals. The crucial difference is that he represents their journey as decisively modern, celebrating the ease and romance of travel by car across North America's newly created network of intracontinental highways.

In *On the Road*, Kerouac displaces the contradictions associated with his own French Canadian identity onto his protagonist, the Italian American Sal Paradise. On the one hand, Sal is an ethnic American who occupies the position of an outsider with which Kerouac so often identified. Indeed, according to the categories of the day, Italians were considered more visibly "ethnic" than were French Canadians. In the same letter in which Kerouac accounted for the deracination of *The Town and the City*, he observed that French Canadians were able to pass "because they look Anglo-Saxon, when the Jews, the Italians, and others cannot."[39] In assuming an Italian American persona, Kerouac figuratively darkens himself. On the other hand, Sal is not dark enough to escape association with the tedium and banality of whiteness. Like so many of Kerouac's protagonists, he seeks out encounters with people of color, who he believes will provide him with an immediacy and soulfulness lacking in his own life. In Denver, he walks through "the colored section, wishing I were a Negro, feeling that the best the white world had offered was not enough ecstasy for me." But his fantasies have less to do with blackness per se than with a series of infinitely interchangeable racial substitutions: "I wished I were a Denver Mexican, or even a poor overworked Jap, anything but what I was so drearily, a 'white man' disillusioned" (180). In this passage, Sal speaks as the Kerouac whose desire to be of another race is nothing so much as a wish to escape his own whiteness, a self-rending longing to be anything other than what he is. In *On the Road*, the exhaustion of whiteness is countered by the lure of contact with the Other, enticing Sal, Dean, and Stan to diverge from their more familiar east-west trajectory to make the frenzied, sleepless journey "magic south."

Built into Kerouac's account is a certain awareness that his characters' impressions of Mexico are so deeply informed by desire that they have very little to do with the scenes before their eyes. "To our amazement," Sal enthuses, "it looked exactly like Mexico. It was three in the morning, and fellows in straw hats and white pants were lounging by the dozen against battered pocky storefronts" (274). What is most striking about these fantasies is their regressive quality. With childlike naïveté, the three men behave as if they are the first travelers ever to cross the "magic border" (273). "We bought three bottles of cold beer—*cerveza* was the name for beer," Sal explains, apparently delighted at the prospect of different words to describe the same thing, and at the foreign sounds of Spanish. Treating the Mexican currency like a toy, Sal is just as excited by the quantity of pesos he receives for his dollars as what they can buy. "We gazed and gazed at our wonderful Mexican money that went so far," he continues, "and played with it and looked around and smiled at everyone" (275–76). The exchange value of money suddenly takes a back seat to the infantile pleasure of possessing the coins. Like a small boy awake past his bedtime, Dean enjoins his friends to "*think* of these cats staying up all hours of the night" (276). Sal is delighted to find, "The *old men* are so cool and grand and not bothered by anything. There's no *suspicion* here, nothing like that" (278). Retreat into a state of childish wonder enables the travelers to imagine themselves liberated from the responsibilities that burdened them on domestic soil. Not surprisingly, Mexico is figured here as an antidote to the authoritarianism and homogeneity the Beats associated with the United States.

The travelers also find larger, collective stories of origin that may help them to rescript the disturbing course of American, and possibly human, history. The ancestors of the "cool and grand" old men lounging on the city streets are the indigenous folk Sal sees in the countryside: "not at all like the Pedros and Panchos of silly civilized American lore . . . they were not fools, they were not clowns; they were great, grave Indians and they were the source of mankind and the fathers of it" (280–81). Kerouac writes Mexicans out of modern historical time by elevating them to mythic status, positioning them as guides in the Anglo-American travelers' search for their own prehistoric origins. Kerouac calls these aboriginals the Fellahin, a term he adopted from Oswald Spengler's *Decline of the West*.[40] According to Spengler, the "fellah-peoples" exist in an alternative temporality. Their primitive simplicity evokes the premodern past but also represents a future that will endure after the demise of a decadent West. As Spengler described them, the Fellahin are "earth-children of an unborn culture, great young souls . . . their unbelievable dynamism, the birth-pangs of a whole new world, not the death throes of your overlived meaning."[41] Kerouac would draw on Spengler's theory throughout his career, identifying the Fellaheen with both Mexican Indians and French Canadians, whose persistent, earthy virtues he saw as the antithesis of a corrupt and soulless modernity. In *On the Road*, as Sal and friends move farther into Mexico, the concept of the Fellahin underlies the connections they imagine among the ancient cultures of Asia, Africa, and Mexico.

Sal's impressions of Mexico get jumbled together with images of other remote geographic locales and peoples; just as earlier he had conflated black, Mexican, and Japanese Americans. As the narrative unfolds, a spatial journey that began with his contemplation of a real map and required passage across a real national divide becomes a form of time travel. The travelers' individual regression takes place against the backdrop of a more pervasively atavistic culture, in which the Fellahin peoples of the world appear virtually interchangeable with one another. They find "Old men [who] sat on chairs in the night and looked like Oriental junkies and oracles" (275) and "thatched huts with African-like bamboo walls" (279) as they drive

> across the world and into the places where we would finally learn ourselves among the Fellahin Indians of the world, the essential strain of the basic primitive, wailing humanity that stretches in a belt around the equatorial belly of the world from Malaya (the long fingernail of China) to India and the great subcontinent to Arabia to Morocco to the selfsame deserts and jungles of Mexico and over the waves to Polynesia to mystic Siam of the Yellow Robe and on around, on around. (280)

Both the ancestors and the unwitting vanguard of a postapocalyptic era, the Fellahin exist in blissful ignorance about the horrors of modernity since they "didn't know that a bomb had come that could crack all our bridges and roads and reduce them to jumbles, and we would be as poor as they someday, and stretching out our hands in the same, same way" (298). The juxtaposition of atomic bomb and Fellahin introduces two competing models of history, one that revolves in perpetual and unchanging cycles; and one in which progress has already wrought the potential for self-destruction. Having seen the fearsome consequences of civilization, the travelers look to the Fellahin as a prototype for an alternative historical imaginary that speaks to both past and future.

At bottom, however, their goal is less historical insight than to "learn ourselves." Whereas an earlier generation of travelers, influenced by the ideals of the Mexican revolution, saw possibilities of social transformation in the indigenous *campesinos*, the Beats sought out the Fellahin as part of the quest for pure self-knowledge. Having crossed the border, Dean raves of his ability to "*understand* the world as, really and genuinely speaking, other Americans haven't done before us" (276). This desire to look anew at the world outside of U.S. borders is a laudable goal. But what Dean calls worldly understanding seems a lot like the exploration of his own consciousness. The farther they move away from the United States, the deeper they probe into themselves. Arriving at a destination they describe as the birthplace of all human civilization, Dean thinks he has "found people like himself" (280). Liberated from the baggage of his own overdeveloped culture, Dean presumes the ability to turn his gaze outward to comprehend and master all that he sees. Of course, what is actually happening is the reverse as the Mexican landscape and people are incorporated into his increasingly grandiose subjectivity.

The terminus of their journey across space and into the self is the Mexican capital, where a barrage of noise, dirt, and speed distinguishes city from country. Mexico City, as Sal perceives it, is at once a vast metropolis and the chaotic, infantile landscape of the unconscious. There, the travelers see "thousands of hipsters" (200) and bohemians who they take to be mirror images of themselves. They also discover that "the great and final wild uninhibited Fellahin-childlike city that we knew we would find at the end of the road" (302) is governed by an ahistorical, mythic sense of time far different from anything they have known before. Having traveled through space to travel within, Sal's ultimate destination is the untapped depths of selfhood. For Dean, who defined his journey as the always-elusive quest for IT, Mexico City cannot be the end of his travels. Wherever he is, IT lies somewhere else in wait of his pursuit. Compelled by the need for constant motion, Dean takes off back across the border, abandoning Sal to the agonies of dysentery.

Sal's affliction legitimates, in a literal way, the warning received at the border about the dangers of Mexican tap water. This is also a more figurative moment in which Kerouac humbles his character, showing the consequences of his arrogant fantasies of incorporation and mastery. For Sal and Dean, the Mexican capital represents the untamed bacchanalian reaches of the unconscious, a place where the self is so all-encompassing that it loses any awareness of others. Having opened to a foreign culture, Sal's body now violently rejects his earlier excesses. One consequence of his illness, then, might be the development of a more modest and reciprocal approach to difference, in which self and other gradually learn mutual acceptance. But because this episode of physical sickness is so closely aligned with Dean's fickleness, its status as a cautionary tale about American hubris abroad is subordinated to a lesson about the fragile intimacies of the road and the limits of a friendship. It becomes part of a recurring pattern in Kerouac's work, in which concerns about the realization of self and resolution of personal relationships subsume flashes of potential insight about the Other. This pattern is confirmed by the fact that *On the Road* does not end in Mexico, but in Sal's return to the United States and tentative reconciliation with Dean. The last paragraph of the novel finds him once again looking from east to west as he sits on a pier in New York and thinks of California. To preserve his friendship with Dean, as well as his identity as a discrete individual and a U.S. citizen, Sal must leave his Mexican adventures behind.

Although *On the Road* closes by reorienting Sal along an east-west trajectory, movement from north to south continued to be a definitive feature of Kerouac's own life. He returned to Mexico many times and it became— along with Franco-American Lowell—one of the two poles of his transnational "visions of America." In Kerouac's mind, north and south were not opposites, as they so often are in images of the North American continent. Instead, he frequently brought them together in mutually enlightening ways. Disillusioned with the course of history in the modern United States, Kerouac sought alternatives in the timeless, soulful figures of the Fellahin, whom he associated not only with Mexican Indians but also with the French Canadian peasantry. Overlooking geographic and cultural differences, he often uses imagery in which one group serves to evoke the other. In *Doctor Sax*, the mother of Jack's boyhood friend G. J. wears "vestments like dresses of old Mexican mothers in tortilla dark interiors of stone";

Jack's own French Canadian *Mémère* hurries through the streets "on solid peasant feet, no wavering, like the mothers of Mexico hurrying barefoot in the rain"; and he describes "her secret snaky knowledge about death as uncanny as the Fellaheen dog that howls in the muddy alleys of Mazatlan."[42] Jack makes similar connections in *Visions of Gerard*, where he observes his mother working in the kitchen "with that heartbreaking, slow, fumbly motion of mothers of the world, like old Indian Mothers who've pounded tortillas and boiled mush across clanks of millenniums and wind-howl."[43] In *Maggie Cassidy*, the crucified Jesus hanging in the home of Jack's girlfriend has feet that look "like the winter cold feet of the poor Mexican worker you see in the street."[44] In *Tristessa*, Jack observes "two ladies go down the sidewalk slowly, the way Mexican women aye French Canadian women go to church in the morning" (83) and he finds that Tristessa's attempt to speak English "sound[s] like my old French Canadian Aunt in Lawrence."[45] And in *Mexico City Blues*, Kerouac writes that "Indian songs in Mexico . . . / are like the little French Canuckian / songs my mother sings."[46] In each case, a woman creates the occasion for Canada and Mexico to serve as analogies for each other, with the author providing the link between these seemingly dissimilar poles. It was through the feminine—associated with the Fellahin qualities of earthiness, religiosity, and maternal and/or sexual feeling—that Kerouac believed he was able to access profound connections that lie beneath disparities in language, culture, and history. Given Kerouac's conviction that the "fellah-peoples" of the world were unchanging and interchangeable, it is not surprising that French Canadians and Mexican Indians would be conjoined in his mind. In his own variant of primitivism, the amodern folk at one end of the continent look and act much like those at the other.

More rarely, however, Kerouac writes with a latent awareness of shared circumstances that might give these comparisons a more convincing sociohistorical weight. According to his biographer, Paul Maher Jr., "Kerouac viewed Mexico City as similar in many ways to Lowell. As with his hometown, the noon sunlight fell on the close-knit communities that sprawled outward from the hub of Mexico City, and those who lived and died by the guiding light of Catholicism populated these quarters predominantly. There were the downtrodden trekking to and from the hot fields and shops at sunset."[47] As Maher's description implies, Kerouac was attuned to similarities in the economic conditions and social organizations of Lowell and Mexico City. Both were home to working-class populations clustered in insular, devoutly Catholic communities. Both had been relatively isolated from the forces of Americanization that were rendering other parts of the continent more homogenous. However, Kerouac also shows an understanding of the real limits to this analogy, outside of his own imagination.

In a scene near the end of *Desolation Angels*, Kerouac stages a more surprising and literal encounter between these two North American antipodes when he takes his French Canadian *Mémère* to visit Mexico. In response to her surprise at finding Indians there, Jack explains, "'*Oui*—Indians just like the American Indians but here the Spaniards did not destroy them' (in French). 'Ici les espanols sont marie avec les Indiens'" [Here the Spaniards married the Indians].[48] Here, Jack does not flatten history, as Kerouac's invocations of the Fellahin are wont to do, instead gesturing to the differences between Spanish and Anglo-American colonialism. In contrast to the violent policies of Indian removal practiced north of the U.S. border, he tells *Mémère*, the Spanish intermarried with the Indians, giving rise to Mexico's mestizo population. So too, he implies that the circumstances that generated the Mexican mestizo are akin to those that produced the Canadian Métis to be found in the Kerouacs' own genealogy. As the descendants of Indians and European settlers, the Kerouacs share a common historical experience with the Mexican people they encounter. Jack's mother's pleasure and surprise at the religiosity of the Indians suggests that shared Catholicism might be further grounds for mutual understanding.

Yet Kerouac is also aware that such cross-cultural recognition can only go so far. When *Mémère* tries to speak to a group of Tarahumara Indians in her "Quebecois Iroquois French" they seem alarmed at being addressed by a white tourist and are unable to respond.[49] Jack, so often the character who imagines an easy identification with the other, must explain their silence. Here, linguistic differences, which Kerouac so often treats as an inspiration, become an unsurpassable barrier. Racial and class differences, which Kerouac so often seeks to transcend or elide, make the prospect of communication impossible. This scene can thus be read as an allegory for the encounter between Quebec and Mexico that was so important to Kerouac's thought, providing him with an occasion to reflect on the potential for, and extreme difficulty of, identification across the lines of language, culture, and nation.

Jack Duluoz brings his *Mémère* to Mexico in the hope of realizing a longstanding desire for the two poles of his world—the Franco-American Lowell of his childhood and the Mexico of his adult inspiration—to meet and recognize each other. He writes that, as the result of their trip, his *Mémère* "understood Mexico and why I had come there so often even tho I'd get sick of dysentery or lose weight or get pale."[50] *Mémère* sees the allure of Mexico, but she also enables her son to acknowledge the limits of cross-cultural reciprocity. In this sense Kerouac is aware that it is only in his imagination that sustained connections between Canada and Mexico occur, adding crucial dimensions to his creative endeavor. Together, they are essential to Kerouac's understanding of the Fellahin as an alternative to a corrupt and decadent West, his innovative play with sound and language, and his vision of an America that was a continent, rather than a country. In turn, Kerouac's experiments with narrative and poetic form; his invention of the irreverent, soulful figure of the beatnik; and his stories of American travel would exert a powerful influence on literary cultures in Canada and Mexico. As they import Beat themes and aesthetics across cultural and linguistic borders, Canadian and Mexican authors contribute to the transnational afterlife of Jack Kerouac while breaking away from what they saw as the restrictive traditions of their own national literatures. As we will see, however innovative their work may be, their visions of America are far more culturally and geographically delimited than are Kerouac's. His intrepid border crossing, willingness to identify with the Other, and appropriation of the language and identity of the people he encountered during his travels attests to a distinctive blend of adventurousness, arrogance, and naïveté. It is this combination that also enabled him to take a vast, multilingual, culturally heterogeneous North America as his purview in a way that no one who has yet come after has been able to emulate.

Killing Off the Father (of the Beats): Kerouac among the Quebecois

For Kerouac, French Canada was always tied to an irretrievable childhood, the loss of his brother Gerard, and his beloved *Mémère*. At the same time that he associated Canada with a vanishing past, however, Quebec was undergoing a period of rapid modernization. As was true elsewhere on the continent, unprecedented economic expansion in the years following World War II led to a corresponding rise in prosperity and conspicuous consumption. For the first time, the province saw a decline in religious practice, and a professionalization of its workforce.[51] Women increasingly sought employment outside of the home, demanding the same forms of parity as their counterparts south of the U.S. border. Indeed, during the last fifteen years of Kerouac's life (the period when he was seeking his Francophone past by traveling to Quebec and France), Quebec moved into the future, rocked by many of the same social and political upheavals that were taking place elsewhere in the world. In the year before Kerouac's death, Montreal hosted the 1967 World's Exposition, where the Quebec pavilion was designed to impress visitors with its atmosphere of sleek modernity.[52] Influenced by his contact with radical black nationalism, Pierre Vallières issued his influential 1968 manifesto, *Les Nègres blancs d'Amérique* (*White Niggers of America*), which argued that the Quebecois were a colonized people akin to the blacks of North America and called on them to shake off the yoke of Anglophone oppression. Invoking Marxism and third world liberation movements, underemployed workers paralyzed the region with strikes, culminating in 1971 with the most massive general strike ever seen in North America.[53] Students at McGill and George Williams (now Concordia) University engaged in mass protests decrying racism and prejudice against Franco-Americans.[54] And Montreal saw the emergence of a counterculture much like those to be found in San Francisco, New York, Toronto, or Mexico City. It became a gathering place for the kind of young people the increasingly conservative Kerouac described disdainfully as "the hippie flower children out in the park with their peanut butter sandwiches and their live-and-let-live philosophy."[55] In his autobiography, Jack Todd, an American military resister who took refuge in Canada, recalled spending his first day in Montreal, "sit[ting] in the sunshine for an afternoon playing guitars with a group of French hippies."[56] His colleague at the tabloid publication where he worked had "hair down to his waist and a beard to his chest," a look that would have made him at home among hippies and political radicals in many cities throughout Europe and North America.[57]

For all that Quebec's cultural and political upheavals shared with other parts of the world, they were also distinctive in that they were motivated by the drive to attain national independence and preserve Franco-American language and culture. Canada's Francophone minority had long been disadvantaged by its lack of political power and employment and educational opportunities. Spurred on by national liberation movements around the globe, the movement for a separate Quebec gained momentum in the 1960s, with concerns over the revival and preservation of the French language as its central platform.[58] Mounting frustration at the marginalization of French Canada led to the formation of the more mainstream Parti Québécois and the radical Front de liberation du Québec (FLQ), which agitated for the abolition of English as the language of government and education, and for the independence (or, in its terms, decolonization) of the province. Authors and artists played a central role in the articulation of Quebec nationalism.[59] The emergence of small, local presses dedicated to the promotion of secular, French Canadian literature enabled a new generation of Quebecois writers to publish and circulate their work.[60] They positioned themselves against a long history of prejudice and exclusion by an

Anglophone majority, which saw French Canadians as lacking in culture and identity and urged them to assimilate.[61] In her widely read poem, "Speak White," Michèle Lalonde enjoined the Quebecois to cast off the constraints of textbook French and English, replacing it with the colloquial, working class intonations of *joual*.[62] The Quebecoization of Kerouac is an outgrowth of this movement.

Since the early 1970s, French Canadian authors have claimed the American icon known as the "King of the Beats" as their own. Although Kerouac became famous in the United States soon after the 1957 publication of *On the Road*, it took some time for the significance of his French Canadian roots to be recognized, a delay Pierre Anctil attributes to the more conservative cultural climate in the province.[63] In 1972, the notion of a Franco-American Kerouac took off with the publication of Victor-Lèvy Beaulieu's *Jack Kerouac: Essai-poulet* (*Kerouac: A Chicken-Essay*) and a special issue of the journal *Devoir* devoted to Kerouac. Beaulieu's *Kerouac* and Jacques Poulin's 1984 novel *Volkswagen Blues* are two of the most important and well-known French Canadian works to contend with Kerouac and his legacy. In the wake of the separatist movement of the 1960s and 1970s, each appropriates Kerouac as part of a broader commitment to the creation of distinctive Quebecois literary voices. At the same time that their work grows out of nationalist agendas, it also represents the expansion and internationalization of Quebecois literature in that it reaches across borders to assert kinship with a celebrated American author whose literature is set predominantly in the United States. For both Beaulieu and Poulin, the act of identification is tinged with aggression and hostility. As they seek to revitalize the notion of a Franco-American history and culture, each emphasizes the tragic, moribund elements of the Kerouac legend, suggesting that the future of Quebecois writing must be secured by escaping from his shadow.

Although Beaulieu's *Kerouac: L'enfant-poulet* is often treated as a straightforward literary biography, it is also an autobiographical account of Beaulieu's intense oedipal identification with and attempt to write in the wake of his celebrated forebear. Beaulieu was already an accomplished writer by the time he completed *Kerouac*, the second in a series of idiosyncratic critical biographies of the authors he most admired, including Victor Hugo, Herman Melville, Jacques Ferron, Tolstoy, and Voltaire. The presence of Hawthorne, Melville, and Kerouac in Beaulieu's pantheon has led the critic Jonathan Weiss to claim that he is the Quebecois writer most strongly oriented toward the U.S. literary canon.[64] However, Weiss underemphasizes the significance of Beaulieu's attempts to reinvent Kerouac as an expatriated Franco-American. Indeed, Beaulieu's primary agenda is to reorient the story

of Kerouac's life and work around the author's Francophone heritage, beginning with his childhood in Lowell and ending with his symbolic return, in middle-age and failing health, to home and mother.[65] On the one hand, Beaulieu affirms that Kerouac's representation of childhood and devotion to his mother capture essential values that are vanishing from French Canadian culture. On the other, he sees Kerouac's perpetual homelessness and unsatisfied longings as representative of the worst excesses incurred by the Franco-American encounter with modernity.

Beaulieu's style pays tribute to Kerouac's spontaneous bop prosody in his use of ellipses, parentheses, spaces, and blocks of capitalized text that make his sentences into visual images whose appearance on the page is as meaningful as the words themselves. When they are used in excess or in unconventional places, these symbols evoke the pauses, digressions, mistakes, and interruptions associated with the writing process, suggesting that we are witnessing the act of creation, rather than a carefully edited revision. They also press at the limits of language, gesturing to affective states that cannot be expressed in words alone. At one point, Beaulieu pays homage to the tongue of Kerouac's childhood by creating an imaginary dialogue between Jack and *Mémère* written entirely in *joual*. *Kerouac* is thus a biography that also performatively enacts Kerouac's stylistic influence on French Canadian letters. However, in contrast to Kerouac himself, who at his best was a manically productive writer, Beaulieu makes the impediments to his own writing—exhaustion, writer's block, crying babies, family obligations, and other distractions—a major part of his story.

Beaulieu concentrates heavily on the biographical details of Kerouac's Franco-American childhood and the works that most directly represent this chapter in the author's life, since he is making the Freudian claim that these formative years set the terms for all of Kerouac's subsequent experiences. He dwells on the historical circumstances that brought Kerouac's parents and grandparents from Quebec to New England, seeing them as essential context for understanding the author's literary production. In contrast to the typical view of Kerouac as the avatar of a radical bohemian subculture, Beaulieu argues that he clung to traditional ideas about religion and sexuality that "were not American but French Canadian well-anchored within oneself—The Quebec of before 1960 . . . Jack was so French Canadian in his ideas about love, holiness and paradise" (140).[66] Beaulieu's Kerouac is not the charismatic "King of the Beats" but a perpetual outsider who was never really accepted by his cohort (particularly Allen Ginsberg, who—in Beaulieu's imagination—is constantly making snide remarks about Kerouac's Canuck identity), and whose adult life was a series of failed attempts to escape the inexorable pull of his heritage. "Poor Jack," he taunts, "what the hell were you doing there with all those pirates of life? Did you want so much to forget Lowell, and your whole Canuck existence—and your fat Father and your Mother whom you pitied even when you disguised them as characters?" (70–71). In his survey of Kerouac's oeuvre, Beaulieu finds the Lowell works to be deeply revealing of the author's oedipal attachments to family and childhood, and his other writings as all more or less unsuccessful efforts to sever the melancholic bonds to his French Canadian past.

To put French Canada at the heart of his biography requires Beaulieu to reevaluate the significance of the locations that were central to Kerouac's writing. Beaulieu attributes a certain realism to Kerouac's Lowell works, which he associates with their capacity to capture the truth of Franco-American experience. For example, the surreal *Doctor Sax*, he claims, "provides the best documentation we possess on Franco-American life in the 1920s and 30s" (27). However, Beaulieu contends that Kerouac's capacity to serve as autoethnographer vanishes once he leaves Lowell behind. Dismissing the Mexico section of *Desolation Angels*, Beaulieu writes, "for anybody who has read Malcolm Lowry's *Under the Volcano* there can't be any other book but that one" (108). Elsewhere he describes Kerouac's literary geography as "a three-dimensional fictional world" consisting of "Frisco (the beat universe), Mexico (a wild, exotic universe, source of hallucinogens, holy land of mushrooms that would make Ginsberg write his *Yage Letters* where we see a kind of transposition of the Oriental myth of initiation by wise old men) and New York (the universe of his mother's exile, that of the past, with its Quebecois appurtenances)" (75). In this passage, Kerouac's New York—the New York of Columbia University and the West End bar, Times Square, and the downtown hipster scene—is reduced to "the universe of his mother's exile" and Mexico to a convenient source of drugs since, for Beaulieu, these places were important only as detours in Kerouac's inevitable move back to his French Canadian origins, embodied in the figure of *Mémère*. "If he never became a real beatnik," Beaulieu asserts, "it was because of his Mother to whom he always returned after his fabulous voyages 'in the crazy American night'" (75). According to the Freudian terms of Beaulieu's account, Kerouac's foreign adventures, his encounters with new experiences and people different from himself, are overwritten by the primal need to reunite with his mother. Beaulieu's biography deemphasizes the heady pleasures of travel—of being cut loose from the responsibilities of work, home, and family—that inform so much of Kerouac's work and are so essential to the beatnik lifestyle, replacing them with a picture of Kerouac the transplanted French Canadian and perpetual exile.

As much as Beaulieu's book is the story *of* Jack Kerouac, it is also an account of Beaulieu's intense identification *with* Jack Kerouac. When he writes about the southern migration of Kerouac's parents and grandparents he is prompted to add that his own grandparents stayed behind in Quebec. When he writes of Kerouac's 1962 trip to France, he mentions that he also went to France in search of his roots. And when he is describing the experience of reading *Visions of Gerard*, he notes that it makes him "think about the great novel I've always wanted to write" (40). While identification with his more famous and accomplished compatriot might be empowering, Beaulieu instead represents himself as a victim, at one point throwing up his authorial hands in despair and proclaiming, "Nothing was ever so difficult for me as this unwritable book" (160). He describes writing as a form of possession in which all efforts to distance himself from Kerouac ultimately collapse into autobiography. Interrupting the story of Kerouac to describe the other things he is doing—sitting in a café, riding a bus, lying in bed listening to the baby cry—Beaulieu makes *Kerouac* as much about the difficult process of creation, and about the burden of having Kerouac as a literary forebear, as it is about Kerouac himself.

Much as he admires Kerouac's portrait of Franco-American culture, Beaulieu also claims to detest his subject, who he sees as the embodiment of the depressing fate of Quebecois literature. Although Kerouac never lived in Quebec, he represents "the Québécois novelist in all his misery, intellectually retarded, a great literary auntie, and so like all of us that we could no longer be anything but projections of ourselves" (146). Beaulieu relegates Kerouac, along with Marie-Claire Blais, to the "cesspool of our afflictions and our failures and our wanderings and our cultural aches and pains and our alienation and our colonization" (166). Kerouac is the Quebecois author in exile, "so like all of us" that his homelessness bespeaks the collective suffering and dispossession of his people. If Kerouac was unable to shed his oedipal attachments, the survival of a younger generation of Quebecois writers relies on the ability to overcome the pathological version of the family romance he represents. Beaulieu, whose wife and baby hover in the background of the narrative, attempts to do so by distancing himself from Kerouac's infantile and irresponsible sexual posturing. Yet he nonetheless suffers from the very "afflictions" and "cultural aches and pains" he associates with Kerouac, his biography enacting the difficulties involved in disentangling himself from his subject. At the same time that so much of his work's stylistic and affective registers are indebted to his precursor,

Beaulieu frames the act of writing as a confrontation intended to banish the specter of Kerouac so that the living author can carry on. There is thus a deep ambivalence running through *Kerouac: A Chicken-Essay*, the first extended attempt to come to terms with the French Canadian Kerouac. It is at once an homage and an exorcism of a literary forebear who never actually lived on Canadian ground, but who is said to represent certain truths, both appealing and repulsive, of Franco-American culture of his time.

Whereas Beaulieu emphasized Kerouac's ties to his Franco-American family and childhood home, Jacques Poulin's 1984 novel *Volkswagen Blues* is interested in Kerouac the traveler. Its story about traveling the highways of North America is clearly indebted to *On the Road*. Poulin's Kerouac embodies the spirit of the *voyageur*, a classic figure in Quebecois literature, who is given a decidedly modern twist in that his protagonist's means of conveyance is the eponymous Volkswagen bus. Far more geographically expansive than Beaulieu's biography, *Volkswagen Blues* embraces, rather than seeking to foreclose, the wanderlust that characterized Kerouac's life and career. Its protagonist is a forty-year-old Quebecois writer named Jack Waterman, who leaves his home in Montreal in search of his missing brother Theo. He follows Theo's trail from Gaspé to San Francisco in the company of a Métis woman nicknamed la Grande Sauterelle [the big grasshopper]. Their journey across the continent is also a trip into the past, as they rediscover important places and events in the history of Franco North America. La Grande Sauterelle is on a quest of her own, traveling the continent and reconnecting with the history of European-Indigenous contact in the hope of better understanding her mixed heritage. Invoking this history, she often provides a corrective to the more familiar narratives of discovery and settlement they encounter in books and museums. Like all road narratives, the novel is structured episodically, following the characters as they move across the continent to their final stop in San Francisco, where they discover Theo, so badly afflicted by dementia and "creeping paralysis" that he is no longer able to recognize his brother.

Volkswagen Blues is Poulin's first novel set outside of Quebec, and it is part of the development of what Mary Jean Green has described as the "geographical expansion of the Quebec fictional world" that took place during the 1980s.[67] Grouping Poulin with writers like Jacques Godbout and Nicole Broussard, Green argues that "even writers like these, who can be considered *Quebecois pure laine*, see their world as extending beyond the borders of Quebec itself, and they see themselves as positioned at the intersection of a multiplicity of cultural forces."[68] A number of critics have described *Volkswagen Blues* as a novel that moves away from more traditional concerns with *québécitude* and toward the exploration of *l'américanité*, the place of Franco-Canadian culture within the Americas.[69] Yet despite the fact that *Volkswagen Blues* is often described as a "post-Kerouac" novel, the significance of its debt to *On the Road* has not been explored in any detail.[70] I will argue that Poulin, much like Beaulieu, writes a work that pays tribute to Kerouac, only to conclude by leaving Kerouac behind, his usefulness for the living Quebecois author exhausted.

Volkswagen Blues shares Kerouac's preoccupation with the intermingling of French and English languages. Poulin, who has worked as a professional translator, inscribes the challenges and possibilities of crossing linguistic borders into his narrative about travel across national borders. Jonathan Weiss has noted that the novel announces its concern with translation in the title itself, which reads the same in English as its does in French.[71] It evokes a hybrid, worldly culture by juxtaposing "blues," connoting the spread of African American cultural forms throughout the continent, and "Volkswagen," a German import brought to America through the global trade in durable goods. "Volkswagen blues," the title of the original Francophone version of the novel, presumes a reader who requires no translation because Quebec is already sutured into the transnational economy and fully participant in the cultural life of the American continent. Written in French, *Volkswagen Blues* is liberally peppered with the English words and phrases that its characters encounter even before they cross the border into the United States. The novel is rife with linguistic encounters between Franco- and Anglo-America, from the use of English-language slang words like "bum" and "cross checking," to the lyrics of songs, signs, and titles of books and albums. The extent to which these effects resist translation only becomes fully evident in the English version, which is unable to capture the Kerouackian multilingualism of the French original.

At the novel's outset, we might be tempted to see its protagonist as a figure for Kerouac. Yet despite his auspicious name, Jack Waterman is an anti-Kerouac whose writing methods and outlook on life could not be further from the Beats. He is the author of five novels, "two of which were, by and large, failures."[72] Although he fantasizes about being possessed by inspiration, in reality, Waterman is "patient and persistent but bereft of inspiration or even impulses, he went to work at the same time every day and, thanks to methodical and dogged work habits, managed to turn out his daily page" (31). In one portentous scene, Jack visits a bookstore in Montreal, where he finds only his two failures in stock, shelved uninvitingly in the back along with other Quebecois literature. After scanning one book with a critical eye, he returns it to the shelf and buys, instead, a map of the United States (23).

This early episode—in which Jack lays aside his own work in favor of a foreign map—suggests that his creative future depends on the ability to travel beyond national borders, coming to know, rather than insulating himself from, the American continent of which he is a part.

Like the travelers in *On the Road*, Poulin's characters move from north to south, rather than east to west, to reach their ultimate destination. The difference is that, whereas *On the Road* substitutes the Italian American Sal Paradise for the Franco-American Kerouac, *Volkswagen Blues* seeks to foreground, rather than suppress, its author's French Canadian origins, and to underscore the role of the French in the exploration and conquest of the New World. So too, Poulin replaces the vague evocations of America's mythic past found in Kerouac with a more specific and probing historical understanding. When they plot their trip on the map (in a scene reminiscent of Sal and his friends planning their journey to the "magic south") la Grande Sauterelle likens it to "the first French explorations in America" she has read about in old Canadian history books (15). Like the early explorers, their journey begins in Gaspé, "where Jacques Cartier had discovered Canada" (193) in 1534. In the local museum, they find "a very large and beautiful map of North America" depicting "the vast territory that belonged to France in the mid-eighteenth century, a territory that extended from the Arctic to the Gulf of Mexico and west as far as the Rocky Mountains: it was an astonishing and very moving sight" (9–10). The map reminds them that the French once occupied much of the continent. Contemplating it from the small corner of North America that still claims a connection to its French roots, they find it "astonishing" because it bespeaks the grand, but temporary, course of imperial possession. At the same time that it celebrates the continent's Franco-American heritage, this scene complicates the idea that the French "discovered" America. Hanging alongside the map of French North America, Jack and la Grande Sauterelle find "an equally impressive map that depicted North America before the arrival of the whites; the map was strewn with the names of Indian tribes" (10). The populous, precontact America depicted by the Indian map puts the history of empire into perspective. This scene is the first of many in which the history and culture of indigenous America surface to trouble more conventional understandings of the exploration and settlement of the continent. Although *Volkswagen Blues* shares Kerouac's concern with America's indigenous past, the Indians in the novel are nothing like the voiceless, primitive Fellahin of *On the Road*. Instead, they are historical agents who played pivotal roles in the political, military, and cultural history of North America.

As much as *Volkswagen Blues* is concerned with colonial history, it also tells stories about North America's more recent past. Over the course of their travels, Jack and la Grande Sauterelle often come across living reminders that they are retracing not only the paths of early pioneers and explorers but also those of the Beats and hippies who rode North America's highways just a few decades before. They come across numerous signs that the continent they are discovering for themselves is Jack Kerouac's America one generation removed, such as a hobo who claims to have met Kerouac during his travels, and Theo's arrest record, which lists *On the Road* among his possessions. These intimations of Kerouac intensify as they approach the Beat metropolis of San Francisco. In the historic City Lights bookstore, they turn up a book called *Beat Angels* that contains a photograph of Lawrence Ferlinghetti, Allen Ginsberg, Jack Hirschman, Bob Kaufman, and one "unidentified man" (201) gathered around a table. The image is reproduced, with its original caption, on the page in *Volkswagen Blues*, where Poulin uses fiction to solve the historical riddle posed by the anonymous man, who Jack recognizes as his brother Theo. In one of many scenes where fictional characters cross the stage of history, Theo is inserted into an important moment in America's cultural past. Here, he is a testament to the depressing fate of the Quebecois author, who is doomed to be the unidentified figure at a literary gathering where he is surrounded by celebrated U.S. American writers.

If Theo is the man in the photograph, we must surmise that it is he, rather than Jack, who is the more apt figure for Kerouac in *Volkswagen Blues*. And if the brash, adventurous Theo is the embodiment of Kerouac's style and sensibility, Poulin closes the novel by relegating him to an unrecoverable past. Everywhere they go in San Francisco, Jack and la Grande Sauterelle are reminded that the chapter of American history represented by the Beats has come to a close. These revelations set the stage for the discovery of an aged and gray-haired Theo, overcome by "creeping paralysis" that has confined him to a wheelchair. Jack's brother, the figure most closely associated with the artistic foment of the Beats and the political idealism of the counterculture, is unable to move or communicate. But the incapacitation of Theo and the culture he represents is not as tragic as it might initially seem. This is a life-changing moment for Jack, who has been able to produce only plodding and earnest literature while working in the shadow of his brother. His disappointing confrontation with Theo, the travels that made it possible, and the lessons taught to him by la Grande Sauterelle are the source of insight that may inspire him to write a different kind of novel in the future. At the end of *Volkswagen Blues*, Jack is bound for Quebec and ready to begin writing, leaving Theo and la Grande Sauterelle behind in

San Francisco. Fittingly, Poulin's novel ends with a return, for having emphasized the importance of travel to the Quebecois discovery of l'amérique, it also announces the importance of maintaining ties to people and place by bringing those discoveries home.

For both Poulin and Beaulieu, Kerouac is a presence to contend with, but also to overcome. They are among the first of a number of Franco-American authors who would reclaim Keraouc's legacy to announce the arrival of a literature newly committed to shedding its traditional isolation and making a place for itself in America without abandoning its Francophone origins.[73] They attempt this task by appropriating a figure who has been claimed as the most American of authors, while at the same time showing him—and the America he depicted—to be vitally informed by French history and culture. In the case of Beaulieu and Poulin, these acts of appropriation are colored by animosity for the less-than-benevolent ghost of Kerouac, who haunts Quebecois literature from outside its borders. Each work concludes that the specter of Kerouac must be eliminated or paralyzed in order for its author to find his voice. While the channeling of Kerouac leads to imaginative and formally innovative narrative production, Beaulieu and Poulin narrow the geographic and cultural coordinates that defined Kerouac's America. Their turn to deeper and more particularized representations of history is also a move away from the vast temporal and spatial panoramas that comprise Kerouac's literary world. Specifically, the chaotic, vital Mexicanisms that color Kerouac's America are off the map for these French Canadian writers, whose continent stops at the United States' southern border. As we will see, a similar process took place at the other end of Kerouac's America, where a youthful cohort of Mexican authors imported Beat themes and aesthetics in an attempt to remake Mexican literature, while forgetting his Franco-American origins.

The Fellahin and the Beatnik: Kerouac among the Mexicans

When Jack Kerouac visited Mexico he believed he had discovered soulful Fellahin living in a primitive temporality of their own, but he also found beatniks and hipsters who were full participants in American modernity. As Ellis Amburn describes, "When Neal and Jack reached Mexico City in June 1950, Mexican hipsters had already preceded them, establishing a beachhead on Redondas Street, the scene of what Kerouac called 'beat (poor) Mexican nightlife,' where they peddled dope and crucifixes."[74] The sight of these hipsters crowding the streets must have driven home the realization that Kerouac and his friends were not explorers of virgin land, as they sometimes claimed to be, but travelers who, having crossed the border, would become witnesses to Mexico's own bohemian scenes. Even Sal Paradise, who is so moved by his encounter with the Fellahin in *On the Road*, must acknowledge the "thousands of hipsters in floppy straw hats and long-lapeled jackets over bare chests" (300) he observes in the Mexican capital. In *Desolation Angels* Kerouac writes of drinking and carousing with a group of rowdy Mexican medical students, prompting his realization that there are "whole gangs of Mexican hipsters . . . Some of them even write poetry, as I found out later, and have their regular Master-Disciple relationship just like in America or London."[75] Not only had Mexicans created their own beatnik subculture, but they also were writing about it in ways very similar to their Anglo-American counterparts. From this perspective, Kerouac is not the father of the Beats, but a representative of a more pervasive cultural phenomenon emerging at roughly the same moment in different locations around the world. Indeed, the terms of Kerouac's description suggest that the beatnik persona he came to embody was influenced, at least in part, by the people he encountered during his Mexican travels.

Kerouac's simultaneous evocation of the Fellahin and the beatnik must be read as a response to the jarringly uneven quality of modernity in the Mexican capital, where untutored *campesinos* could be found alongside prosperous, cosmopolitan city-dwellers. This is the context that gave rise to La Onda, a label that refers to both a literary cohort and the Mexican counterculture that flourished between 1966 and 1972 from which its name is derived. The Onderos differ from the post-Kerouac Quebecois writers in that their work reflects a more indirect engagement with the Beats and the Anglo-American counterculture they inspired. They are less concerned with Kerouac the icon than with the themes, lifestyles, and aesthetic techniques he and his cohort came to represent as they were imported into a Mexican context. While the Onderos adulate the modernity of the Anglo-American Beats and their successors, they also strongly repudiate their tendency to associate Mexico with primitive folk cultures and untainted natural settings.

The interest in Anglo-American countercultures is part of the Onderos' self-fashioning as hip, youthful, and cosmopolitan. According to Cynthia Steele, *La Onda* is a "term that has been applied both to the counterculture and its narrative equivalent [and it] derives from the slang term *estar en onda*, 'to be with it' or 'in,' suggesting its connection with a yearning to be contemporary, to not be *fresa* ('straight,' 'uptight,' bourgeois), even—or perhaps especially—in the midst of underdevelopment."[76] Steele's gloss is useful because it highlights the Onderos' rejection of Western stereotypes about Mexico's economic and cultural backwardness, as well as the conservative values of the Mexican bourgeoisie. Literally translated as "the wave," La Onda is also associated with the electronic mass media that made U.S. popular culture increasingly accessible to Latin Americans.[77] Enamored of cars, rock music, and urban spaces, the Onderos aspire to share a rebellious cosmopolitan subculture with other young people from around the world, but especially the United States. As Carlos Monsiváis described the phenomenon, "La onda aparece como hambre de 'contemporaneidad,' una vez establecida como modelo de lo 'contemporáneo' la cultura juvenil de Norteamérica" [La Onda appears to be hungry for "contemporaneity" once the youth culture of North America is established as a model of the "contemporary"].[78] For the Onderos, a cool, youthful contemporaneity is inextricably bound up with the English language and the popular cultures of Anglo-America.

La Onda is the product of a historical moment of intensified political and economic connections between Mexico and the United States. The Mexican state tended to be nationalistic and isolationist, focused on domestic affairs rather than on the outward-directed realm of foreign policy.[79] Since independence in 1821, Mexico's relations with the United States had been strained, at times erupting into armed conflict. Tensions between the two nations began to ease after Mexico served as an important ally during the Second World War, emerging as a crucial line of defense in the escalating cold war. Much like Quebec, Mexico's population had been predominantly rural and Catholic until the middle of the twentieth century. It too saw a period of rapid modernization in the postwar decades, as its economy opened to the United States and religious and social strictures began to relax. However, Quebec of the 1960s was in the throes of the intensely nationalistic separatist movement, while Mexico was looking abroad in an effort to solidify economic and cultural ties to its northern neighbor. As Mexico's official development strategy shifted from radical redistribution to capital accumulation, its border opened to foreign investment and products, and it actively sought a North American tourist market.[80] Beginning in the 1960s, the favorable business climate attracted such corporations as GM, Ford, Chrysler, RCA, and Zenith to Mexico.[81] The presence of transnational industries, consumer items, English-speaking tourists, and popular film and music from North America made ordinary Mexican citizens increasingly familiar with the language and culture of the United States. Their responses ranged from enthusiasm to charges of cultural imperialism and fear that Mexico would lose a sense of its own traditions.

On the literary scene, a group of authors, all under thirty, expressed the mood of their generation in "una literatura sobre jóvenes escrita desde la juventud misma" [a literature written by and about young people].[82] Their success was enabled by the emergence of the prestigious Editorial Joaquín Mortiz, a press whose Serie del Volador imprint was dedicated to the publication of innovative, experimental fiction.[83] Foremost among them were José Agustín, Gustavo Sainz, and Parménides García Saldaña, whose bestselling novels and short stories were influential among young readers, although largely decried by the literary establishment.[84] Whereas Kerouac and his cohort treated Mexico as an exotic antidote to modern life, Mexican authors resisted the conventional view of Latin American underdevelopment by espousing an attitude of hip cosmopolitanism. They thought that fast cars and rock music were far more romantic than the colorful landscapes and indigenous peasants associated with state-sanctioned Mexican nationalism. The teenage characters in their fiction thirst for knowledge about Europe and North America that would align them with an international youth culture dispersed in space, but drawn together by common tastes in music, entertainment, and styles of dress. Yet however worldly their frame of reference, the Onderos were no more interested in Canada than the Quebecois were interested in Mexico. Their *norteamérica* ended at the United States' northern border.

The Onderos embrace an aesthetic of youthful spontaneity that is forged, in part, through their rejection of literary predecessors. Just as Kerouac would eschew traditional rules of order and composition, the Onderos announce their irreverence for the traditional Mexican canon while also drawing on many of its established tropes and narrative concerns.[85] As Manuel de Jesús Hernández-Gutiérrez has argued, the Onderos are distinguished from earlier generations by their relative disinterest in issues of Mexican history or national identity. According to Luis Leal: "The young writers did not want to be identified as partisan to specifically Mexican causes, or accused of writing under the influence of major national writers. They wanted Mexican literature to be considered as part of Western letters. It did not interest them to write exclusively for the Mexican people, nor the Spanish-speaking countries, but rather to be translated and read in other countries."[86] Conceiving of the break with national literary tradition in generational terms, the Onderos saw young people as both their subject and intended audience. "Habíamos despotricado," Agustín wrote of himself and Gustavo Sainz, "él *just for the sake of it* y yo por ardido, en contra del Centro Mexicano de Escritores, especialmente en contra de Juan Rulfo y (horror parricida) de Juan José Arreola. Presumíamos de estar-al-día en literatura contemporánea, la gringa en particular" [We had ranted and raved, [Sainz] just for the sake of it and me with vehemence, against the Mexican

Writers Center, especially Juan Rulfo and (parricidal horror) Juan José Ar-
reloa. We thought ourselves up to date on contemporary literature, particularly from the United States].[87] At once a description and a performance of
Agustín's unorthodox spanglish, the phrase "just for the sake of it" evokes
the spontaneity so important to the Beat generation. Agustín manifests his
disregard for established literary institutions and ancestors Arreola and
Rulfo by representing himself as hip and ultramodern.[88] The urgency of
his rebellion stems from the fact that these patriarchs have been so closely
identified with national literature. The Onderos perceive the canon of Latin
American authors that has set the terms for Mexican literature as limited
and parochial, the international acclaim for the work of Octavio Paz, Rulfo,
or Carlos Fuentes only contributing to stereotypes about Mexican backwardness.[89]

While the Onderos share the Beats' irreverence for literary forefathers,
their rebellion assumes a different form. Rather than literally fleeing from
adult responsibilities, the teenagers in their fiction tend to remain within
narrowly circumscribed areas of Mexico City that include the middle-class
neighborhoods of Navarte, La Condesa, and the hip Zona Rosa. There, they
often find themselves under the curious gaze of Western tourists in search
of historic ruins and quaint colorful folk. The Onderos transform Mexico
City into a contact zone where vacationers clash with a local population
that wants nothing to do with such outdated clichés.[90] This figurative borderland is very different from Mexico's actual border with the United States,
where intercultural dynamics unfold in the shadow of the vast political
and economic inequities between the two nations. In the Onderos' Mexico City, *chilangos* (local residents) occupy positions of authority in relation
to Western visitors. Unlike the diffident, welcoming natives of tourist bro-
chures, these Mexican teenagers are crude and disrespectful. For example,
when the protagonist of Agustín's *De perfil* [In Profile] realizes that a group
of North American sightseers has observed him smoking an illicit cigarette,
he rants,

Me importa un pito que me vean, canallas, para eso soy joven, para hacer
lo que se me antoje, para correr, pegar de brincos y fumar hasta el ombligo.
Qué les importa lo que haga, gringos ancianos. Mocos güeyes!, les hago vio-
lines y gestos que seguramente no comprenden: sonríen como buenos turis-
tas que son. Qué país.

[I don't give a shit if they saw me, jerks, that's why I'm young, to do what I
please, to run, jump around, and smoke until I'm blue in the face. What do

I care what those old gringos do? Snotty S.O.B.'s! I gave them the finger and gestures they surely don't understand: they smile like the good tourists they are. What a country.][91]

Later, the tourists approach "con cara de muy monos, sonriendo y toda la cosa" [with cute faces, smiling and the whole bit] and attempt to communicate with him in an incomprehensible Spanish.[92] He responds with a mental catalogue of the useless English he has learned in school: "What do you do today Sir? My little dog is name little Peluso. My sister has a doll. The doll es pretty. Very. How old are you? Very old thank you and you? I am very old too thank you too."[93] Agustín represents the inability to communicate as a form of resistance against becoming a "native" in the eyes of the Western tourists. As I have argued, Kerouac employed similar forms of interlingualism because he was delighted by the sound of foreign words, and often privileged their aesthetic qualities over their meaning. Agustín employs these strategies with a different purpose, robbing language of its meaning as a gesture of defiance against the cultural and political dominance of English that the Anglo-American tourists represent.

Agustín's 1973 novel *Se está haciendo tarde* [It's getting late] makes even more pointed connections among English, the global economy, and the rise of a Mexican counterculture. Its setting is Acapulco, where a nomadic population of hippies, wealthy tourists, and seasonal workers speak in a confusion of tongues. Although the resort is saturated by Western commercial interests, the narrative's vacuous characters seem uninterested in benefiting from a Mexican economy bolstered by tourism and foreign investment. As the protagonist Rafael is driven through the streets by his friend Virgilio, "Dos hippies pedían aventón bajo un letrero que decía ACAPULCO WELCOMES YOU, cerca del Club de Pesca, y Virgilio los ignoró, se siguió de largo. Por todas partes letreros en ingles" [Near the Fishing Club, two hippies were hitchhiking under a sign that read ACAPULCO WELCOMES YOU, and Virgil ignored them and drove on. Everywhere signs in English].[94] In a moment of obvious irony, Virgilio undermines the sign's welcoming gesture to English-speaking tourists by refusing to pick up the hippies, who are not its intended audience anyway. However, it is impossible to ignore the billboards that pepper the landscape with slogans addressed to foreign consumers. One reads: "EASY NON-STOP FLIGHTS TO NEW YORK, L.A., AND SAN FRANCISCO, WHERE THE ACTION IS!"[95] Another commands: "INVEST IN ACAPULCO THE LAND OF EXTRA PROFIT!"[96] The availability of easy nonstop flights indicates how much times have changed since Kerouac's long drive, but also Agustín's very different emphasis on modern Mexico's commercial ties with the United States. Against this backdrop, Rafael—who ekes out a living as a tarot card reader—Virgilio, and two Canadian women pass the day trading insults, driving aimlessly, drinking to excess, and finally dropping acid. These patently unproductive diversions stand in jarring contrast to the ads that promote Acapulco as a site of economic expansion.

With their simple messages spelled out in immense, block letters, the billboards in *Se está haciendo tarde* cast a long shadow. The Onderos may reside far from the U.S. border, but they are constantly reminded that their powerful neighbor to the north has mined the country for investment and travel opportunities. Through their disrespectful eyes, gringo tourists appear ignorant and foolish. Although important, these cross-cultural encounters are relatively rare in La Onda's fiction, which is concerned primarily with the daily activities and struggles of Mexican teenagers. Writing in a manner reminiscent of Kerouac's spontaneous prosody, the Onderos refuse to edit or hierarchize, seeking instead to capture the quality and texture of the protagonists' everyday experience in all of its repetitive tedium. Their focus on the mundane activities of contemporary life appears more radical in the context of a Latin American literary canon dominated by magical realism.

More Holden Caulfield than Neal Cassady, the *rebeldes sin causa* rely on the security of home and parents, however unsatisfactory, as a foundation for their nonconformity. Instead of lighting out for uncharted territory, they show their disrespect for authority through fumbling, illicit sex, stolen cigarettes, and drinking. Much like their North American contemporaries, these young men move restlessly between one friend's home and another's, from bars to parties, restaurants, cafés, and city parks. Being alone, particularly in the privacy of one's own bedroom, often leads to the kind of frustration and rage expressed by Gabriel Guia, the protagonist of *La tumba* [The Tomb], "En veces me dan ganas de poner una bomba en todo el mundo, acabar con todos" [Sometimes I feel like bombing the entire world, to get rid of them all].[97] A far cry from the Fellahin Kerouac imagines as innocent survivors of nuclear holocaust, Guia, in this fit of adolescent angst, fantasizes that he is the agent of global destruction. His outburst is a reminder that Mexican teenagers are haunted by the same cold war images of atomic apocalypse as their counterparts in the United States.

The cityscapes that are the setting for the Onderos' fiction are also strikingly different from the Fellahin Mexico Kerouac described. Their primary settings are the upper-middle-class urban neighborhoods where their characters live, recreate, and go to school. Although typically located in the vast, sprawling Mexican capital, these narratives are pervaded by a feeling of claustrophobia. Teenage protagonists respond to the restrictions of their immediate surroundings by inventing highly localized vocabularies and rituals, while simultaneously expressing affinities with larger, more dispersed communities of consumers. Their sensibility thus seems a by-product of the urban space they inhabit, manifesting the qualities anthropologist Néstor García Canclini associates with contemporary Mexico City:

> The disintegration of the city as a result of demographic expansion and urban sprawl diminishes the organizational significance of the historic center and shared public spaces that once encouraged common experiences in the Mexican capital. Territorial expansion and the massification of the city that reduced interaction among neighborhoods are processes that date from the 1950s to the present, precisely the same period in which radio, television, and video spread throughout the city. These are the new, invisible electronic links that have reorganized relations among inhabitants in a more abstract and depersonalized manner, while connecting us all to a transnational symbolic order.[98]

By the time the Onderos began writing in the mid-1960s, Mexico City's more traditional, centralized urban core was already giving way to the series of dispersed localities García Canclini describes. Mass media was beginning to create the transnational communities of consumers that would often supplant local or national affiliations later in the twentieth century. This context explains a tension at the heart of La Onda's fiction, which is rooted in a specific time and place, while looking outward to more abstract and disembodied forms of collectivity. Setting their fiction within a cacophonous, modern city filled with cars, television, and rock music, the Onderos resist the stereotype of Mexican underdevelopment promoted by North American film and literature. They also reject the quaint, colorful folkways of the state-sanctioned *indigenismo* intended to promote nationalism and attract foreign tourists of the kind depicted in *De perfil* and *Se está haciendo tarde*. The modernity advanced by their fiction is thus particular to the Mexican context, but it belongs to a Mexico saturated by economic and cultural interests that are transnational in scope.

To show off their literacy, the Onderos look not to great Mexican authors, but to the cultures of Western Europe and the United States. Gabriel Guia catalogues his purchase of records by "Satchmo, Adderly, Debussy, and Grieg" and books by Verlaine, Beckett, and Kerouac.[99] Agustín's *rebeldes* drop these names to indicate their avant-garde tastes. Familiarity with high art and literature that might be a sign of nerdish conformity (or what Kerouac called "tedious intellectualness,"[100] OTR 7) north of the border grants

worldliness to Mexican teenagers who chafe at the constraints of an oppressive national culture. Amid such predictable topics as friends, sex, and
rock music, their conversations often turn toward matters of culture. During these rather implausible moments, the characters seem directly to voice
the tastes and ambitions of their authors. At a party, a character named
Ziper scolds his friends for thinking that he invented the concept of "pop-
scribbling": "No han leído nada de literatura pop? En el Village, después
del tramp-writing, es la onda en turno" ["Haven't you read any pop literature? In the Village, it was the next new wave after tramp writing"].[101] In
Ziper's version of radical literary history, New York's Greenwich Village is
not a particular place but a symbolic geography. He aspires to participate
in an international community of readers who would understand his allusion to "el Village" and the bohemian cohorts that congregated there. Later
that evening, the protagonist's cousin Esteban criticizes a friend's painting,
"Pinta horrible, puras indias gordas, fofas, cubistas. Válgame Dios, cubistas
en esta época! Que país" ["He paints horribly, only fat, flabby, cubist indians. Good god, cubists in this era! What a country"].[102] Ironic and preten-
tious as they may be, Esteban's complaints also bespeak his knowing contemporaneity. Rejecting the derivative art of painters who continue to work
with postrevolutionary themes and styles, the urbane teenagers of La Onda
locate themselves within a culturally progressive, modernized Mexico far
different from the underdeveloped zones so striking to the North American
traveler.

The Onderos' cultural literacy is wide-ranging and democratic. Indeed,
more important than avant-garde art and literature is the Anglo-American
rock music that provides a soundtrack for their everyday activities. If Kerouac's spontaneous prosody was an attempt to reproduce in writing the
jazz and bop of his time, La Onda's fiction is the literary counterpart to the
rocanrol that was increasingly popular among Latin American consumers
in the 1960s and 1970s. As Eric Zolov has shown, the promotion of North
American bands south of the border gave rise to numerous Mexican imitators and spurred the development of a broader youth counterculture.[103] The
stories in Parménides García Saldaña's collection *El rey criollo* [King Creole]
are saturated with references to rock and rock music. Likewise, Agustín titles
his memoir of the 1960s *El rock de la carcel* [Jailhouse Rock], acknowledging the centrality of Elvis to his life during this formative period. His 1996
study of the Mexican counterculture includes a section whose title, "El lado
oscuro de la luna" [the dark side of the moon], pays tribute to Pink Floyd,
with chapters on punks, "rock mexicano," and "bandas." Explaining his

distinctive use of colloquial language, Agustín cited rock music as an inspiration: "*De perfil* realmente no era literatura, al menos tal como se le concebia entonces. Era una proposición distinta: como el rock, se trataba de fundir alta cultura y cultura popular, legitimar artisticamente de una vez por todas el lenguaje coloquial" ["Its true, *De perfil* wasn't really literature, at least not as it was conceived of back then. Rather, it was a new proposition: as with rock, it sought to fuse high and popular culture, to legitimate artistically once and for all a colloquial language"].[104] Modeling his fiction on the rhythms and cadences of rock, Agustín claims to have invented a hybrid alternative to known literary forms.

Although rock music was initially marketed to Mexican elites, the Onderos embraced it as an opportunity to break away from their own bourgeois origins by transgressing rigid class barriers. Their early fiction anticipates the powerful allure *rocanrol* would exert for working-class Mexicans in the 1970s and 1980s. As Elena Poniatowska writes, "Quiénes sostienen en México el rock? Los jodidos, los fregados, los chavos que viven en las colonias más pobres" [Who maintains rock in Mexico? The down and out, the fucked-over, the kids who live in the poorest colonies].[105] Having captured the prized middle-class consumer demographic, rock took hold in Mexico among more economically and socially marginalized audiences. These fans may not have understood its English-language lyrics, but they responded to its connotations of *desmadre*, or vulgar disregard for social conventions and established figures of authority.[106] Taking advantage of these associations, the Onderos use rock music to illuminate alternating currents of shallowness and a more genuine urge toward rebellion within their privileged adolescent protagonists.

Some ten years after the sounds of jazz and bop provided a soundtrack for Kerouac's improvisational sketches, Anglo-American rock music enabled La Onda's radical experimentation with language. Rock lyrics play an important part in making Saldaña's work into what Juan Bruce-Novoa has called an "interlingual text," writing that exploits the juncture between two linguistic traditions while remaining stubbornly resistant to translation.[107] Beginning each story with the Spanish translation of a Rolling Stones song, Saldaña uses these lyrics to satirize the superficiality of his bourgeois, teenage protagonists, and also to portray more serious registers of rage and frustration. Like Poulin's *Volkswagen Blues*, Saldaña's *El rey criollo* could not be translated into any one language without diffusing the unsettling effects of Spanish prose interrupted by banal rock lyrics in English. Saldaña's language, a distinctive hybrid of Anglo-American rock and the colloquial speech of working-class *chilangos* and young people, demands a reader who is multilingual and, ideally, versed in contemporary music as well as literary history.

It is in the innovative use of language that La Onda most evidently moves beyond imitation of Anglo-American forms to become a unique countercultural expression in its own right. Like the post-Kerouac Quebecois, the Onderos recognized language as a domain of political struggle, which would allow them to claim affiliation with young people around the globe, while simultaneously reaffirming their ties to specific localities within Mexico City. And like the Quebecois adoption of *joual*, they made use of vernacular idioms that had previously been used only in speech, understanding the new language that resulted as a political statement. Recognizing the importance of linguistic experimentation to literature's oppositional potential, Octavio Paz observed that "when a society decays, it is language that is the first to become gangrenous. As a result, social criticism begins with grammar and the reestablishing of meanings."[108] La Onda's early fiction coincides with violent clashes between the Mexican state and student protestors demanding freedom of expression. Its language suits the mood of restless frustration among Mexican youths, who often speak less because they have something urgent to say than because they are compelled to announce their capacity for self-expression. In the context of long-standing government repression of free speech—climaxing in the massacre of student demonstrators at Tlatelolco in 1968—this assertion of one's voice has broadly political connotations.[109] As if to claim this right to freedom of expression, circular and repetitive dialogues may go on for pages with no apparent concern for narrative expediency. Agustín is known for the invention of defiant, unlovely compound words such as "circuloliterariomodernistas," "de alto wattage," and "seudoBeatnik." This is the impure, hybrid language of a metropolis shaken by the fusion of cultures resulting from globalization.

Whether they seek to access rebellious currents among young people or to criticize the superficiality of Mexico's privileged classes, La Onda's colloquialisms remain virtually untranslatable. One unanticipated consequence of such linguistic innovation is that even though these texts aspire to an international audience, they have rarely been read outside of Mexico. The same is true of their Quebecois counterparts Beaulieu and Poulin. Although *Volkswagen Blues* has received some attention by Anglophone Canadian critics, the English-language version of *Kerouac: A Chicken-Essay* is long out of print. The crucial role of translation, marketing, and distribution in forming a canon of world literature is often overlooked in discussions of literary influence.[110] But questions that might seem to reside entirely in the realm of literary value in fact have everything to do with the production and circulation of books themselves. Countercultures, which may wish to imagine themselves exempt from the marketplace, are no exception. Not only did the American Beats and hippies who crossed national borders enjoy the privilege of a U.S. passport, but editors, publishers, and reviewers have guaranteed that their experiences will be transmitted posthumously to readers around the world. Their Mexican and Quebecois counterparts, no matter how inventive and worldly in scope, are constrained by the borders of nation and language.

The story of Kerouac's North America provides a revealing look at the possibilities and obstacles to the circulation of culture across national and linguistic borders. Describing this iconic American author as *North American* underscores the importance of French Canada and Mexico to Kerouac's literary production, vectors of his life and career that are lost when the interpretation of his work and influences remains centered on the U.S. context. Reading across borders, we see the importance of transnational mobility to Kerouac's creative endeavor, as well as the tangled routes traveled by his work and reputation, which give rise to innovative forms of literary expression in both Quebec and Mexico. As I have argued, the adaptation of post-Kerouac themes and aesthetics in these contexts cannot be seen as mere imitation or as a sign of the inevitable homogenization of American culture. Taking these dynamics of appropriation seriously offers us a fresh view of Kerouac as an American author, and introduces less familiar voices into the field of North American literary history. A more expansive understanding of the category of American literature reveals underexamined pockets of creative production in places that Kerouac viewed predominantly through the lens of nostalgic primitivism. But even as they imagine themselves participating in a cosmopolitan cultural scene, and as their geographic horizons broaden, the post-Kerouac Quebecois remain uninterested in Mexico, while the Mexican authors are equally uninterested in Canada. However unwittingly, these writers treat the United States as the conduit to participation in a greater American literary scene. Only in Kerouac do we find the imagination of an America that includes Canada and Mexico, as well as the United States, and attempts—however misguided, at times—to think about Canada and Mexico independently of the United States. By reading across borders, we thus come to understand what Kerouac leaves out, and also what is unique about his capaciously multicultural, multilingual visions of America.

CHAPTER FIVE

Continental Ops: Crossing Borders in North American Crime Narrative

A case involving women, money, and murder. A darkened room where two men confront each other. A disillusioned investigator. The friend who betrayed him by "going Mexican." The intimacies of male bonding sundered. Forty years after Raymond Chandler's classic *The Long Goodbye* (1951) told this story, Michael Connelly revives it in his best-selling crime thriller, *The Black Ice* (1993).[1] Both novels are set in Los Angeles, where their detective-protagonists struggle to preserve the reputations of friends who appear to have committed suicide under suspicious circumstances. Both crimes have ties to Mexico that require the detective to travel there during the course of his investigation. In the end, the alleged victims are found alive, having faked their own deaths to get away with murder. Each man's slide into degeneracy is indicated by his increasing identification with Mexico, and the transformation of his physical features from white to "Mexican." His passage across the border signals the surrender of his values, relationships, and core aspects of his identity.

This is where the similarities between Connelly and Chandler come to an end. Published in the same year as the signing of Nafta, *The Black Ice* reflects the extent to which relations between the United States and its closest neighbors have changed in the decades since the publication of *The Long Goodbye*. Although Connelly's protagonist Harry Bosch is as tough-minded and individualistic as Chandler's Philip Marlowe, he operates in a world where the professional private eye is obsolete. A lone detective is no match for the transnational crime rings that plague contemporary Los Angeles. The files, computer databases, and institutional resources needed to track their movements are available only to those working within a law enforcement agency. Unlike Marlowe, Bosch is not a private eye but a member of the Los Angeles Police Department, where his breaches of protocol cause constant friction with his superiors. Whereas Marlowe's case concerns interpersonal, domestic matters—a bad marriage leads to conflicts over love, money, and ultimately, murder—Bosch's concerns rivalry among powerful international drug cartels. And whereas Marlowe's border is a sparsely populated frontier at the edge of civilization, Bosch's borderlands are teeming with foot and vehicular traffic, commerce, and industrial activity. In order to continue his investigation on the other side/*al otro lado*, he must contend with a foreign system of government and collaborate with his Mexican counterparts.

When Chandler's Marlowe remarks, "Tijuana is not Mexico. No border town is anything but a border town," he indicates the marginality of the region to national affairs, a perspective very similar to that of the travelers in Jack Kerouac's *On the Road*.[2] As a resident of Los Angeles, he believes that border towns are isolated and provincial. This view would become increasingly untenable in the decades that followed, as North America's borderlands were transformed into primary arteries in the global economy and undocumented immigration and smuggling came to be seen as problems of national security. Along the U.S.-Mexico border, the post–World War II period saw rapid development spurred by the buildup of U.S. military bases, a booming tourist industry, and the arrival of the *maquiladoras*, all of which solidified ties between the two nations and positioned the region as a hub of transnational, commercial activity.[3] The "world's longest undefended border" between the United States and Canada acquired similar importance in 1989 with the implementation of the Canada-U.S. Free Trade Agreement. With the signing of Nafta, Mexico joined in a trilateral commitment to opening the continent's borders, enabling the movement of goods and services and the increasing integration of the three economies. Although national borders had originally functioned to protect citizens from attack and preserve territorial integrity, these accords signaled the arrival of an era in which open borders would be essential to the region's economic prosperity.

This market-driven push to erode borders coincided with the U.S. government's recognition of cross-border crime as a problem of national security, a shift that had obvious consequences for Canada and Mexico.[4] The loosening of economic borders that gave rise to legally sanctioned forms of globalization also encouraged the internationalization of a brand of criminals political scientist Peter Andreas describes as "clandestine transnational actors (CTAs), defined as nonstate actors who operate across national borders in violation of state laws and who attempt to evade law enforcement efforts."[5] This type of criminal poses new challenges for law enforcement agencies whose jurisdictional authority ends at national borders.[6] As Bartosz H. Stanislawski has argued, international policing efforts have lagged far behind the evolution of powerful clandestine networks, which seek out "black spots" in the vicinity of national border regions that "are formally part of the country but are out of effective government control."[7] The most wealthy and powerful of these networks command a sphere of influence dispersed far beyond the borderlands where their operations are based. As reflected in *The Black Ice*, these new circumstances have made U.S. borders with Canada and Mexico into popular settings for contemporary crime fiction, which takes its cue, in part, from the changing conditions of North American crime.

Material changes in relations among North America's three nation-states have thus coincided with the evolution of detective fiction itself, which has increasingly recognized links between crimes against individuals and the transnational criminal networks that operate on the underside of the global economy. However, to see the detective novel as a simple reflection of its historical context is to lose sight of its status as literature and, more specifically, as a type of genre fiction.[8] The preceding chapters have examined North American culture through the lens of shared historical experiences, especially generative moments of transnational cultural production, and key figures who articulate a trans-American sensibility. This book has not yet devoted a chapter to questions of genre, which, I will argue, offer yet another fruitful device for understanding the uneven relationship between North American cultural forms, the nation-state, and the continent. Genre fiction provides a particularly apt lens for comparative analysis because— within the confines of fixed formulas and conventions—it reflects the collective beliefs and values of a given community of readers at a particular moment in time. As Fredric Jameson puts it, "genres are essentially literary *institutions*, or social contracts between a writer and a specific public, whose function is to specify the proper use of a particular cultural artifact."[9] At its most basic level, the detective genre registers disruptions in the social order, seeking imagined resolutions to problems of morality, justice, and the law that may seem insurmountable outside the domain of fiction. The investigator's task is to restore the status quo by ferreting out wrongdoing and absolving the innocent of blame. Detective fiction tends to place less emphasis on the solution to the crime than on the investigative process, which exposes persistent, but otherwise invisible, tensions within the social fabric. Although those tensions are put to rest when the case is closed, the detective story often ends with a troubling sense of disconnection between the social problems it reveals and generic demands for resolution. Thus, despite the fact that many critics see the detective genre as an inherently conservative form, its ability to expose contradictions between the systemic causes of crime and their imagined solutions have, at various moments, made it a compelling tool of social critique.[10]

Because their themes and conventions have proved to be extremely portable, detective novels can now be found in virtually any part of the world.[11] In North America, where hard-boiled crime writers first transformed the genre in the 1920s, detective fiction has migrated from its origins in major cities such as New York, Chicago, and Los Angeles to a diversity of new locations, stretching from Quebec to Chiapas.[12] Yet despite the growing internationalism of crime fiction, scholars have continued to study it within discrete national or linguistic traditions. This means that we know a good deal about direct lines of literary influence—the impact of the British tradition on Anglo-American or Canadian hard-boiled writers, or the Spanish *novela negra* on the Mexican *neopoliciaco*, for instance—but far less about how writers from different traditions would respond to common regional problems.

This chapter is about how detective novels from Canada, the United States, and Mexico have approached the subject of cross-border crime, and what those representations tell us about how North Americans view their closest neighbors. We might expect continental integration to make these novels look more similar, but I find that detective fiction, much like the post-Kerouac Quebecois and Mexican literatures examined in the previous chapter, often works strenuously to assert the presence of national and cultural borders, to insist on the ways it is *unlike* its generic counterparts on the other side/*al otro lado*. More specifically, I am concerned with how the detective novel represents the interrelation of crime, government, and civil society in a variety of regional settings. In what follows, I examine the work of three authors—John Farrow, Rolando Hinojosa, and Paco Ignacio Taibo II—who use the detective genre to reflect on problems of justice that span national borders but must be resolved via local institutions. Each of these writers has worked extensively in other genres, turning to the detective novel as a vehicle for addressing new contradictions that arise within a North America where globalization is unevenly eroding national borders. Each appropriates a particular kind of detective novel—the ratiocinative (Farrow), the police procedural (Hinojosa), and the hard-boiled (Taibo)—as his vehicle for social and literary critique, adopting and reconfiguring its generic conventions to address new circumstances of production, circulation, and reception. An analysis of their work must begin with the fundamental contradiction between a genre that almost effortlessly crosses national borders and the divergent opportunities for aspiring authors of detective fiction to publish their work in different national contexts. At the level of plot, further contradictions include the rhetoric of open borders and the realities of their increasing militarization, the growing magnitude and dispersal of crime networks and the local and/or national remedies currently in place to address it, and the desire for transnational community and the continued power and allure of the nation-state. Each author arrives at narrative closure by seeking to resolve those contradictions with fantasies of civic order that bespeak very different understandings of literature's relationship to the social world. These understandings, in turn, tell us how far North Americans are from a shared culture, or common notions of justice.

The Canadianist Detective Fiction of John Farrow

When Emile Cinq-Mars, the protagonist of Canadian John Farrow's two detective novels, *City of Ice* (1999) and *Ice Lake* (2001), looks across the Atlantic, he imagines himself a successor to his favorite literary investigator, Sherlock Holmes, and his Canadian surroundings as a New World version of Britain: "Montreal was renowned, indeed legendary, for crime—that was where he would go. . . . The city would become his London."[13] This passage provides a revealing clue about the kind of detective novel Farrow imagines himself to be writing. Given his stated anxiety about the marginality of Canadian letters, it is no accident that he turns to the most famous literary detective of all time. The allusion to Holmes suggests an effort to write Canadian fiction that acknowledges its ties to Europe, while distinguishing itself from the U.S. culture that has long threatened to engulf or absorb it. Substituting contemporary Montreal for Victorian London, he acknowledges Canada's enduring ties to imperial Britain and tellingly ignores the very different type of crime writing inspired by North American cities such as New York, Chicago, and Los Angeles. So too, Farrow's protagonist favors the ratiocinative mode perfected by the reserved, cerebral Holmes, and implicitly rejects the rough, cynical style of the hard-boiled detective introduced to the genre by U.S. writers in the 1930s. Yet Farrow inserts Cinq-Mars into a very different world than that of his Victorian precursor. In his novels, the old-school investigator is forced into reluctant confrontation with contemporary forms of wrongdoing involving transnational corporations, post–cold war organized crime syndicates, and ruthless biker gangs. This tension between the vast scope and sophistication of present-day criminal underworlds, and the detective's nostalgia for a just, orderly, and autonomous Canada, is key to the meaning and purpose of Farrow's crime writing.

It is not surprising that Cinq-Mars finds his role model in the British Sherlock Holmes, having no tradition of well-known Canadian literary detectives to speak of. Farrow has explained his turn to detective fiction as an attempt to reach a broader audience after becoming disillusioned with the small readership attained by his more explicitly literary novels (written under his given name, Trevor Ferguson), *High Water Chants*, *Onyx John*, and *The Fire Line*. "Being overlooked as Canadians is common to our literature," he remarked in an interview, "Canadian writers are a little slow in answering the call to crime fiction, they feel a taint."[14] As Farrow points out, there has been relatively little crime writing about Canada. Indeed, many North Americans would be hard-pressed to think of a single detective novel written by a Canadian or set north of the 49th parallel. Instead, the mention of Canada brings to mind the most peaceable and law-abiding of cultures, epitomized in the nonthreatening figure of the Mountie and the national motto, "peace, order, and good government."

This view is perpetuated by crime narratives coming from the United States, which express little interest in Canada, save for the fact that it shares the nation's northern border. Although it served as a haven for bootleggers during Prohibition and its border region has long supported a thriving traffic in contraband, Canada is essentially nonexistent in U.S. American representations of transnational crime. Terrence Malick's film *Badlands* (1973) is a good example. It tells the story of Kit Carruthers, a garbage collector who tries unsuccessfully to escape across the northern border after a brutal crime spree. But because he never makes it, Canada serves as little more than a fantasy of evading the law. Canada plays a more significant role in Brian de Palma's 1987 *The Untouchables*. Set during the Prohibition era, the film is about an undercover team assigned to combat liquor smuggling across the United States' northern border. In contrast to the frisson of cultural and racial difference found in representations of the U.S.-Mexico borderlands, *The Untouchables* underscores the extent to which Canada looks exactly like the United States, and Canadians are virtually indistinguishable from their American antagonists. A few years later, two successful U.S. TV series about crime and detection incorporated Canadian settings, which were notable primarily because Canada has so rarely been portrayed as a venue for criminal activity. One is David Lynch's *Twin Peaks*, which includes a subplot about the activities of French Canadian brothers involved in smuggling illegal drugs across the U.S.-Canadian border. Many of the sinister figures in the series also have some association with One-Eyed Jack's, a casino located just north of the U.S. border. So too, much of the *X-Files* was filmed in Vancouver, and the mysteries tracked by its detectives often require travel between Canada and the United States. In a testament to the paucity of such representations, Canadian fans kept track of the culturally specific Canadian references that popped up in particular episodes.[15] However, in neither case do we find fully developed Canadian characters or depictions of Canadian efforts to police cross-border crime.

It was not until relatively recently that Canadians attempted to develop their own distinctive versions of the detective novel. Although they have been writing detective fiction since the nineteenth century, Canadian authors have typically been grouped together with their British, French, or U.S. counterparts. As Priscilla Walton puts it, "Canadianicity is erased from histories of crime fiction."[16] Nowhere is this erasure more evident than in the career of Canadian Kenneth Millar, who moved to California and became the detective novelist Ross MacDonald. MacDonald's assimilation into the canon of American hard-boiled fiction makes sense, since there is very little that identifies his work as Canadian. "It is only recently that Canadians as *Canadians* have begun to make their mark in crime fiction," Walton writes. "Perhaps because writers like MacDonald were perceived as American, contemporary writers tend to foreground Canadianicity in their texts."[17] As Walton uses it, the concept of "Canadianicity" seems to refer simply to the adoption of local settings and vernaculars by authors born in Canada. However, it is worth stretching the implications of this category, since "Canadianicity" can serve as a potentially useful way of considering how Canadian detective novels may reflect views about crime and civic order that are distinct from their counterparts in other regions of North America. Without resorting to simplistic claims about national character, it is possible to say that, in North America, relations between citizens and systems of governmentality vary greatly from one regional and/or national context to another. As I will argue, even when North American detective novels share a common interest in documenting the proliferation of cross-border crime, they express differing beliefs about what constitutes lawless activity, the social environments that nurture it, and how it should be combated.

Farrow underscores the Canadianicity of his detective novels through thick descriptions of Montreal and its environs. As with other authors in this chapter, his detective fiction creates parallels between the investigation of crime and the investigation of the history and nature of a place. In *Ice Lake*, Farrow looks back to the founding of Montreal, claiming that its geographic position at the crux of major trade routes has always made it an ideal breeding ground for transnational crime. Globalization has exacerbated the problem, putting ordinary citizens at ever-greater risk. Each of Farrow's detective novels focuses on a border zone—the Port of Montreal in *City of Ice* and the Mohawk Akwesasne reserve that spans the U.S.-Canadian border in *Ice Lake*—as a point of particular vulnerability, where crime thrives in the gaps between different local and national law enforcement agencies. They depict Montreal itself as a violent place, home to CIA-sponsored search-and-destroy missions, international biker gangs, the Russian Mafia, and corrupt corporations whose malfeasance has repercussions far beyond Canadian borders. Local law enforcement is often in the pocket of organized crime, bombs explode in public, and kidnapping and murder occur with alarming frequency. By elaborating the sinister activities of Montreal's criminal networks, Farrow unsettles the stereotype of Canada as North America's peaceable attic. Instead, he shows it to be an epicenter for events that threaten the security of the entire continent. As he explained in an interview,

> We have criminal gangs interconnected with international gangs, and gangs that are popular with the public despite their murderous ways. We have a long-standing tradition of using the American border (remember Prohibition) for illicit import and export and to evade the FBI and CIA. Russian, Chinese, Jamaican, Italian and Irish gangs all flourish, in addition to our hometown French gangs, particularly the most brutal chapter in existence of the Hell's Angels. Montreal is also known as the city where Middle East terrorists have cells that plot against American targets. I think the material here for a criminal series is bottomless.[18]

Here, Farrow's enthusiasm for the narrative possibilities of Montreal's criminal underworlds is palpable and his Cinq-Mars novels work strenuously to establish its viability as a location for great crime writing.

Although neither novel ends by defeating crime networks that plague contemporary Quebec, Farrow uses the process of crime fighting to bring imaginary resolution to one of Canada's most well known problems: the conflict between British and French that has threatened to divide the nation. He sets the stage in *City of Ice*, where law enforcement has been distracted by linguistic factionalism in its ranks. As Farrow explains, "the English-French dichotomy is a facet of Montreal life and by bringing it right into the squad care and the office area, I'm able to explore a relationship that must cross a cultural divide."[19] The tensions between Anglo and Francophone Canada touch Cinq-Mars directly when—despite his protests—he is paired with the English-speaking John Mathers, whose respectful competence gradually erodes the older detective's antipathy to collaboration. If Cinq-Mars imagines himself a modern-day Sherlock Holmes, Mathers is his Doctor Watson. By working together effectively over two novels, the detectives save the lives of many civilians, thwart the activities of Montreal's international biker gangs, bring down a Russian drug lord, and halt the wrongdoing of a multinational pharmaceutical manufacturer. One way to read this partnership is as an allegory about an Anglophone writer working in Quebec and seeking the respect of the Francophone community. But Farrow suggests that the resolution of Franco-Anglophone conflict has far broader significance, since it impacts the security of the entire continent and the world beyond.

In Farrow's novels, the successful partnership between Cinq-Mars and Mathers stands in contrast to the strained relationship between U.S. and Canadian law enforcement agencies. Despite the scope of the crimes he portrays, Farrow rejects the idea—widely shared among North American policy makers and politicians—that they can best be combated through binational collaboration with the United States. In each novel, the unfolding narrative of investigation reveals the negative impact of proximity to the United States and the necessity for Canadian independence on matters of law enforcement and the dispensation of justice. Cross-border crime may affect both U.S. and Canadian citizens, but there is no sense that Canadian investigators could benefit from the information or resources of their southern counterparts. Instead, Farrow's novels create scenarios in which local Canadian police (sometimes in collaboration with national forces such as the Mounties) are pitted against transnational criminal antagonists. In *Ice Lake*, a Canadian drug manufacturer is conducting illegal experiments that have killed scores of AIDS patients in the eastern United States. Given that a number of deaths occur in New York City, the NYPD might be expected to play a significant part in the investigation. Instead, the American detectives don't arrive in Montreal until the case is nearly solved, only to alienate their Canadian counterparts with ignorant comments about Canadian lingual politics and the organization of Canadian law enforcement.[20] Cinq-Mars greets them with an intimidating speech about the brutality of the Montreal gangs, concluding sarcastically, "I wouldn't want you thinking you've crossed into a safe country. It's not safe if you're law enforcement. . . . Show them your gold shields and tell them you're from New York, they might not be impressed" (IL, 430). Here, Farrow reverses the conventional view of Canada as a bland, nonviolent place by underscoring the ruthlessness of Montreal's gangs and implying that the NYPD's reputation for toughness has not traveled across the border. Cinq-Mars's allegations of inadequacy are borne out when the NYPD officers prove inconsequential to the investigation. Together, Cinq-Mars and Mathers save the life of a woman in danger and expose the president of the pharmaceutical company. In the process, Cinq-Mars reminds the culprit that he is lucky to be in Canada rather than the United States, where he might receive the death penalty. However, the detective cannot eradicate the larger problem of corporate malfeasance, tied as it is to greedy shareholders, unethical business practices, and Canada's porous border with the United States.

Indeed, the challenge to civic order and justice arising from Canada's proximity to the United States is one of the persistent themes of Farrow's crime fiction. Early in the first Cinq-Mars novel, we learn that the detective, who spent much of his career working in petty crime, has recently become the foremost member of his squad. His rapid elevation is due to a secret informant, who provides him with tips about the activities of the Mafia, the CIA, and other clandestine groups. By the second novel, his anonymous source is revealed to be the cynical, unprincipled CIA agent Selwyn Norris. Although he allegedly works on behalf of the law, Norris knowingly puts civilians in danger and resorts to murdering his antagonists, rather than bringing them to trial under the U.S. legal system. He justifies his activities unconvincingly by claiming they serve the interest of defeating a larger opponent. Cinq-Mars acknowledges that his partnership with Norris allows him to save lives, but he finds the agent's methods abhorrent. This unwanted collaboration contrasts with the functional partnership between Anglo and Francophone detectives, becoming a figure for the problem of Canada's unavoidable contamination by the corrosive values and institutions of the United States.

Given the scope of the crimes portrayed by Farrow's novels, the reserved, aging, backward-looking Cinq-Mars may seem like an odd protagonist. And Sherlock Holmes may seem an ill-chosen role model for a detective who makes his living by combating the criminal netherworlds of contemporary Montreal. But these novels are as much about the impossibility of being Holmes as they are about successfully becoming him; time and again, they portray the loss of clear distinctions between right and wrong; and the impossibility of maintaining strict boundaries in a world touched everywhere by transnational crime. And as much as the melancholic, old-fashioned Cinq-Mars is the protagonist of these novels, so is the contemporary city of Montreal, a crossroads where many cultures collide and mingle, and a haven for illicit activities of all kinds. While Cinq-Mars laments the irrecoverable loss of traditional values and social organizations to transnational crime, he also charts a course through vibrant urban settings that offer rich possibilities for transnational crime writing. Farrow's detective novels aspire to show the superiority of Canadian society, law enforcement, and systems of justice at the same time that they are enamored of the clandestine networks that promise to put Montreal and the U.S.-Canadian border on the map of North American crime fiction. In order to keep these tensions in play, Farrow's protagonist must operate at a certain remove from the worlds he investigates, retreating at the end of each novel to his farm in the Montreal suburbs. It is to the United States' southern border and beyond that we must now turn to find detectives who grow out of, and are fully implicated by, the border zones where they live and work.

The Borderlanders and the Police: Rolando Hinojosa

The Canadian Emile Cinq-Mars takes Sherlock Holmes as his model because he has neither a similarly well-known Canadian precursor nor a tradition of crime writing about the U.S.-Canadian border and its environs to follow. Although Mexican literature has been plagued by a similar paucity of notable detectives, the U.S.-Mexico borderlands has long been a popular setting for North American crime writers. Reading their work—much of which is set in a California marked by its proximity to Mexico—one might conclude that, until the late twentieth century, the law stopped at the United States' southern border. This is particularly true of hard-boiled fiction, a genre invented in North America. In the work of its classic practitioners, Mexico is essentially outside the law, a space where the police are incompetent and corrupt, and where criminals, perverts, and losers go to indulge their appetites for vice. Whereas Canada is believed to be uninteresting because of its similarity to the United States, Mexico is defined by its otherness, and North American writers have long exploited the frisson of cultural and linguistic difference to be found at the U.S.-Mexico border. Outlaw Mexico is at once dangerous and seductive to streetwise Anglo detectives who walk a fine line at the edge of morality and lawfulness. Criminals who flee south to escape identification often end up losing themselves altogether, engulfed by the tantalizing prospect of "going Mexican."

The association of Mexico with moral degeneracy can be found in a novel as recent as Connelly's *The Black Ice*. It can be traced to such early works of hard-boiled fiction as Dashiell Hammett's 1927 story, "The Golden Horseshoe," in which a petty criminal escapes into Mexico, where he assumes the identity of a dead man in order to extort money from his wife back in the United States.[21] A more extreme metamorphosis occurs in Chandler's *The Long Goodbye*, where the fickle and deceptive Terry Lennox undergoes plastic surgery, his darkened skin and changed features literally transforming him into a Mexican. He enhances these surgical alterations with an overly expressive body language, effeminate perfume, and dainty eyebrows.[22] Lennox represents the extent of his fall as a descent from north to south when he explains to Marlowe, "I was born in Montreal. I'll be a Mexican national pretty soon now."[23] Behind this terse statement is an imagined geography in which Montreal is the place of his virtuous origins, whereas becoming a "Mexican national" will conclude his slide into utter degradation, permanently severing the bond of friendship he shared with Marlowe. The most extended hard-boiled representation of Mexico occurs in James M. Cain's novel *Serenade* (1937), in which Anglo-Americans travel south of the border to indulge their most naked, bestial instincts. Cain's protagonist, the U.S. American John Howard Sharp, describes the penchant for violence he discovers in the Mexican populace: "About half the population of the country go around with pearl-handled automatics on their hips, and the bad part about these guns is that they shoot, and after they shoot nothing is ever done about it."[24] In the mode of D. H. Lawrence, Cain's Mexico is a place of elemental savagery, where an innate brutality combines with a total absence of law enforcement that makes it a haven for criminal activity.

Orson Welles would try to challenge these stereotypes in his 1957 film noir *Touch of Evil*, which pits the tough, honest Mexican detective Miguel Vargas against the corrupt American Hank Quinlan. The plot reverses the conventions of hard-boiled fiction by featuring a Mexican protagonist who is committed to collaborating with U.S. law enforcement agencies. But Welles's vision of neighborly community is undermined by his decision to cast Charlton Heston as Vargas, as if no actual Mexicans were qualified to play the part. The spectacle of a white actor in brownface turns the character's Mexican nationality into a matter of race, implying that a person could not be simultaneously white and Mexican. Heston's garbled Spanish further distinguishes him from the actual Spanish speakers in the film. Despite the fact that Vargas is part of a police force, he seems to operate in isolation from his colleagues, since he is the only Mexican law enforcement figure to appear during the entire movie, which otherwise relegates Mexicans to predictable roles as cartoonish villains, drug addicts, and vandals. Many of these clichés endure in *Traffic* (2000), Steven Soderbergh's more recent depiction of cross-border crime. The film's manifest intent is to indict the U.S. War on Drugs, laying blame for its failure on both sides of the border. It shows how law enforcement efforts are defeated by internal police corruption, the drug habits of U.S. consumers, and the powerful Mexican cartels that supply them. Yet this attempt at even-handedness is undermined by familiar visual and narrative stereotypes that depict Mexico as a place of lawless violence. Whereas the United States is pictured in cool blues, the Mexican scenes are shot through a lurid yellow filter that suggests an atmosphere of corruption and decay. This visual device is echoed at the level of plot, which is weighted heavily toward the well-rounded stories of families in the United States, its Mexican sequences focusing almost exclusively on the depravity that extends from ordinary cops to wealthy drug cartels, the military, and the highest levels of government.

Beginning in the 1980s, Chicano/a authors began to challenge such narrative clichés about the border by writing detective fiction that featured more well-developed Mexican and Mexican American characters in the context of complex, historically informed representations of border culture.[25] In their hands, a very different picture of cross-border crime and investigation begins to emerge. Rolando Hinojosa is one of the earliest and most acclaimed Chicano authors to work in the detective genre. Like Farrow, he is a writer of more deliberately literary fiction who made a self-conscious decision to try his hand at crime narrative. Like Farrow, Hinojosa's detective novels, *Partners in Crime* (1985) and *Ask a Policeman* (1998) portray a border society whose order is disrupted by the intrusion of lawless activity. He too uses the fantasy of teamwork between men from different cultural contexts—in this case Anglo and Mexican American—to bring imagined resolution to conflicts that divide the region. However, what is distinctive about Hinojosa is that his fictional world spans the international border, devoting equal amounts of attention to the United States and Mexico. Where Farrow expressed antipathy toward binational collaboration, Hinojosa imagines the sharing of information and resources as essential to the well-being of a region that is of vital importance to the continent. And where Farrow appropriated the ratiocinative tradition of his British precursors, whose protagonists rely on individual intelligence and problem-solving abilities, Hinojosa's chosen mode is the police procedural. Following the investigative process in exhaustive detail, he uses the detective novel to expose the destructive effects of organized crime on the values, institutions, and social networks of the border region. For Hinojosa, crime cannot be easily distinguished from the legally sanctioned, but equally damaging, impact of national government and transnational capital. The police procedural is a form that allows him to explore the possibilities of systemic change from within the local law enforcement institutions that, he believes, are best equipped to combat the corrosive forces of big government, corporations, and international crime syndicates alike.

Hinojosa's crime novels are part of his ongoing effort to create a complex portrait of Mexican American community through the use of multiple perspectives and genres. An understanding of his larger literary project helps to clarify his rather surprising turn to popular formula fiction some twelve years after the publication of his first novel, *Estampas del valle y otras obras* (*Sketches of the Valley and Other Works*). Hinojosa's Klail City cycle, which has been compared in complexity and scope to William Faulkner's Yoknapatawpha or Gabriel García Márquez's Macondo, consists of a series of interrelated novels about the fictional communities of Barrones, Tamaulipas, and Belken County, Texas, the southernmost point of land entry into Mexico.[26] The portrait of a hybrid border culture provided by the Klail City novels is rooted in Hinojosa's own experiences as a native of Mercedes, Texas, of mixed Anglo-Latino heritage.[27] All of his fiction is set within a relatively narrow geographic locale that closely resembles the place of his birth. However, Hinojosa has always written with an awareness of the region's place within a broader American context. As he describes it, "I am Mexicano and I'm a Texas Mexican. But if I was born in this country . . . I can draw from all over the world for my work. What I'm contributing . . . is really American literature."[28] Hinojosa insists on situating Chicano culture within America, but his is an America that extends across the borders of the United States to Mexico and beyond.[29] "Chicano Literature is a United States literature," he writes, "but it is also a literature of the Americas, as Martí so clearly saw and labelled the New World."[30] Informed by such cosmopolitan convictions, Hinojosa's novels are firmly rooted in a local community that spans the U.S.-Mexico border, where "going Mexican" is a fact of everyday life, rather than a sign of irreparable decline.

Partners in Crime and *Ask a Policeman* share many of the same underlying themes that characterize other works in the Klail City cycle; however, they are distinguished by their concern with institutions dedicated to the preservation of law and order, exposing the damaging effects of transnational crime on a border community, and exploring conflicts between local and national authority. On the most basic level, Hinojosa explains his foray into detective fiction as a means of bringing visibility to the rising violence and social unrest that the transnational drug trade introduced to the U.S.-Mexico border region.[31] Like many contemporary crime writers, he resists clear distinctions between legal and illegal activity, showing how the operations of big government and the transnational economy actually enable the emergence of organized crime. However, there is more to his detective fiction than the documentation of crime, and his decision to write in the mode of police procedural provides further insight about the meaning of these novels. Given a history in which Mexican-Americans have often been ill served by the U.S. legal system, it makes sense that Chicano writers have avoided a type of detective novel whose sympathies lie with law enforcement. Instead, they tend to write about private detectives working on behalf of populations who have been wronged by established legal authorities. However, in Hinojosa's hands, the police procedural becomes a means to critique institutions of law enforcement from within and to imagine their vital role in the formation of a more just and equitable social order. The transnational structure of the communities he writes about enables him to explore what happens when an investigation crosses national borders, requiring various state agencies to cooperate with one another, and to criticize the absence of a functional binational system of law enforcement.

Partners in Crime and *Ask a Policeman* are the most plot-driven, linear contributions to his Klail City series, which is known for its fragmentary, impressionistic narrative style. They follow Lieutenant Rafael Buenrostro and his colleagues as they investigate a series of violent murders involving both U.S. and Mexican nationals. The turn to realism enables Hinojosa to address social issues more directly, but the detective genre's demand for closure also allows him to imagine solutions that affirm binational partnership as key to the future well-being of the borderlands. His detective novels show the region's vulnerability to forces of transnational crime as well as to lawful institutions that threaten to centralize and standardize its systems of governance, creating a sharp divide between one side of the border and another, transforming local economies, and fragmenting traditional social organizations. They conclude by affirming the value of local over national government, which they represent not only as inept at crime solving but also as often responsible for creating the circumstances that enable its proliferation.

In Hinojosa's novels, geography is essential both to the emergence of transnational crime and the formation of the complex social ecosystem it disrupts. Like Farrow, Hinojosa takes the detective novel as an opportunity for the investigation of place, as well as of crime. Life in the twin towns of Barrones, Tamaulipas, and Klail City, Texas, is unimaginable without the ability to traverse the border freely, since their social, cultural, and economic systems are completely interdependent. As some sociologists have recognized, border communities tend to be hostile to centralized government and to legislation they see as out of touch with the practical realities of life in a binational region.[32] In the case of the U.S.-Mexico borderlands, this sensibility is enhanced by distance from seats of federal power. Hinojosa writes as a borderlander who affirms the efficacy of the local over and against the cumbersome and inadequate mechanisms of national governance. When a case requires U.S. and Mexican colleagues to work together, they gather at the Lone Star restaurant for a night that "was business, and it was visiting as well; a fine, old valley custom, on both banks of the River. Newcomers chafed, but they either succumbed to the habit or they didn't succeed."[33] Borderlanders have their own jokes, rituals, and codes, which have more to do with membership in a regional community than with citizenship or native language, since most are bilingual. They are suspicious of outsiders or "*fuereños*" (PC, 117), who must submit to local custom in order to secure the necessary cooperation of regional authorities.[34]

In this environment, Hinojosa creates a detective protagonist who is ideally equipped to combat transnational crime. Compared to the awkward Cinq-Mars, who remains an outsider to the urban netherworlds he investigates, Rafael Buenrostro has a more organic relationship to the place where he lives and works. The Texan detective is a lifelong border dweller who succeeds not through the intellectual acrobatics of the Holmesian tradition, or the tips of anonymous informants, but through hard work, patience, and the ability to collaborate well with others. In the context of Hinojosa's fictive Valley, these qualities make him uniquely suited to cross-border investigation and to resolve historic antagonisms between Anglos and Mexicans in the region. The Chicano Buenrostro has good reason to resent Anglos, given that his father was the victim of a racially motivated murder. But by the second novel, the detective has married an Anglo woman and reconciled with his father-in-law, who may have been responsible for the death of Buenrostro's own father. Moreover, Buenrostro works closely with a team of Anglo colleagues. After fifteen years with his Anglo partner Sam Dorson, the two men enjoy a relationship so intimate it is rumored that "they could read each other's minds."[35] Their success in combating the clandestine networks that thrive in the U.S.-Mexican border zone comes from their deep familiarity with local culture, their sense of when it is appropriate to bend the rules, and their willingness to cooperate with Mexican law enforcement agencies. Interpersonal relationships are crucial to the smooth functioning of the Belken County Homicide Squad, where Buenrostro and Dorson are old friends as well as co-workers. These associations span the border, since many members of the U.S. law enforcement community have friends and relatives in Mexico. Thus, Hinojosa extends the demands of partnership that are a requisite feature of the police procedural into many aspects of his protagonist's life, suggesting that his career is a model for a social order in which Anglos and Mexicans cooperate to defeat the corrosive power of institutions, legal and illegal, that have infiltrated the borderlands.

In keeping with the broader themes of the Klail City cycle, Hinojosa's detective novels are as concerned with establishing a portrait of a functional transborder community as they are with depicting the crime that disrupts it. In *Ask a Policeman*, he portrays the bustle of legitimate activity at the international border as an alternative to the harmful world of illicit, transnational crime. For example, in one descriptive passage, we learn that "the old neighborhood across from the fort, dating back to the 1850s, was now a crowded block of cheap stores and fast-food places catering mostly to the Mexican nationals who crossed the bridge daily. Many came to shop and spend American dollars, and more came to earn their dollars as maids, store clerks, gardeners, painters, carpenters, janitors, and still others to serve as pick-up day laborers paid for work done on the spot" (AP, 32). The mid-nineteenth-century fort is an architectural landmark that recalls a prior moment when the border was not an integrated cultural ecosystem but a zone of military contestation. What was once the site of armed conflict has become a thriving commercial district where businesses owned by U.S. citizens are supported by Mexicans, who work at low-wage jobs on the U.S. side of the border. Here, Hinojosa provides a portrait of effective transnational symbiosis in which the labor of Mexicans, as well as the income they spend north of the border, is essential to the well-being of the U.S. economy. The United States, in turn, supplies them with employment and commercial opportunities. This passage attests to inequities between one side of the border and the other, but more importantly, it establishes a contrast between a healthy mode of cross-border interdependence and the disorder introduced by transnational crime.

The motivation behind Hinojosa's turn to detective fiction, however, is to document the escalation of cross-border crime in the Rio Grande Valley. Published in 1985 and 1998, his crime novels depict events that unfold between 1972 and 1976, just one year after Richard Nixon coined the term *war on drugs* in 1971 as part of his campaign to restore "law and order" to the United States.[36] This declaration of war was bracketed by the passage of the Controlled Substances Act in 1970 and the formation of the Drug Enforcement Agency in 1973. Hinojosa's novels are thus set at the beginning of a period that would have a momentous impact on U.S.–Latin American relations. As it escalated under Ronald Reagan, the War on Drugs made the narcotics trade vastly lucrative, damaging the economies and political stability of many Central and South American nations and taking countless civilian lives. Hinojosa records the impact of these developments on a border community. As he explains in *Partners in Crime*, "Mexican oil and Valley cotton had traditionally brought in much of the revenue; in Nineteen

Seventy-two, drugs and their artificial affluence were forcing their way into the economy" (115). In Hinojosa's account, not only has the drug trade introduced high levels of violence to the region, but it has also attracted criminals from elsewhere in the hemisphere, along with the unwanted attention of national governments in Mexico City and Washington, DC. We see this evolution over the course of the two novels. *Partners in Crime* focuses primarily on the activities of local crime families, whose relatively small-scale operations serve as a contrast to the far more gruesome violence in *Ask a Policeman*, which is attributed, at least in part, to the intrusion of criminal elements from South America and Canada into the region.

Where *Partners in Crime* and *Ask a Policeman* move beyond documentary is in the parallelisms they create between the drug trade and the destructive presence of national governments and transnational capital in the borderlands, as well as the solutions they imagine to these problems. Hinojosa's detective novels use the narrative of criminal investigation to reveal the contradictions underlying national policies regarding drugs and border management, which profess a commitment to law and order while actually making border regions more dangerous and impeding the work of local law enforcement agencies. From this perspective, the problem with big-time organized crime is that it inevitably leads to violence and it introduces outsiders into a community that relies on enduring ties among its members. In these respects, the national governments in Washington, DC and Mexico City are little different from the criminal elements that are their alleged antagonists. Both represent an alien presence that disrupts the Rio Grande Valley's intimate, binational social organization, and both are all too willing to use punitive methods that put the public in danger.

Hinojosa's decision to write a police procedural dictates that his sympathies will necessarily lie with law enforcement. Indeed, in an interview he remarked that he deliberately sought to avoid the figure of "the crooked cop," which he saw as a cliché of leftist writing.[37] In his hands, writing about the institution and practice of law enforcement from within becomes a vehicle for reform, enabling him to criticize the failures of national government and to imagine alternatives devised by borderlanders themselves. On the U.S. side, the position of national government is embodied by the district attorney Chip Valencia, who advocates for an increased military presence along the border and whose hawkish politics often lead to clashes with Buenrostro and Dorson, who seek to avoid violence at all costs. In *Partners in Crime*, the two detectives demonstrate their commitments by going unarmed into their showdown with José Antonio Gómez, the last remaining member of a crime family responsible for countless deaths on both sides of the border. Hinojosa confirms the rightness of their position when, work-ing closely with their Mexican counterparts, the detectives bring Gómez down, his only injury a self-inflicted gunshot wound. His novel ends with a fantasy in which the best way to eradicate transnational crime is collabo-ration between local law enforcement officers from both sides of the bor-der. The innocent are unharmed, the culprit is snagged, and justice can be served. The tensions between local and national authority are resolved by communities that are competent to regulate themselves. This is not simply a local matter, since problems of border management threaten the eco-nomic well-being and security of the entire continent. At the same time, the growing importance of the borderlands makes such felicitous localisms un-likely. Thus, Hinojosa's detective novels chart the tensions between the del-icate binational equilibrium of a border community, and the forces—crim-inal and legal—that constantly endanger its survival.

The Independent Eye of the Mexican *Neopoliciaco*: Paco Ignacio Taibo II

At the same time that Hinojosa was beginning his Klail City cycle, the Latin American *neopoliciaco* was coming into its own, epitomized in the work of Paco Ignacio Taibo II, the most well-known and prolific Mexican detec-tive novelist of his generation. Like Farrow and Hinojosa, Taibo has writ-ten in multiple genres, turning the detective novel into a vehicle for pro-gressive social criticism. The most explicitly political of the three authors, the left-leaning Taibo looks to the detective novel for its capacity to expose social problems and inspire readers to "see the world through somebody else's eyes."[38] As he explains, "Mexican society is full of disinformation, hid-den things, strange stories behind reality, behind appearances. I felt when I was twenty years old that the mystery structure of storytelling was a very good front for Mexican society. Disinformation is the biggest Mexican art of the twentieth century. Therefore I decided mystery was the field to talk about society."[39] In keeping with these insights, his detectives are investiga-tors and social critics who unmask the wrongdoing of governments, corpo-rations, and organized crime while giving voice to the ordinary citizens it injures.

Beyond the particular content of his novels, Taibo sees his adoption of a lowly form of formula fiction as a gesture of solidarity with the reading publics who constitute its primary audience. He fashions himself after the Anglo-American hard-boiled crime writers of the 1920s and 1930s, whose gritty cynicism, identification with the down-and-out, and concern with the social causes of lawlessness are ideally suited to his political sympathies. At the same time, he attempts to produce a form of crime writing that is indelibly marked by, and expresses the collective unconscious of, its Mexican origins. As I will argue, the particularly dark and chaotic nature of Taibo's fictional world makes the kind of ending demanded by the detective genre highly problematic. He addresses this difficulty via narrative denouement that are deliberately anticlimactic, sensational, or utterly irresolute. An author who has consistently pressed at the limits of the detective genre, Taibo takes his experimentation to new extremes in *Muertos incómodos* (*The Uncomfortable Dead*), a serial novel coauthored with Subcomandante Marcos, spokesperson for the Zapatista Army of National Liberation that has occupied territory in Chiapas since 1994. This collaborative, dialogic narrative experiments with the possibility of writing detective fiction that fingers systemic wrongdoing as such, rather than the guilty individuals who are merely its symptoms. Its two-part ending manages at once to cohere to recognizable generic conventions and take the genre in new directions designed to address the pervasive, dispersed, and institutionalized nature of transnational crime in the twenty-first century.

Taibo's appropriation of the hard-boiled mode must be understood in the context of the history of the Latin American detective novel. Whereas the Anglo-American detective novel flourished in the first half of the twentieth century, critics generally agree that noteworthy examples of the genre did not begin to appear in Mexico until much later. As is the case in Canada, Mexican authors did not attempt to produce specifically Mexican forms of detective fiction until relatively recently. Detective fiction in translation, which had been popular with Latin American readers since the nineteenth century, reached its apogee in the 1930s and 1940s, inspiring a host of Mexican imitators to take advantage of a ready market in the 1950s.[40] By all accounts, their work did little to venture beyond the generic formulas that had been established by their foreign counterparts. As Persephone Braham explains, "until the 1970s the field of Latin American detective fiction was both limited and derivative. Through simulation or parody, authors engaged the marginal status and formulaic nature of detective narrative to dramatize Latin America's peripheral position with respect to modern Western culture."[41] Things changed with the arrival of detective novelists such as Taibo, Jorge Ibargüengoitia, Carmen Boullosa, and Gabriel Trujillo Muñoz, who rejected their Hispanic predecessors as derivative and conventional ("a generation of parodists and imitators," in Taibo's words[42]), while seeking to create a distinctively Mexican version of the genre. These authors came of political age in the 1960s, as part of a generation of intellectuals that was galvanized by the October 1968 massacre of student protestors in the Plaza de las Tres Culturas. They found an avenue for social critique in the hard-boiled detective novel, making its leftist sentiments far more overt than any of their Anglo-American precursors.[43] The decision to embrace a degraded form of popular literature was itself seen as a political act, a reaction against the difficult, experimental fiction of the boom generation and the sophisticated readership it imagined. As Taibo explains, "in the end of the 1960s, when I started writing, most of the young writers of my generation were mad about *form*. I was extremely bored by that. They were producing novels that nobody could read, a kind of doctors' language, in which a doctor can understand another doctor but nobody else. . . . They were producing novels where they were losing the readers; there was no space for storytellers and readers. So this was a kind of reaction: to go back to storytelling."[44] Thus, the Mexican *neopoliciaco* was born.

The *neopoliciaco* is modeled after the hard-boiled fiction of Chandler, Dashiell Hammett, and Chester Himes, who were admired by contemporary Latin American authors for their proletarian values and their ability to address a popular readership while maintaining a commitment to literary style. Himes's influence is particularly apparent in the *neopoliciaco*'s depiction of Mexico as a place of near-anarchic corruption, where a dysfunctional state apparatus has given free reign to criminals, while ignoring the needs of ordinary citizens. The impact of the events of 1968 is evident in these novels' disdain for the state and official institutions, and skepticism about the possibilities of justice. They reflect the widespread distrust of official authorities that has arisen among Latin Americans who have experienced decades of short-lived and unreliable government regimes. In a context where crime almost invariably involves the state, it is crucial that the investigator be a private eye who obeys no authority other than his own moral code. This figure, who has come to seem outdated to many U.S. detective writers, is taken up by authors of the Mexican *neopoliciaco* as the fitting embodiment of a David-and-Goliath struggle in which the people are pitted against crime syndicates, police, and the state. The detective's most hated antagonists are not individuals but institutions, including the U.S. and Mexican governments, which both perpetrate and condone acts of lawless violence that endanger the citizens they are intended to serve.

Taibo conceives of his detective fiction as the organic outgrowth of a chaotic, wild Mexico City, which is the epicenter of his literary universe. "Somebody told me it was impossible to do a crime fiction novel in Mexico because that was an Anglo-Saxon genre," he claimed, "so I decided that it was a wise idea to go into this tradition and show that nothing is impossible in literature."[45] His treatment of the city pays homage to Raymond Chandler, who reimagined sunny Southern California through the dark, gritty atmospherics of hard-boiled *noir*. Like the British Chandler, who claimed California as his adopted home, Taibo is a Spanish immigrant who settled permanently in Mexico City. Just as Chandler's Marlowe is a product of particular California locales and lifestyles, Taibo's detective Hector Belascoarán Shayne is born of an urban, Mexican context, which, for better or worse, is the place where he most belongs. But, as Taibo describes it, these places give rise to very different kinds of hard-boiled writing. Comparing his setting to Chandler's, he remarked in an interview: "the differences are in the structure of the lone hero, the outsider: a vocation for solitude, a fidelity to friends (in Marlowe's case) and to certain obsessions (in Belascoarán Shayne's case). Raymond Chandler's character moves within rational histories whereas mine is surrounded by a chaotic atmosphere, Kafkaesque and corrupt: Mexico City."[46] Here, Taibo acknowledges his debt to Chandler, while emphasizing the specific qualities of the Mexican capital—a city so vast and anarchic that it makes Los Angeles of the 1930s and 40s seem like a small town—that must necessarily generate a unique kind of detective fiction. For Taibo, this means writing novels touched with fantasy, sensational violence, and a sense of the absurd. His protagonist is prone to flights of metaphysical speculation that would have been anathema to the grounded, pragmatic Philip Marlowe.

The one-eyed, melancholic Belascoarán Shayne is the imperfect offspring of his urban environment. In *Días de combate* (published in English as *Calling All Heroes*), the first novel in the series, he walks the streets of this massive, decentralized, modern metropolis:

> The city opened up to him like a monster, like the fetid entrails of a whale, or the insides of a discarded tin can. In its few hours of sleep, the sleep of a tired man, of a worker worn out by his labor, the city became a character, a subject, signals, and would blow breezes full on strange intentions. The jungle of television antennas was bombarded by wavelengths, messages, commercials. The asphalt, the shop windows, the walls, the cars, the *taco* vendor stalls, the stray dogs all made room for him at the beat of his steps.[47]

In this passage, Taibo personifies the city to underscore the absolute synchrony between his protagonist and the place he lives and works. Indeed, Belascoarán Shayne experiences his ambivalent, impassioned attachment to the Mexican capital as far more meaningful than his relationships with other human beings. Departing from the realism of the Chandlerian mode, the "strange intentions" of Taibo's Mexico City include the occasional intrusion of the fantastic, as when Belascoarán Shayne, having been killed off at the close of *No habrá final feliz* (*No Happy Ending*), is revived in the next novel in the series, *Regreso a la misma ciudad y bajo la lluvia* (*Return to the Same City*). Taibo explains this turn of events by situating them within the history of Latin American magical realism, as well as Mexicans' particular obsessions with death and resurrection. "The magic is not entirely my fault. Appeal to the cultural traditions of a country whose history teems with resurrections."[48] Writing for and expressing the consciousness of his Mexican readership, Taibo's detective fiction thus combines the gritty realism of the Anglo-American hard-boiled with the magical, absurdist tendencies of Latin American literary tradition.

The Belascoarán Shayne novels use the investigative process as a mechanism to expose the contradictions between the fickle edifice of lawfulness and the widespread corruption of Mexican institutions, an abhorrence of violent crime and a sense that violence is often the only means of securing justice within a rotten political system, and a desire to punish guilty individuals coupled with an awareness that their crimes are far larger and more systemic than any one person. Typically, Belascoarán Shayne is hired to solve a fairly conventional problem such as a theft, a missing person, or a murder, only to discover that it is tied in to vast criminal conspiracies that reach across national borders and into the highest levels of institutional authority. Seemingly isolated and ordinary acts of wrongdoing are ultimately symptoms of a more pervasive malfeasance on the part of the Mexican and U.S. governments, the Mexican police and military, the CIA, drug traffickers, Nicaraguan contras, organ smugglers, and Cuban gangsters. Although the crimes Belascoarán Shayne investigates are nearly always transnational in scope, Taibo expresses no faith in the prospect of collaboration between local or national law enforcement agencies, given the extreme corruption of officials on either side of the border. Indeed, he finds little hope for law enforcement of any kind, since his investigations uncover collusion between criminal networks and institutions that are supposed to dispense justice and ensure public safety.

Taibo's detective fiction typically concludes by thematizing the difficulty of imagining a resolution to crimes that result from such deep, systemic corruption. Often the Mexican investigator can find no other recourse than killing his antagonists. This puts Taibo in a complicated position, since his novels risk condoning acts of violence as extreme as those committed by his antagonists. On the one hand, they suggest that murder is sometimes necessary in the pursuit of justice. On the other, they are careful not to make it the solution that brings closure to the novel. Thus, they insist that violence may be one unfortunate step in the investigative process, but it cannot secure an end to the pervasive wrongdoing the narrative has exposed. In *An Easy Thing*, Belascoarán Shayne is working three cases at once: attempting to solve the murders of two managers in the Delex Steel Corporation, investigating the cause of a young girl's self-destructive behaviors, and pursuing rumors that Emilio Zapata is alive and living in a cave outside of Mexico City. At the novel's end, Belascoarán Shayne implicates the president of the company in the murders, and then breaks his jaw, reflecting that "happy endings weren't made for Mexico."[49] His next move is to blow up the bowling alley that is the meeting place for the men who harassed the teenage girl. In the wake of these violent acts, Belascoarán Shayne seeks out the aged cave dweller. Although he is unable to prove the man's identity, their cordial meeting closes the novel with the possibility that the revolutionary values Zapata stood for may still be alive and well, if buried, in contemporary Mexico. Given Taibo's ongoing search for a heroic Mexican past, and his sympathy with the political goals of the revolution, this historic encounter must be read as a sign of hope for the present. True, the discovery of a man who may be Zapata cannot erase the violence Belascoarán Shayne has just committed. However, his remark that "where there's good faith, that's all that matters"[50] implies that his more destructive activities may be in the service of promoting a better Mexico, rather than simply the result of nihilistic despair.

In his evolving quest to write detective fiction expressing the intense atmospherics and moral complexities of contemporary Mexico, Taibo explores another alternative in *Muertos incómodos*, a novel written with Subcomandante Marcos, which was published serially in the left-leaning Mexican daily newspaper *La Jornada* between December 2004 and February 2005, and then appeared as a book later that year. Exploiting the popular appeal of the detective genre, the two authors sought to reach the widest possible readership by making each installment immediately available via the Internet, and arranging for the completed novel to be translated into multiple languages.[51] The collaborative process is integral to the form of *Muertos incómodos*, which consists of chapters alternately written by Taibo, featuring the world-weary Hector Belascoarán Shayne, and by Marcos, featuring a naive, unpolished Zapatista detective named Elias Contreras (who also happens to be dead, having been slain in combat some time before). In certain ways, Taibo finds his ideal partner in the charismatic guerilla leader, who has always seen literature as a vital tool for building a social revolution. At the same time, Taibo has denied that "books are vehicles for

social propositions."[52] In contrast to Marcos, whose writing is overtly ideological, Taibo believes that literature has a more indirect capacity to influence its readers by opening their eyes to alternative perceptions of the
world. The two authors make no effort to cover over their differences: Belascoarán Shayne is characteristically "tied to [Mexico city] by an umbili-
cal cord" and often veers from the course of the investigation into metaphysical speculation, while Contreras—a peasant who is utterly unfamiliar
with the ways of the city—cautions that Zapatistas "should definitely *not*
enter into metaphysical considerations," concentrating instead on the rebels' more concrete political agendas.[53] Emerging from these disparate literary voices, which often contradict, repeat, or stray from one another, the
structure of *Muertos incómodos* models a form of collectivity that also allows
for individual differences among its participants.

Nowhere are the authors' differences more apparent than in the visions
of justice each advances at the novel's end. The tangled plot of *Muertos incómodos* brings Belascoarán Shayne and Contreras together in their hunt
for a truly bad man named Morales, who is guilty of murdering members
of Mexico's leftist opposition, conspiring to sell the rich natural resources
of Chiapas to foreign interests, belonging to a sinister ultra-right-wing secret society called El Yunque, and participating in Mexico's Dirty War. Eventually, it becomes clear that Morales cannot be a single individual: "Could
there be three Moraleses? A single shape-shifting mutant Morales? Five of
them? Fifty? A trio? The Moraleses?" (161) Belascoarán Shayne ponders.
These questions are never answered. Indeed, there are multiple Moraleses,
since the real culprit the two men are pursuing is "the system" itself. As Contreras puts it, "THE murderer is not going to return to the scene of the crime,
simply because the murderer *is* the scene of the crime. The murderer is the
system. Yes! The system. When there's a crime, you have to go looking for
the culprit upstairs, not downstairs. The Evil is the system, and the Bad are
those that serve the system" (63). In the end, each detective has a chance to
finger at least one Morales. Contreras tracks his back to Chiapas, where the
guilty man is arrested by the "autonomous justice authorities of the Good
Governance Boards" (236) erected by the Zapatistas as an alternative to the
"bad government" of the Mexican state (239). Marcos proves the moral
superiority of the Zapatistas, who mete out a nonviolent form of punishment to a man responsible for many deaths. However, at the end of his
contribution to the novel, the sentence is undermined by the very institutions that once supported Morales's wrongdoing. The Zapatistas intercept a
phone call among high-level intelligence officials from several nations who
agree that Morales must be "terminated" to prevent him from disclosing

their covert operations. Marcos's conclusion thus decisively identifies a culprit, brings him to trial, and then condemns the guilty to certain death, while allowing the Zapatistas to keep their hands clean.

Taibo, who has the last word, writes a far more violent and ambiguous ending in which Belascoarán Shayne tracks his Morales down to an office in Mexico City's highest building, the Torre Latinoamericana. After the detective asks himself despairingly, "What was he supposed to do with this character? Who was he supposed to turn him over to? In Mexico?" (263), he pushes the guilty man off the observation deck. As in several other Belascoarán Shayne novels, the detective resorts to violence because he knows the corruption of the Mexican legal system will prevent justice from being served in any other way. In a manner typical of Taibo, the novel does not end with the death of Morales. No sooner does Belascoarán Shayne exit the building, than he thinks he sees "two or three Moraleses" on his way home and is disturbed to find that, throughout the day "Moraleses kept turning up in the most unlikely places" (265). In contrast to Marcos, Taibo's conclusion does not shy away from murder, while at the same time implying that the systemic crimes Morales represents cannot be eradicated with the death of any one individual since others will invariably appear to take his place.

Muertos incómodos makes no effort to be coherent, to bring its two authorial voices into dialogue, or to supply a unified conclusion to the tangled plotlines they create. The novel's refusal to provide decisive closure must be seen as a part of its meaning, laying bare contradictions that might be resolved by a more generically conventional ending. It is difficult to imagine an Anglo-American counterpart to *Muertos incómodos*, which emerges out of a context in which culture and politics have been much more closely entwined than they are in the United States or Canada. Among the three North American nations, only Mexico had a revolution that put art and literacy at the center of its projects of social reform. But Mexico also has a long history of repressing dissent, of treating literature as a more dangerous and meaningful form of expression than it is elsewhere on the continent. In this context, what makes Taibo's project unusual is his decision to voice his protest via a genre that has often been used to expose wrongdoing, but very rarely to promote social change. His detective novels do so somewhat counterintuitively, not by providing his readers with a plan of action, but by reminding them of the differences between life and fiction. In *Frontera Dreams* (*Sueños de frontera*), we learn that "Belascoarán, unlike the authors of crime novels, liked complex stories, but only those in which nothing happened,"[54] while in *No Happy Ending*, he realizes that "he needed to figure out his next move. If this were a mystery novel, it would have all become clear to him; even when the detective was uncertain, at least his uncertainty was always clear. It was nothing like this" (111). Belascoarán Shayne's problem, of course, is that he thinks he is a person when in fact he is a character in a detective novel. But his musings might give the reader pause to reflect on the aptness of his insight that life, unlike detective novels, does not provide easy closure where the guilty are identified and justice is served. Having enabled the reader to see the world through Belascoarán Shayne's point of view, Taibo leaves us to figure out how to act in our own world, where nothing much happens, where cause and effect are rarely clear, but where nonetheless it is necessary to preserve a sense of right and wrong. In this realization, he suggests, lie the seeds of political awareness and the possibility of social reform.

Looked at together, contemporary North American detective novels from three very different cultural contexts provide a revealing example of what Jameson called an "ideology of form," the implicit beliefs and values that reside in a work's generic structure. It is not only that each author chooses to write detective fiction, as opposed to another genre, but that he also seeks out the type of detective fiction best suited to address the social problems he imagines it can expose and resolve. Concerned with the absence of Canadian voices and settings in the detective genre, John Farrow appropriates the Holmesian tradition, which elevates the detective above the social worlds he investigates, emphasizing his superior knowledge and intellect, only to show its inadequacy to the vast and brutal crime scenes of contemporary Montreal. His breaks with the ratiocinative mode bespeak the tensions in his effort to illustrate Canada's moral and institutional superiority, but also to assert its viability as a location for crime fiction. Rolando Hinojosa takes the Rio Grande Valley as the setting for detective fiction that is steeped in the particularities of local culture but is also intended to occupy a place within a broader trans-American literary corpus. His police procedurals sympathize with officers of the law and believe in the potential of local institutions to combat the damaging intrusion of national governments and transnational capital into the U.S.-Mexico border region. Writing as a borderlander, he affirms the value of binational teamwork and selective adherence to procedure for creating reform. And Paco Ignacio Taibo II's hard-boiled *neopoliciacos* insist that the detective operate independently of all institutional authority, recognizing that he may need to resort to violence in the pursuit of justice. Working within a Mexican context, Taibo is the most cynical of the three about the efficacy of official law enforcement institutions and the most hopeful about literature's capacity to produce social change. Reading their work comparatively allows us to see how generic forms do cultural work, in this case providing very different responses to the shared phenomenon of crime within an increasingly integrated North America and to the situation of the crime writer seeking an audience for his work.

One unexpected consequence of studying cross-border crime narrative comparatively is that it shows the tenacity of nationalism within a transnational literary form. We might think that authors concerned with the internationalization of North American crime would also be interested in imagining international solutions to the problems it causes. But with the exception of Hinojosa's fully integrated cross-border society, these authors envision the nation as an alternative to the unwelcome Americanization of the continent. Through the character of Emile Cinq-Mars, John Farrow expresses nostalgia for the conservative social values he associates with rural Quebec. Enraptured as they are by the vibrant brutality of transnational crime, his novels nonetheless seek symbolic healing for Canada's historic divisions and advocate for insulating the nation against absorption by the United States. Paco Iganacio Taibo's Coke-guzzling, hard-boiled protagonist reflects a more affirming view of U.S. culture while expressing a similar degree of alarm about the consequences of U.S. political hegemony on the continent. He uses the detective novel to advance a more hopeful form of *mexicanidad* that is associated neither with the decay of contemporary Mexican society nor with official modes of nationalism advanced by the Mexican state.

In this chapter, the purpose of comparative, transnational analysis is to study how a genre travels and the fascinating things it can reveal as it is absorbed into a new context. Genre fiction provides an ideal opportunity for comparison because it assumes multiplicity. By definition, a work of genre fiction cannot exist in isolation. Instead, it must identify itself via its participation in a literary tradition with recognizable conventions. From the perspective of reception, genres make sense only if they are read comparatively, since it is possible to understand their formulaic structures as formulaic only by being familiar with other works from the same generic category. Genres are telling documents of the institutions and values that are important to a given society. When they migrate across borders, it becomes especially apparent which values travel and which are rooted in a very particular place and time. The detective novel, which explores the commission of crime, its social consequences, and the restoration of order, has proved to be a vital medium for North Americans to reflect on their place in an increasingly integrated continent where people and things move, sometimes effortlessly, across national borders, but where the mechanisms of order and justice remain, for the most part, the province of local and national authorities. The novels I have discussed in this chapter are a testament to the productive mobility of culture, but they also tell us how far we are from anything like a continental community.

CHAPTER SIX

The Northern Borderlands and Latino/a Canadian Diaspora

The title of Carmen Aguirre's play *¿Que Pasa with La Raza, eh?* (2000) offers an enticing fusion of linguistic and cultural referents.[1] "La raza," a synonym for *la gente* or *el pueblo* (the people), refers to the imagined community of Latin Americans of diverse races and backgrounds. The juxtaposition of English and Spanish words implies an audience familiar with both languages. Most intriguingly, the interjection "eh" at the end of a question written largely in Spanish gestures to a Canadian interlocutor. Beginning with the inverted question mark particular to Spanish and ending with Canadian English, Aguirre's title announces a drama that will span the hemisphere. In its representation of Latino/a community, the play addresses such familiar themes as the perils of border crossing, the exploitation of migrant workers, encounters with racism, and the struggle to define a cohesive cultural identity.[2] What makes *¿Que Pasa?* distinctive is that, where we might expect it to be set somewhere in the southwestern United States, it actually takes place in Vancouver. Its Latino/a characters' search for self-definition unfolds in the context of a critique of Canadian multiculturalism, and it refers to "America" as a synonym for the entire hemisphere rather than for the United States alone. Evoking the well-known "Upside-Down Map" sketched by Joaquín Torres-García in 1943, an enormous, upside-down map of Latin America hangs behind an otherwise bare stage. At the beginning of the play, a slide projects the words "South America," also upside-down, onto the map as a way of introducing a performance that will confuse the familiar geographies of Latino/a diaspora. But rather than literally turning the map on its head, as this image might suggest, *¿Que Pasa?* moves the border north, giving center stage to Canadian Latino/a communities that are virtually unknown south of the 49th parallel.

Latino/as in Canada? Aguirre's play might produce a feeling of vertigo among many North Americans, who associate a Latino/a presence with the southern rather than the northern reaches of the continent.[3] However, ¿Que Pasa? gives voice to a small but growing population of Latino/as residing north of the U.S.-Canadian border. Despite their numbers, it is worth paying attention to the cultural representations they have generated because they are harbingers of demographic shifts that promise to make Latino/as an increasingly significant part of the Canadian nation and, as such, they offer fresh perspectives on the North American continent that is the subject of this book. They are indicative of new connections between Canada and Latin America that destabilize the United States from its position as the mediator of continental relations and as the desired endpoint of all Latino/a migration. And they provide yet another reason for including Canada in any account of the history and culture of the American hemisphere. As we have seen in preceding chapters, Canada's fate is tied to the United States, Mexico, and its southern neighbors not only by an accident of geography but by parallel histories of European colonialism, the conquest of indigenous peoples, nation-building, and struggles over slavery and freedom. In the present, Canada shares Latin American concerns with the potentially detrimental effects of free trade, the regional impact of globalization, and the ubiquity of U.S. culture industries. But like the United States, it has become a major destination for immigrants because of its political stability and promise of economic opportunity. As Latino/a Canadians develop the opportunities and resources to represent their experiences, they draw attention to the circumstances that are shrinking historic divisions between Canada and the rest of the Americas.

One of the most articulate voices to reflect on Canada's place in the Americas is that of the author, performer, and director Guillermo Verdecchia. Born in Argentina, Verdecchia was a young boy when his family immigrated to Canada in an effort to escape political corruption and economic uncertainty. Having left their home in the late 1960s, they managed to avoid the "dirty war" carried out under the military dictatorship of Jorge Rafael Videla.[4] They settled in Kitchener, Ontario, where, as he describes it, "there was nothing to do but eat doughnuts and dream of elsewhere."[5] As a classically trained actor who needed to earn a living, Verdecchia found himself cast into stereotypically "Latino" roles. As an author, he had greater freedom to criticize the homogeneity of the Canadian mainstream, challenging his readers/viewers to think about difference in more complicated ways. In the 1990s, Verdecchia wrote the play *Fronteras Americanas/American Borders* (1993) and short story collection *Citizen Suarez* (1997), two works that are at once intensely personal and reflective of broader sociopolitical concerns of their moment, such as debates about continental integration surrounding the signing of Nafta and controversies over the quincentennial of the "discovery" of America. Positioning himself against conservatives like author Neil Bissoondath, Verdecchia used the experiences of Latino/a Canadians to explore the productive tensions arising from multiple cultural allegiances, as well as evolving relations between north and south that were changing Canada's place in the Americas.[6]

Whereas other chapters have looked comparatively at cultures of Canada, the United States, and Mexico, this chapter focuses on a single author whose work is, to my knowledge, unique in its efforts to claim the borderlands for Latino Canadian culture. The reading that follows takes its cue from the title *Fronteras Americanas*, which prompts us to read both the play and short story collection as centrally concerned with redefining the location and significance of the borders between north and south. By the 1990s, this emphasis on borderlands would be rather unsurprising in the work of a U.S. Latino/a author. However, Verdecchia situates his reflections in a decidedly Canadian context where borders have a very different resonance, and where allusions to Latino/a and Latin American cultures have very little resonance at all. Although his work is influenced by the art and politics of U.S. Chicano/as, he is wary of the tendency to conflate all Latino/a border cultures with the U.S.-Mexico borderlands, as well as the erasure of Canada from accounts of inter-American culture that focus exclusively on relations between the United States and Latin America. So too, he turns a critical eye on the Canadian mainstream for its distant and ill-informed posture toward Latin America.

The view of American borders offered by *Fronteras Americanas* and *Citizen Suarez* must be seen as a form of situated knowledge that emerges from Verdecchia's identity as a Latino Canadian who claims Canada as his long-time home. These works are interesting because they press their audiences toward a more capacious and varied view of the borderlands that enhances and challenges the perspectives offered by U.S.-Mexico border studies. The latter tends to condemn borders for restricting human mobility, perpetuating inequalities, and creating artificial divisions among people and environments. The Canadian vantage reminds us that borders can also be a means of protection and a guarantor of rights and services to those who reside within them. Whereas the United States' border with Mexico is associated with a history of violence and dispossession, there has been no armed conflict between the United States and Canada since the War of 1812. Instead, their shared border provides a model of peaceable coexistence designed to enable, rather than impede, the flow of goods and people from one side to the other. As we saw in chapter 2, crossing the U.S.-Canadian border was so important to escaping slaves that they equated Canada with the biblical Promised Land. In the twentieth century, many Canadians looked to their southern border as the last line of defense against the hegemony of U.S. culture and politics.[7] Many are proud of policies that distinguish Canada from the United States, such as government-funded health insurance, legalization of gay marriage, state-sanctioned multiculturalism, and absence of the death penalty. Their demands for more stringent border management are motivated by quite different political convictions than those articulated by the U.S. conservatives who advocate the erection of a massive fence along the border with Mexico. To be sure, Canada has its own strains of xenophobia, but the call to reinforce the border with the United States often has more to do with a desire to protect Canada's culture and political system from engulfment by its southern neighbor. Unlike the United States, Canada has only one border of any consequence, and the majority of its population lives within one hundred miles of it.[8] It has no border region comparable to the U.S. Southwest, with its distinctive culture and distance from centers of national power. Instead, Canada as a whole is often characterized as a "border society," a view maintained by Verdecchia himself. As Roger Gibbens explains of the Canadian border region, "the most important impact comes not from proximity of the international boundary itself, but from the more general proximity of the United States."[9] Thus, without romanticizing Canada as the antithesis to all that is wrong with the United States, we can still acknowledge that including it in a discussion of the continent—and the hemisphere—encourages us to think about the differences between American borderlands, and the relationships between nation and region that they engender.

This is one of the central insights of Verdecchia's *Fronteras Americanas* and *Citizen Suarez,* which experiment with a range of narrative and theatrical devices that seek to integrate Canada into a portrait of American borderlands. In what follows, I will argue that the play's open-ended, performative structure is better suited to reflecting on the meaning and consequences of Canada's borders with Latin America than is the short story collection. However, the limitations of *Citizen Suarez* are instructive since they can help us to better understand the possibilities and perils of translating a Chicano/a understanding of borderlands to other American locales. While the play effectively appropriates many of the political concerns of the U.S. Chicano/a borderlands into a Canadian context, where they resonate in fresh and surprising ways, the stories provide a narrower range of viewpoints that threaten to evacuate the questions raised by *Fronteras Americanas* of political content, turning them instead into problems of individual psychology. Read as a pair, however, the two works constitute a powerful and distinctive commentary on the changing place of Canada within a greater American hemisphere. As the subjects of this book's final chapter, they also point the way toward an expanding geographical frame that looks outward to connect particular North American places to the Americas and the world.

Latino/a Canadian Diasporas

Citizen Suarez and *Fronteras Americanas* are about a Latino/a population in Canada that has largely gone unnoticed in the United States, which has been preoccupied with its own struggles over immigration. This oversight is not surprising, given that Latino/as constitute a far larger and more significant demographic presence north of the Canadian border. Whereas there are some 35 million Latino/as in the United States, comprising 12.5 percent of the total population,[10] there are only 500,000 to 800,000 in all of Canada.[11] And whereas Mexican Americans have occupied the southwestern borderlands region since before it belonged to the United States, the majority of Latino/as in Canada arrived during the second half of the twentieth century. In the decades following World War II, Canada, which was seeking to augment its labor force, proved a more welcoming destination than the United States, which turned away many Latin American political refugees because of their suspected communist leanings.[12] Their numbers began to increase as political dissidents fled the Cuban Revolution in 1953, then the military dictatorships that rose to power in the 1970s and 1980s in Brazil, Uruguay, Chile, and Argentina. In the 1980s, civil wars in Nicaragua, Guatemala, and El Salvador drove Central American migrants north in search of refuge and economic opportunity. They were subsequently joined by growing numbers of Mexicans, discouraged by the United States' hostility toward immigrants under the presidency of George W. Bush.[13] Since the signing of Nafta, the establishment of commercial relations between Canada and Mexico has brought more educated, white-collar Latinos north. Today, the largest Spanish-speaking population lives in Quebec, where some express their affinity for the new immigrant group by calling themselves "Latinos du Nord."[14] There are also sizeable Latino/a communities in Vancouver, Toronto, Ottawa, Edmonton, and Winnipeg.[15]

Among the migrants from Latin America are significant numbers of authors, artists, and intellectuals. Until recently, many maintained the stance of political exiles who continued to identify with their place of origin, seeing their residence in Canada as a necessity rather than a choice.[16] They wrote of the violence and repression in their home countries, nostalgia for the people and places they had left behind, and the difficulties of adjustment to a new environment. Others turned to forms of modernist experimentation that were devoid of all references to the immediate social or political context. They tended to write in Spanish and to publish with Spanish or Latin American presses, which limited the audiences who read and responded to their work.

Only more recently has there been an attempt among Latino/a Canadians to move away from the experience of exile and toward cultural forms that express a hyphenated Canadian identity. As Alberto Gomez explains of a young generation of Latino/a artists,

> Often the sons and daughters of political refugees fleeing dictatorships in the southern cone, bitter wars in Central America, or economic impoverishment, they did not choose to settle here. Yet their formation of language and identity is also shaped by experiences of growing up in Canada. Caught between history and place, memories of political conflict clash with the pull of consumer culture. Living between languages and dreams, they sense they are "aliens" in the society in which they exist and from which they come. In Latin America they are identified as "different" for the way they speak Spanish and for their North American acculturation; in Canada, they are immigrants, newcomers, hyphenated citizens.[17]

Unable to identify completely either with Canada or particular Latin American homelands, this second generation seeks modes of belonging that are not tied to the nation-state. Verdecchia observes that it is only in the context of Canada that diverse Latin American constituencies—individuals who once fiercely identified as Mexican, Peruvian, Argentinean, Guatemalan, Venezuelan, and the like—become Latino/as, casting aside their prejudices against one another in order to build communities and political coalitions.[18] Declaring themselves members of *la raza*, the Canadian migrants recognize connections to Latino/as from many different parts of the American hemisphere. At the same time that they are determined to stay in Canada, they challenge the myth of the nation as a harmonious, multicultural mosaic by speaking out about their encounters with injustice and racial prejudice. Poet Janet Romero articulates these tensions in "Canadá," a title that announces the Latino/a presence that is transforming the nation from within. The verses express greater ambivalence as they catalogue the opportunities offered by the new land:

Its how we spoke about it, Canadá, tierra de oportunidad
      land of opportunity
           oportunidades
    muchas, muchas oportunidades
      come the opportunity at ridicule[19]

Verdecchia announces himself as a part of this divided sensibility when he proclaims at the end of *Fronteras Americanas*: "I am a hyphenated person but I am not falling apart, I am putting together. I am building a house on the border" (78). With this statement, he declares his intention to make a home where he is, rejecting both the exile's longing for an unattainable point of origin and the traveler's belief that constant movement can solve his problems. Although Verdecchia is not affiliated with any particular Latino/a community, the politics and aesthetics of his work are indebted, at least in part, to U.S. Latino/a art and criticism. As he recalls, the discovery of Teatro Campesino, the performance art of Guillermo Gomez-Peña, the poetry of Juan Felipe Herrera, and the scholarship of Juan Flores and George Yúdice was "a revelation."[20] He felt that these authors and artists "gave him permission" to express his lifelong sensation of being an "imposter, an alien" within Canadian society, but also to insist on his right to claim Canada as his adopted home.[21] Such sentiments are thematized in *Citizen Suarez* and *Fronteras Americanas*, the works that are most evocative of Verdecchia's own biography. From a variety of different perspectives, they draw on his boyhood experiences as an Argentinean immigrant, and his subsequent efforts to build a career as a well-respected member of Toronto's theatrical and literary communities. At the same time, they also reflect on broader questions about Canada's changing role in the Americas at a moment of intensified concern about the integration of the continent and the hemisphere. In their choice of genre, both works manifest a commitment to the representation of collective experience. *Fronteras Americanas* is a play that gives voice to two characters from distinct economic and social backgrounds who suggest the diversity of Latino/a Canadian populations. *Citizen Suarez* uses the short story form to portray many different geographic locations and points of view. In these works, Verdecchia thus provides multiple examples of the contemporary phenomena that tie Latin America and Canada together, painting a revised portrait of the American hemisphere in which Canada plays an integral part.

Fronteras Americanas: A Continental View of the Borderlands

Written in 1991–92 and first performed in 1993, Guillermo Verdecchia's one-person play *Fronteras Americanas/American Borders* coincided with the controversial quincentennial of Columbus's arrival in the Americas and the signing of Nafta. Both events underscored Canada's interconnection to the continent and the hemisphere. Whether the quincentennial was seen as a cause for celebration or a commemoration of the brutalities of conquest, it represented a history of indigenous dispossession and European settlement in the New World that Canada shared with its American neighbors. Two years later, Nafta looked like the first step toward a more integrated continental community. Canada's decision to participate represented a significant shift in its foreign policy, which recognized deep and enduring ties to the United States, but had traditionally ignored the rest of the hemisphere. Nafta ushered in a new era of economic interrelation, creating an unprecedented bond between Canada and Mexico and opening the way for subsequent accords that might include Central and Latin America. *Fronteras Americanas* provides a Canadian perspective on the human consequences of this regional integration. More specifically, it reflects on how Canadian understandings of home and nation are being transformed by a greater awareness of belonging to an inter-American community.

The primary audience of Verdecchia's play is Canadian, and it has been performed predominantly in Canadian venues before the middle-class, white constituencies that make up the majority of Canada's Anglophone theatergoing audiences. Although it resonates with the work of U.S. Latino/a authors and performance artists, Verdecchia claims his primary influences came from Brechtian modernism, and the Toronto alternative theater scene of which he was a part. He cites the edgy, experimental plays of Daniel Brooks, Daniel MacIvor, John Mighton, Ken Garnhum, Djanet Sears, and Monica Mojica as his most explicit sources of inspiration.[22] Verdecchia explains that the play was conceived in part as a personal endeavor to understand his own feelings of alienation as a "hyphenated Canadian" and in part as a challenge to a theatrical world that did not reflect the diversity of Toronto's population on stage.[23]

From the beginning, *Fronteras Americanas* insistently challenges prevailing understandings of Canadianness by insisting on Canada's necessary entanglements with a greater American hemisphere. At one point in the play, a slide projected onto the stage quotes Carlos Fuentes: "Every North American, before this century is over, will find that he or she has a personal frontier with Latin America" (54). In the context of Verdecchia's play,

Fuentes's pronouncement suggests that "American borders" can no longer be understood to refer exclusively to the particular corridor dividing the United States from Mexico, since the entire continent has become a contact zone where Anglo and Latin America meet up, clash, and interpenetrate. This point is emphasized in the published version, where a footnote explains that Fuentes made this statement while delivering the prestigious Canadian Massey lectures sponsored by the University of Toronto. The fact that Fuentes would receive this honor is evidence of newfound ties between Canada and Mexico. "This 1984 Massey Lecture elegantly explores, in great detail, the divisions expressed by the Mexico–North America border," it reads. "Although Fuentes focuses almost exclusively on the U.S., his analysis and insights provide a useful perspective for Canadians" (79). Fuentes's perspective is useful because it draws Canadians' attention to the U.S.-Mexico borderlands, a region that should be of vital interest as the nation confronts a new population of Latino/a immigrants.

In *Fronteras Americanas*, Fuentes's expanded sense of American borders is reiterated by a character named Verdecchia, who explains to the audience, "when I say AMERICA I don't mean the country, I mean the continent. Somos todos Americanos. We are all Americans" (20). His assertion echoes Latin American thinkers from Simón Bolívar to José Martí, who argued for the importance of regional solidarity under the banner of a collective American identity. Looking back to older models of hemispheric community, Verdecchia envisions America as a single continent. But what makes his perspective new is that he speaks as a Latin American in Canada; his reference to the continent positions Canadian themes and settings within a broader American framework. Indeed, despite gestures toward the legacy of pan-Americanism, Verdecchia describes *Fronteras Americanas* as "an intensely Canadian play."[24] The importance of his Canadian context is made visible in the film version, *Crucero/Crossroads*, in which a Canadian flag hangs prominently in the background during an early scene. It is further emphasized in the play when he delivers a monologue called "An Idiosyncratic History of America" that lists the War of 1812, the establishment of the Dominion of Canada in 1867, and the Montreal Canadiens' winning the Stanley Cup for hockey in 1969 alongside a seemingly random series of watershed moments in U.S. and Latin American history, such as the building of the pyramid at Teotihuacan, Columbus's arrival in America, the U.S.-Mexican War of 1846, and the election of Richard Nixon to the U.S. presidency (29–32). The overall effect of this catalogue is to carve out a role for Canada in historical narratives that have traditionally focused on other parts of the Americas.

As these examples suggest, *Fronteras Americanas* is less a narrative than a performative collage of voices and "found objects" such as quotations, video and film clips, and sounds and images lifted from other sources. What holds these disparate materials together are monologues delivered by a character named Verdecchia and his more edgy, streetwise alter ego, the Latino Facundo Morales Segundo, who goes by the ironically adopted Canadian name Wideload McKenna. The anxiety-ridden, middle-class Verdecchia is at once an autobiographical figure and a fictional character who confuses the line between presentation and representation. Early in the play, he laments that he feels lost, although he can locate himself quite specifically "in Toronto, at 30 Bridgman Avenue" (20). As the play continues, he delivers a series of confessional speeches that describe his family's departure from Argentina, childhood encounters with cultural intolerance in Kitchener, Ontario, and his eventual return to the place of his birth. "I Am Going Home—all will be resolved, dissolved, revealed" (36), he tells himself as he plans to visit Argentina for the first time as an adult. But Verdecchia undermines his own assertion, giving the spectator reason to believe his quest will be unsuccessful, since he discloses that his knowledge of "home" has come largely through travel guides, Spanish classes, friends, and three viewings of the film *Missing*.

It is not surprising, then, that Verdecchia's fantasy of homecoming is shattered, proving that his goal of recovering an authentic point of origin is an impossibility. In Buenos Aires, his foreignness is manifest in a bout of food poisoning. His vomiting is a literal symptom of his inability to digest Argentinean culture, regardless of how fervently he believes that it should be familiar and palatable. Recounting the feverish haze of sickness, he says, "I throw up in the bidet and I just want to go home—but I'm already there—aren't I?" (50). His confusion reaches its climax at this point of bodily vulnerability, which instantiates his discovery that he feels no greater sense of belonging in Argentina than he does in Canada. The experience of childhood dislocation, followed by many years of identification with a lost homeland, has left him in a state of uncomfortable liminality. When he announces, "All sides of the border have claimed and rejected me" (51), he suggests that the border is less a specific location than a powerful figure for those who understand themselves as belonging to more than one culture, and thus unable to feel at home in any one geographical place.

Through a series of fragmented monologues, *Fronteras Americanas* charts Verdecchia's evolution (with the help of his therapist and a visit to a "Border Brujo") from a position of loss and alienation to recognition of the productive tensions arising from multiple allegiances. "This is where I work," he tells himself upon his return to Canada, "this is where I make the most sense, in this Noah's ark of a nation" (74). The metaphor of the ark suggests that Canada is a place where diverse peoples must coexist to ensure their mutual survival. The ark is also a temporary home, one that is always in motion. In this, it is an apt figure for the widespread dislocation of things and people at the end of the twentieth century. "I am learning to live the border," Verdecchia intones at the play's end, "I have called off the Border Patrol. I am a hyphenated person but I am not falling apart, I am putting together. I am building a house on the border." He then turns to the audience with a direct challenge: "And you? Did you change your name somewhere along the way? Does a part of you live hundreds or thousands of kilometres away? Do you have two countries, two memories? Do you have a border zone?" (78). Verdecchia's confessional narrative ends when he ruptures the divide between performer and spectator, his questions implicating the viewer by suggesting that living on a "border zone" of some kind has become a virtually universal American condition.

To understand what is happening when Verdecchia breaks through the fourth wall, it is useful to follow Diana Taylor's distinction between the archive and the repertoire. She describes the archive as a storehouse where documents and other types of material evidence are preserved for posterity. In contrast to the stasis of the archive is the repertoire, a source of living, "embodied memory," such as "performances, gestures, orality, movement, dance, singing," forms of expression that are considered to be "ephemeral, nonreproducible knowledge."[25] According to Taylor, in the Americas, repertoires have served as a repository of counternarratives for those left on the margins of official histories of conquest and nation-building. Describing such inter-American repertoires as Spanish *pastorelas* (shepherds' plays) and mock battles between *moros y cristianos*, Taylor argues that "the repertoire allows for an alternative perspective on historical processes of transnational contact and invites a remapping of the Americas, this time following the traditions of embodied practice."[26] Whereas the archive aspires to preserve its contents intact, the repertoire can change in response to different historical contexts and geographic locations.

Fronteras Americanas foregrounds these forms of embodied knowledge when it becomes a collaboration between actor and spectators, who together must continually reenact the discovery of borders named by its title. For Verdecchia, performance is a vital medium because it allows the actor to connect directly with his audience and because it can evolve over time, in response to current events and changes in venue and audience. As he explains in the preface, "*Fronteras Americanas* is part of a process, part of a much larger attempt to understand and invent. As such, it is provisional, atado con alambre [strung together with wire]. In performance, changes were made nightly depending on my mood, the public, our location, the arrangement of the planets" (13).[27] Relinquishing control over the production of his work, Verdecchia writes, "I hope that anyone choosing to perform this text will consider the possibilities of making (respectful) changes and leaving room for personal and more current responses" (13). Framing the play in such terms ensures that it will function as a repertoire of collective experience that exists in dynamic relation to the context of its performance.

Fronteras Americanas is not simply a collaboration between Verdecchia the character and the audience, since the play itself consists of two voices whose monologues eventually merge into one. The second character is the much rougher, more confrontational Wideload, who at various points calls himself a "Chicano," while also admitting, "I wasn't born in East L.A. I wasn't born in de Southwest U.S.A. I wasn't even born in Méjico" (26). Both parts are played by the same actor, a device that gestures to a *latinidad* that transcends class and national borders. This decision is significant for Verdecchia, an actor whose elite training has allowed him to escape the kind of ethnic typecasting he encountered during his early career.[28] Instead of passing as part of the cultural mainstream, Verdecchia outs himself through his identification with an unmistakably Latino character, as if to suggest that acknowledgment of one virtually requires recognition of the other. While Wideload might strike some as a mere compendium of offensive racial clichés, Verdecchia's deployment of stereotypes is strategic. He describes Wideload as a self-conscious composite of the many bad Latino parts he had auditioned for over the years, with an admiring nod to the performative politics of Luis Valdez's *Zoot Suit* and Teatro Campesino.[29] In the film version, Wideload's performance and garb are styled after the Mexican American Pachuco, a type that would be familiar to many U.S. spectators, but far less so to the Canadians Verdecchia imagined as his primary audience. But however veiled it might remain, the insertion of Chicanismo into the play is a meaningful symbolic gesture. According to Michelle Habell-Pallán, Chicano/a popular culture has been appropriated by a new generation of Latino/a Canadians, who have seized on its association with militant oppositionality to articulate an ethnic identity that resists the cozy version of cultural pluralism promulgated by the state.[30] In the Canadian context, Chicano is a referent that floats free from its attachment to the highly specific geographic locales mentioned by Wideload, becoming instead a signifier for a proud and defiant Latino/a ethnic nationalism. If

Verdecchia represents the internal conflicts of the assimilated middle-class Latino Canadian, Wideload is his unruly, irrepressible double and the two cannot be disentangled.

Although his dialect is clichéd, Wideload's speeches challenge Anglo stereotypes about Latino/as by claiming aggressively that south of the border "dere's no pinche Taco Bell for thousands of miles" (22), critiquing representations of Latino/as in Anglo-American popular culture, and debunking propaganda surrounding the War on Drugs. While many aspects of this character are familiar, what makes the Latino Wideload remarkable is that he resides in Canada and that Canadian culture is central to his subjectivity as an occupant of the borderlands. When he says that he lives "in the border," he explains "for you people from outa town" that he is referring to "Queen and Lansdowne," an ethnically and economically mixed Toronto neighborhood. He challenges spectators to confront their own entrenched racial assumptions, but also offers himself as a guide who can lead them through the demographic and cultural changes of an integrating America. His character is thus a testament to Latino/as' growing geographic dispersal, as well as the diversity of Latino/as to be found Canada. Latino/as can no longer be described by reference to a single region of origin or arrival, since they have come to inhabit many different parts of the American continent. In doing so, they have expanded the perimeters of the borderlands and its varied cultures.

Absent Verdecchia's voice, Wideload would be little more than an ethnic stereotype, undermining his own critiques by confirming the audience's preconceptions about the Otherness of Latino/a immigrants. However, issuing from the mouth of the same actor, the voices of Wideload and Verdecchia attest to the diversity and complexity of Latino/a experiences in Canada. As the play continues, the differences between their characters become less pronounced until they deliver the final speech in one voice. It is also crucial that, throughout the play, the two personas speak directly to the audience, modulating the tone and substance of their performances in accordance with the responses they elicit on any given night. The spectators of *Fronteras Americanas*—which was often performed with the house lights partially illuminated—could not sit passively as if unaffected by the dramas unfolding onstage. Instead they had to recognize that they too are implicated in the events that brought Verdecchia/Wideload before them. In this, *Fronteras Americanas* moves beyond the representation of Verdecchia's own experiences, or even the particular experiences of Latino/a Canadians, to become an exploration of Canada's changing place on the American continent. In *Citizen Suarez*, Verdecchia would experiment with a new genre, attempting to broaden his portrayal of inter-American filiation with stories told from a variety of perspectives and set in many different geographical locations.

"Have we crossed a border?": The Many Americas of *Citizen Suarez*

Published four years after *Fronteras Americanas*, Verdecchia's short story collection *Citizen Suarez* picks up where the play left off, continuing its exploration of the political conditions that induced Latin Americans to relocate to Canada, the difficulties of adjustment to alien environments, the troubling stereotypes of Latino/as that exist in Canadian culture, and, ultimately, the rich forms of artistic and political expression that can arise out of the migrant's hyphenated sensibility. Seizing on the play's central theme, *Citizen Suarez* exports "the borderlands" from its expected location along the U.S.-Mexico border to multiple settings in Canada, the United States, and Latin America. Like *Fronteras Americanas*, this collection does not treat borderlands as a specific region, but as a name for the many places where multiple cultures encounter, fuse, and clash with one another. Some stories deal with the literal crossing of national borders: the difficult adjustments of the eponymous Suarez family after moving to Canada from an unspecified Latin American country, a troubled Canadian traveling through northwest Argentina, a Mexican Canadian en route to his father's birthplace in Morelos. Others evince the more diffuse effects of human and cultural migration throughout the hemisphere with descriptions of a store selling Peruvian goods in downtown Toronto; Spanish-language TV playing in Anglo-American homes; and a Latin American general who uses torture techniques learned at the U.S. sponsored School of the Americas. In a paradigmatic scene from the story "Letter from Tucuman," the unnamed protagonist writes:

> The bus stops. In the middle of nothing. We are all asked to get out and proceed to the little shack off the side of the road. Have we crossed a border? Not that I know of. . . . But here are a bunch of soldiers looking very bored in rumpled uniforms checking our passports and chain smoking cigarettes. No explanation is offered. Nothing exciting happens; no questions are asked. We all troop back onto the bus. (78)

This passage identifies the protagonist as a traveler who observes, but remains untouched by, the potentially "exciting" disruptions endured by those living under an oppressive military regime. Although the soldiers seem ineffectual, their very presence attests to the militarization of many American borders, as well as the political repression that has prompted Latin Americans to emigrate since the 1950s. At the same time, the question raised in this scene might serve as an allegory for a collection that understands American borders as something far more dispersed and inchoate than the literal boundary lines between neighboring nations. So pervasive is the contemporary experience of actual and figurative border crossing, the protagonist's confusion suggests, that it has become quite unremarkable. "Have we crossed a border?" could thus serve as a refrain for virtually every story in the collection.

Whereas *Fronteras Americanas* is marked by the varied influences of Brechtian drama, alternative Canadian theater, and U.S. Latino/a literature and performance art, *Citizen Suarez* is even more stylistically varied, its approach changing from one story to another as if searching for a mode capable of representing the experiences of characters in a wide variety of situations and places. Some stories evoke the themes and style of Alice Munro, who perfected the depiction of seething undercurrents running beneath the deceptive quiet of small-town Canadian life. But many others insert elements of magical realism, touches of the absurd, and a tendency toward metaphysical speculation that is clearly derived from Latin American literary tradition. These sources are allegorized in "The Dream of the Library," in which an Argentinean Canadian vacationing in Buenos Aires encounters the ghost of Jorge Luis Borges in the *Biblioteca Nacional*. There, they engage in conversation about the capital city and the protagonist's search for a book he recalls from childhood. The story appears to establish a neat, if unsurprising, account of literary influence in which the most renowned of all Argentinean authors imparts his wisdom to a Canadian successor. However, despite the most obvious clues, the protagonist never guesses the identity of his august interlocutor. In this sense, "The Dream" is less a predictable fantasy of literary transmission, than an ironic parable about its failure since the Canadian seems unable to recognize the fact that he has literally collided with a literary heritage resulting from Canada's newfound ties to Latin America. In its sometimes comic, double-edged, or understated appropriation of Anglo and Latin American themes and styles, *Citizen Suarez* thus can be read as an attempt to portray the cultural fusion arising from Canada's emerging links to the American hemisphere.

In *Citizen Suarez*, Latin America is not only a source of nostalgia and literary inspiration or an appealing travel destination, it is also a place torn by political crises and economic instability that make permanent residence there untenable. With the exception of two stories set in Argentina, references to Latin America are vague, as if the problems depicted in individual stories could occur in any number of places. For example, the collection opens with a dark satire about the unwitting martyrdom of a university student named Oscar. His problems begin when he wears a necktie that violates the code of mourning imposed by the state after the death of "La Señora," a thinly fictionalized Eva Peron. The breech of sartorial protocol that begins as a joke is soon taken up by various opposition groups, setting off widespread rebellion and prompting harsh retaliatory measures by the ruling military regime. In the end, Oscar is tortured and shot, and "his body, along with several others, was heaved into a pit in a garbage dump" (22), the offending tie blown away by the wind. The story of Oscar's ridiculous and ultimately tragic predicament reveals the routine and arbitrary violence of a dictatorship unable to tolerate the slightest gesture of dissent. The brutality and repression of an unnamed Latin American country are similarly depicted in a story called "Winter Comes to the Edge of the World," narrated through the flashbacks of a political dissident who has sought refuge in Canada. There, she thinks obsessively of her disappeared comrades, detention camps, and "Falcons cruising the street" (122). Her miscarriage of a pregnancy resulting from her affair with Julio, one of her comrades, is a metaphor for the impossibility of life-affirming consequences emerging from such a bleak environment. In the title story, "The Several Lives of Citizen Suarez," a math professor named Octavio Suarez leaves his homeland to escape a climate of censorship and anti-intellectualism. The collection ends with a story that is harshly critical of the elite citizens of a fictional Latin American nation named Ixturria. Living in gated compounds where they are surrounded by imported luxuries, the characters are oblivious of the class warfare and political turmoil taking place around them. After a friend affiliated with the political resistance is murdered, the protagonist completes his retreat from reality by marrying a member of his close-knit social circle. These stories provide a rationale for the Latino/a Canadian diaspora by showing the untenability of return, regardless of the difficulties of life in the new country. They also lend an ironic cast to the nostalgia some characters express toward a lost Latin American homeland, echoing Verdecchia's discovery in *Fronteras Americanas* that recovery of origins is an impossible fantasy.

Despite the fact that Canada offers a refuge from the crises plaguing many Latin American countries, it is hardly a panacea in these stories. The characters in *Citizen Suarez* face many of the same dilemmas of alienation and cultural intolerance articulated in *Fronteras Americanas*. In his 1991 performance, *The Noam Chomsky Lectures* (co-written and performed with Daniel Brooks), Verdecchia elaborates the contradictions between Canada's reputation as a nation of peacekeepers and its implication in violence and injustice around the globe. As he puts it, "the real Canadian traditions are quiet complicity and hypocritical moral posturing. This nation of quiet diplomats, of peacekeepers, is in fact a nation of quiet profiteers, a nation that has enriched itself on the misery and destruction of millions of lives all over the globe."[31] While this point is never made so directly in *Citizen Suarez*, it seems to lie behind the portrayal of Canadian culture in many stories. In "Citizen Suarez," the prosperous Toronto suburbs are banal and colorless. The protagonist of "Winter Comes" appreciates that Canada shelters her from political repression, but also feels that she is "exiled to the edge of the world" in an "empty white and grey place" (123). Here, the rather clichéd reference to Canada's coldness and whiteness takes on added resonance when it is used to describe racial intolerance, as well as the weather. The story "Money in the Bank" further develops the portrait of Canadian racial insensitivity in its depiction of a Latino actor's struggle for professional legitimacy. On the set of a TV movie-of-the-week, the makeup artist paints his face brown, prompting him to reflect incredulously, "I have nothing against brown but if they wanted brown they could have hired a brown actor, no? I ask Make-up why she's going so dark with the base and she says 'You're the Cook aren't you? The Latino Cook?'" (87). Her questions equate Latinidad with dark skin and manual labor, underscoring the racial biases that persist despite Canada's official commitment to preserving ethnic diversity. The protagonist finds himself caught in a vicious cycle: although he is trained to be a serious actor, his livelihood relies on broadcast television, where the one-dimensional roles he is forced to play will be seen by thousands of Canadian viewers, thereby reinforcing the stereotypes that limit his acting opportunities. "Money in the Bank" thus takes us beyond the new immigrant's feelings of isolation and exclusion to depict the more abiding prejudices faced by non-Anglo Canadians.

These dilemmas are crystallized in the struggles of Fernando Suarez, the ambivalent "citizen" of the title story, who seeks to remain on the border, uncomfortably straddling multiple cultures in the face of his parents' determination to assimilate by becoming Canadian citizens. The teenaged Fernando resists claiming membership in any one national community, attempting to preserve the parts of his identity—and the special forms of knowledge—that have come through the transformative experience of moving from one culture to another. When his parents inform him that the entire family will become citizens, he fears he will lose "his position as a foreigner and his knowledge of the double or perhaps multiple lives he lived [which] was for him a recondite and marvelous wound" (46). Unable to stop them from completing the process, he feels a deep sense of loss at the possibilities he has given up. Fernando is representative of many characters in Verdecchia's fiction who affirm the perspective that comes from being "a hyphenated person." At the same time, his story underscores the fact that such ambivalence can only be appreciated from the relative safety and comfort of Canada, where one does not have to worry about being beaten, shot, or imprisoned for failing to conform.

In its multiple portraits of the encounter between Anglo and Latin America, *Citizen Suarez* illustrates the portability of the borderlands concept that has become an organizing paradigm for much recent work in American, Canadian, and Mexican studies. The notion of borders as places where disparate cultures clash, converge, and produce hybrid forms of expression is a suggestive model for understanding contact zones of many kinds. The state of mind famously described by Gloria Anzaldúa in *Borderlands/La Frontera*, which comes from bearing "the emotional residue of an unnatural boundary," might characterize any number of liminal situations, as she suggests by linking the struggles of U.S.-Mexico border dwellers with those of women, people of color, and queers.[32] But it also raises the kinds of questions that have troubled some Chicano/a critics, who ask whether something gets lost when a specific locale—and the populations, history, and culture associated with it—is translated into a more general figure for cultural and geographical crossings of all kinds.[33] For Chicano/as, the borderlands refers specifically to the "third country" along the two-thousand-mile border between the United States and Mexico. Border culture emerged out of the rich fusion of the many different ethnic and national groups that passed through and settled in an area where daily life was influenced by conflicts over land, repressive immigration policies, the exploitation of migrant workers, and racial intolerance. The Chicano/a movement born in the region during the 1960s was decidedly working class in orientation, although students and middle-class Mexican Americans would also be important participants. It arose out of political struggles to improve the working conditions of Mexican agricultural laborers, to redress the claims of landowners who had been progressively stripped of their property, and to create a sense of solidarity and ethnic pride among Mexican Americans.[34] The Chicano/a art and literature that emerged from this environment often seeks to give voice to populations that have been denied representation, telling the stories of colonization of land, perilous border crossings, and constant fear of *la migra*.

It is true that many of the stories in *Citizen Suarez* are also about an underrepresented population—Latin Americans in Canada; however, the collection tends to focus on well-educated, middle-class migrants and travelers, meaning that the struggles of the most marginalized border-crossers are muted. Verdecchia's characters move across national boundaries with relative ease. The friction they experience comes more from the psychological effects of cultural dislocation than from encounters with the law, dire poverty, or intolerable working conditions. Fernando Suarez, who agonizes about the loss of self that might come with the assumption of Canadian citizenship is a case in point. The challenge he faces is not the possibility of arrest or deportation, but his own indecision. Verdeccia's fiction is about the more privileged group of Latin American migrants who travel by plane rather than crossing dangerous rivers and deserts by foot. They come to a place with relatively generous immigration policies, particularly toward those who are white and middle class, and who have the resources to arrange their arrival in advance. They must work for a living, but they are professors, actors, and writers, rather than manual laborers. Thus, they may feel the same emotional frisson that Anzaldúa describes, but they are spared the material suffering associated with so many U.S.-Mexico border crossings.

When issues of class friction arise in *Citizen Suarez*, they surface as unexpected eruptions, rather than being the center of narrative attention. For example, in "The Several Lives," Fernando remembers an encounter that took place before the move to Canada, when a lunch at a restaurant with his father was interrupted by a boy begging for food. Fernando "believed he was related to the boy in some way. . . . The boy was Fernando in some way, the boy Fernando might have become if they hadn't emigrated perhaps" (45). The confrontation might have taught Fernando an enduring lesson about inequality and the potential of empathy to reach others across class lines. But there is no evidence that Fernando's fantasy of identification is reciprocated, or that the meeting has any marked influence on the subsequent course of his life. Relocation to Canada frees him from the prospect of poverty and starvation, conditions that are relegated to the margins of a narrative filtered through the perceptions of more well educated, financially secure characters.

A similar glimpse across class lines occurs in "Letter from Tucuman," where the protagonist, a Canadian traveler, turns down his taxi driver's offer of a guided tour through the Argentinean city. Later he realizes that the driver needed the money to buy a birthday present for his daughter. Instead of doing anything to rectify the situation, he sinks into depression, "incapacitated, by all the sadness ever: the lonely dead no one ever mourned; the hundreds of thousands of lost souls, hurled into salty darkness in the bottom of a man-made lake or a cold stinking cell. I am sad for all those whose turn will never come, those who wait and wait and wait" (81). This is the melodramatic and self-indulgent sadness of a traveler who has enough of life's basic comforts that he can wallow in his own emotional pain without translating it into any meaningful effort to help others. "Letter from Tucuman" is representative of a more general pattern in *Citizen Suarez*, in which the kind of racial and economic tensions that arise on the U.S.-Mexico borderlands are marginalized in favor of more middle-class problems. Moments of narrative friction remind us that such inequities exist, but they are not the primary concern of any of these stories.

As someone accustomed to working in the collective medium of performance, Verdecchia is less successful at representing others through the more private, individualized mode of narrative fiction, in which—despite its geographic and situational diversity—all characters threaten to collapse into versions of the same middle-class subjectivity. Read alone, *Citizen Suarez* might thus have little to say to readers of Chicano/a literature, who expect representations of the borderlands to engage issues of social justice more directly. However, taken as part of Verdecchia's broader literary project, the collection contributes to an expansive and varied portrait of Latino/a diaspora in the Americas. The political problems it depicts, concerning life under violent and repressive military dictatorships, are somewhat different from those afflicting the U.S.-Mexico borderlands, but they are hardly inconsequential. In this, *Citizen Suarez* suggests that perhaps Canada, where diverse Latin American migrants come together as Latino/as, would be a promising location for finding common ground between disparate forms of political and cultural struggle arising at American borders. It echoes this conviction at the level of style and content, in its fusion of Anglo and Latin American sensibilities.

Of the works Verdecchia has produced over the course of his literary career, *Fronteras Americanas* and *Citizen Suarez* are the two that deal most directly with the author's experiences of border crossing and migration in the Americas. However, the themes they address—the causes and effects of an expanding Latino/a diaspora (particularly the role of the United States in enabling the rise of military dictatorships), the productive and uncomfortable consequences of cultural dislocation—and the critical perspectives they offer on Canada's changing place in the Americas and the world, persist through many of the plays he has written, directed, and performed. Verdecchia's 1997 play about the first Gulf War, *A Line in the Sand* (with Marcus Youssef), examines borders in a more global context through the story of a Canadian soldier and a Palestinian teenager who meet on a line in the Qatari desert.[35] Eight years later, his play (with Marcus Youssef and Camyar Chai), *The Adventures of Ali & Ali and the Axes of Evil: A Divertimento for Warlords*, satirized the political contradictions surrounding the War on Terror through the antics of the eponymous Ali Hakim and Ali Ababwa, refugees from the fictional Arab nation of Agraba. Although much of the performance is concerned with the United States' role in the Middle East, it is directed at Canadian audiences, who are incited to recognize Canada's complicity in enabling the war to continue. Together, these works depict Canada's increasing involvement in international affairs, suggesting that its status as a border nation is relevant not only to its relations with the United States but also with the larger global community. They imply that Canada's intensifying ties to Latin America are a paradigm for the perils and promise of full engagement with a global community.

Verdecchia is a fitting subject for the final chapter of a book devoted to tracing unexpected lines of contact across the North American continent and to unsettling predictable narratives about north and south. Not only does his work represent the increasing interconnections between Canada and Latin America, it also expands the southern reaches of the continent beyond Mexico's border with Guatemala. In doing so, it returns to an earlier vision—both troubling and hopeful—of an integrated American hemisphere. For pre–World War II generations, the notion of a unified America was tied to a belief in the continent's shared political commitments and cultural sensibilities, as well as in its isolation from the rest of the world. Without claiming such cohesion, Verdecchia nonetheless aspires to erode Canada's historic sense of distance from Latin America through the connective imagery of shared borders.

Verdecchia's comparative approach to the borderlands allows him to imagine the need for solidarities among Latino/a Canadians, U.S. Chicano/as, and other Latin Americans that might be less apparent in a place dominated by a larger and/or more singular Latino/a presence. As I have suggested, his deterritorialization of the borderlands may be attributed, at least in part, to his experience as a Latino living in Canada, rather than the United States, where the border with Mexico has become virtually synonymous with the very notion of borderlands. His work is an example of how Latino/a Canadian culture complicates the U.S.-centric view that "the border" refers exclusively to the place where the United States and Mexico meet. Drawing on the oppositional connotations of U.S.-Mexican border culture, it unmoors the borderlands from their particular location to show how the hemisphere itself has become a crucible for the complex intermixture of Anglo and Latin Americas. It does so without losing sight of the nation, which has the power to enable liberating forms of movement, to force the desperate flight of its citizens, and to constrict routes of freedom and economic opportunity. By introducing Canadian characters and settings, his work gives new coordinates for locating "El Norte," while at the same time disrupting the binary between north and south with a necessary third term.

The Nafta Superhighway and the Limits of North American Community

When Guillermo Verdecchia announced in his 1993 play, *Fronteras Americanas*, "when I say AMERICA I don't mean the country, I mean the continent. Somos todos Americanos. We are all Americans," he was deliberately trying to be provocative.[1] Addressing the relatively homogenous, middle-class audiences who attend the Canadian theater, he described the continent as a vast borderlands where nobody could avoid being touched by demographic shifts that were shrinking the globe and changing Canada's relation to the American hemisphere. Verdecchia intended to startle his spectators by revealing the Latinoization of Canada and asking them to imagine themselves as "Americanos," residents of a continent as well as a nation.[2] But when he made these pronouncements he could not have imagined how controversial the prospect of continental integration could become, how deeply resistant Canadians, U.S. Americans, and Mexicans would be to the prospect of understanding themselves as part of a unified North America.

The trouble began some ten years after the first performances of *Fronteras Americanas*, when rumors swept the Internet that the leaders of Canada, Mexico, and the United States were conspiring to implement a European-style North American Union. Their plans were unfolding behind closed doors, the story went, without public conversation or the mandate of their voting constituencies. At the heart of the controversy was a 2005 initiative called the Security and Prosperity Partnership (SPP), jointly authored by the governments of the three North American nations. By all accounts, the SPP is a mundane organization designed to facilitate dialogue about matters of security and commerce that would be of mutual concern to its participants. But conspiracy theorists saw it as the first step in an effort to engineer a continental union by stealth. Republican congressman Ron Paul of Texas described it as "an unholy alliance of foreign consortiums and officials from several governments," and conservative commentator Phyllis Schlafly wrote indignantly, "'We the people' of the United States were never asked if we want to be 'integrated' with Mexico and Canada, two countries of enormously different laws, culture, concepts of government's role, economic system, and standard of living."[3] A related area of concern focused on North America's SuperCorridor Coalition (NASCO), a nonprofit, trinational coalition of business and transportation agencies whose stated goal was to improve transportation infrastructure on the continent. When opponents of North American union saw a map posted on the organization's home page depicting the flow of North American commercial traffic, alarm bells went off. NASCO claimed that it was simply a representation of current realities, but anticontinentalists hotly disagreed, insisting that it was a blueprint for a "NAFTA superhighway" that would stretch from Winnipeg to Mexico City. The legend of the Nafta superhighway gathered steam, appearing in editorials and letters-to-the-editor of major newspapers, and on a segment of Lou Dobbs's *Moneyline*. By 2007, nineteen state legislatures had adopted resolutions opposed to plans for a trinational political entity.[4] More than a decade after the implementation of Nafta, many residents of North America (particularly the United States), it seemed, could not have been further from Guillermo Verdecchia's conclusion that "we are all Americans."

There is little evidence to support the charge that top-secret plans to construct a North American superhighway are underway, or that presidents Calderón, Bush, and Harper are quietly negotiating the formation of a North American Union that will obliterate the nation-state as we know it. Instead, these stories seem destined to join the ranks of such robust urban legends as the Kentucky Fried Rat, alligators in the New York City sewers, and Elvis sightings. It is easy to dismiss them as the rantings of deranged xenophobes, since some of the most vocal protests have emerged from Congressman Paul, the John Birch Society, and conservatives like Schlafly, and Jerome Corsi, coauthor of *Unfit for Command*, the book-length attack on presidential candidate John Kerry's service during the Vietnam War. When they come from these quarters, it is clear that objections to the Nafta superhighway are bound up with anti-Mexican sentiment. As one Mexican blogger wrote accusingly, "la superautopista del TLCAN parece ser un artificio electoral republicano para evidenciar y explotar uno de los grandes miedos estadounidenses: la inevitable cercanía con México y los mexicanos" [the Nafta superhighway seems like a Republican electoral artifice to demonstrate and exploit one of the great U.S. American fears: the inevitable proximity to Mexico and Mexicans].[5] As this author observes, in the United

States, antipathy toward the idea of a North American union often goes hand in hand with animosity toward one's Mexican neighbors.

While there is much truth to his allegation, opposition to the idea of continental integration is not limited to xenophobes and isolationists, nor is it the exclusive concern of U.S. residents. Protests have been voiced by trade unionists, environmentalists, members of the antiglobalization movement, the progressive Council of Canadians, and the leftist Mexican organization Centro de investigaciones económicas y políticas de acción comunitaria (CIEPAC). Their resistance has less to do with xenophobia than with fears that democratic government is being superseded by corporations, who are not subject to the dictates of the voting public or oversight by national regulatory agencies. Given how many North Americans of varied political persuasions have been captivated by the myth of the Nafta superhighway and the North American Union, their concerns are worth taking seriously, no matter how fictitious the actual initiatives for continental integration may be. At bottom, they point to the fact that the majority of ordinary North Americans identify as residents of nations and/or regions, not of continents, and that many like national borders just as they are. In their eyes, North America is the unwanted brainchild of politicians, economists, and transnational corporations bent on consolidating their power and financial well-being. Not only do they have no aspiration toward belonging to a continental union, they also actively oppose it. It seems that Canadians, U.S. Americans, and Mexicans are not prepared to become North Americans simply because they are told that it is economically advantageous to relax the trade barriers and political systems dividing the three nations.

This should not be surprising news. Over the course of this book, we have seen the tenacity of local and national differences exemplified time and again. For every author or artist who articulates a longing for borderless community or transnational solidarity, there is another who uses art or literature to redraw the boundaries that matter. The fugitive slaves who escaped into Canada and Mexico celebrated the borders that signaled their arrival on free soil. The national borders of the United States are essential to the imagined geography of slave narratives, which were written at a moment when the rhetoric of continentalism was, more often than not, employed by advocates of slavery seeking new territory to colonize. Whereas the most vocal opponents of the North American Union come from the United States, Mexicans and Canadians have a longer and more consistent tradition of concern about the erosion of cultural borders. In the twentieth century, the specificities of black Canadian and Mexican experience have frequently been eclipsed by African American culture and history—which is often taken to stand in for all black experience on the continent—or by those naysayers who deny the presence of blackness in Canada and Mexico altogether. Literature, visual arts, and performance have become repositories where the particularities of Afro-Mexican and Canadian cultures are preserved and recreated by younger generations seeking an Americanness that is not synonymous with the United States. The borders of nation and region were equally important to Canadians and Mexicans as the work and legend of Jack Kerouac acquired international currency. Beginning in the 1960s, authors in Canada and Mexico drew inspiration from Kerouac's legacy, while appropriating it to address the distinctive political and aesthetic concerns of their own local contexts. In this sense, their work is at once local and transnational, reflecting the possibilities and limits of the circulation of cultural influence. Similar ambitions motivate contemporary detective novelists from Canada and Mexico, who attempt to escape the shadow of their more well-known U.S. American counterparts by producing crime writing that remains true to its Canadian and Mexican settings but that also speaks to an international readership. In all of these cases, local and national particularity is marshaled as a defense against the prospect of cultural homogeneity that threatens to accompany the economic and/or political integration of the continent. Significantly, these expressions of anticontinentalism come from across the ideological spectrum, suggesting that the desire to protect or reinforce national borders does not belong exclusively to any one political position and that it is therefore all the more important to understand the motivations, as well as the content, of such proposals.

At the same time that it reveals a strong tradition of North American nationalism, *Continental Divides* has considered many examples of communities who live in defiance of national borders and have developed cultural traditions dedicated to imagining and sustaining cross-border society over many generations. The work of Thomas King and Leslie Marmon Silko pays homage to Indian ancestors whose lands and people were divided by the European conquest, and affirms the formation of transnational social and political networks in the present day. Similarly, novelist Rolando Hinojosa has devoted his literary career to depicting a transnational community that straddles the current U.S.-Mexico border, and has its origin in a time before the border existed. His fictional Valley is both a reflection of the realities he perceives in his south Texas home and a projection of an imagined social world tied together by binational networks of family and friends, shared customs, systems of local governance, and bilingual communication that persist despite the efforts of national governments to reinforce the border as a line of separation. Borders are a less literal presence in the short stories and plays of Guillermo Verdecchia, a fact that I have attributed to his location in Canada, far from an actual border with Latin America. His work is nonetheless deeply invested in depicting the virtues and necessities of border crossing. It simultaneously thematizes the experiences of Latino Canadians, and enacts them at the level of form by fusing Anglo, Latin American, and Chicano/a styles and sensibilities. In this way, he performatively enacts the erosion of borders resulting from the movement of people and things around the Americas and the world. In each of these cases, the border is a figure for conflicts between the needs and aspirations of particular groups, and the failures of, demands, and/or restrictions imposed by the nation-state.

The urge to erode borders and break down rigid nationalisms is not always prompted by economic need and political oppression. As we have seen, more voluntary forms of continentalism were embraced by the artists and writers who gathered in Mexico City during the 1920s in search of a revolutionary synthesis of culture and politics that was grounded in a distinctively American (but not necessarily national) sense of history and aesthetics. They were followed by the mobile Beat and countercultural generations of the 1950s and 1960s, who traveled in the hope of finding political and artistic inspiration through contact with a foreign Other. While in some instances, the activities of these travelers amount to little more than cultural tourism, in other cases artistic and political expression is genuinely enhanced by the ability to cross borders with an openness to the exchange of ideas and experiences, as well as a desire to recover traditions that existed long before the current borders were set in place. Yet the fact remains that among the many North American artists, authors, travelers, migrants, and refugees who affirm the value and necessity of border crossing, it would be difficult to argue that any envision an integrated continent where borders are eliminated altogether. Jack Kerouac's America might come closest, were it not for the fact that his creative inspiration relies so deeply on the presence of borders between self and Other, the familiar and the foreign. And even the most fervent calls for cross-border community are rooted in specific places rather than aspiring to a truly borderless continent.

North America has been fortunate not to have endured the devastating events that helped to turn the warring nations of Europe into a continent. The relative peacefulness of North America's three nations for nearly a hundred years has had the ironic effect of enhancing, rather than diminishing, their sense of difference from one another. In its most troublesome form, that sentiment leads to the kinds of racism and xenophobia that underlie demands for a wall along the U.S.-Mexico border or that see foreign terrorists seeping into the United States via Canada and Mexico. So too, the imbalance of power on the continent has long inspired more legitimate Canadian and Mexican fears that becoming North American would mean being absorbed by the orbit of U.S. politics and culture.

Indeed, the richness of North American culture—as it is represented in literature, visual arts, and film—comes largely from the failures of large-scale integration, deriving its energies instead from the very unsystematic mingling of diverse languages, traditions, environments, and political sensibilities in actual borderlands and other zones of contact. Perhaps the most hopeful lesson to emerge from the controversy over the Nafta superhighway is that it highlights a gap between the beliefs and actions of ordinary people and the economic trends that are often said to penetrate the deepest crevices of daily life, robbing citizens of agency and political voice. While nation-states and multinational corporations are seeking to better their position within the global economy by moving toward the formation of integrated regional blocs, there is no such movement toward homogeneity, standardization, or totalizing synthesis in the domain of North American culture.

As this book draws to a close, it cannot claim to have identified a set of distinctively North American cultural traditions or to have traced the decline of the nation-state and the increasing unification of the continent. Instead we are reminded of how different from one another Canadians, U.S. Americans, and Mexicans continue to be, as well as the tremendous internal variations within and across the borders of each of these three vast nations. In the realm of culture, at least, the prospect of an integrated North America seems an impossibility for the foreseeable future, although the continent is home to many smaller, functional cross-border communities. As I have argued, to equate the North America that is my subject with the North America of politicians, security experts, economists, or the naysayers of the Nafta superhighway is to miss the point. I have tried to advance a very different understanding of continents that does not simply reinforce prevailing configurations of economic and military power. Instead, the continent, as I have envisioned it over the proceeding chapters, is a heuristic frame designed to enable comparative perspectives and to bring into view alternative histories and cultural formations that might be obscured by an exclusive emphasis on the nation-state, or by too-close attention to any one region. These alternatives become apparent only by approaching North America as a shifting geographical assemblage with multiple vectors extending outward across the globe. From this perspective, it is possible to imagine infinite circuits of connection that are not, like the Nafta super-highway, based purely on the imperatives of commercial trade, but also on constant, multidirectional exchange of populations, ideas, and values. Without idealizing a nonexistent continental community, my goal has thus been to chart the lengthy and often unrecognized traditions of neighborly exchange, both hostile and amicable, that have left an imprint on North America's varied cultures.

NOTES

INTRODUCTION

1. Douglas Todd, "Cascadia: Naïve Dream or the Next Frontier?" *Vancouver Sun*, May 6, 2008, at http://www.canada.com/vancouversun/news/story.html?id=c325b778-869d -4bef-a2e2-03b1789c6049, accessed June 27, 2008.

2. Somewhat ironically, opponents of immigration have used similar maps of the imagined Chicano nation to project a dystopian future in which Mexicans reclaim the United States by stealth, at http://www.limitstogrowth.org/WEB-text/aztlan.html, accessed June 5, 2006.

3. Throughout this study, my analysis focuses both on individual works of literature, art, or other expressive forms, and on the broader culture that gives rise to them. I use *culture* in its core anthropological sense, to mean the social contexts and historical processes that make possible, shape, and are shaped by imaginative productions. The simplest definition of this sense of *culture* is articulated by Stephen Greenblatt, who described it as "a particular network of negotiations for the exchange of material goods, ideas, and . . . people" that at once constrains and enables the subjects who operate within it. See Stephen Greenblatt, "Culture," in *Critical Terms for Literary Study*, ed. Frank Lentricchia and Thomas McLaughlin (Chicago: University of Chicago Press, 1995), 229.

4. Benedict Anderson, *Imagined Communities: Reflections on the Origin and Spread of Nationalism* (London and New York: Verso, 1991).

5. Edmundo O'Gorman, *The Invention of America: An Inquiry into the Historical Nature of the New World and the Meaning of Its History* (Bloomington: Indiana University Press, 1961).

6. Martin Lewis and Kären E. Wigen, *The Myth of the Continents: A Critique of Metageography* (Berkeley: University of California Press, 1997), 10.

7. Lewis and Wigen, *The Myth of the Continents*, 25–26; Walter Mignolo, "Misunderstanding and Colonization: The Reconfiguration of Memory and Space," *South Atlantic Quarterly* 92, no. 2 (1993): 209–60; O'Gorman, *Invention of America*; Eviatar Zerubavel, *Terra Cognita: The Mental Discovery of America* (New Brunswick, NJ: Rutgers University Press, 1992), 5.

8. Aníbal Quijano and Immanuel Wallerstein, "Americanicity as a Concept, or the Americas in the Modern World-System," *International Social Science Journal* 44, no. 4 (1992): 549–57.

9. Arthur P. Whitaker, *The Western Hemisphere Idea: Its Rise and Decline* (Ithaca, NY: Cornell University Press, 1954), 1–21.

10. Alan K. Hendrikson, "The Power and Politics of Maps," in *Reordering the World: Geopolitical Perspectives on the Twenty-First Century* (Boulder, CO: Westview Press, 1999), 60.

11. Thomas Jefferson, "A Hemisphere to Itself," to Alexander von Humboldt, December 6, 1813, at http://odur.let.rug.nl/~usa/P/tj3/writings/brf/jef1224.htm, accessed June 26, 2007.

12. On the Monroe Doctrine, see Gretchen Murphy, *Hemispheric Imaginings: The Monroe Doctrine and Narratives of U.S. Empire* (Durham, NC: Duke University Press, 2005); Dexter Perkins, *A History of the Monroe Doctrine* (Boston: Little, Brown, 1963); Whitaker, *The Western Hemisphere Idea*, 97–100.

13. Anna Brickhouse, *Transamerican Literary Relations and the Nineteenth-Century Public Sphere* (Cambridge and New York: Cambridge University Press, 2004).

14. Franklin D. Roosevelt, "First Inaugural Address," March 4, 1933, at http://www.feri .org/common/news/details.cfm?QID=2067&clientid=11005, accessed July 9, 2007.

15. Hendrikson, "Power and Politics of Maps," 60; Murphy, *Hemispheric Imaginings*; Whitaker, *The Western Hemisphere Idea*.

16. Whitaker, *Western Hemisphere Idea*, 155.

17. Eugene Staley, "The Myth of the Continents," *Foreign Affairs* 19, no. 3 (1941): 482.

18. Staley, "Myth of the Continents," 494.

19. Ibid., 486.

20. Hendrikson, "Power and Politics of Maps," 60–61.

21. Whitaker, *Western Hemisphere Idea*, 154–77; David Ryan, *U.S. Foreign Policy in World History* (New York and London: Routledge, 2000), 149.

22. Murphy, *Hemispheric Imaginings*, 145–58.

23. Lewis and Wigen, *Myth of the Continents*, 162–69.

24. On American studies and area studies, see Paul A. Bové, "Can American Studies Be Area Studies?" in *Learning Places: The Afterlives of Area Studies*, ed. Masao Miyoshi and Harry Harootunian (Durham, NC: Duke University Press, 2002), 206–30.

25. Zerubavel, *Terra Cognita*, 42.

26. James D. Drake, "Appropriating a Continent: Geographical Categories, Scientific Metaphors, and the Construction of Nationalism in British North America and Mexico," *Journal of World History* 15, no. 3 (2004): 323–57.

27. C. G. Fenwick, "Canada and the Monroe Doctrine," *American Journal of International Law* 32, no. 4 (1938): 782–85; Whitaker, *Western Hemisphere Idea*, 150–53; and John Herd Thompson and Stephen J. Randall, *Canada and the United States: Ambivalent Allies* (Athens: University of Georgia Press, 2002), chaps. 5 and 6.

28. Maxwell A. Cameron and Brian W. Tomlin, *The Making of NAFTA: How the Deal Was Done* (Ithaca, NY: Cornell University Press, 2000), 2.

29. Cameron and Tomlin, *Making of NAFTA*, 5–6.

30. See http://www.theonion.com/onion3818/mexi-canadianoverpass.html.

31. Gary Clyde Hufbauer and Jeffrey J. Schott, *NAFTA Revisited: Achievements and Challenges* (Washington DC: Institute for International Economics, 2005), 18.

32. For comparative perspectives on Nafta and the EU, see Peter Andreas and Thomas J. Biersteker, eds., *The Rebordering of North America: Integration and Exclusion in a New Security Context* (New York and London: Routledge, 2003); Kirsten Appendini and Sven Bislev, eds., *Economic Integration in NAFTA and the EU* (New York: St. Martin's Press, 1999); A. S. Bhalla, *Regional Blocs: Building Blocks or Stumbling Blocks* (New

York: St. Martin's Press, 1997); Emanuel Brunet-Jailly, *Comparing Local Cross-Border Relations under the EU and NAFTA* (Orono, ME: Canadian-American Center, 2004); Francesco G. Duina, *The Social Construction of Free Trade: The European Union, NAFTA, and MERCOSUR* (Princeton, NJ: Princeton University Press, 2006); Thomas C. Fischer, *The Europeanization of America: What Americans Need to Know about the European Union* (Durham, NC: Carolina Academic Press, 1995); Nicholas V. Ginaris, *The North American Free Trade Agreement and the European Union* (Westport, CT: Praeger, 1998); Demetrios G. Papademetriou and Debora Waller Meyers, "Overview, Context, and a Vision for the Future," in *Caught in the Middle: Border Communities in an Era of Globalization,* ed. Papademetriou and Meyers (Washington DC: Carnegie Endowment for Peace, 2001), 1–40; the essays in Peter Hakim and Robert E. Litan, eds., *The Future of North American Integration: Beyond NAFTA* (Washington, DC: Brookings Institution Press, 2002).

33. Robert Pastor, "NAFTA Is Not Enough: Steps toward a North American Community," in Hakim and Litan, eds., *Future of North American Integration,* 87.

34. Perrin Beatty, "Canada in North America: Isolation or Integration?" in Hakim and Litan, eds., *Future of North American Integration,* 52–53.

35. Pastor, "NAFTA Is Not Enough," 90.

36. Rebecca Morales, "Dependence or Interdependence: Issues and Policy Choices Facing Latin Americans and Latinos," in *Borderless Borders: U.S. Latinos, Latin Americans, and the Paradox of Interdependence,* ed. Frank Bonilla, Edwin Meléndez, Rebecca Morales, and María de los Angeles Torres (Philadelphia: Temple University Press, 1998), 9.

37. Naomi Klein, "The Rise of the Fortress Continent," *The Nation* (February 3, 2003): 10.

38. Drake, "Appropriating a Continent."

39. Anne E. Kingsolver, *NAFTA Stories: Fears and Hopes in Mexico and the United States* (Boulder, CO: Lynne Rienner Publishers, 2001), 204.

40. Shelly Fisher Fishkin, "Crossroads of Cultures: The Transnational Turn in American Studies," *American Quarterly* 57, no. 1 (2005): 17–57; Robert Gross, "The Transnational Turn: Rediscovering American Studies in a Wider World," *Journal of American Studies* 34 (2000): 373–93; Ursula Heise, "Ecocriticism and the Transnational Turn in American Studies," *American Literary History* 20, nos. 1–2 (2008): 381–404.

41. Among the many critics who have called for, and explored the significance of, these developments in the field, the most influential voices include Jane C. Desmond and Virginia R. Dominguez, "Resituating American Studies in a Critical Internationalism," *American Quarterly* 48 (Fall 1996): 475–90; Claire Fox and Claudia Sadowski-Smith, "Theorizing the Hemisphere: Inter-Americas Work at the Intersection of American, Canadian, and Latin American Studies," *Comparative American Studies* 2, no. 1 (2004): 41–74; Paul Giles, "Transnationalism and Classic American Literature," *PMLA* 118, no. 1 (2003): 62–77; Kirsten Silva Gruesz, "The Occluded History of Transamerican Literature," in *Critical Latin American and Latino Studies,* ed. Juan Poblete (Minneapolis: University of Minnesota Press, 2003), 121–37; Gregory S. Jay, "The End of American Literature," *College English* 53 (March 1991): 264–81; Amy Kaplan, "'Left Alone with America': The Absence of Empire in the Study of American Culture," in *The Cultures of United States Imperialism,* ed. Amy Kaplan and Donald Pease (Durham, NC: Duke University Press, 1993), 3–21; John Muthyala, "Reworlding America: The Globalization of American Studies," *Cultural Critique* 47 (Winter 2001): 91–119; Carolyn Porter, "What We Know That We Don't Know: Remapping American Literary Studies," *American Literary History* 6 (Fall 1994): 467–526; John Carlos Rowe, ed., *Post-Nationalist American Studies* (Berkeley: University of

California Press, 2000); Rowe, "Nineteenth-Century U.S. Literary Culture and Trans-nationality," *PMLA* 188, no. 1 (2003): 78–89; Robert McKee Irwin, "¿Qué hacen los nuevos americanistas? Collaborative Strategies for a Postnationalist American Studies," *Comparative American Studies* 2, no. 3 (2004): 303–23 and "*Ramona* and Post-nationalist American Studies: On Our America and the Mexican Borderlands," *American Quarterly* 55, no. 4 (2003): 539–67.

42. See, for example, Marc Shell, *American Babel: Literatures of the United States from Ab-naki to Zuni* (Cambridge, MA: Harvard University Press, 2002) and the essays in Werner Sollors, *Multilingual America: Transnationalism, Ethnicity, and the Languages of American Literature* (New York: New York University Press, 1998).

43. Janice Radway, "What's in a Name?" *American Quarterly* 51, no. 1 (1999): 1–32; Amy Kaplan, "Violent Belongings and the Question of Empire Today," *American Quarterly* 56, no. 1 (2004): 1–18; Fishkin, "Crossroads of Cultures"; Emory Elliot, "Diver-sity in the United States and Abroad: What Does It Mean When American Studies Is Transnational?" *American Quarterly* 59, no. 1 (2007): 1–25.

44. On the internationalisms of previous generations of critics, see Michael Denning, *The Cultural Front: The Laboring of American Culture in the Twentieth Century* (Lon-don and New York: Verso, 1996), 130–32; Robert Gross, "The Transnational Turn"; and Samuel Truett and Elliott Young, "Making Transnational History: Nations, Re-gions, and Borderlands," in *Continental Crossroads: Remapping U.S.-Mexico Border-lands History*, ed. Truett and Young (Durham, NC: Duke University Press, 2004), 1–32. Original sources include Randolph S. Bourne, "Trans-National America," in *Theories of Ethnicity: A Classical Reader*, ed. Werner Sollers (New York: New York Uni-versity Press, 1996), 93–108; Henry Nash Smith, *Virgin Land: The American West as Symbol and Myth* (Cambridge, MA: Harvard University Press, 1978); and Louis Hartz, *The Liberal Tradition in America: An Interpretation of American Political Thought since the Revolution* (New York: Harcourt Brace, 1955).

45. For examples of critics who overstate the insularity of prior scholarship, see Des-mond and Dominguez, "Resituating American Studies in a Critical International-ism"; Fishkin, "Crossroads of Cultures"; Kaplan, "Left Alone with America" and "Vi-olent Belongings"; Muthyala, "Reworlding America"; Donald E. Pease and Robyn Wiegman, "Futures," in *The Futures of American Studies* (Durham, NC: Duke Univer-sity Press, 2002), 1–42.

46. For two overviews of American studies that remark on the ascendance of the border-lands model, see Kaplan, "Left Alone with America," 3–21 and Linda Kerber, "Di-versity and the Transformation of American Studies," *American Quarterly* 41, no. 3 (1989): 415–31. While hardly exhaustive, the following list includes some of the most well-known and influential works of borderlands criticism: Gloria Anzaldúa, *Borderlands/La Frontera: The New Mestiza* (San Francisco: Spinsters/Aunt Lute, 1987); Mary Pat Brady, *Extinct Lands, Temporal Geographies: Chicana Literature and the Ur-gency of Space* (Durham, NC: Duke University Press, 2002); Hector Calderón and José David Saldívar, eds., *Criticism in the Borderlands: Studies in Chicano Literature, Culture, and Ideology* (Durham, NC: Duke University Press, 1991); Debra A. Cas-tillo and Maria Socorro Tabuenca de Cordoba, *Border Women: Writing from La Fron-tera* (Minneapolis: University of Minnesota Press, 2002); Claire F. Fox, *The Fence and the River: Culture and Politics at the U.S.-Mexico Border* (Minneapolis: University of Minnesota Press, 1999); Guillermo Gómez-Peña, *The New World Border: Prophe-cies, Poems, and Loqueras for the End of the Century* (San Francisco: City Lights, 1996); Carl Gutiérrez-Jones, *Rethinking the Borderlands: Between Chicano Culture and Legal*

Discourse (Berkeley: University of California Press, 1995); Lawrence Herzog, *Where North Meets South: Cities, Space, and Politics on the U.S.-Mexico Border* (Austin: University of Texas Press, 1990); Monika Kaup, *Rewriting North American Borders in Chicano and Chicana Narrative* (New York: Lang, 2001); José Limón, *American Encounters: Greater Mexico, the United States, and the Erotics of Culture* (Boston: Beacon Press, 1998); David Lorey, *The U.S.-Mexican Border in the Twentieth Century: A History of Economic and Social Transformation* (Wilmington, DE: SR Books, 1999); David Maciel, *El Norte: The U.S.-Mexico Border in Contemporary Cinema* (San Diego: Institute for Regional Studies of the Californias, 1990); Oscar J. Martínez, *Border People: Life and Society in the U.S.-Mexico Borderlands* (Tucson: University of Arizona Press, 1994) and *Troublesome Border* (Tucson: University of Arizona Press, 1998); Scott Michaelson and David E. Johnson, eds., *Border Theory: The Limits of Cultural Politics* (Minneapolis: University of Minnesota Press, 1997); José David Saldívar, *Border Matters: Remapping American Cultural Studies* (Berkeley: University of California Press, 1997); Sonia Saldívar-Hull, *Feminism on the Border: Chicana Gender Politics and Literature* (Berkeley: University of California Press, 2000).

47. Herbert Bolton, *The Spanish Borderlands: A Chronicle of Old Florida and the Southwest* (New Haven, CT: Yale University Press, 1921).

48. Anzaldúa, *Borderlands/La Frontera*, 25.

49. Ibid., 19.

50. Exceptions include Rachel Adams and Sarah Casteel, "Canada and the Americas," a special issue of *Comparative American Studies* 3, no. 1 (March 2005); Sarah Casteel, *Second Arrivals: Landscape and Belonging in Contemporary Writing of the Americas* (Charlottesville: University of Virginia Press, 2007); Sarah Casteel and Patrick Imbert, eds., *Canada and Its Americas: Transnational Navigations* (Montreal and Kingston: McGill-Queen's University Press, forthcoming); Earl Fitz, *Rediscovering the New World: Inter-American Studies in a Comparative Context* (Iowa City: University of Iowa Press, 1991); Patrick Imbert, *Consensual Disagreement: Canada and the Americas* (Ottawa: University of Ottawa Press, 2005); Claudia Sadowski-Smith, *Border Fictions: Empire, Globalization, and Writing at the Borders of the United States* (Charlottesville: University of Virginia Press, 2008).

51. Roger Gibbens, "Meaning and Significance of the Canadian-American Border," in *Borders and Border Politics in a Globalizing World*, ed. Paul Ganster and David E. Lorey (Lanham, MD: SR Books, 2004), 151–67, and Bruno Ramirez, "Borderland Studies and Migration: The Canada/United States Case," in *Repositioning North American Migration History: New Directions in Modern Continental Migration, Citizenship, and Community*, ed. Marc S. Rodriguez (Rochester, NY: University of Rochester Press, 2004).

52. Gibbens, "Meaning and Significance of the Canadian-American Border," 162.

53. Truett and Young, eds., *Continental Crossroads*, 13.

54. See, for example, Martin Albrow, *The Global Age: State and Society beyond Modernity* (Cambridge: Polity Press, 1996); Arjun Appadurai, *Modernity at Large: Cultural Dimensions of Globalization* (Minneapolis: University of Minnesota Press, 1996); Manuel Castells, *The Rise of the Network Society* (New York and Oxford: Blackwell Publishers, 1996) and *The Internet Galaxy: Reflections on The Internet, Business, and Society* (Oxford: Oxford University Press, 2001); Jürgen Habermas, *The Postnational Constellation: Political Essays* (Cambridge: Polity Press, 2001); Ankie Hoogvelt, *Globalisation and the Postcolonial World: The New Political Economy of Development* (London: Macmillan, 1997); Masao Miyoshi, "A Borderless World? From Colonialism to Transnationalism and the Decline of the Nation-State," *Critical Inquiry* 19, no. 4 (1993):

726–51; Jean-Marie Guéhenno, *The End of the Nation-State* (Minneapolis: University of Minnesota Press, 1996); Jan Aart Scholte, *Globalization: A Critical Introduction* (New York: St. Martin's Press, 2000); Malcolm Waters, *Globalization* (London: Routledge, 1995).

CHAPTER ONE

It has been a challenge to find appropriate terminology for this chapter, since each of North America's nation-states employs a different vocabulary to describe its indigenous people. They are First People or First Nations in Canada, Native Americans *in the United States, and* indios *or* personas indígenas *in Mexico. Because I did not want to privilege the vocabulary of any one national context, I have decided to use the more general terms* Native North American, Indian, *and* indigenous people *interchangeably.* Indian *is the term most commonly used by nearly all of the authors and artists discussed in the chapter.*

1. On Aquash, see Johanna Brand and Warren Almand, *The Life and Death of Anna Mae Aquash* (Toronto: Lorimer, 1993); Antoinette Clara Claypoole, *Who Would Unbraid Her Hair: The Legend of Annie Mae* (Ashland, OR: Anam Cara Press, 1999); and Steve Hendricks, *The Unquiet Grave: The FBI and the Struggle for the Soul of Indian Country* (New York: Thunder's Mouth Press, 2006).

2. Shelley Niro, "The Border: Artist's Statement," in *The Contemporary Native American Photoart of Shelley Niro* (Hamilton, NY: Longyear Museum of Anthropology, Colgate University, 1997), 8–9.

3. John Muthyala, "*Almanac of the Dead*: The Dream of the Fifth World in the Borderlands," *Literature Interpretation Theory* 14 (2003): 357–85; 358.

4. Amy Kaplan, "'Left Alone with America': The Absence of Empire in the Study of American Culture," in *Cultures of United States Imperialism*, ed. Amy Kaplan and Donald E. Pease (Durham, NC: Duke University Press, 1993), 3–21; Scott Michaelson and David E. Johnson, "Border Secrets," in *Border Theory: The Limits of Cultural Politics* (Minneapolis: University of Minnesota Press, 1997), 1–42; Amritjit Singh and Peter Schmidt, "On the Borders between U.S. Studies and Postcolonial Theory," in *Postcolonial Theory and the United States: Race, Ethnicity, and Literature*, ed. Amritjit Singh and Peter Schmidt (Jackson: University Press of Mississippi, 2000), 3–69.

5. David E. Lorey, *The U.S.-Mexican Border in the Twentieth Century: A History of Economic and Social Transformation* (Wilmington, DE: Scholarly Resources, 1999).

6. Here I echo the argument made by John Muthyala in "Border Cultures in the Borderlands," in *Reworlding America: Myth, History, and Narrative* (Athens: Ohio University Press, 2006), 107.

7. Philip J. Deloria, *Indians in Unexpected Places* (Lawrence: University Press of Kansas, 2004), 11–12.

8. R. David Edmunds, "Native Americans and the United States, Canada, and Mexico," in *A Companion to American Indian History*, ed. Philip J. Deloria and Neal Salisbury (Malden, MA: Blackwell Publishers, 2004), 416.

9. Eileen M. Luna-Firebaugh, "The Border Crossed Us: Border Crossing Issues of the Indigenous Peoples of the Americas," *Wicazo Sa Review* (Spring 2002): 159–81.

10. This is the subject of many of the essays in G. Malcolm Lewis, ed., *Cartographic Encounters: Perspectives on Native American Mapmaking and Map Use* (Chicago: University of Chicago Press, 1998). See also J. B. Harley, *The New Nature of Maps: Essays in the History of Cartography* (Baltimore: Johns Hopkins University Press, 2001), chap. 6; Alan Morantz, *Where Is Here? Canada's Maps and the Stories They Tell* (Toronto:

Penguin, 2002), 24–52; and Mark Warhus, *Another America: Native American Maps and the History of Our Land* (New York: St. Martin's Press, 1997).

11. D. W. Meinig, *The Shaping of America: A Geographical Perspective on 500 Years of History* (New Haven, CT: Yale University Press, 1996), 1: 232.

12. On the history of Indians in the United States, see Edmunds, "Native Americans and the United States, Canada, and Mexico," and Jeanne Guillemin, "The Politics of National Integration: A Comparison of United States and Canadian Indian Administration," *Social Problems* 25, no. 3 (1978): 319–32; on Indians in Canada see Edmunds, "Native Americans and the United States, Canada, and Mexico," Guillemin, "Politics of National Integration," and Roger L. Nichols, *Indians in the United States and Canada: A Comparative History* (Lincoln: University of Nebraska Press, 1998); on Indians in Mexico see Alexander S. Dawson, *Indian and Nation in Revolutionary Mexico* (Tucson: University of Arizona Press, 2004) and Mark A. Burkholder, "An Empire beyond Compare," 115–50, Ross Hassig, "The Collision of Two Worlds," 79–112, Robert W. Patch, "Indian Resistance to Colonialism," 183–212, all in *The Oxford History of Mexico*, ed. Michael Meyer and William H. Beezley (Oxford and New York: Oxford University Press, 2000). For some of the few comparative approaches to the conquest, see Edmunds, "Native Americans and the United States, Canada, and Mexico," and Gregory Evans Dowd, "Wag the Imperial Dog: Indians and Overseas Empires in North America, 1650–1776," both in Deloria and Salisbury, eds., *A Companion to American Indian History*. For comparative approaches to Indians in Canada and Mexico, see Curtis Cook and Juan D. Lindau, eds., *Aboriginal Rights and Self-Government: The Canadian and Mexican Experience in North American Perspective* (Montreal and Kingston: McGill-Queen's University Press, 2000).

13. Gregory S. Camp, "Working Out Their Own Salvation: The Allotment of Land in Severalty and the Turtle Mountain Chippewa Band, 1870–1920," *American Indian Culture and Research Journal* 14, no. 2 (1990): 19–38, and Nancy J. Peterson, "History, Postmodernism, and Louise Erdrich's *Tracks*," *PMLA* 109, no. 5 (1994): 982–94.

14. Camp, "Working Out Their Own Salvation," 19.

15. Rachel Hays, "Cross-Border Indigenous Nations: A History," *BorderLines* 4, no. 1 (1996): 1–4; Luna-Firebaugh, "Border Crossed Us," 166, 170–72; Valerie Taliman, "Borders and Native Peoples: Divided, but Not Conquered," *Native Americas* 18, no. 1 (2001): 4; Charles Wilkinson, *Blood Struggle: The Rise of Modern Indian Nations* (New York: W. W. Norton, 2005), 301; and Ofelia Zepeda, "Autobiography," in *Here First: Autobiographical Essays by Native American Writers*, ed. Arnold Krupat and Brian Swann (New York: Modern Library, 2000), 408. Thanks to Silvio Torres-Saillant for directing me to the Zepeda essay.

16. Full text is available at http://www.earlyamerica.com/earlyamerica/milestones/jaytreaty/text.html, accessed September 29, 2007.

17. Kristina Nilson Allen, "Homeland Insecurity," *Cultural Survival Quarterly* 30, no. 3 (2006): 18–23; Luna-Firebaugh, "Border Crossed Us," 165–70.

18. Cited in Taliman, "Borders and Native Peoples," 6.

19. Alison Brysk, "Turning Weakness into Strength: The Internationalization of Indian Rights," *Latin American Perspectives* 23, no. 2 (1996): 43.

20. Brysk, "Turning Weakness into Strength," 45.

21. Elizabeth Cook-Lynn, *Why I Can't Read Wallace Stegner and Other Essays* (Madison: University of Wisconsin Press, 1996), 93. See also Craig S. Womack, *Red on Red: Native American Literary Separatism* (Minneapolis: University of Minnesota Press, 1999); Robert Warrior, *Tribal Secrets: Recovering American Indian Intellectual Traditions*

(Minneapolis: University of Minnesota Press, 1995); and Jace Weaver, Craig Womack, and Robert Warrior, eds., *American Indian Literary Nationalism* (Albuquerque: University of New Mexico Press, 2006).

22. Arnold Krupat and Michael A. Elliot, "American Indian Fiction and Anticolonial Resistance," in *Columbia Guide to American Indian Literatures of the United States since 1945*, ed. Eric Cheyfitz (New York: Columbia University Press, 2006). As Shari Hundorf has reminded me, despite their explicit calls for tribal specificity, these critics' own work suggests the interconnections among tribal nations.

23. Leslie Marmon Silko, "The Border Patrol State," in *Yellow Woman and a Beauty of the Spirit* (New York: Simon and Schuster, 1996), 122–23.

24. Thomas King, *The Truth about Stories: A Native Narrative* (Minneapolis: University of Minnesota Press, 2005), 149. In keeping with this view, Jace Weaver has described King's perspective as "pan-Indian," in *That the People Might Live: Native American Literatures and Native American Community* (New York: Oxford University Press, 1997).

25. King, *Truth about Stories*, 102.

26. Jeffrey Canton, "Coyote Lives," in *The Power to Bend Spoons*, ed. Beverly Daurio (Toronto: Mercury Press, 1998), 92.

27. Taliman, "Borders and Native Peoples," 6.

28. In ibid., 7.

29. In this, I disagree with the reading of *Truth and Bright Water* in *Border Crossings: Thomas King's Cultural Inversions* by Arnold Davidson, Priscilla Walton, and Jennifer Andrews (Toronto: University of Toronto Press, 2003), which emphasizes the subversive power of King's comedy to overcome the obstacles that confront his indigenous characters. As King represents it, the economic and social problems of the community in the novel cannot be solved through humor or comic inversion.

30. In his interview with Jeffrey Canton, Thomas King claims that despite the differences among Indian people, "what remains the same is the firm base that we have in places—even if sometimes the places aren't our own to begin with" (Canton, "Coyote Lives," 92).

31. J. R. Miller, *Skyscrapers Hide the Heavens: A History of Indian-White Relations in Canada* (Toronto: University of Toronto Press, 1991), chap. 9.

32. On the White Paper of 1969, see Miller, *Skyscrapers Hide the Heavens*, 238–39.

33. C. E. S. Franks, "Indian Policy: Canada and the United States Compared," in *Aboriginal Rights and Self Government*, 221–63.

34. Edmunds, "Native Americans and the United States, Canada, and Mexico," 411–12.

35. Thomas King, *Truth and Bright Water* (New York: Atlantic Monthly Press, 1999), 1. All subsequent references will be cited parenthetically in the text.

36. On the trope of the suicidal plunge, see Laura Romero, "Vanishing Americans: Gender, Empire, and New Historicism," in *American Literary Studies: A Methodological Reader*, ed. Michael A. Elliott and Claudia Stokes (New York: New York University Press, 2003).

37. "NAFTA sparks bloody clashes in Mexico (Canadian Native leaders plan trip to Chiapas to support uprising)," *Windspeaker* 11, no. 22 (1994): 3; Jack D. Forbes, "A Native American Perspective on NAFTA," *Cultural Survival Quarterly* 17, no. 4 (1994): 3; Tom Goldtooth, "NAFTA and Native Americans: An Agenda for Transnational Termination?" *The Circle* 13, no. 1 (1999): 12; Valerie Taliman, "NAFTA Threatens Native Sovereignty and Threatens Indigenous Economies," *The Circle* 13, no. 1 (1999):

13; and Valerie Taliman, "NAFTA May Clip Native Treaty Rights," *Indian Country* 13, no. 17 (1993): A1.

38. Miller *Skyscrapers Hide the Heavens*, 260–63; Nichols, *Indians in the United States and Canada*, 233, 245.

39. Jennifer Andrews and Priscilla L. Walton write that "King's depictions of border crossings may offer a subversive vision of how Natives performatively can revise stereotypes to achieve their own goals, but there is always an awareness that such victories are momentary and subject to national retrenchment" (Andrews and Walton, "Rethinking Canadian and American Nationality: Indigeneity and the 49th Parallel in Thomas King," *American Literary History* 18, no. 3 [2006]: 606).

40. Barbara E. Mundy, *The Mapping of New Spain: Indigenous Cartography and the Maps of the Relaciones Geográficas* (Chicago: University of Chicago Press, 1996), xvi.

41. For other readings of the map, see Virginia E. Bell, "Counter-Chronicling and Alternative Mapping in *Memoria del Fuego* and *Almanac of the Dead*," *MELUS* 25, no. 3/4 (2000): 5–30; Ann Brigham, "Productions of Geographic Scale and Capitalist-Colonialist Enterprise in Leslie Marmon Silko's *Almanac of the Dead*," *MFS: Modern Fiction Studies* 50, no. 2 (2004): 303–31; Shari Huhndorf, "Picture Revolution: 'Tribal Internationalism' and the Future of the Americas in Leslie Marmon Silko's *Almanac of the Dead*," in *Mapping the Americas: The Transnational Politics of Contemporary Native Culture* (Ithaca, NY: Cornell University Press, 2009).

42. Silko's 1999 novel, *Gardens in the Dunes*, is also international in scope, since its protagonists travel from the U.S. Southwest to Europe, but its concerns are narrower and it focuses on individual characters rather than groups.

43. Arnold Krupat, *Turn to The Native: Studies in Criticism and Culture* (Lincoln: University of Nebraska Press, 1996), 52.

44. Silko, "The Border Patrol State," 115.

45. Ibid., 114.

46. Ibid., 123.

47. Ibid., 122.

48. Thomas Irmer, "An Interview with Leslie Marmon Silko," at www.altx.com/interviews/Silko.html, accessed December 7, 2006.

49. Leslie Marmon Silko, *Almanac of the Dead* (New York: Penguin, 1991), 759. All subsequent references will be cited parenthetically in the text.

50. Jerome M. Levi, "A New Dawn or a Cycle Restored? Regional Dynamics and Cultural Politics in Indigenous Mexico, 1978–2001," in *The Politics of Ethnicity: Indigenous Peoples in Latin American States*, ed. David Maybury Lewis (Cambridge, MA: Harvard University Press, 2002), 16.

51. Isain Mandujano, "Mexico's Southern Border: A Virtual Line," *World Press Review* 48, no. 9 (2001), at http://www.worldpress.org/, accessed December 19, 2006; June Nash, "The Reassertion of Indigenous Identity: Mayan Responses to State Intervention in Chiapas," *Latin American Research Review* 30, no. 3 (1995): 7–41.

52. Nash, "Reassertion of Indigenous Identity," 30–32.

53. Velia Jaramillo, "Mexico's 'Southern Plan': The Facts" *World Press Review* 48, no. 9 (2001), at http://www.worldpress.org/, accessed December 19, 2006.

54. For more on the significance of Yaquis in *Almanac of the Dead*, see Muthyala, *Reworlding America*, chap. 4.

55. Luna-Firebaugh, "Border Crossed Us," 167, 173–74; Hays, "Cross-Border Indigenous Nations," 2–3.

56. Patch, "Indian Resistance to Colonialism," in Meyer and Beezley, eds., *Oxford History of Mexico,* 181–211.

57. Channette Romero, "Envisioning a 'Network of Tribal Coalitions': Leslie Marmon Silko's *Almanac of the Dead,*" *American Indian Quarterly* 26, no. 4 (2002): 637.

58. On the nationalist framing of the rebellion, see Mark T. Berger, "Romancing the Zapatistas: International Intellectuals and the Chiapas Rebellion," *Latin American Perspectives* 28, no. 2 (March 2001): 149–70.

59. Edmundo O'Gorman, *The Invention of America; An Inquiry into the Historical Nature of the New World and the Meaning of Its History* (Bloomington: Indiana University Press, 1961).

CHAPTER TWO

1. Alice Walker, *By the Light of My Father's Smile* (New York: Random House, 1998).

2. Diana Taylor, *The Archive and the Repertoire: Performing Cultural Memory in the Americas* (Durham, NC: Duke University Press, 2003), 20.

3. As anthropologist Bobby Vaughn observes, Afro-Mexicans tend to identify as Mexican rather than as members of the black diaspora. See "Afro-Mexico: Blacks, Indígenas, Politics, and the Greater Diaspora," in *Neither Enemies nor Friends: Latinos, Blacks, Afro-Latinos,*" ed. Anani Dzidzienyo and Suzanne Oboler (New York: Palgrave, 2005), 117–36.

4. Kathleen Brogan, "American Stories of Cultural Haunting: Tales of Heirs and Ethnographers," *College English* 57, no. 2 (1995): 158–59.

5. Robin Winks, *The Blacks in Canada: A History* (Montreal: McGill-Queen's University Press, 1997), 235.

6. Winks, *Blacks in Canada,* 143.

7. Ibid., chap. 8.

8. Ibid., 171–76.

9. Quoted in ibid., 253.

10. Martin Luther King Jr., *Conscience for Change: Massey Lectures, Seventh Series* (Toronto: Canadian Broadcasting Corporation, 1967), 1.

11. Quoted in Bruce Allen Dick, ed., *The Critical Response to Ishmael Reed* (Westport, CT: Greenwood Press, 1999), 134.

12. Ishmael Reed, *Flight to Canada* (New York: Atheneum, 1989), 88.

13. Ashraf Rushdy, *Neo-Slave Narratives: Studies in the Social Logic of a Literary Form* (New York: Oxford, 1999).

14. Winks, *Blacks in Canada,* 241.

15. Harriet Jacobs, *Incidents in the Life of a Slave Girl: The Classic Slave Narratives,* ed. Henry Louis Gates Jr. (New York: Penguin, 1987), 503.

16. *The Rev. J. W. Loguen, as a Slave and as a Freeman: A Narrative of Real Life* (New York: Negro Universities Press, 1968), 305.

17. Cited in Frances Smith Foster, *Witnessing Slavery: The Development of Ante-Bellum Slave Narratives* (Madison: University of Wisconsin Press, 1979), 89.

18. Frances E. W. Harper, "The Air of Freedom," in *The Freedman's Book,* ed. Lydia Maria Francis Child (Boston: Ticknor and Fields, 1865), 243.

19. Harriet Beecher Stowe, *Uncle Tom's Cabin* (New York: Signet, 1981), 413.

20. Joseph Mensah, *Black Canadians: History, Experiences, Social Conditions* (Halifax: Fernwood Publishing, 2002); Jason H. Silverman, *Unwelcome Guests: Canada West's Response to American Fugitive Slaves, 1800–1865* (Millwood, NY: Associated Faculty Press, 1985); and Winks, *Blacks in Canada.*

21. George Elliot Clarke, *Odysseys Home: Mapping African-Canadian Literature* (Toronto: University of Toronto Press, 2002), 33.

22. Rinaldo Walcott, *Black Like Who? Writing Black Canada* (Toronto: Insomniac Press, 2003), 29.

23. Winks, *Blacks in Canada*, 270.

24. On Delany in Canada, see Dorothy Sterling, *The Making of an Afro-American: Martin Robinson Delany* (New York: Da Capo Press, 1996).

25. Robert Levine, *Martin Delany, Frederick Douglass, and the Politics of Representative Identity* (Chapel Hill: University of North Carolina Press, 1997), 200.

26. Martin Delany, *Blake; or, the Huts of America* (Boston: Beacon Press, 1970), 30.

27. Delany, *Blake*, 143.

28. Ibid., 152.

29. In Richard Newman, Patrick Rael, and Philip Lapsansky, eds., *Pamphlets of Protest: An Anthology of Early African-American Protest Literature, 1790–1860* (New York: Routledge, 2001), 230.

30. Gregg Crane, "The Lexicon of Rights, Power, and Community in *Blake*: Martin R. Delany's Dissent from *Dred Scott*," *American Literature* 68, no. 3 (1996): 527–53.

31. Martin R. Delany, *The Condition, Elevation, Emigration, and Destiny of the Colored People of the United States and Official Report of the Niger Valley Exploring Party* (New York: Arno Press, 1968), 178.

32. Martin Delany, "Political Destiny," in Newman, Rael, and Lapsansky, eds., *Pamphlets of Protest*, 238–39.

33. Delany, "Political Destiny," 234.

34. Ibid., 235.

35. Cited in Quintard Taylor, *In Search of the Racial Frontier: African Americans in the American West, 1528–1990* (New York: Norton, 1998), 38–39.

36. On the Black Seminoles, see Kenneth W. Porter, *The Black Seminoles: History of a Freedom-Seeking People* (Gainesville: University Press of Florida, 1996); Rosalie Schwartz, *Across the Rio to Freedom: U.S. Negroes in Mexico* (El Paso: Texas Western Press, 1975); and Ronnie C. Tyler, "Fugitive Slaves in Mexico," *Journal of Negro History* 57, no. 1 (1972): 1–12.

37. Schwartz, *Across the Rio to Freedom*, 40–41.

38. Benjamin Lundy, *The Life, Travels, and Opinions of Benjamin Lundy* (New York: Augustus M. Kelley, 1971), 96. On Lundy, see also Schwartz, *Across the Rio to Freedom*.

39. D. W. Meinig, *The Shaping of America: A Geographical Perspective on 500 Years of History* (New Haven, CT: Yale University Press, 1993), 2: 298; and Schwartz, *Across the Rio to Freedom*.

40. Schwartz, *Across the Rio to Freedom*, 29.

41. Cited in Meinig, *Shaping of America*, 2: 305.

42. Schwartz, *Across the Rio to Freedom*, 29.

43. Josefina Zoraida Vázquez and Lorenzo Meyer, *The United States and Mexico* (Chicago: University of Chicago Press, 1985), 28–29.

44. This greater atmosphere of racial tolerance had its roots in the Old World Spain, where slavery was understood to be a temporary condition and cultural pluralism was the norm. See Patricia Seed, *American Pentimento: The Invention of Indians and the Pursuit of Riches* (Minneapolis: University of Minnesota Press, 2001); and Jaime Rodríguez, "The Emancipation of America," *American Historical Review* 105, no. 1 (2000): 131–53; "La Antigua Provincia de Guayaquil en la época de la Independencia," in *Revolución, independencia y la nuevas naciones de América*, coord. Jaime E.

Rodríguez O. (Madrid: Fundación Mapfre Tavera, 2005), 511–56; and "Ciudadanos de la Nación Española: Los indígenas y las elecciones constitucionales en el Reino de Quito," in *La mirada esquiva: Reflexiones históricas sobre la interacción del Estado y la ciudadanía en los Andes,* ed. Marta Irurozqui (Madrid: Consejo Superior de Investigaciones Científicas, 2005).

45. Schwartz, *Across the Rio to Freedom,* 7.

46. Schwartz, *Across the Rio to Freedom,* and Taylor, *In Search of the Racial Frontier,* 37.

47. Vázquez and Meyer, *United States and Mexico,* 18.

48. Schwartz, *Across the Rio to Freedom,* 37.

49. Foster, *Witnessing Slavery,* 118.

50. See Jeff Guinn, *Our Land before We Die: The Proud Story of the Seminole Negro* (New York: Putnam, 2002), and Porter, *Black Seminoles.*

51. Porter, *Black Seminoles,* 6.

52. Cited in Porter, *Black Seminoles,* 9.

53. On Mexican help to fugitive slaves, see Neil Foley, *The White Scourge: Mexicans, Blacks, and Poor Whites in Texas Cotton Culture* (Berkeley: University of California Press, 1997); Taylor, *In Search of the Racial Frontier;* Schwartz, *Across the Rio to Freedom;* and Ruthe Winegarten, *Black Texas Women: 150 Years of Trial and Triumph* (Austin: University of Texas Press, 1995).

54. Taylor, *In Search of the Racial Frontier,* 41.

55. John Hope Franklin and Loren Schweninger, *Runaway Slaves: Rebels on the Plantation, 1790–1860* (New York: Oxford, 1999), 115.

56. Franklin and Schweninger, *Runaway Slaves,* 115.

57. Ibid., 26.

58. Ronnie Tyler and Laurence R. Murphy, *Slave Narratives of Texas* (Austin: Encino Press, 1974), 68.

59. Tyler and Murphy, *Slave Narratives of Texas,* 69.

60. Frederick Law Olmsted, *A Journey through Texas* (New York: Burt Franklin, 1969), 454.

61. Olmsted, *Journey through Texas,* 324.

62. Ibid., 325.

63. Ibid., 326.

64. The research of anthropologist Bobby Vaughn has been particularly instrumental in identifying the African elements of black Mexican cultures in Veracruz and Costa Chica. See Vaughn, "Blacks in Mexico: A Brief Overview," at http://www.mexconnect .com/mex_/feature/ethnic/bv/brief.htm, accessed February 5, 2007; "Mexico in the Context of the Transatlantic Slave Trade," *Diálogo* 5 (2001): 1–11; and Vaughn and Ben Vinson III, *Afroméxico: El pulso de la población negra en México* (Mexico City: Fonda de Cultura Economica, 2004).

65. There is a growing body of scholarship on blacks in Mexico, beginning with Gonzalo Aguirre Beltrán's *La población negra de México* (Mexico City: Ediciones Fuente Cultural, 1946). See also Herman Lee Bennett, *Lovers, Family, Friends: The Formation of Afro-Mexico, 1580–1910* (Durham, NC: Duke University Press, 1993); Patrick James Carroll, *Blacks in Colonial Veracruz: Race, Ethnicity, and Regional Development* (Austin: University of Texas Press, 1991); Nicole von Germeten, *Black Blood Brothers: Contrafraternities and Social Mobility for Afro-Mexicans* (Gainesville: University Press of Florida, 2006); Marco Polo Hernández Cuevas, *African Mexicans and the Discourse on Modern Nation* (Dallas: University Press of America, 2004); Colin Palmer, *Slaves of the White God* (Cambridge, MA: Harvard University Press, 1976); Martha Menchaca, *Recovering History, Constructing Race: The Indian, Black, and White Roots of Mexican*

Americans (Austin: University of Texas Press, 2001); Vaughn and Vinson, *Afroméxico*; Ben Vinson, *Bearing Arms for His Majesty: The Free-Colored Militia in Colonial Mexico* (Palo Alto, CA: Stanford University Press, 2001).

66. Patrick J. Carroll, "Africa in the Americas: Blacks in Mexico," at http://www.humanities -interactive.org/newworld/africa/blacks_in_mexico.htm, accessed February 5, 2007.

67. Beltrán, *Población negra*, 200; Vaughn, "Blacks in Mexico."

68. Carroll, "Africa in the Americas"; Steve Sailer, "Where Did Mexico's Missing Blacks Go?" UPI May 8, 2002, at http://www.isteve.com/2002_Where_Did_Mexicos_Blacks _Go.htm, accessed October 29, 2007.

69. Dedra S. McDonald, "To Be Black and Female in the Spanish Southwest: Toward a History of African Women on New Spain's Far Northern Frontier," in *African American Women Confront the West, 1600–2000*, ed. Quintard Taylor and Shirley Ann Wilson Moore (Norman: University of Oklahoma Press, 2003), 32–52.

70. Rushdy, *Neo-Slave Narratives*, chap. 1.

71. Winks, *Blacks in Canada*, 194–95.

72. On recent work of historic designation, see Shannon Ricketts, "Commemorating the Underground Railroad in Canada," *CRM* 5 (1999): 33–34; and Ricketts, "Canadian Terminals on the Underground Railroad," *Journal of the Ontario History and Social Sciences Teachers' Association* (Winter 2001): n.p.

73. Winks, *Blacks in Canada*, 233.

74. Clarke, *Odysseys Home*, 31.

75. Lawrence Hill, "Black Like Us: Canada Is Not Nearly as Integrated as We Like to Think," *Globe and Mail*, February 9, 2000.

76. George Elliot Clarke, "Another Great Thing," *Canadian Literature* 165 (Summer 2000): 139–41.

77. Charles T. Davis and Henry Louis Gates Jr., "Introduction: The Language of Slavery," in *The Slave's Narrative*, ed. Charles T. Davis and Henry Louis Gates Jr. (Oxford: Oxford University Press, 1985), xxiii (emphasis in original).

78. Lawrence Hill, *Any Known Blood* (New York: Morrow, 1997), 436. All subsequent references will be cited parenthetically in the text.

79. See Winks, *Blacks in Canada*, 267–69, on Brown's actual visit to Canada.

80. See Fred Landon, "Canadian Negroes and the John Brown Raid," *Journal of Negro History* 6, no. 2 (1921): 174–82, and Winks, *Blacks in Canada*, 267–69.

81. Mary Ann Shadd, "A Plea for Emigration, or Notes of Canada West" (1852), in Newman, Rael, and Lapsansky, eds., *Pamphlets of Protest*, 199–213.

82. Toni Morrison, *Beloved* (New York: Plume, 1987).

83. Lori Lansens, *Rush Home Road* (Boston: Little, Brown, 2002), 152. All subsequent references will be cited parenthetically in the text.

84. John Sayles, "Introduction," in *Men with Guns & Lone Star* (London: Faber and Faber, 1998), viii. All subsequent references will be cited parenthetically in the text.

85. Michael Harper, "Gayl Jones: An Interview," *Massachusetts Review* 18, no. 4 (1977): 706.

86. Charles H. Rowell, "An Interview with Gayl Jones," *Callaloo* 16 (1982): 40.

87. Gayl Jones, *Corregidora* (Boston: Beacon Press, 1975), 9.

88. Jones, *Corregidora*, 80.

89. Ibid., 59.

90. Sarika Chandra, "Interruptions: Tradition, Borders, and Narrative in Gayl Jones's *Mosquito*," in *After the Pain: Critical Essays on Gayl Jones*, ed. Fiona Mills and Keith Mitchell (New York: Peter Lang, 2006), 137–53.

91. Henry Louis Gates Jr., "Sanctuary," *New York Times Book Review*, November 14, 1999,

14; Tom Leclair, review of *Mosquito, Salon*, January 12, 1999, at http://www.salon
.com/books/sneaks/1999/01/12sneaks.html (accessed April 14, 2009); Tamala M.
Edwards, review of *Mosquito, Time*, February 8, 1999, 72.

92. Carrie Tirado Bramen, "Speaking in Typeface: Characterizing Stereotypes in Gayl
Jones's *Mosquito," MFS: Modern Fiction Studies* 49, no. 1 (2003): 124–54.

93. Gayle Jones, *Mosquito* (Boston: Beacon Press, 1999), 615. All subsequent references
will be cited parenthetically in the text.

94. A number of critics have pointed out the novel's interest in cross-cultural community, and particularly in the possibilities of forging ties between African Americans
and other ethnic groups. See, for example, Chandra, "Interruptions"; Casey Claybough, "Afrocentric Recolonizations: Gayl Jones's 1990s Fiction," *Contemporary Literature* 46, no. 2 (2005): 243–74; and Fiona Mills, "Telling the Untold Tale: Afro-
Latino/a Identifications in the Work of Gayl Jones," in Mills and Mitchell, eds., *After
the Pain*, 91–115.

95. On the erasure of blackness in Mexican arts and letters, see Hernández Cuevas, *African Mexicans and the Discourse of Modern Nation*.

96. Guillermo Sánchez de Anda, *Yanga: Un guerrero negro* (Mexico City: Círculo Cuadrado,
1998), 126.

97. Sánchez de Anda, *Yanga*, 37.

98. Ibid., 39.

99. Amanda Claybaugh, *The Novel of Purpose: Literature and Social Reform in the Anglo-
American World* (Ithaca, NY: Cornell University Press, 2007).

100. Sánchez de Anda, *Yanga*, 36.

101. Ibid., 63.

102. Vaughn, "Mexico in the Context of the Transatlantic Slave Trade," 1–11; and Vaughn,
"Afro-Mexico," 118–36.

CHAPTER THREE

1. Edward Weston, *The Daybooks of Edward Weston*, vol. 1, ed. Nancy Newhall (Millerton, NY: Aperture, 1973), 136.

2. For example, see Shari Benstock, *Women of the Left Bank: Paris, 1900–1940* (Aus-
tin: University of Texas Press, 1986); Sara Blair, "Modernism and the Politics of
Culture," in *The Cambridge Companion to Modernism*, ed. Michael Levenson (Cambridge: Cambridge University Press, 1999), 157–73; Ann Douglas, *Terrible Honesty:
Mongrel Manhattan in the 1920s* (New York: Farrar, Straus, Giroux, 1995); Deborah
Parsons, *Streetwalking the Metropolis: Women, the City, and Modernity* (Oxford: Oxford University Press, 2000); Susan Squier Merril, *Virginia Woolf and London: The
Sexual Politics of the City* (Chapel Hill: University of North Carolina Press, 1985);
and Andrew Thacker, *Moving through Modernity: Space and Geography in Modernism* (Manchester: Manchester University Press, 2003) for site-specific studies of
modernism. There is also a related scholarship on modernist bohemias. See Andrea Barnet, *All-Night Party: The Women of Bohemian Greenwich Village and Harlem,
1913–1930* (Chapel Hill, NC: Algonquin Books of Chapel Hill, 2004); Christine
Stansell, *American Moderns: Bohemian New York and the Creation of a New Century*
(New York: Henry Holt 2000); and Ross Wetzsteon, *Republic of Dreams: Greenwich Village, The American Bohemia, 1910–1960* (New York: Simon and Schuster,
2001).

3. Peter Wollen, *Raiding the Icebox: Reflections on Twentieth-Century Culture* (New York
and London: Verso, 1993), 194.

4. On Latin American *modernismo*, see Bart L. Lewis, "Modernism," in *Mexican Literature: A History*, ed. David William Foster (Austin: University of Texas Press, 1994); Cathy L. Jrade, *Modernismo, Modernity, and the Development of Spanish American Literature* (Austin: University of Texas Press, 1998); and Anthony L. Geist and José B. Monleón, "Modernism and Its Margins: Rescripting Hispanic Modernism," in *Modernism and Its Margins: Reinscribing Cultural Modernity from Spain and Latin America*, ed. Geist and Monleón (New York and London: Garland, 1999), xvii–xxxv.

5. Carlos Monsiváis, "Anita Brenner and the Mexican Renaissance," foreword to *Anita Brenner: A Mind of Her Own*, by Susannah Joel Glusker (Austin: University of Texas Press, 1998), xi.

6. Cited in Alice Gambrell, "A Courtesan's Confession: Frida Kahlo and Surrealist Entrepreneurship," in *Women Intellectuals, Modernism, and Difference: A Transatlantic Culture, 1919–1945* (Cambridge: Cambridge University Press, 1997), 59.

7. Thomas Benjamin, "Rebuilding the Nation," in *The Oxford History of Mexico*, ed. Michael Meyer and William H. Beezley (New York and Oxford: Oxford University Press, 2000), 470.

8. Friedrich E. Schuler, "Mexico and the Outside World," in Meyer and Beezley, eds., *Oxford History of Mexico*, 506.

9. Anita Brenner, *The Wind That Swept Mexico: The History of the Mexican Revolution, 1910–1942* (New York and London: Harper and Brothers, 1943), 13. All subsequent references will be cited parenthetically in the text.

10. Helen Delpar, *The Enormous Vogue of Things Mexican: Cultural Relations between the United States and Mexico, 1920–1935* (Tuscaloosa: University of Alabama Press, 1992), 16.

11. This phrase comes from Delpar, *Enormous Vogue of Things Mexican*. On Anglo-American interest in Mexico of the 1920s and 30s, see also Drewey Wayne Gunn, *American and British Writers in Mexico, 1556–1973* (Austin: University of Texas Press, 1974) and Frederick B. Pike, *The United States and Latin America: Myths and Stereotypes of Civilization and Nature* (Austin: University of Texas Press, 1992).

12. Edward Weston, *Daybooks of Edward Weston*, vol. 2, ed. Nancy Newhall (New York: Horizon Press, 1961), 244.

13. On John Reed, see Delpar, *Enormous Vogue of Things Mexican*, 20; on Reed and Turner, see John A. Britton, *Revolution and Ideology: Images of the Mexican Revolution in the United States* (Lexington: University Press of Kentucky, 1995), 36–40.

14. Delpar, *Enormous Vogue of Things Mexican*, chap. 1, and Britton, *Revolution and Ideology*.

15. Paul Hollander, *Political Pilgrims: Western Intellectuals in Search of the Good Society* (New Brunswick, NJ: Transaction Publishers, 1998).

16. Delpar, *Enormous Vogue of Things Mexican*, 52.

17. Benjamin, "Rebuilding the Nation," 474.

18. Cited in Anita Brenner, *Idols behind Altars* (New York: Payson and Clark, 1929), 255. All subsequent references will be cited parenthetically in the text.

19. Wollen, *Raiding the Icebox*, 194–95.

20. Britton, *Revolution and Ideology*, 51.

21. Olivier Debroise, *Mexican Suite: A History of Photography in Mexico*, trans. Stella de Sá Rego (Austin: University of Texas Press, 2001), 202.

22. Glusker, *Anita Brenner*, 46.

23. Kenneth Rexroth, *An Autobiographical Novel*, ed. Linda Hamalian (New York: New Directions, 1991), 344.

24. Langston Hughes, *I Wonder as I Wander* (New York: Hill and Wang, 1993), 295.

25. Laura Mulvey, with Peter Wollen, "Frida Kahlo and Tina Modotti," in *Visual and Other Pleasures* (Bloomington: Indiana University Press, 1989), 95, 96.

26. Shirlene Soto, *The Emergence of the Modern Mexican Woman: Her Participation in Revolution and Struggle for Equality, 1910–1940* (Denver: Arden Press, 1990), 100.

27. On feminism in Mexico, see Gabriela Cano, "The *Porfiriato* and the Mexican Revolution: Constructions of Feminism and Nationalism," in *Nation, Empire, Colony: Historicizing Gender and Race*, ed. Ruth Roach Pierson and Nupur Chaudhuri (Bloomington: Indiana University Press, 1998), 106–20; Anna Macias, "Women and the Mexican Revolution, 1910–1920," *Americas* 37, no. 1 (1980): 53–82; Julia Tuñón Pablos, *Women in Mexico: A Past Unveiled*, trans. Alan Hynds (Austin: University of Texas Press, 1999); and Soto, *Emergence of the Modern Mexican Woman*.

28. Letizia Argenteri, *Tina Modotti: Between Art and Revolution* (New Haven, CT: Yale University Press, 2003), 52.

29. Roy Newquist, interview with Katherine Anne Porter, *McCall's*, August 1965, 137.

30. Cited in William L. Nance, "Katherine Anne Porter and Mexico," *Southwest Review* 55, no. 2 (1970): 145–46.

31. Newquist, interview with Katherine Anne Porter, 142.

32. Porter was highly inconsistent on these views, and would at times contradict them by claiming that she had always wanted to go to Europe instead of Mexico. In 1946, she wrote to her nephew Paul Porter, "Darling what would you do in Mexico? Go to university there? Don't run away anywhere, for anything. Don't go anywhere unless you have a real reason. . . . I wanted for years to go to Europe, but I kept getting little jobs that took me back to Mexico." Cited in Mark Busby, "Katherine Anne Porter and Texas: Ambivalence Deep as the Bone," in *From Texas to the World and Back: Essays on the Journeys of Katherine Anne Porter*, ed. Mark Busby and Dick Heaberlin (Fort Worth: Texas Christian University Press, 2001), 137.

33. Cited in Thomas Walsh, *Katherine Anne Porter and Mexico: The Illusion of Eden* (Austin: University of Texas Press, 1992), 1.

34. Walsh, *Katherine Anne Porter and Mexico*, 111.

35. Nance, "Katherine Anne Porter and Mexico," 145.

36. Newquist, interview with Katherine Anne Porter, 141.

37. Katherine Anne Porter, introduction to *The Itching Parrot*, in *Mutual Impressions: Writers from the Americas Reading One Another*, ed. Ilan Stavans (Durham, NC: Duke University Press, 1999), 219.

38. Walsh, *Katherine Anne Porter and Mexico*, 5–6.

39. Katherine Anne Porter, "Where Presidents Have No Friends," in *The Collected Essays and Occasional Writings of Katherine Anne Porter* (New York: Delacorte Press, 1970), 415.

40. Walsh, *Katherine Anne Porter and Mexico*, 59.

41. Katherine Anne Porter, "A Letter from Mexico," in *Uncollected Early Prose of Katherine Anne Porter*, ed. Ruth M. Alvarez and Thomas F. Walsh (Austin: University of Texas Press, 1993), 135.

42. Katherine Anne Porter, *Outline of Popular Arts and Crafts*, in *Uncollected Early Prose of Katherine Anne Porter*, 138.

43. Ibid., 165.

44. Ibid.

45. Ibid.

46. Porter, "A Letter from Mexico," 133.

47. Katherine Anne Porter, "Old Gods and New Messiahs," review of *Idols behind Altars*, by Anita Brenner, in *"This Strange, Old World" and Other Book Reviews by Katherine Anne Porter*, ed. Darlene Harbour Unrue (Athens: University of Georgia Press, 1991), 86.

48. Porter, *Outline of Popular Arts and Crafts*, 170.

49. Ibid., 139.

50. Ibid., 150.

51. Alvarez and Walsh, introduction to "Children of Xochitl," in *Uncollected Early Prose*, 73.

52. Porter, "Children of Xochitl," 75.

53. Ibid., 79.

54. Ibid., 80.

55. Ibid., 82.

56. José E. Limón, *American Encounters: Greater Mexico, the United States, and the Erotics of Culture* (Boston: Beacon Press, 1998), 37.

57. Walsh, *Katherine Anne Porter and Mexico*, 83.

58. Katherine Anne Porter, "María Concepción," in *The Collected Essays and Occasional Writings of Katherine Anne Porter* (New York: Delacorte Press, 1970), 3.

59. Porter, "María Concepción," 6.

60. Ibid., 8.

61. Ibid., 20.

62. Hank Lopez, "A Country and Some People I Love," interview with Katherine Anne Porter, *Harper's*, 1965, 58.

63. Porter, "Old Gods and New Messiahs," 84, 88.

64. Glusker, *Anita Brenner*, 81.

65. Ibid., 58.

66. See ibid., 104–7 on the reception of *Idols*.

67. Richard D. Woods, "Anita Brenner: Cultural Mediator for Mexico," *Studies in Latin American Popular Culture* 9 (1990): 214.

68. Cited in Glusker, *Anita Brenner*, 37.

69. Cited in ibid., 38.

70. Alan Knight, "Racism, Revolution, and *Indigenismo*: Mexico, 1910–1940," in *The Idea of Race in Latin America, 1879–1940*, ed. Richard Graham (Austin: University of Texas Press, 1990), 74.

71. Debroise, *Mexican Suite*, 174–82.

72. Katherine Anne Porter, "Mexico's Thirty Long Years of Revolution," in *"This Strange, Old World,"* 122.

73. Argenteri, *Tina Modotti*, 61.

74. Walsh, *Katherine Anne Porter and Mexico*, 166.

75. Andrea Noble, *Tina Modotti: Image, Texture, Photography* (Albuquerque: University of New Mexico Press, 2000), 61–63.

76. Glusker, *Anita Brenner*, 68.

77. Ibid., 69.

78. Ibid., 68.

79. There are numerous biographies about Modotti's life and work, which include Patricia Albers, *Shadows, Fire, Snow: The Life of Tina Modotti* (New York: Clarkson Potter, 1999); Argenteri, *Tina Modotti*; Mildred Constantine, *Tina Modotti: A Fragile Life* (San Francisco: Chronicle, 1993); Margaret Hooks, *Tina Modotti: Photographer and*

Revolutionary (London: Pandora, 1993); Sarah M. Lowe, *Tina Modotti: Photographs* (New York: Harry N. Abrams, 1995); Mulvey, "Frida Kahlo and Tina Modotti"; Elena Poniatowska, *Tinísima* (Mexico City: Era, 1992).

80. Rexroth, *Autobiographical Novel*, 344.

81. Recently some critics have provided more extensive formal analysis as a corrective to the biographical emphasis of Modotti scholarship. See Carol Armstrong, "This Photography Which Is Not One: In the Gray Zone with Tina Modotti," *October* 101 (Summer 2002): 19–52; and Noble, *Tina Modotti*.

82. Cited in Lowe, *Tina Modotti: Photographs*, 36.

83. Cited in Noble, *Tina Modotti*, 36.

84. Lowe, *Tina Modotti: Photographs*, 21.

85. Ibid., 37–38.

86. Weston, *Daybooks*, 1:136.

87. Although the relationship between Modotti and Weston is typically understood as one of student and teacher, Carol Armstrong makes a convincing argument that, in certain instances, Modotti pioneered techniques that later appeared in Weston's photography.

88. Poniatowska, *Tinísima*, 51.

89. Noble, *Tina Modotti*, 93.

90. Michael Denning, *The Cultural Front: The Laboring of American Culture in the Twentieth Century* (London and New York: Verso, 1996).

CHAPTER FOUR

1. See, for example, Ellis Amburn, *Subterranean Kerouac: The Hidden Life of Jack Kerouac* (New York: St. Martin's Press, 1998); Ann Charters, *Kerouac* (New York: St. Martin's Press, 1994); Tom Clark, *Jack Kerouac: A Biography* (New York: Marlowe, 1995); Paul Maher, *Kerouac: The Definitive Biography* (Lanham, MD: Taylor Trade Publishing, 2004); Dennis McNally, *Desolate Angel: Jack Kerouac, the Beat Generation, and America* (Cambridge, MA: Da Capo Press, 2003); Gerald Nicosia, *Memory Babe: A Critical Biography of Jack Kerouac* (Berkeley: University of California Press, 1983); David Sandison, *Jack Kerouac: An Illustrated Biography* (Chicago: Chicago Review Press, 1999); Matt Theado, *Understanding Jack Kerouac* (Columbia: University of South Carolina Press, 2000); Steve Turner, *Jack Kerouac: Angelheaded Hipster* (New York: Viking, 1996).

2. Jack Kerouac, *Selected Letters, 1940–1956*, ed. Ann Charters (New York and London: Viking, 1995), 229.

3. Nicosia, *Memory Babe*, 21.

4. Richard S. Sorrell, "Novelists and Ethnicity: Jack Kerouac and Grace Metalious as Franco-Americans," *MELUS* 9, no. 1 (1982): 39.

5. Sorrell, "Novelists and Ethnicity," 39.

6. Maher, *Kerouac: The Definitive Biography*, 3–4.

7. Jack Kerouac, *Lonesome Traveler* (New York: Grove Press, 1990), v.

8. Jack Kerouac, *Doctor Sax* (New York: Buccaneer Books, 1975), 7.

9. Jack Kerouac, *Visions of Gerard* (New York: Penguin, 1991), 4.

10. Kerouac, *Visions of Gerard*, 64.

11. Ibid., 85.

12. Jack Kerouac, *Book of Sketches* (New York: Penguin, 2006), 398. Although beyond the scope of this chapter, there is also much to be said about how and why Kerouac associated his literary scene with the "homosexual arts."

13. Jack Kerouac, *The Subterraneans* (New York: Grove Press 1994), 3, 79.

14. Jack Kerouac, *Desolation Angels* (New York: Paragon Books, 1979), 331.

15. On Kerouac's attraction to the other, see Jonathan Paul Eburne, "Trafficking in the Void: Burroughs, Kerouac, and the Consumption of Otherness," *MFS: Modern Fiction Studies* 43, no. 1 (1997): 53–92; Robert Holton, "Kerouac among the Fellahin: *On the Road* to the Postmodern," *MFS: Modern Fiction Studies* 41, no. 2 (1995): 265–83; Manuel Luis Martinez, *Countering the Counterculture: Reading Postwar American Dissent from Jack Kerouac to Tomás Rivera* (Madison: University of Wisconsin Press, 2003); Brendon Nichols, "The Melting Pot That Boiled Over: Racial Fetishism and the *Lingua Franca* of Jack Kerouac's Fiction," *MFS: Modern Fiction Studies* 49, no. 3 (2003): 524–49; Jon Panish, "Kerouac's *The Subterraneans*: A Study of 'Romantic Primitivism,'" *MELUS* 19, no. 3 (1994): 107–23.

16. On the importance of French to Kerouac's writing, see Carole Allamand, "La voix du paradis: La québécitude de Jack Kerouac," *Etudes françaises* 40, no. 1 (2004): 131–48 and Ann Douglas, "'Telepathic Shock and Meaning Excitement': Kerouac's Poetics of Intimacy," *College Literature* 27, no. 1 (2000): 8–26.

17. Kerouac, *Subterraneans*, 3.

18. Kerouac, *Selected Letters*, 228–29.

19. Tim Hunt, *Kerouac's Crooked Road: Development of a Fiction* (Berkeley: University of California Press, 1996), xx. See also Allamand, "La voix du paradis," 131–48.

20. Kerouac, *Visions of Gerard*, 85.

21. Ibid., 14.

22. Kerouac, *Vanity of Duluoz* (New York: Penguin, 1994), 32.

23. Kerouac, *Selected Letters*, 228.

24. Kerouac, *Subterraneans*, 103–4. My translation, with thanks to Monika Giacoppe for help.

25. Kerouac, *Selected Letters*, 229.

26. Jack Kerouac, *Maggie Cassidy* (London: André Deutsch, 1959), 84.

27. Daniel Belgrad, *The Culture of Spontaneity: Improvisation and the Arts in Postwar America* (Chicago: University of Chicago Press, 1998). See Andrew Ross, "Hip, and the Long Front of Color," in *No Respect: Intellectuals and Popular Culture* (New York and London: Routledge, 1989), 65–101 on the allure of blackness for the white hipster of the 1950s.

28. Kerouac, *Desolation Angels*, 221.

29. Daniel Belgrad, "The Transnational Counterculture: Beat-Mexican Intersections," in *Reconstructing the Beats*, ed. Jennie Skerl (New York: Palgrave-Macmillan, 2004), 29.

30. In James T. Jones, *A Map of "Mexico City Blues": Jack Kerouac as Poet* (Carbondale: Southern Illinois University Press, 1992), 52.

31. Maher, *Kerouac: The Definitive Biography*, 255; Nicosia, *Memory Babe*, 414.

32. Allen Ginsberg, "Ready to Roll," in *Reality Sandwiches* (San Francisco: City Lights Books, 1966), 64.

33. Kerouac, *Desolation Angels*, 234.

34. Jack Kerouac, "Mexico Fellahin," in *Lonesome Traveler*, 23; Kerouac, *Tristessa* (New York: Penguin, 1992), 55; Kerouac, *Mexico City Blues* (New York: Grove Press, 1959), 134.

35. Charters, *Kerouac*, 226.

36. Kerouac, *Tristessa*, 42.

37. On *Mexico City Blues*, see Jones, *A Map of "Mexico City Blues,"* and Glenn Sheldon, *South of Our Selves: Mexico in the Poems of Williams, Kerouac, Corso, Ginsberg, Levertov, and Hayden* (Jefferson, NC: McFarland, 2004).

38. Jack Kerouac, *On the Road* (New York: Penguin, 1991), 265. All subsequent references will be cited parenthetically in the text.

39. Kerouac, *Selected Letters*, 229.

40. On Kerouac and the Fellahin, see Holton, "Kerouac among the Fellahin"; Nicosia, *Memory Babe*, 390; Jones, *A Map of "Mexico City Blues,"* 63–66.

41. Quoted in Maher, *Kerouac: The Definitive Biography*, 113.

42. Kerouac, *Doctor Sax*, 14, 182, 115.

43. Kerouac, *Visions of Gerard*, 5.

44. Kerouac, *Maggie Cassidy*, 33.

45. Kerouac, *Tristessa*, 83, 10.

46. Kerouac, *Mexico City Blues*, 12.

47. Maher, *Kerouac: The Definitive Biography*, 213.

48. Kerouac, *Desolation Angels*, 343. My translation, with thanks to Monika Giacoppe for help.

49. Ibid., 344.

50. Ibid.

51. John Dickinson and Brian Young, *A Short History of Quebec* (Montreal and Kingston: Queen's University Press, 2003), 303–44; Myrna Kotash, *Long Way from Home: The Story of the Sixties Generation in Canada* (Toronto: James Lorimer, 1980), 209–10.

52. Pierre Berton, *The Last Good Year* (Toronto: Doubleday Canada, 1997), 280.

53. Dickinson and Young, *Short History of Quebec*, 320; Kotash, *Long Way from Home*, 238.

54. Dickinson and Young, *Short History of Quebec*, 320, 325.

55. Jack Kerouac, *Good, Blonde, and Others* (San Francisco: Grey Fox Press, 1993), 193.

56. Jack Todd, *Desertion in the Time of Vietnam* (New York: Houghton Mifflin, 2001), 223.

57. Todd, *Desertion in the Time of Vietnam*, 232.

58. Berton, *Last Good Year*, 314.

59. Dickinson and Young, *Short History of Quebec*, 337.

60. E. D. Blodgett, "Francophone Writing," in *Cambridge Companion to Canadian Literature*, ed. Eva-Marie Kröller (New York: Cambridge University Press, 2004), 61.

61. Blodgett, "Francophone Writing," 52.

62. Kotash, *Long Way from Home*, 214.

63. Pierre Anctil, "Jack Kerouac anachronique," *Voix et images* 3, no. 13 (1988): 408–12.

64. Jonathan Weiss, "Victor-Lèvy Beaulieu: Écrivain américain," *Etudes françaises* 19, no. 1 (1983): 41–57.

65. Ray Ellenwood, "Victor-Lèvy Beaulieu and the Québeckization of American Literature," in *Context North America: Canadian/U.S. Literary Relations*, ed. Camille R. La Bossière (Ottawa: University of Ottawa Press, 1994), 92.

66. Victor-Lèvy Beaulieu, *Jack Kerouac: A Chicken-Essay*, trans. Sheila Fischman (Toronto: Coach House Press, 1975), 140. All subsequent references will be cited parenthetically in the text. For a similar argument, see Armand Chartier, "Jack Kerouac, franco-américain," *Revue d'histoire littéraire du Québec et du Canada français* 12 (1986): 83–96.

67. Mary Jean Green, "The Quebec Novel Today: Multiple Perspectives," *French Review* 67, no. 6 (1994): 924.

68. Green, "The Quebec Novel Today," 924–25.

69. Laurent Mailhot, "Volkswagen Blues, de Jacques Poulin, et autres 'histoires américaines' du Québec," *Oeuvres et critiques* 14, no. 1 (1989): 19–28; Anne Marie Miraglia, "L'amérique et l'américanité chez Jacques Poulin," *Urgences* 34 (1991): 34–45;

Jonathan Weiss, "Une lecture américaine de Volkswagen Blues," *Etudes françaises* 21, no. 3 (1985): 89–96.

70. Critics who have linked Poulin to Kerouac include D. F. Rogers, the unnamed author of "Jacques Poulin," in *Canadian Writers since 1960*, ed. W. H. New (Detroit: Gale Research, 1986), 898; Miraglia, "L'amérique et l'américanité chez Jacques Poulin"; Marie-Lyne Piccione, "Au rendez-vous des doublures: Volkswagen Blues de Jacques Poulin," *Annales du Centre de recherches sur l'Amérique Anglophone* 21 (1996): 121–28.

71. Weiss, "Une lecture américaine de *Volkswagen Blues*."

72. Jacques Poulin, *Volkswagen Blues*, trans. Sheila Fischman (Toronto: Cormorant Books, 1988), 23. All subsequent references will be cited parenthetically in the text.

73. See, for example, Jean Babineau, *Vortex* (Moncton: Éditions Perce-Neige), 2001; Gerald LeBlanc, *Moncton Mantra*, trans. Jo-Anne Elder (Toronto: Guernica, 2001); and the songs and poetry of Zachary Richard. For Anglophone Canadian appropriations of Kerouac, see Ken McGoogan, *Visions of Kerouac* (Toronto: Willow Avenue Books, 2007), and Ray Robertson, *What Happened Later* (Markham, ON: Thomas Allen, 2007).

74. Amburn, *Subterranean Kerouac*, 154.

75. Kerouac, *Desolation Angels*, 247.

76. Cynthia Steele, *Politics, Gender, and the Mexican Novel, 1968–1988: Beyond the Pyramid* (Austin: University of Texas Press, 1992), 112.

77. Eric Zolov, *Refried Elvis: The Rise of the Mexican Counterculture* (Berkeley: University of California Press, 1999).

78. Carlos Monsiváis, "La naturaleza de la onda," in *Amor perdido* (Mexico City: Biblioteca Era, 1977), 236. All translations are mine, unless otherwise indicated.

79. Jorge I. Domínguez and Rafael Fernández de Castro, *The United States and Mexico: Between Partnership and Conflict* (New York and London: Routledge, 2001).

80. Zolov, *Refried Elvis*, 235.

81. Oscar J. Martinez, *Troublesome Border* (Tucson: University of Arizona Press, 1988).

82. José Agustín, *La contracultura en México: La historia y el significado de los rebeldes sin causa, los jipitecas, los punks y las bandas* (Mexico City: Grijalbo, 1996), 95.

83. Danny J. Anderson, "Creating Cultural Prestige: Editorial Joaquín Mortiz," *Latin American Research Review* 31, no. 2 (1996): 15.

84. The term *La Onda* was first applied to this group of authors by Margo Glantz, with the encouragement of Saldaña. Margo Glantz, comp., *Onda y escritura en Mexico: Jóvenes de 20 a 33* (Mexico City: Siglo Veintiuno Editores, 1971). Agustín has been more resistant to the concept than Saldaña, who was a close friend until his untimely death. His short story, "Cual es La Onda?" (*Diálogos* 10, no. 1 [1974]: 11–13), deals parodically with the bourgeois pretensions of this group. However, he also leveled the more serious accusation that Glantz's critical treatment misunderstood the group's scope and complexity. José Agustín, *El rock de la carcel* (Mexico City: Editores Mexicanos Unidos, 1986), 78–79. See also Elena Poniatowska, "La literatura de la Onda," in *¡Ay, vida no me mereces!* (Mexico City: Joaquín Mortiz, 1985), 169–213, for an account of those dynamics.

85. Juan Bruce-Novoa, "*La Onda* as Parody and Satire," in *José Agustín: "Onda" and Beyond*, ed. June C. D. Carter and Donald L. Schmidt (Columbia: University of Missouri Press, 1986), 37–55.

86. Leal cited in Manuel de Jesús Hernández-Gutiérrez, "Mexican and Mexican-American Literary Relations," in *Mexican Literature: A History*, ed. David William Foster (Austin: University of Texas Press, 1994), 388.

87. Agustín, *El rock de la cárcel*, 10.
88. Cited in John Kirk, "The Development of an *Ondero*," in Carter and Schmidt, eds., *José Agustín*, 17.
89. Ironically, as Anderson has shown, both the more elitist experimental fiction of the Latin American boom writers and the youthfully irreverent work of the Onderos were published by the same press, the Editorial Joaquín Mortiz, which "actively encouraged both these trends" (Anderson, "Creating Cultural Prestige," 3).
90. The notion of the contact zone comes from Mary Louise Pratt, *Imperial Eyes: Travel Writing and Transculturation* (New York: Routledge, 1992). It has been usefully augmented to describe the Mexican context by Claudio Lomnitz-Adler in *Deep Mexico, Silent Mexico: An Anthropology of Nationalism* (Minneapolis: University of Minnesota Press, 2001).
91. José Agustín, *De perfil* (Mexico City: Joaquín Mortiz, 1966), 282.
92. Agustín, *De perfil*, 285.
93. Ibid.
94. José Agustín, *Se está haciendo tarde* (Mexico City: Joaquín Mortiz, 1973), 134.
95. Agustín, *Se está haciendo tarde*, 135.
96. Ibid., 136.
97. José Agustín, *La tumba* (Mexico City: Grijalbo, 1978), 26.
98. Néstor García Canclini, *Consumers and Citizens: Globalization and Multicultural Conflicts*, trans. George Yúdice (Minneapolis: University of Minnesota Press, 2001), 74.
99. Agustín, *La tumba*, 78.
100. Kerouac, *On the Road*, 7.
101. Agustín, *De perfil*, 164.
102. Ibid., 168.
103. Zolov, *Refried Elvis*.
104. Cited in ibid., 161.
105. Poniatowska, "La literatura de la Onda," in *¡Ay, vida no me mereces!*, 175.
106. Zolov, *Refried Elvis*, 27, 160. Zolov notes that rock music's movement from top to bottom of the class hierarchy in Mexico is the opposite of its trajectory in the United States and Britain, where it emerged as a working-class cultural form and then caught on with middle-class young people.
107. Juan Bruce-Novoa, *Retrospace: Collected Essays on Chicano Literature* (Houston: Arte Público, 1990) 49.
108. Octavio Paz, *The Other Mexico: Critique of the Pyramid*, trans. Lysander Kemp (New York, Grove Press, 1972), 48.
109. Ibid.
110. Lawrence Venuti makes an important contribution to such discussion by foregrounding translation as both a form of labor and creative activity. His *Scandals of Translation: Toward an Ethics of Difference* (New York: Routledge, 1998) is an effort to rescue translation from its marginality within intellectual, legal, and corporate discourse.

CHAPTER FIVE

1. Raymond Chandler, *The Long Goodbye* (New York: Vintage Books, 1992); Michael Connelly, *The Black Ice* (New York: Warner Books, 1993).
2. Chandler, *Long Goodbye*, 37.
3. Peter Andreas and Timothy Snyder, eds., *The Wall around the West: State Borders and Immigration Controls in North America and Europe* (Lanham, MD: Rowman and Little-

field, 2000); Lawrence A. Herzog, *Where North Meets South: Cities, Space, and Politics on the U.S.-Mexico Border* (Austin: University of Texas Press, 1990); David E. Lorey, *The U.S.-Mexican Border in the Twentieth Century: A History of Economic and Social Transformation* (Wilmington, DE: Scholarly Resources, 1999); Oscar J. Martínez, *Border People: Life and Society in the U.S.-Mexico Borderlands* (Tucson: University of Arizona Press, 1994); Claudia Sadowski-Smith, ed., *Globalization on the Line: Culture, Capital, and Citizenship at U.S. Borders* (New York: Palgrave, 2002).

4. Peter Andreas, "Redrawing the Line: Borders and Security in the Twenty-First Century," *International Security* 28, no. 2 (2003): 78–111, at 83–91.

5. Andreas, "Redrawing the Line," 78. For other sources on the rise of transnational crime, see Peter Andreas, *Policing the Globe: Criminalization and Crime Control in International Relations* (New York: Oxford University Press, 2006); Gargi Bhattacharyya, *Traffick: The Illicit Movement of People and Things* (London: Pluto Press, 2005); Stephen E. Flynn, "The False Conundrum: Continental Integration Versus Homeland Security," in *The Rebordering of North America*, ed. Peter Andreas and Thomas J. Biersteker (New York and London: Routledge, 2003), 110–27; Tom Farer, ed., *Transnational Crime in the Americas* (New York: Routledge, 1999); Robert J. Johnston, "Terror and Organized Crime: Old Fears, New Foes, Newer Threats," in *Of Fears and Foes: Security and Insecurity in an Evolving Global Political Economy*, ed. Joseph V. Ciprut (Westport, CT: Praeger, 2000); Willem van Schendel and Itty Abraham, eds., *Illicit Flows and Criminal Things: States, Borders, and the Other Side of Globalization* (Bloomington: Indiana University Press, 2005); Paul R. Viotti, *International Relations and World Politics: Security, Economy, Identity* (Upper Saddle River, NJ: Prentice Hall, 2001); Phil Williams and Dimitri Vlassis, eds., *Combating Transnational Crime: Concepts, Activities, and Responses* (London and Portland, OR: Frank Cass, 2001).

6. Bartosz H. Stanislawksi, "Transnational 'Bads' in the Globalized World: The Case of Transnational Organized Crime," *Public Integrity* 6, no. 2 (2004): 155–70.

7. Stanislawski, "Transnational 'Bads' in the Globalized World," 161.

8. On the detective novel as genre, see Franco Moretti, *Signs Taken for Wonders: Essays in the Sociology of Literary Forms*, trans. Susan Fischer, David Forgacs, and David Miller (London: Verso, 1983); Catherine Nickerson, *The Web of Iniquity: Early Detective Fiction by American Women* (Durham, NC: Duke University Press, 1998); Dennis Porter, *Pursuit of Crime: Art and Ideology in Crime Fiction* (New Haven, CT: Yale University Press, 1981); Martin Priestman, ed., *Cambridge Companion to Crime Fiction* (New York and Cambridge: Cambridge University Press, 2003).

9. Fredric Jameson, *The Political Unconscious: Narrative as a Socially Symbolic Act* (Ithaca, NY: Cornell University Press, 1981), 106.

10. On the conservatism of the detective novel, see Kathleen Gregory Klein, *Woman Detective: Gender and Genre* (Urbana: University of Illinois Press, 1988); Moretti, *Signs Taken for Wonders*; and Dennis Porter, *Pursuit of Crime: Art and Ideology in Detective Fiction* (New Haven, CT: Yale University Press, 1981).

11. The table of contents of a collection like *The Post-Colonial Detective* illustrates the genre's international diversity.

12. On the diversity of the contemporary crime novel, see Hans Bertens and Theo D'haen, *Contemporary American Crime Fiction* (New York: Palgrave, 2001); Dorothea Fischer-Hornung and Monika Mueller, eds., *Sleuthing Ethnicity: The Detective in Multiethnic Crime Fiction* (Madison, NJ: Fairleigh Dickinson University Press, 2003); Adrienne Johnson Gosselin, ed., *Multicultural Detective Fiction: Murder from the "Other Side"* (New York: Garland, 1999); Kathleen Gregory Klein, ed., *Diversity and Detective*

Fiction (Bowling Green, OH: Bowling Green State University Popular Press, 1999); Kathleen Gregory Klein, *The Woman Detective*; Peter Messent, ed., *Criminal Proceedings: The Contemporary American Crime Novel* (Chicago: Pluto Press, 1997); Richard B. Schwartz, *Nice and Noir: Contemporary American Crime Fiction* (Columbia: University of Missouri Press, 2002); Priscilla Walton and Manina Jones, eds., *Detective Agency: Women Rewriting the Hard-Boiled Tradition* (Berkeley: University of California Press, 1999).

13. John Farrow, *City of Ice* (New York: Random House, 1999), 220. All subsequent references will be cited parenthetically in the text.

14. J. Kingston Pierce, "The Cold Truth about John Farrow," *January Magazine*, August 2001, at http://www.januarymagazine.com/profiles/jfarrow.html, accessed April 4, 2005.

15. The show's Canadian referents are carefully tracked on "The Canadian Connection," at http://ccr.ptbcanadian.com, accessed April 7, 2005.

16. Priscilla L. Walton, "Murder Ink: Detective Fiction in Canada," in *Pop Can: Popular Culture in Canada*, ed. Lynne Van Luven and Priscilla L. Walton (Scarborough, ON: Prentice Hall Allyn and Bacon Canada, 1999), 50–55; at 50. As part of the project of recovering the "Canadianicity" of the detective genre, Canadians have recently sought to restore the reputation of the prolific Victorian detective writer Grant Allen, who was born in Ontario. See Therese Greenwood, "Canadian Festival Honours Crime-Writing Pioneer," *Mystery Readers Journal* 19, no. 4 (2003–04): 9–10.

17. Walton, "Murder Ink," 50. David Skene-Melvin, *Canadian Crime Fiction* (Shelburne, ON: Battered Silicon Dispatch Box, 1996), and many of the essays in the Cool Canadian Crime issue of *Mystery Readers Journal* 19, no. 4 (2003–04) make a similar point.

18. Pierce, "The Cold Truth about John Farrow."

19. Ibid.

20. John Farrow, *Ice Lake* (Toronto: HarperCollins Canada, 2001), 425–26.

21. Dashiell Hammett, "The Golden Horseshoe," in *The Continental Op* (New York: Random House, 1974).

22. Chandler, *Long Goodbye*, 370.

23. Ibid., 377.

24. James M. Cain, *Three by Cain* (New York: Vintage, 1989), 7.

25. On Chicano/a detective fiction, see Ralph Rodriguez, *Brown Gumshoes: Detective Fiction and the Search for Chicano/a Identity* (Austin: University of Texas Press, 2005).

26. This comparison is made by Elizabeth Espadas, "Bridging the Gap: Rolando Hinojosa's Writings in Their Latin American Dimension," *MACLAS Latin American Essays* 1 (1987): 7–15, and Wilson Neate, "The Function of Belken County in the Fiction of Rolando Hinojosa: The Voicing of Chicano Experience," *Americas Review* 18, no. 1 (1990): 92–102, and by Hinojosa himself in Rolando Hinojosa-Smith, "Commentary," *World Literature Today* 3–4 (Summer 2001): 64–72.

27. Barbara Strickland, "Rolando Hinojosa-Smith: Crossing Literary Borders," *Austin Chronicle*, August 29, 1997.

28. Rolando Hinojosa, "The Boss I Work for Dialogue: Leslie Marmon Silko & Rolando Hinojosa" (1987), in *Conversations with Leslie Marmon Silko*, ed. Ellen L. Arnold (Jackson: University of Mississippi Press, 2000), 94.

29. For example, see Espadas, "Bridging the Gap."

30. Rolando Hinojosa, "Chicano Literature: An American Literature with a Difference,"

in *The Rolando Hinojosa Reader: Essays Historical and Critical*, ed. José David Saldívar (Houston: Arte Público Press, 1985), 43.

31. Hinojosa-Smith, "Commentary."

32. Martínez, *Border People*, 23–24.

33. Rolando Hinojosa, *Partners in Crime* (Houston: Arte Público Press, 1985), 173. All subsequent references will be cited parenthetically in the text.

34. As Hinojosa remarks of his own borderlander identity, "I was born on the Texas-Tamaulipas border, not far from where the Rio Grande flows into the Gulf of Mexico and not far from the last two engagements of the Civil War. The territory was surveyed by the Spanish army and settled by Spanish subjects in the 1850s, and the people who settled there had a sure sense of identity. That self-confidence remains, and the Valleyites, with all their good and bad points, have one reply when asked where they hail from: 'I'm from the Valley.' They name no town unless pressed to do so." Hinojosa-Smith, "Commentary."

35. Rolando Hinojosa, *Ask a Policeman* (Houston: Arte Público Press, 1998), 183. All subsequent references will be cited parenthetically in the text.

36. On the War on Drugs, see Ted Galen Carpenter, *Bad Neighbor Policy: Washington's Futile War on Drugs in Latin America* (New York: Palgrave Macmillan, 2003); Jorge Chabat, "Drug Trafficking in U.S.-Mexico Relations: What You See Is What You Get," in *Drug Trafficking in the Americas*, ed. Bruce M. Bagley and William O. Walker III (Coral Gables, FL: University of Miami, North-South Center, 1994); Farer, ed., *Transnational Crime in the Americas*, 29–35; Alan L. McPherson, *Intimate Ties, Bitter Struggles: The United States and Latin America since 1945* (Washington DC: Potomac Books, 2006); Richard H. Friman, *NarcoDiplomacy: Exporting the U.S. War on Drugs* (Ithaca, NY: Cornell University Press, 1996); Curtis Marez, *Drug Wars: The Political Economy of Narcotics* (Minneapolis: University of Minnesota Press, 2004); William O. Walker, ed., *Drugs in the Western Hemisphere: An Odyssey of Cultures in Conflict* (Wilmington, DE: Scholarly Resources, 1996).

37. Danilo H. Figueredo, "Ask a Mystery Writer: A Conversation with Rolando Hinojosa," *MultiCultural Review* (September 1999): 27.

38. In John F. Baker, "No Happy Endings," *Boston Review*, February/March 2001, at http://bostonreview.net/BR26.1/taibo.html (accessed April 14, 2009).

39. In Baker, "No Happy Endings."

40. Persephone Braham, *Crimes against the State, Crimes against Persons: Detective Fiction in Cuba and Mexico* (Minneapolis: University of Minnesota Press, 2004), and Ilan Stavans, *Antiheroes: Mexico and Its Detective Novel*, trans. Jesse H. Lytle and Jennifer A. Mattson (Madison, NJ: Fairleigh Dickinson University Press, 1997).

41. Braham, *Crimes against the State, Crimes against Persons*, ix.

42. Cited in Stavans, *Antiheroes*, 146.

43. Braham, *Crimes against the State, Crimes against Persons*, xiii. On the emergence of Leftist detective fiction in the U.S.-Mexico border region, see Claire Fox, "Left Sensationalists at the Transnational Crime Scene: Recent Detective Fiction from the U.S.-Mexican Border," in *World Bank Literature*, ed. Amitava Kumar (Minneapolis: University of Minnesota Press, 2003), 184–200.

44. In Baker, "No Happy Endings."

45. Ibid.

46. Cited in Stavans, *Antiheroes*, 145.

47. Cited in Jorge Hernández Martín, "Paco Ignacio Taibo II: Post-Colonialism and the

Detective Story in Mexico," in *The Post-Colonial Detective*, ed. Ed Christian (New York: Palgrave, 2001), 168.

48. Paco Ignacio Taibo II, "A Note from the Author," in *Return to the Same City*, trans. Laura Dail (New York: Mysterious Press, 1996), n.p.

49. Paco Ignacio Taibo II, *An Easy Thing*, trans. William I. Neuman (Scottsdale, AZ: Poisoned Pen Press, 2002), 228.

50. Taibo, *An Easy Thing*, 236.

51. Richard Boudreaux, "Mexico's Rebel with a Cause and a Knack for Prose," *Los Angeles Times*, December 26, 2004, A3; James C. McKinley, "Solution to a Stalled Revolution: Write a Mystery Novel," *New York Times*, December 13, 2004, A4; Luis Hernandez Navarro, "Cosas del pasado," *La Jornada*, January 18, 2005; Jo Tuckman, "Subcomandante Marcos Pens New Twist to Zapatista Struggle," *The Guardian*, December 20, 2004, 11.

52. Baker, "No Happy Endings."

53. Paco Ignacio Taibo II and Subcomandante Marcos, *The Uncomfortable Dead (What's Missing Is Missing)*, trans. Carlos Lopez (New York: Akashic Books, 2006), 42, 64. All subsequent references will be cited parenthetically in the text.

54. Paco Ignacio Taibo II, *Frontera Dreams*, trans. Bill Verner (El Paso, TX: Cinco Puntos Press, 2002), 106.

CHAPTER SIX

1. Carmen Aguirre, *¿Que Pasa with La Raza, eh?* in *Along Human Lines: Dramas from Refugee Lives*, ed. George Seremba, Carmen Aguirre, and Ann Lambert (Winnipeg: Blizzard, 2000), 51–107.

2. Michelle Habell-Pallán, "'Don't Call Us Hispanic': Popular Latino/a Theater in Vancouver," *Latino/a Popular Culture*, ed. Michelle Habell-Pallán and Mary Romero (New York: New York University Press, 2002), 174–75.

3. On the history of Canadian involvement in Latin America, see J. C. M. Ogelsby, *Gringos from the Far North: Essays in The History of Canadian-Latin American Relations, 1866–1968* (Toronto: Macmillan Company of Canada, 1976).

4. On Argentina's "dirty war," see Martin Edward Andersen, *Dossier secreto: Argentina's desaparecidos and the Myth of the "Dirty War"* (Boulder, CO: Westview Press, 1993); Iain Guest, *Behind the Disappearances: Argentina's Dirty War against Human Rights and the United Nations* (Philadelphia: University of Pennsylvania Press, 1990); Paul H. Lewis, *Guerillas and Generals: The "Dirty War" in Argentina* (Westport, CT: Praeger, 2002); Diana Taylor, *Disappearing Acts: Spectacles of Gender and Nationalism in Argentina's "Dirty War"* (Durham, NC: Duke University Press, 1997); Thomas C. Wright, *State Terrorism in Latin America: Chile, Argentina, and International Human Rights* (New York: Rowman and Littlefield, 2007).

5. Gillermo Verdecchia, *Fronteras Americanas/American Borders* (Toronto: Coach House Press, 1993), 28. All subsequent references will be cited parenthetically in the text.

6. Neil Bisoondath, *Selling Illusions: The Cult of Multiculturalism in Canada* (Toronto: Penguin, 2002).

7. Bryce Traister, "Risking Nationalism: NAFTA and the Limits of the New American Studies," *Canadian Review of American Studies/Revue canadienne d'ètudes américaines* 27, no. 3 (1997): 191–204.

8. Roger Gibbens, "Meaning and Significance of the Canadian-American Border," in

Borders and Border Politics in a Globalizing World, ed. Paul Ganster and David E. Lorey (Lanham, MD: SR Books, 2005), 153.

9. Gibbens, "Meaning and Significance of the Canadian-American Border," 157.

10. At http://pewhispanic.org/files/factsheets/2.pdf, accessed June 14, 2006.

11. At http://migration.ucdavis.edu/MN/more.php?id=3071_0_2_0, accessed June 14, 2006.

12. Thomas C. Wright and Rody Oñate, *Flight from Chile: Voices of Exile* (Albuquerque: University of New Mexico Press, 1998).

13. San Grewal, "Latin Boon for Brand Canada: Divisive Immigration Politics in the U.S. Are Pushing Talented Latinos Further North," *Toronto Star*, August 4, 2007, at http://www.thestar.com/article/243034, accessed July 21, 2008; Danna Harman, "Mexicans Head North for a Better Life. Way North," *Christian Science Monitor*, October 28, 2005, at http://www.csmonitor.com/2005/1028/p01s04-woam.html, accessed July 25, 2007; and Chris Hawley, "Canada Is Wooing Mexican Immigrants," *Arizona Republic*, May 3, 2005, at http://www.azcentral.com/arizonarepublic/news/articles/0503canada03.html, accessed July 25, 2007.

14. Julie Barlow, "Nous, les Latinos du Québec," *L'actualité*, June 1, 2007, at http://www.lactualite.com/article.jsp?content=20070510_154246_5377, accessed July 21, 2008.

15. Hugh Hazleton, "Quebec Hispanico: Themes of Exile and Integration in the Writing of Latin Americans Living in Quebec," *Canadian Literature* 142–43 (Autumn–Winter 1994), and Andrew Machalski, *Hispanic Writers in Canada: A Preliminary Survey of the Activities of Spanish and Latin-American Writers in Canada*, ed. Michael S. Batts (Ottawa: Department of the Secretary of State of Canada, 1988).

16. Habell-Pallán, "Don't Call Us Hispanic," 175; Alberto Gomez, "Where the South and the North Meet: Latino/a Identity and Cultural Heterogeneity," *a-r-c* 1 (November 2000), at http:///a-r-c.gold.ac.uk/a-r-c_Three, 33, accessed June 22, 2006.

17. Gomez, "Where the South and the North Meet," 3.

18. Personal conversation, July 13, 2007. A similar point is made by Karleen Pendleton Jiménez in "Lengua Latina: Latina Canadians (Re)constructing Identity through a Community of Practice," in *Learning, Teaching, and Community: Contributions of Situated and Participatory Approaches to Educational Innovation*, ed. Lucinda Pease-Alvarez and Sandra R. Schecter (Mahwah, NJ: Lawrence Erlbaum, 2005), 235–56.

19. Cited in Pendleton Jiménez, "Lengua Latina," 248.

20. In particular, he mentions Juan Flores and George Yúdice, "Living Borders/Buscando America: Languages of Latino/a Self-Formation," *Social Text* 24 (1990): 57–84; Guillermo Verdecchia, personal conversation, July 13, 2007.

21. Guillermo Verdecchia, personal conversation, July 13, 2007.

22. E-mail correspondence, July 17, 2007.

23. Personal conversation, July 13, 2007.

24. Ibid.

25. Diana Taylor, *The Archive and the Repertoire: Performing Cultural Memory in the Americas* (Durham, NC: Duke University Press, 2005), 20.

26. Taylor, *The Archive and the Repertoire*, 20.

27. My translation.

28. *Canadian Theatre Encyclopedia*, at http://www.canadiantheatre.com/dict.pl?term=Verdecchia%2C%20Guillermo (accessed December 12, 2007).

29. Personal conversation, July 13, 2007.

30. Habell-Pallán, "Don't Call Us Hispanic."

31. Daniel Brooks and Guillermo Verdecchia, *The Noam Chomsky Lectures* (Toronto: Coach House Press, 1991), 33.

32. Gloria Anzaldúa, *Borderlands/La Frontera: The New Mestiza* (San Francisco: Aunt Lute Books, 1999), 25.

33. See, for example, Mary Pat Brady, "The Fungibility of Borders," *Nepantla: Views from the South* 1, no. 1 (2000): 171–90; Claire Fox, *The Fence and the River: Culture and Politics at the U.S.-Mexico Border* (Minneapolis: University of Minnesota Press, 199); and Debra A. Castillo and María Socorro Tabuenca Córdoba, *Border Women: Writing from La Frontera* (Minneapolis: University of Minnesota Press, 2002).

34. Ignacio M. García, *Chicanismo: The Forging of a Militant Ethos among Mexican Americans* (Tucson: University of Arizona Press, 1997).

35. Marcus Youssef and Guillermo Verdecchia, *A Line in the Sand* (Burnaby, BC: Talonbooks, 1997).

EPILOGUE

1. Guillermo Verdecchia, *Fronteras Americanas/American Borders* (Toronto: Coach House Press, 1993), 20.

2. Personal conversation, July 13, 2007.

3. Ron Paul, "A North American United Nations?" August 28, 2006, at http://www.house.gov/paul/tst/tst2006/tst082806.htm, accessed November 13, 2007, and Phyllis Schafly, "Scholars Explain Bush's SPP," October 10, 2007, at http://www.eagleforum.org/column/2007/oct07/07-10-10.html, accessed November 13, 2007.

4. Christopher Hayes, "The NAFTA Superhighway," *The Nation* (August 27, 2007), at http://www.thenation.com/doc/20070827/hayes, accessed August 29, 2007.

5. At http://mexicanosalgrito.blogspot.com/2007/08/just-thought.html, accessed August 14, 2007, my translation.

BIBLIOGRAPHY

Adams, Rachel, and Sarah Casteel. "Canada and the Americas." Special issue of *Compara-tive American Studies* 3, no. 1 (March 2005).

Aguirre, Carmen. *¿Que Pasa with La Raza, eh?* In *Along Human Lines: Dramas from Refugee Lives*, edited by George Seremba, Carmen Aguirre, and Ann Lambert, 51–107. Winni-peg: Blizzard, 2000.

Agustín, José. *La contracultura en México: La historia y el significado de los rebeldes sin causa, los jipitecas, los punks y las bandas.* Mexico City: Grijalbo, 1996.

———. "Cual es La Onda?" *Diálogos* 10, no. 1 (1974): 11–13.

———. *De perfil.* Mexico City: Joaquín Mortiz, 1966.

———. *El rock de la cárcel.* Mexico City: Editores Mexicano Unidos, 1986.

———. *Se está haciendo tarde.* Mexico City: Joaquín Mortiz, 1973.

———. *La tumba.* Mexico City: Grijalbo, 1978.

Albers, Patricia. *Shadows, Fire, Snow: The Life of Tina Modotti.* New York: Clarkson Potter, 1999.

Albrow, Martin. *The Global Age: State and Society beyond Modernity.* Cambridge: Polity Press, 1996.

Allamand, Carole. "La voix du paradis: La québécitude de Jack Kerouac." *Etudes françaises* 40, no. 1 (2004): 131–48.

Allen, Kristina Nilson. "Homeland Insecurity." *Cultural Survival Quarterly* 30, no. 3 (2006): 18–23.

Alvarez, Ruth M., and Thomas F. Walsh, eds. *Uncollected Early Prose of Katherine Anne Por-ter.* Austin: University of Texas Press, 1993.

Amburn, Ellis. *Subterranean Kerouac: The Hidden Life of Jack Kerouac.* New York: St. Mar-tin's Press, 1998.

Anctil, Pierre. "Jack Kerouac anachronique." *Voix et images* 3, no. 13 (1988): 408–12.

Andersen, Martin Edward. *Dossier secreto: Argentina's desaparecidos and the Myth of the "Dirty War."* Boulder, CO: Westview Press, 1993.

Anderson, Benedict. *Imagined Communities: Reflections on the Origin and Spread of Nation-alism.* London and New York: Verso, 1991.

Anderson, Danny J. "Creating Cultural Prestige: Editorial Joaquín Mortiz." *Latin American Research Review* 31, no. 2 (1996): 3–41.

Andreas, Peter. *Policing the Globe: Criminalization and Crime Control in International Rela-tions.* New York: Oxford University Press, 2006.

———. "Redrawing the Line: Borders and Security in the Twenty-First Century." *International Security* 28, no. 2 (2003): 78–111.

Andreas, Peter, and Thomas J. Biersteker, eds. *The Rebordering of North America: Integration and Exclusion in a New Security Context*. New York and London: Routledge, 2003.

Andreas, Peter, and Timothy Snyder, eds. *The Wall around the West: State Borders and Immigration Controls in North America and Europe*. Lanham, MD: Rowman and Littlefield, 2000.

Andrews, Jennifer, and Priscilla L. Walton. "Rethinking Canadian and American Nationality: Indigeneity and the 49th Parallel in Thomas King." *American Literary History* 18, no. 3 (2006): 600–617.

Anzaldúa, Gloria. *Borderlands/La Frontera: The New Mestiza*. San Francisco: Spinsters/Aunt Lute, 1987.

Appadurai, Arjun. *Modernity at Large: Cultural Dimensions of Globalization*. Minneapolis: University of Minnesota Press, 1996.

Appendini, Kirsten, and Sven Bislev, eds. *Economic Integration in NAFTA and the EU*. New York: St. Martin's Press, 1999.

Argenteri, Letizia. *Tina Modotti: Between Art and Revolution*. New Haven, CT: Yale University Press, 2003.

Armstrong, Carol. "This Photography Which Is Not One: In the Gray Zone with Tina Modotti." *October* 101 (Summer 2002): 19–52.

Baker, John F. "No Happy Endings." *Boston Review*. February/March 2001. Accessed December 13, 2007 at http://bostonreview.net/BR26.1/taibo.html.

Barnet, Andrea. *All-Night Party: The Women of Bohemian Greenwich Village and Harlem, 1913–1930*. Chapel Hill, NC: Algonquin Books of Chapel Hill, 2004.

Beatty, Perrin. "Canada in North America: Isolation or Integration?" In *The Future of North American Integration: Beyond NAFTA*, edited by Peter Hakim and Robert E. Litan, 31–72. Washington, DC: Brookings Institution Press, 2002.

Beaulieu, Victor-Lèvy. *Jack Kerouac: A Chicken-Essay*. Translated by Sheila Fischman. Toronto: Coach House Press, 1975.

Belgrad, Daniel. *The Culture of Spontaneity: Improvisation and the Arts in Postwar America*. Chicago: University of Chicago Press, 1998.

———. "The Transnational Counterculture: Beat-Mexican Intersections." In *Reconstructing the Beats*, edited by Jennie Skerl, 27–40. New York: Palgrave-Macmillan, 2004.

Bell, Virginia E. "Counter-Chronicling and Alternative Mapping in *Memoria del Fuego* and *Almanac of the Dead*." *MELUS* 25, no. 3/4 (2000): 5–30.

Beltrán, Gonzalo Aguirre. *La población negra de Mexico*. Mexico City: Ediciones Fuente Cultural, 1946.

Benjamin, Thomas. "Rebuilding the Nation." In *The Oxford History of Mexico*, edited by Michael Meyer and William H. Beezley, 467–502. New York and Oxford: Oxford University Press, 2000.

Bennett, Herman Lee. *Lovers, Family, Friends: The Formation of Afro-Mexico, 1580–1910*. Durham, NC: Duke University Press, 1993.

Benstock, Shari. *Women of the Left Bank: Paris, 1900–1940*. Austin: University of Texas Press, 1986.

Berger, Mark T. "Romancing the Zapatistas: International Intellectuals and the Chiapas Rebellion." *Latin American Perspectives* 28, no. 2 (2001): 149–70.

Bertens, Hans, and Theo D'haen. *Contemporary American Crime Fiction*. New York: Palgrave, 2001.

Berton, Pierre. *The Last Good Year*. Toronto: Doubleday Canada, 1997.

Bhalla, A. S. *Regional Blocs: Building Blocks or Stumbling Blocks?* New York: St. Martin's Press, 1997.

Bhattacharyya, Gargi. *Traffick: The Illicit Movement of People and Things.* London: Pluto Press, 2005.

Bisoondath, Neil. *Selling Illusions: The Cult of Multiculturalism in Canada.* Toronto: Penguin, 2002.

Blair, Sara. "Modernism and the Politics of Culture." In *The Cambridge Companion to Modernism*, edited by Michael Levenson, 157–73. Cambridge: Cambridge University Press, 1999.

Blodgett, E. D. "Francophone Writing." In *Cambridge Companion to Canadian Literature*, edited by Eva-Marie Kröller, 49–69. New York: Cambridge University Press, 2004.

Bolton, Herbert E. *The Spanish Borderlands: A Chronicle of Old Florida and the Southwest.* New Haven, CT: Yale University Press, 1921.

Boudreaux, Richard. "Mexico's Rebel with a Cause and a Knack for Prose." *Los Angeles Times*, December 26, 2004, A3.

Bourne, Randolph S. "Trans-National America." In *Theories of Ethnicity: A Classical Reader*, edited by Werner Sollers, 93–108. New York: New York University Press, 1996.

Bové, Paul A. "Can American Studies Be Area Studies?" In *Learning Places: The Afterlives of Area Studies*, edited by Masao Miyoshi and Harry Harootunian, 206–30. Durham, NC: Duke University Press, 2002.

Brady, Mary Pat. *Extinct Lands, Temporal Geographies: Chicana Literature and the Urgency of Space.* Durham, NC: Duke University Press, 2002.

Braham, Persephone. *Crimes against the State, Crimes against Persons: Detective Fiction in Cuba and Mexico.* Minneapolis: University of Minnesota Press, 2004.

Bramen, Carrie Tirado. "Speaking in Typeface: Characterizing Stereotypes in Gayl Jones's *Mosquito*." *MFS: Modern Fiction Studies* 49, no. 1 (2003): 124–54.

Brand, Johanna, and Warren Almand. *The Life and Death of Anna Mae Aquash.* Toronto: Lorimer, 1993.

Brenner, Anita. *Idols behind Altars.* New York: Payson and Clark, 1929.

———. *The Wind That Swept Mexico: The History of the Mexican Revolution, 1910–1942.* New York and London: Harper and Brothers, 1943.

Brigham, Ann. "Productions of Geographic Scale and Capitalist-Colonialist Enterprise in Leslie Marmon Silko's *Almanac of the Dead*." *MFS: Modern Fiction Studies* 50, no. 2 (2004): 303–31.

Brogan, Kathleen. "American Stories of Cultural Haunting: Tales of Heirs and Ethnographers." *College English* 57, no. 2 (1995): 149–65.

Brooks, Daniel, and Guillermo Verdecchia. *The Noam Chomsky Lectures.* Toronto: Coach House Press, 1991.

Bruce-Novoa, Juan. "*La Onda* as Parody and Satire." In *José Agustín: "Onda" and Beyond*, edited by June C. D. Carter and Donald L. Schmidt, 37–55. Columbia: University of Missouri Press, 1986.

———. *Retrospace: Collected Essays on Chicano Literature, Theory, and History.* Houston: Arte Público Press, 1990.

Brunet-Jailly, Emanuel. *Comparing Local Cross-Border Relations under the EU and NAFTA.* Orono, ME: Canadian-American Center, 2004.

Brysk, Alison. "Turning Weakness into Strength: The Internationalization of Indian Rights." *Latin American Perspectives* 23, no. 2 (1996): 38–57.

Burkholder, Mark A. "An Empire beyond Compare." In *The Oxford History of Mexico*, edited by Michael Meyer and William H. Beezley, 115–50. New York and Oxford: Oxford University Press, 2000.

Busby, Mark. "Katherine Anne Porter and Texas: Ambivalence Deep as the Bone." In *From Texas to the World and Back: Essays on the Journeys of Katherine Anne Porter*, edited by Mark Busby and Dick Heaberlin, 133–48. Fort Worth: Texas Christian University Press, 2001.

Cain, James M. *Three by Cain*. New York: Vintage, 1989.

Calderón, Hector, and José David Saldívar, eds. *Criticism in the Borderlands: Studies in Chicano Literature, Culture, and Ideology*. Durham, NC: Duke University Press, 1991.

Cameron, Maxwell A., and Brian W. Tomlin. *The Making of NAFTA: How the Deal Was Done*. Ithaca, NY: Cornell University Press, 2000.

Camp, Gregory S. "Working Out Their Own Salvation: The Allotment of Land in Severalty and the Turtle Mountain Chippewa Band, 1870–1920." *American Indian Culture and Research Journal* 14, no. 2 (1990): 19–38.

The Canadian Connection. April 7, 2005. At http://ccr.ptbcanadian.com.

Canclini, Néstor García. *Consumers and Citizens: Globalization and Multicultural Conflicts*. Translated by George Yúdice. Minneapolis: University of Minnesota Press, 2001.

———. "Latins or Americans: Narratives of the Border." *Canadian Journal of Latin American and Caribbean Studies*" 23, no. 46 (1998): 117–31.

Cano, Gabriela. "The *Porfiriato* and the Mexican Revolution: Constructions of Feminism and Nationalism." In *Nation, Empire, Colony: Historicizing Gender and Race*, edited by Ruth Roach Pierson and Nupur Chaudhuri, 106–20. Bloomington: Indiana University Press, 1998.

Canton, Jeffrey. "Coyote Lives." In *The Power to Bend Spoons*, edited by Beverly Daurio, 90–97. Toronto: Mercury Press, 1998.

Carpenter, Ted Galen. *Bad Neighbor Policy: Washington's Futile War on Drugs in Latin America*. New York: Palgrave Macmillan, 2003.

Carroll, Patrick J. "Africa in the Americas: Blacks in Mexico." Humanities Interactive. April 2, 2007. At http://www.humanities-interactive.org/newworld/africa/blacks_in_mexico.htm.

———. *Blacks in Colonial Veracruz: Race, Ethnicity, and Regional Development*. Austin: University of Texas Press, 1991.

Casteel, Sarah. *Second Arrivals: Landscape and Belonging in Contemporary Writing of the Americas*. Charlottesville: University of Virginia Press, 2007.

Casteel, Sarah, and Patrick Imbert, eds. *Canada and Its Americas: Transnational Navigations*. Montreal and Kingston: McGill-Queen's University Press, forthcoming.

Castells, Manuel. *The Internet Galaxy: Reflections on The Internet, Business, and Society*. Oxford: Oxford University Press, 2001.

———. *The Rise of the Network Society*. New York and Oxford: Blackwell Publishers, 1996.

Castillo, Debra A., and Maria Socorro Tabuenca de Cordoba. *Border Women: Writing from La Frontera*. Minneapolis: University of Minnesota Press, 2002.

Chabat, Jorge. "Drug Trafficking in U.S.-Mexico Relations: What You See Is What You Get." In *Drug Trafficking in the Americas*, edited by Bruce M. Bagley and William O. Walker III. Coral Gables, FL: University of Miami, North-South Center, 1994.

Chandler, Raymond. *The Long Goodbye*. New York: Vintage Books, 1992.

Chandra, Sarika. "Interruptions: Tradition, Borders, and Narrative in Gayl Jones's *Mosquito*." In *After the Pain: Critical Essays on Gayl Jones*, edited by Fiona Mills and Keith Mitchell, 137–53. New York: Peter Lang, 2006.

Charters, Ann. *Kerouac*. New York: St. Martin's Press, 1994.

Chartier, Armand. "Jack Kerouac, franco-américain." *Revue d'histoire littéraire du Québec et du Canada français* 12 (1986): 83–96.

Clark, Tom. *Jack Kerouac: A Biography*. New York: Marlowe, 1995.

Clarke, George Elliot. "Another Great Thing." *Canadian Literature* 165 (Summer 2000): 139–41.

———. *Odysseys Home: Mapping African-Canadian Literature*. Toronto: University of Toronto Press, 2002.

Claybaugh, Amanda. *The Novel of Purpose: Literature and Social Reform in the Anglo-American World*. Ithaca, NY: Cornell University Press, 2007.

Claybough, Casey. "Afrocentric Recolonizations: Gayl Jones's 1990s Fiction." *Contemporary Literature* 46, no. 2 (2005): 243–74.

Claypoole, Antoinette Clara. *Who Would Unbraid Her Hair: The Legend of Annie Mae*. Ashland, OR: Anam Cara Press, 1999.

Connelly, Michael. *The Black Ice*. New York: Warner Books, 1993.

Constantine, Mildred. *Tina Modotti: A Fragile Life*. San Francisco: Chronicle, 1993.

Cook, Curtis, and Juan D. Lindau, eds. *Aboriginal Rights and Self-Government: The Canadian and Mexican Experience in North American Perspective*. Montreal and Kingston: McGill-Queen's University Press, 2000.

Cook-Lynn, Elizabeth. *Why I Can't Read Wallace Stegner and Other Essays*. Madison: University of Wisconsin Press, 1996.

"Cool Canadian Crime." *Mystery Readers Journal* 19, no. 4 (2003–04): 3–4.

Crane, Gregg. "The Lexicon of Rights, Power, and Community in *Blake*: Martin R. Delany's Dissent from *Dred Scott*." *American Literature* 68, no. 3 (1996): 527–53.

Cuevas, Marco Polo Hernández. *African Mexicans and the Discourse on Modern Nation*. Dallas: University Press of America, 2004.

Davidson, Arnold, Priscilla Walton, and Jennifer Andrews. *Border Crossings: Thomas King's Cultural Inversions*. Toronto: University of Toronto Press, 2003.

Davis, Charles T., and Henry Louis Gates Jr. "Introduction: The Language of Slavery." In *The Slave's Narrative*, edited by Charles T. Davis and Henry Louis Gates Jr., xi–xxxiii. Oxford: Oxford University Press, 1985.

Dawson, Alexander S. *Indian and Nation in Revolutionary Mexico*. Tucson: University of Arizona Press, 2004.

Debroise, Olivier. *Mexican Suite: A History of Photography in Mexico*. Translated by Stella de Sá Rego. Austin: University of Texas Press, 2001.

Delany, Martin. *Blake; or, the Huts of America*. Boston: Beacon Press, 1970.

———. *The Condition, Elevation, Emigration, and Destiny of the Colored People of the United States and Official Report of the Niger Valley Exploring Party*. New York: Arno Press, 1968.

———. "Political Destiny of the Colored Race on the American Continent." In *Pamphlets of Protest: An Anthology of Early African-American Protest Literature, 1790–1860*, edited by Richard Newman, Patrick Rael, and Philip Lapsansky, 226–39. New York: Routledge, 2001.

Deloria, Philip J. *Indians in Unexpected Places*. Lawrence: University Press of Kansas, 2004.

Delpar, Helen. *The Enormous Vogue of Things Mexican: Cultural Relations between the United States and Mexico, 1920–1935*. Tuscaloosa: University of Alabama Press, 1992.

Denning, Michael. *The Cultural Front: The Laboring of American Culture in the Twentieth Century*. London and New York: Verso, 1996.

Desmond, Jane C., and Virginia R. Dominguez. "Resituating American Studies in a Critical Internationalism." *American Quarterly* 48 (Fall 1996): 475–90.

Dick, Bruce Allen, ed. *The Critical Response to Ishmael Reed*. Westport, CT: Greenwood Press, 1999.

Dickinson, John, and Brian Young. *A Short History of Quebec*. Montreal and Kingston: Queen's University Press, 2003.

Domínguez, Jorge I., and Rafael Fernández de Castro. *The United States and Mexico: Between Partnership and Conflict*. New York and London: Routledge, 2001.

Douglas, Ann. "'Telepathic Shock and Meaning Excitement': Kerouac's Poetics of Intimacy." *College Literature* 27, no. 1 (2000): 8–26.

———. *Terrible Honesty: Mongrel Manhattan in the 1920s*. New York: Farrar, Straus, Giroux, 1995.

Dowd, Gregory Evans. "Wag the Imperial Dog: Indians and Overseas Empires in North America, 1650–1776." In *A Companion to American Indian History*, edited by Philip J. Deloria and Neal Salisbury, 46–67. Malden, MA: Blackwell Publishers, 2004.

Drake, James D. "Appropriating a Continent: Geographical Categories, Scientific Metaphors, and the Construction of Nationalism in British North America and Mexico." *Journal of World History* 15, no. 3 (2004): 323–57.

Duina, Francesco G. *The Social Construction of Free Trade: The European Union, NAFTA, and MERCOSUR*. Princeton, NJ: Princeton University Press, 2006.

Eburne, Jonathan Paul. "Trafficking in the Void: Burroughs, Kerouac, and the Consumption of Otherness." *MFS: Modern Fiction Studies* 43, no. 1 (1997): 53–92.

Edmunds, R. David. "Native Americans and the United States, Canada, and Mexico." In *A Companion to American Indian History*, edited by Philip J. Deloria and Neal Salisbury, 397–421. Malden, MA: Blackwell Publishers, 2004.

Edwards, Tamala M. Review of *Mosquito*, by Gayl Jones. *Time*, February 8, 1999, 72.

Ellenwood, Ray. "Victor-Lèvy Beaulieu and the Québeckization of American Literature." In *Context North American: Canadian/U.S. Literary Relations*, edited by Camille R. La Bossière, 89–95. Ottawa: University of Ottawa Press, 1994.

Elliot, Emory. "Diversity in the United States and Abroad: What Does It Mean When American Studies Is Transnational?" *American Quarterly* 59, no. 1 (2007): 1–25.

Espadas, Elizabeth. "Bridging the Gap: Rolando Hinojosa's Writings in Their Latin American Dimension." *MACLAS Latin American Essays* 1 (1987): 7–15.

Farer, Tom, ed. *Transnational Crime in the Americas*. New York: Routledge, 1999.

Farrow, John. *City of Ice*. New York: Random House, 1999.

———. *Ice Lake*. Toronto: HarperCollins Canada, 2001.

Fenwick, C. G. "Canada and the Monroe Doctrine." *American Journal of International Law* 32, no. 4 (1938): 782–85.

Figueredo, Danilo H. "Ask a Mystery Writer: A Conversation with Rolando Hinojosa." *MultiCultural Review* (September 1999): 26–27.

Fischer-Hornung, Dorothea, and Monika Mueller, eds. *Sleuthing Ethnicity: The Detective in Multiethnic Crime Fiction*. Madison, NJ: Fairleigh Dickinson University Press, 2003.

Fischer, Thomas C. *The Europeanization of America: What Americans Need to Know about the European Union*. Durham, NC: Carolina Academic Press, 1995.

Fishkin, Shelly Fisher. "Crossroads of Cultures: The Transnational Turn in American Studies." *American Quarterly* 57, no. 1 (2005): 17–57.

Fitz, Earl. *Rediscovering the New World: Inter-American Studies in a Comparative Context*. Iowa City: University of Iowa Press, 1991.

Flores, Juan, and George Yúdice. "Living Borders/Buscando America: Languages of Latino/a Self-Formation." *Social Text* 24 (1990): 57–84.

Flynn, Stephen E. "The False Conundrum: Continental Integration Versus Homeland Security." In *The Rebordering of North America*, edited by Peter Andreas and Thomas J. Biersteker, 110–27. New York and London: Routledge, 2003.

Foley, Neil. *The White Scourge: Mexicans, Blacks, and Poor Whites in Texas Cotton Culture.* Berkeley: University of California Press, 1997.

Forbes, Jack D. "A Native American Perspective on NAFTA." *Cultural Survival Quarterly* 17, no. 4 (1994): 3.

Foster, Frances Smith. *Witnessing Slavery: The Development of Ante-Bellum Slave Narratives.* Madison: University of Wisconsin Press, 1979.

Fox, Claire F. *The Fence and the River: Culture and Politics at the U.S.-Mexico Border.* Minneapolis: University of Minnesota Press, 1999.

———. "Left Sensationalists at the Transnational Crime Scene: Recent Detective Fiction from the U.S.-Mexican Border." In *World Bank Literature*, edited by Amitava Kumar, 184–200. Minneapolis: University of Minnesota Press, 2003.

Fox, Claire, and Claudia Sadowski-Smith. "Theorizing the Hemisphere: Inter-Americas Work at the Intersection of American, Canadian, and Latin American Studies." *Comparative American Studies* 2, no. 1 (2004): 41–74.

Franklin, John Hope, and Loren Schweninger. *Runaway Slaves: Rebels on the Plantation, 1790–1860.* New York: Oxford, 1999.

Franks, C. E. S. "Indian Policy: Canada and the United States Compared." In *Aboriginal Rights and Self Government*, edited by Curtis Cook and Juan Lindau, 221–63. Montreal: McGill-Queen's University Press, 2000.

Friman, Richard H. *NarcoDiplomacy: Exporting the U.S. War on Drugs.* Ithaca, NY: Cornell University Press, 1996.

Gambrell, Alice. *Women Intellectuals, Modernism, and Difference: A Transatlantic Culture, 1919–1945.* Cambridge: Cambridge University Press, 1997.

García, Ignacio M. *Chicanismo: The Forging of a Militant Ethos among Mexican Americans.* Tucson: University of Arizona Press, 1997.

Gates, Henry Louis, Jr. "Sanctuary." Review of *Mosquito*, by Gayl Jones. *New York Times Book Review*, November 14, 1999, 14.

Geist, Anthony L., and José B. Monleón. "Modernism and Its Margins: Rescripting Hispanic Modernism." In *Modernism and Its Margins: Reinscribing Cultural Modernity from Spain and Latin America*, edited by Geist and Monleón, xvii–xxxv. New York and London: Garland, 1999.

Germeten, Nicole von. *Black Blood Brothers: Confraternities and Social Mobility for Afro-Mexicans.* Gainesville: University Press of Florida, 2006.

Gibbens, Roger. "Meaning and Significance of the Canadian-American Border." In *Borders and Border Politics in a Globalizing World*, edited by Paul Ganster and David E. Lorey, 151–67. Lanham, MD: SR Books, 2005.

Giles, Paul. "Transnationalism and Classic American Literature." *PMLA* 118, no. 1 (2003): 62–77.

Ginaris, Nicholas V. *The North American Free Trade Agreement and the European Union.* Westport, CT: Praeger, 1998.

Ginsberg, Allen. "Ready to Roll." In *Reality Sandwiches*, 64. San Francisco: City Lights Books, 1966.

Glantz, Margo. *Onda y escritura en Mexico: Jóvenes de 20 a 33.* Mexico City: Siglo Veintiuno Editores, 1971.

Glusker, Suzannah Joel. *Anita Brenner: A Mind of Her Own.* Austin: University of Texas Press, 1998.

Goldtooth, Tom. "NAFTA and Native Americans: An Agenda for Transnational Termination? *The Circle* 13, no. 1 (1999): 12.

Gomez, Alberto "Where the South and the North Meet: Latino/a Identity and Cultural Heterogeneity." *Fuse: Art, Media, Politics* 22, no. 4 (2000): 26–32.

Gómez-Peña, Guillermo. *The New World Border: Prophecies, Poems, and Loqueras for the End of the Century.* San Francisco: City Lights, 1996.

Gosselin, Adrienne Johnson. *Multicultural Detective Fiction: Murder from the "Other Side."* New York: Garland, 1999.

Green, Mary Jean. "The Quebec Novel Today: Multiple Perspectives." *French Review* 67, no. 6 (1994): 922–29.

Greenblatt, Stephen. "Culture." In *Critical Terms for Literary Study*, edited by Frank Lentricchia and Thomas McLaughlin, 225–32. Chicago: University of Chicago Press, 1995.

Greenwood, Therese. "Canadian Festival Honours Crime-Writing Pioneer." *Mystery Readers Journal* 19, no. 4 (2003–04): 9–10.

Gross, Robert. "The Transnational Turn: Rediscovering American Studies in a Wider World." *Journal of American Studies* 34 (2000): 373–93.

Gruesz, Kirsten Silva. "The Occluded History of Transamerican Literature." In *Critical Latin American and Latino Studies*, edited by Juan Poblete, 121–37. Minneapolis: University of Minnesota Press, 2003.

Guest, Iain. *Behind the Disappearances: Argentina's Dirty War against Human Rights and the United Nations.* Philadelphia: University of Pennsylvania Press, 1990.

Guillemin, Jeanne. "The Politics of National Integration: A Comparison of United States and Canadian Indian Administration." *Social Problems* 25, no. 3 (1978): 319–32.

"Guillermo Verdecchia." *Canadian Theatre Encyclopedia.* December 12, 2007. At http://www.canadiantheatre.com/dict.pl?term=Verdecchia%2C%20Guillermo.

Guinn, Jeff. *Our Land before We Die: The Proud Story of the Seminole Negro.* New York: Putnam, 2002.

Gunn, Drewey Wayne. *American and British Writers in Mexico, 1556–1973.* Austin: University of Texas Press, 1974.

Gutiérrez-Jones, Carl. *Rethinking the Borderlands: Between Chicano Culture and Legal Discourse.* Berkeley: University of California Press, 1995.

Habell-Pallán, Michelle. "'Don't Call Us Hispanic': Popular Latino/a Theater in Vancouver." In *Latino/a Popular Culture*, edited by Michelle Habell-Pallán and Mary Romero, 174–89. New York: New York University Press, 2002.

Habermas, Jürgen. *The Postnational Constellation: Political Essays.* Cambridge: Polity Press, 2001.

Harley, J. B. *The New Nature of Maps: Essays in the History of Cartography.* Baltimore: Johns Hopkins University Press, 2001.

Harman, Danna. "Mexicans Head North for a Better Life. Way North." *Christian Science Monitor*, October 28, 2005. Accessed July 25, 2007 at http://www.csmonitor.com/2005/1028/p01s04-woam.html.

Hassig, Ross. "The Collision of Two Worlds." In *The Oxford History of Mexico*, edited by Michael Meyer and William H. Beezley, 79–112. New York and Oxford: Oxford University Press, 2000.

Hoogvelt, Ankie. *Globalisation and the Postcolonial World: The New Political Economy of Development.* London: Macmillan, 1997.

Hammett, Dashiell. "The Golden Horseshoe." In *The Continental Op.* New York: Random House, 1974.

Harper, Frances E. W. "The Air of Freedom." In *The Freedman's Book*, edited by Lydia Maria Francis Child, 243. Boston: Ticknor and Fields, 1865.

Harper, Michael. "Gayl Jones: An Interview." *Massachusetts Review* 18, no. 4 (1977): 692–715.

Hartz, Louis. *The Liberal Tradition in America: An Interpretation of American Political Thought since the Revolution*. New York: Harcourt Brace, 1955.

Hawley, Chris. "Canada Is Wooing Mexican Immigrants." *Arizona Republic*, May 3, 2005. Accessed July 25, 2007 at http://www.azcentral.com/arizonarepublic/news/articles/0503canada03.html.

Hayes, Christopher. "The NAFTA Superhighway." *The Nation* (August 27, 2007). Accessed August 29, 2007 at http://www.thenation.com/doc/20070827/hayes.

Hays, Rachel. "Cross-Border Indigenous Nations: A History." *BorderLines* 4, no. 1 (1996): 1–4.

Hazleton, Hugh. "Quebec Hispanico: Themes of Exile and Integration in the Writing of Latin Americans Living in Quebec." *Canadian Literature* 142–43 (Autumn–Winter 1994): 120–35.

Hendricks, Steve. *The Unquiet Grave: The FBI and the Struggle for the Soul of Indian Country*. New York: Thunder's Mouth Press, 2006.

Hendrikson, Alan K. "The Power and Politics of Maps." In *Reordering the World: Geopolitical Perspectives on the Twenty-First Century*, edited by George J. Demko and William B. Wood, 49–70. Boulder, CO: Westview Press, 1999.

Hernández-Gutiérrez, Manuel de Jesus. "Mexican and Mexican-American Literary Relations." In *Mexican Literature: A History*, edited by David William Foster, 385–438. Austin: University of Texas Press, 1994.

Herzog, Lawrence. *Where North Meets South: Cities, Space, and Politics on the U.S.-Mexico Border*. Austin: University of Texas Press, 1990.

Hill, Lawrence. *Any Known Blood*. New York: Morrow, 1997.

———. "Black Like Us: Canada Is Not Nearly as Integrated as We Like to Think." *Globe and Mail*, February 9, 2000, A15.

Hinojosa, Rolando. *Ask a Policeman*. Houston: Arte Público Press, 1998.

———. "The Boss I Work for Dialogue: Leslie Marmon Silko & Rolando Hinojosa" (1987). In *Conversations with Leslie Marmon Silko*, edited by Ellen L. Arnold, 84–96. Jackson: University of Mississippi Press, 2000.

———. "Commentary." *World Literature Today* 3–4 (Summer 2001): 64–72.

———. *Partners in Crime*. Houston: Arte Público Press, 1985.

Hollander, Paul. *Political Pilgrims: Western Intellectuals in Search of the Good Society*. New Brunswick, NJ: Transaction Publishers, 1998.

Holton, Robert. "Kerouac among the Fellahin: *On the Road* to the Postmodern." *MFS: Modern Fiction Studies* 41, no. 2 (1995): 265–83.

Hooks, Margaret. *Tina Modotti: Photographer and Revolutionary*. London: Pandora, 1993.

Hufbauer, Gary Clyde, and Jeffrey J. Schott. *NAFTA Revisited: Achievements and Challenges*. Washington DC: Institute for International Economics, 2005.

Hughes, Langston. *I Wonder as I Wander*. New York: Hill and Wang, 1993.

Huhndorf, Shari. "Picture Revolution: 'Tribal Internationalism' and the Future of the Americas in Leslie Marmon Silko's *Almanac of the Dead*." In *Mapping the Americas: The Transnational Politics of Contemporary Native Culture*. Ithaca, NY: Cornell University Press, 2009.

Hunt, Tim. *Kerouac's Crooked Road: Development of a Fiction*. Berkeley: University of California Press, 1996.

Hutcheon, Linda. *A Poetics of Postmodernism: History, Theory, Fiction*. New York: Routledge, 1988.

Imbert, Patrick *Consensual Disagreement: Canada and the Americas*. Ottawa: University of Ottawa Press, 2005.

Irmer, Thomas. "An Interview with Leslie Marmon Silko." July 12, 2006. At http://www.altx.com/interviews/silko.html.

Irwin, Robert McKee. "¿Que hacen los nuevos americanistas? Collaborative Strategies for a Postnationalist American Studies." *Comparative American Studies* 2, no. 3 (2004): 303–23.

———. "*Ramona* and Postnationalist American Studies: On 'Our America' and the Mexican Borderlands." *American Quarterly* 55, no. 4 (2003): 539–67.

Jacobs, Harriet. *Incidents in the Life of a Slave Girl: The Classic Slave Narratives*, edited by Henry Louis Gates Jr., 333–515. New York: Penguin, 1987.

Jameson, Fredric. *The Political Unconscious: Narrative as a Socially Symbolic Act*. Ithaca, NY: Cornell University Press, 1981.

Jaramillo, Velia. "Mexico's 'Southern Plan': The Facts." *World Press Review* 48, no. 9 (2001). Accessed December 19, 2006 at http://www.worldpress.org/.

Jay, Gregory S. "The End of American Literature." *College English* 53 (March 1991): 264–81.

Jay's Treaty. Accessed September 29, 2007 at http://www.earlyamerica.com/earlyamerica/milestones/jaytreaty/text.html.

Jefferson, Thomas. "A Hemisphere to Itself." Letter to Alexander von Humboldt, December 6, 1813. Accessed June 26, 2007 at http://odur.let.rug.nl/~usa/P/tj3/writings/brf/jef1224.htm.

Johnston, Robert J. "Terror and Organized Crime: Old Fears, New Foes, Newer Threats." In *Of Fears and Foes: Security and Insecurity in an Evolving Global Political Economy*, edited by Joseph V. Ciprut, 187–208. Westport, CT: Praeger, 2000.

Jones, Gayl. *Corregidora*. Boston: Beacon Press, 1975.

———. *Mosquito*. Boston: Beacon Press, 1999.

Jones, James T. *A Map of "Mexico City Blues": Jack Kerouac as Poet*. Carbondale: Southern Illinois University Press, 1992.

Jrade, Cathy L. *Modernismo, Modernity, and the Development of Spanish American Literature*. Austin: University of Texas Press, 1998.

Kaplan, Amy. "'Left Alone with America': The Absence of Empire in the Study of American Culture." In *The Cultures of United States Imperialism*, edited by Amy Kaplan and Donald Pease, 3–21. Durham, NC: Duke University Press, 1993.

———. "Violent Belongings and the Question of Empire Today." *American Quarterly* 56, no. 1 (2004): 1–18.

Kaup, Monika. *Rewriting North American Borders in Chicano and Chicana Narrative*. New York: Lang, 2001.

Kerber, Linda. "Diversity and the Transformation of American Studies." *American Quarterly* 41, no. 3 (1989): 415–31.

Kerouac, Jack. *Book of Sketches*. New York: Penguin, 2006.

———. *Desolation Angels*. New York: Paragon Books, 1979.

———. *Doctor Sax*. New York: Buccaneer Books, 1975.

———. *Good, Blonde, and Others*. San Francisco: Grey Fox Press, 1993.

———. *Lonesome Traveler*. New York: Grove Press, 1990.

———. *Maggie Cassidy*. London: André Deutsch, 1959.

———. *Mexico City Blues*. New York: Grove Press, 1959.

———. *On the Road*. New York: Penguin, 1991.

———. *Selected Letters, 1940–1956*. Edited by Ann Charters. New York and London: Viking, 1995.

———. *The Subterraneans*. New York: Grove Press, 1994.

———. *Tristessa*. New York: Penguin, 1992.

———. *Visions of Gerard*. New York: Penguin, 1991.

King, Martin Luther, Jr. *Conscience for Change: Massey Lectures, Seventh Series*. Toronto: Canadian Broadcasting Corporation, 1967.

King, Thomas. *The Truth about Stories: A Native Narrative*. Minneapolis: University of Minnesota Press, 2005.

———. *Truth and Bright Water*. New York: Atlantic Monthly Press, 1999.

Kingsolver, Anne E. *NAFTA Stories: Fears and Hopes in Mexico and the United States*. Boulder, CO: Lynne Rienner Publishers, 2001.

Kirk, John. "The Development of an *Ondero*." In *José Agustín: "Onda" and Beyond*, edited by June C. D. Carter and Donald L. Schmidt, 9–23. Columbia: University of Missouri Press, 1986.

Klein, Kathleen Gregory. *Woman Detective: Gender and Genre*. Urbana: University of Illinois Press, 1988.

Klein, Kathleen Gregory, ed. *Diversity and Detective Fiction*. Bowling Green, OH: Bowling Green State University Popular Press, 1999.

Klein, Naomi. "The Rise of the Fortress Continent." *The Nation* (February 3, 2003): 10.

Knight, Alan. "Racism, Revolution, and *Indigenismo*: Mexico, 1910–1940." In *The Idea of Race in Latin America, 1879–1940*, edited by Richard Graham, 71–113. Austin: University of Texas Press, 1990.

Kotash, Myrna. *Long Way from Home: The Story of the Sixties Generation in Canada*. Toronto: James Lorimer, 1980.

Krupat, Arnold. *Turn to The Native: Studies in Criticism and Culture*. Lincoln: University of Nebraska Press, 1996.

Krupat, Arnold, and Michael A. Elliot. "American Indian Fiction and Anticolonial Resistance." In *Columbia Guide to American Indian Literatures of the United States since 1945*, edited by Eric Cheyfitz, 127–82. New York: Columbia University Press, 2006.

Landon, Fred. "Canadian Negroes and the John Brown Raid." *Journal of Negro History* 6, no. 2 (1921): 174–82.

Leclair, Tom. Review of *Mosquito*, by Gayl Jones. *Salon*, January 12, 1999. At http://www .salon.com/books/sneaks/1999/01/12sneaks.html.

Levi, Jerome M. "A New Dawn or a Cycle Restored? Regional Dynamics and Cultural Politics in Indigenous Mexico, 1978–2001." In *The Politics of Ethnicity: Indigenous Peoples in Latin American States*, edited by David Maybury Lewis, 3–49. Cambridge, MA: Harvard University Press, 2002.

Levine, Robert. *Martin Delany, Frederick Douglass, and the Politics of Representative Identity*. Chapel Hill: University of North Carolina Press, 1997.

Lewis, Bart L. "Modernism." In *Mexican Literature: A History*, edited by David William Foster, 139–70. Austin: University of Texas Press, 1994.

Lewis, G. Malcolm, ed. *Cartographic Encounters: Perspectives on Native American Mapmaking and Map Use*. Chicago: University of Chicago Press, 1998.

Lewis, Martin, and Kären E. Wigen. *The Myth of the Continents: A Critique of Metageography*. Berkeley: University of California Press, 1997.

Lewis, Paul H. *Guerillas and Generals: The "Dirty War" in Argentina*. Westport, CT: Praeger, 2002.

Limón, José E. *American Encounters: Greater Mexico, the United States, and the Erotics of Culture*. Boston: Beacon Press, 1998.

Lomnitz-Adler, Claudio. *Deep Mexico, Silent Mexico: An Anthropology of Nationalism*. Minneapolis: University of Minnesota Press, 2001.

Lopez, Hank. "A Country and Some People I Love." Interview with Katherine Anne Porter. *Harper's* (1965): 58–67.

Lorey, David E. *The U.S.-Mexican Border in the Twentieth Century: A History of Economic and Social Transformation.* Wilmington, DE: Scholarly Resources, 1999.

Lowe, Sarah M. *Tina Modotti: Photographs.* New York: Harry N. Abrams, 1995.

Luna-Firebaugh, Eileen M. "The Border Crossed Us: Border Crossing Issues of the Indigenous Peoples of the Americas." *Wicazo Sa Review* (Spring 2002): 159–81.

Lundy, Benjamin. *The Life, Travels, and Opinions of Benjamin Lundy.* New York: Augustus M. Kelley, 1971.

Machalski, Andrew. *Hispanic Writers in Canada: A Preliminary Survey of the Activities of Spanish and Latin-American Writers in Canada.* Edited by Michael S. Batts. Ottawa: Department of the Secretary of State of Canada, 1988.

Macias, Anna. "Women and the Mexican Revolution, 1910–1920." *Americas* 37, no. 1 (1980): 53–82.

Maciel, David. *El Norte: The U.S.-Mexico Border in Contemporary Cinema.* San Diego: Institute for Regional Studies of the Californias, 1990.

Maher, Paul. *Kerouac: The Definitive Biography.* Lanham, MD: Taylor Trade Publishing, 2004.

Mailhot, Laurent. "*Volkswagen Blues*, de Jacques Poulin, et autres 'histoires américaines' du Québec." *Oeuvres et critiques* 14, no. 1 (1989): 19–28.

Mandujano, Isain. "Mexico's Southern Border: A Virtual Line." *World Press Review* 48, no. 9 (2001). Accessed December 19, 2006 at http://www.worldpress.org/.

Marez, Curtis. *Drug Wars: The Political Economy of Narcotics.* Minneapolis: University of Minnesota Press, 2004.

Martín, Jorge Hernández. "Paco Ignacio Taibo II: Post-Colonialism and the Detective Story in Mexico." In *The Post-Colonial Detective*, edited by Ed Christian 159–75. New York: Palgrave, 2001.

Martinez, Manuel Luis. *Countering the Counterculture: Reading Postwar American Dissent from Jack Kerouac to Tomás Rivera.* Madison: University of Wisconsin Press, 2003.

Martínez, Oscar J. *Border People: Life and Society in the U.S.-Mexico Borderlands.* Tucson: University of Arizona Press, 1994.

———. *Troublesome Border.* Tucson: University of Arizona Press, 1988.

McDonald, Dedra S. "To Be Black and Female in the Spanish Southwest: Toward a History of African Women on New Spain's Far Northern Frontier." In *African American Women Confront the West, 1600–2000*, edited by Quintard Taylor and Shirley Ann Wilson Moore, 32–52. Norman: University of Oklahoma Press, 2003.

McKinley, James C. "Solution to a Stalled Revolution: Write a Mystery Novel." *New York Times*, December 13, 2004, A4.

McNally, Dennis. *Desolate Angel: Jack Kerouac, the Beat Generation, and America.* Cambridge, MA: Da Capo Press, 2003.

McPherson, Alan L. *Intimate Ties, Bitter Struggles: The United States and Latin America since 1945.* Washington DC: Potomac Books, 2006.

Meinig, D. W. *The Shaping of America: A Geographical Perspective on 500 Years of History.* Vol. 1, Atlantic America, 1492–1800. New Haven, CT: Yale University Press, 1986.

———. *The Shaping of America: A Geographical Perspective on 500 Years of History.* Vol. 2, Continental America, 1800–1967. New Haven, CT: Yale University Press, 1993.

Menchaca, Martha. *Recovering History, Constructing Race: The Indian, Black, and White Roots of Mexican Americans.* Austin: University of Texas Press, 2001.

Mensah, Joseph. *Black Canadians: History, Experiences, Social Conditions.* Halifax: Fernwood Publishing, 2002.

Merino, José. *Mexicanos al Grito*. Accessed August 14, 2007 at http://mexicanosalgrito
.blogspot.com/2007/08/just-thought.html.

Messent, Peter. *Criminal Proceedings: The Contemporary American Crime Novel*. Chicago:
Pluto Press, 1997.

Michaelson, Scott, and David E. Johnson, eds. *Border Theory: The Limits of Cultural Politics*.
Minneapolis: University of Minnesota Press, 1997.

Mignolo, Walter. "Misunderstanding and Colonization: The Reconfiguration of Memory
and Space." *South Atlantic Quarterly* 92, no. 2 (1993): 209–60.

Migration News. "Canada: Immigration, Nafta." *Migration News* 12, no. 1 (2005). Accessed
June 14, 2006 at http://migration.ucdavis.edu/MN/more.php?id=3071_0_2_0.

Miller, J. R. *Skyscrapers Hide the Heavens: A History of Indian-White Relations in Canada*. Toronto: University of Toronto Press, 1991.

Mills, Fiona. "Telling the Untold Tale: Afro-Latino/a Identifications in the Work of Gayl
Jones." In *After the Pain: Critical Essays on Gayl Jones*, edited by Fiona Mills, 91–115.
New York: Peter Lang, 2006.

Miraglia, Anne Marie. "L'amérique et l'américanité chez Jacques Poulin." *Urgences* 34
(1991): 34–45.

Miyoshi, Masao. "A Borderless World? From Colonialism to Transnationalism and the
Decline of the Nation-State." *Critical Inquiry* 19, no. 4 (1993): 726–51.

Monsiváis, Carlos. "Anita Brenner and the Mexican Renaissance." Foreword to *Anita
Brenner: A Mind of Her Own*, by Susannah Joel Glusker, ix–xvi. Austin: University of
Texas Press, 1998.

———. "La naturaleza de la Onda." In *Amor Perdido*, 225–62. Mexico City: Biblioteca Era,
1977.

Morales, Rebecca. "Dependence or Interdependence: Issues and Policy Choices Facing
Latin Americans and Latinos." In *Borderless Borders: U.S. Latinos, Latin Americans, and
the Paradox of Interdependence*, edited by Frank Bonilla, Edwin Meléndez, Rebecca Morales, and María de los Angeles Torres, 1–13. Philadelphia: Temple University Press,
1998.

Morantz, Alan, *Where Is Here? Canada's Maps and the Stories They Tell*. Toronto: Penguin,
2002.

Moretti, Franco. *Signs Taken for Wonders: Essays in the Sociology of Literary Forms*. Translated
by Susan Fischer, David Forgacs, and David Miller. London: Verso, 1983.

Morrison, Toni. *Beloved*. New York: Plume, 1987.

Mulvey, Laura, with Peter Wollen. "Frida Kahlo and Tina Modotti." In *Visual and Other
Pleasures*, 81–107. Bloomington: Indiana University Press, 1989.

Mundy, Barbara E. *The Mapping of New Spain: Indigenous Cartography and the Maps of the
Relaciones Geográficas*. Chicago: University of Chicago Press, 1996.

Murphy, Gretchen. *Hemispheric Imaginings: The Monroe Doctrine and Narratives of U.S. Empire*. Durham, NC: Duke University Press, 2005.

Muthyala, John. "*Almanac of the Dead*: The Dream of the Fifth World in the Borderlands."
Literature Interpretation Theory 14, no. 4 (2003): 357–85.

———. "Reworlding America: The Globalization of American Studies." *Cultural Critique*
47 (Winter 2001): 91–119.

———. *Reworlding America: Myth, History, and Narrative*. Athens: Ohio University Press,
2006.

"NAFTA Sparks Bloody Clashes in Mexico (Canadian Native Leaders Plan Trip to Chiapas
to Support Uprising)." *Windspeaker* 11, no. 22 (1994): 3.

Nance, William L. "Katherine Anne Porter and Mexico." *Southwest Review* 55, no. 2 (1970): 143–53.

Nash, June. "The Reassertion of Indigenous Identity: Mayan Responses to State Intervention in Chiapas." *Latin American Research Review* 30, no. 3 (1995): 7–41.

Navarro, Luis Hernandez. "Cosas del Pasado." *La Jornada*, January 18, 2005. Accessed December 13, 2007 at http://www.jornada.unam.mx/2005/01/18/023a1pol.php.

Neate, Wilson. "The Function of Belken County in the Fiction of Rolando Hinojosa: The Voicing of Chicano Experience." *Americas Review* 18, no. 1 (1990): 92–102.

Newquist, Roy. Interview with Katherine Anne Porter. *McCall's*, August 1965, 89, 137–43.

Nichols, Brendon. "The Melting Pot That Boiled Over: Racial Fetishism and the *Lingua Franca* of Jack Kerouac's Fiction." *MFS: Modern Fiction Studies* 49, no. 3 (2003): 524–49.

Nichols, Roger L. *Indians in the United States and Canada: A Comparative History*. Lincoln: University of Nebraska Press, 1998.

Nickerson, Catherine. *The Web of Iniquity: Early Detective Fiction by American Women*. Durham, NC: Duke University Press, 1998.

Nicosia, Gerald. *Memory Babe: A Critical Biography of Jack Kerouac*. Berkeley: University of California Press, 1983.

Niro, Shelley. "The Border: Artist's Statement." In *The Contemporary Native American Photoart of Shelley Niro*, 8–9. Hamilton, NY: Longyear Museum of Anthropology, Colgate University, 1997.

Noble, Andrea. *Tina Modotti: Image, Texture, Photography*. Albuquerque: University of New Mexico Press, 2000.

Norrell, Brenda. "Indigenous Border Summit Opposes Border Wall and Militarization." October 31, 2006. Accessed November 16, 2006 at http://americas.irc-online.org/amcit/3648.

O'Gorman, Edmundo. *The Invention of America: An Inquiry into the Historical Nature of the New World and the Meaning of Its History*. Bloomington: Indiana University Press, 1961.

Ohmae, K. *The End of the Nation State*. New York: Free Press, 1995.

Olmsted, Frederick Law. *A Journey through Texas*. New York: Burt Franklin, 1969.

Pablos, Julia Tuñón. *Women in Mexico: A Past Unveiled*. Translated by Alan Hynds. Austin: University of Texas Press, 1999.

Palmer, Colin. *Slaves of the White God*. Cambridge, MA: Harvard University Press, 1976.

Panish, Jon. "Kerouac's *The Subterraneans*: A Study of 'Romantic Primitivism.'" *MELUS* 19, no. 3 (1994): 107–23.

Papademetriou, Demetrios G., and Debora Waller Meyers. "Overview, Context, and a Vision for the Future." In *Caught in the Middle: Border Communities in an Era of Globalization*, edited by Demetrios G. Papademetriou and Debora Waller Meyers, 1–40. Washington DC: Carnegie Endowment for Peace, 2001.

Parsons, Deborah. *Streetwalking the Metropolis: Women, the City, and Modernity*. Oxford: Oxford University Press, 2000.

Pastor, Robert. "NAFTA Is Not Enough: Steps toward a North American Community." In *The Future of North American Integration: Beyond NAFTA*, edited by Peter Hakim and Robert E. Litan, 87–117. Washington, DC: Brookings Institution Press, 2002.

Patch, Robert W. "Indian Resistance to Colonialism." In *The Oxford History of Mexico*, edited by Michael Meyer and William H. Beezley, 183–212. New York and Oxford: Oxford University Press, 2000.

Paul, Ron. "A North American United Nations?" *Ron Paul's Texas Straight Talk*. August 28,

2006. Accessed November 13, 2007 at http://www.house.gov/paul/tst/tst2006/tst08 2806.htm.

Paz, Octavio. *The Other Mexico: Critique of the Pyramid*. Translated by Lysander Kemp. New York: Grove Press, 1972.

Pease, Donald E., and Robyn Wiegman. "Futures." In *The Futures of American Studies*, edited by Donald Pease and Robyn Wiegman, 1–42. Durham, NC: Duke University Press, 2002.

Perkins, Dexter. *A History of the Monroe Doctrine*. Boston: Little, Brown, 1963.

Peterson, Nancy J. "History, Postmodernism, and Louise Erdrich's *Tracks*." *PMLA* 109, no. 5 (1994): 982–94.

"Pew Hispanic Center Fact Sheet." University of Southern California, Annenberg School for Communications. Pew Hispanic Center. Accessed June 14, 2006 at http://pew hispanic.org/files/factsheets/2.pdf.

Pierce, J. Kingston. "The Cold Truth about John Farrow." *January Magazine*, August 2001. Accessed April 4, 2005 at http://www.januarymagazine.com/profiles/jfarrow.html.

Piccione, Marie-Lyne. "Au rendez-vous des doublures: *Volkswagen Blues* de Jacques Poulin." *Annales du Centre de recherches sur l'Amérique Anglophone* 21 (1996): 121–28.

Pike, Frederick B. *The United States and Latin America: Myths and Stereotypes of Civilization and Nature*. Austin: University of Texas Press, 1992.

Poniatowska, Elena. "La literatura de la Onda." In *¡Ay, vida no me mereces!* 169–213. Mexico City: Joaquín Mortiz, 1985.

———. *Tinísima*. Mexico City: Era, 1992.

Porter, Carolyn. "What We Know That We Don't Know: Remapping American Literary Studies." *American Literary History* 6 (Fall 1994): 467–526.

Porter, Dennis. *Pursuit of Crime: Art and Ideology in Crime Fiction*. New Haven, CT: Yale University Press, 1981.

Porter, Katherine Anne. "Children of Xochitl." In *Uncollected Early Prose*. Austin: University of Texas Press, 1993.

———. Introduction to *The Itching Parrot*. In *Mutual Impressions: Writers from the Americas Reading One Another*, edited by Ilan Stavans, 198–227. Durham, NC: Duke University Press, 1999.

———. "A Letter from Mexico." In *Uncollected Early Prose*, 131–35.

———. "María Concepción." In *The Collected Essays and Occasional Writings of Katherine Anne Porter*, 3–21. New York: Delacorte Press, 1970.

———. "Mexico's Thirty Long Years of Revolution." In *"This Strange, Old World" and Other Book Reviews by Katherine Anne Porter*, edited by Darlene Harbour Unrue, 121–24. Athens: University of Georgia Press, 1991.

———. "Old Gods and New Messiahs." Review of *Idols behind Altars*, by Anita Brenner, 83–88. In *"This Strange, Old World" and Other Book Reviews*.

———. *Outline of Mexican Popular Arts and Crafts*. In *Uncollected Early Prose*, 136–87.

———. "Where Presidents Have No Friends." In *The Collected Essays and Occasional Writings of Katherine Anne Porter*, 404–15.

Porter, Kenneth W. *The Black Seminoles: History of a Freedom-Seeking People*. Gainesville: University Press of Florida, 1996.

Poulin, Jacques. *Volkswagen Blues*. Translated by Sheila Fischman. Toronto: Cormorant Books, 1988.

Pratt, Mary Louise. *Imperial Eyes: Travel Writing and Transculturation*. New York: Routledge, 1992.

Priestman, Martin, ed. *Cambridge Companion to Crime Fiction*. New York and Cambridge: Cambridge University Press, 2003.

Quijano, Aníbal, and Immanuel Wallerstein. "Americanicity as a Concept, or the Americas in the Modern World-System." *International Social Science Journal* 44, no. 4 (1992): 549–57.

Radway, Janice. "What's in a Name?" *American Quarterly* 51, no. 1 (1999): 1–32.

Ramirez, Bruno. "Borderland Studies and Migration: The Canada/United States Case." In *Repositioning North American Migration History: New Directions in Modern Continental Migration, Citizenship, and Community*, edited by Marc S. Rodriguez, 16–26. Rochester, NY: University of Rochester Press, 2004.

Reed, Ishmael. *Flight to Canada*. New York: Atheneum, 1989.

Rexroth, Kenneth. *An Autobiographical Novel*. Edited by Linda Hamalian. New York: New Directions, 1991.

Ricketts, Shannon. "Canadian Terminals on the Underground Railroad." *Heritage* (Spring 2000): 21–23.

———. "Commemorating the Underground Railroad in Canada." *CRM* 5 (1999): 33–34.

Rodríguez, Jaime. "La Antigua Provincia de Guayaquil en la época de la Independencia." In *Revolución, Independencia y la nuevas naciones de América*, edited by Jaime E. Rodríguez O., 511–56. Madrid: Fundación Mapfre-Tavera, 2005.

———. "Ciudadanos de la Nación Española: Los indígenas y las elecciones constitucionales en el Reino de Quito." In *La mirada esquiva: Reflexiones históricas sobre la interacción del Estado y la ciudadanía en los Andes*, edited by Marta Irurozqui. Madrid: Consejo Superior de Investigaciones Científicas, 2005.

———. "The Emancipation of America." *American Historical Review* 105, no. 1 (2000): 131–53.

Rodríguez, Ralph. *Brown Gumshoes: Detective Fiction and the Search for Chicano/a Identity*. Austin: University of Texas Press, 2005.

Romero, Channette. "Envisioning a 'Network of Tribal Coalitions': Leslie Marmon Silko's *Almanac of the Dead*." *American Indian Quarterly* 26, no. 4 (2002): 623–40.

Romero, Laura. "Vanishing Americans: Gender, Empire, and New Historicism." In *American Literary Studies: A Methodological Reader*, edited by Michael A. Elliott and Claudia Stokes, 41–62. New York: New York University Press, 2003.

Roosevelt, Franklin D. "First Inaugural Address." March 4, 1933. Accessed July 9, 2007 at http://www.feri.org/common/news/details.cfm?QID=2067&clientid=11005.

Rowe, John Carlos. "Nineteenth-Century U.S. Literary Culture and Transnationality," *PMLA* 188, no. 1 (2003): 78–89.

Rowe, John Carlos, ed. *Post-Nationalist American Studies*. Berkeley: University of California Press, 2000.

Rowell, Charles H. "An Interview with Gayl Jones." *Callaloo* 16 (1982): 32–53.

Rushdy, Ashraf. *Neo-Slave Narratives: Studies in the Social Logic of a Literary Form*. New York: Oxford University Press, 1999.

Ryan, David. *U.S. Foreign Policy in World History*. New York and London: Routledge, 2000.

Sadowski-Smith, Claudia. *Border Fictions: Empire, Globalization, and Writing at the Borders of the United States*. Charlottesville: University of Virginia Press, 2008.

Sadowski-Smith, Claudia, ed. *Globalization on the Line: Culture, Capital, and Citizenship at U.S. Borders*. New York: Palgrave, 2002.

Sailer, Steve. "Where Did Mexico's Missing Blacks Go?" UPI, May 8, 2002. Accessed at

Steve Sailer's iSteve Blog, October 29, 2007, at http://www.isteve.com/2002_Where _Did_Mexicos_Blacks_Go.htm.

Saldívar, José David. *Border Matters: Remapping American Cultural Studies*. Berkeley: University of California Press, 1997.

Saldívar-Hull, Sonia. *Feminism on the Border: Chicana Gender Politics and Literature*. Berkeley: University of California Press, 2000.

Sánchez de Anda, Guillermo. *Yanga: Un guerrero negro*. Mexico City: Círculo Cuadrado, 1998.

Sandison, David. *Jack Kerouac: An Illustrated Biography*. Chicago: Chicago Review Press, 1999.

Sayles, John. *Men with Guns & Lone Star*. London: Faber and Faber, 1998.

Schendel, Willem van, and Itty Abraham, eds. *Illicit Flows and Criminal Things: States, Borders, and the Other Side of Globalization*. Bloomington: Indiana University Press, 2005.

Schlafly, Phyllis. "Scholars Explain Bush's SPP." *Eagle Forum*, October 10, 2007. Accessed November 13, 2007 at http://www.eagleforum.org/column/2007/oct07/07-10-10 .html.

Scholte, Jan Aart. *Globalization: A Critical Introduction*. New York: St. Martin's Press, 2000.

Schuler, Friedrich E. "Mexico and the Outside World." In *The Oxford History of Mexico*, edited by Michael Meyer and William H. Beezley, 503–42. New York and Oxford: Oxford University Press, 2000.

Schwartz, Richard B. *Nice and Noir: Contemporary American Crime Fiction*. Columbia: University of Missouri Press, 2002.

Schwartz, Rosalie. *Across the Rio to Freedom: U.S. Negroes in Mexico*. El Paso: Texas Western Press, 1975.

Seed, Patricia. *American Pentimento: The Invention of Indians and the Pursuit of Riches*. Minneapolis: University of Minnesota Press, 2001.

Shadd, Mary Ann. "A Plea for Emigration, or Notes of Canada West" (1852). In *Pamphlets of Protest: An Anthology of Early African-American Protest Literature, 1790–1860*, edited by Richard Newman, Patrick Rael, and Philip Lapsansky, 199–213. New York: Routledge, 2001.

Sheldon, Glenn. *South of Our Selves: Mexico in the Poems of Williams, Kerouac, Corso, Ginsberg, Levertov, and Hayden*. Jefferson, NC: McFarland, 2004.

Silko, Leslie Marmon. *Almanac of the Dead*. New York: Penguin, 1991.

———. "The Border Patrol State." In *Yellow Woman and a Beauty of the Spirit*, 115–23. New York: Simon and Schuster, 1996.

———. *Gardens in the Dunes*. New York, Simon and Schuster, 1999.

Silverman, Jason H. *Unwelcome Guests: Canada West's Response to American Fugitive Slaves, 1800–1865*. Millwood, NY: Associated Faculty Press, 1985.

Singh, Amritjit, and Peter Schmidt. "On the Borders between U.S. Studies and Postcolonial Theory." In *Postcolonial Theory and the United States: Race, Ethnicity, and Literature*, edited by Amritjit Singh and Peter Schmidt, 3–69. Jackson: University Press of Mississippi, 2000.

Skene-Melvin, David. *Canadian Crime Fiction*. Shelburne, ON: Battered Silicon Dispatch Box, 1996.

Smith, Henry Nash. *Virgin Land: The American West as Symbol and Myth*. Cambridge, MA: Harvard University Press, 1978.

Sorrell, Richard S. "Novelists and Ethnicity: Jack Kerouac and Grace Metalious as Franco-Americans." *MELUS* 9, no. 1 (1982): 37–52.

Soto, Shirlene. *The Emergence of the Modern Mexican Woman: Her Participation in Revolution and Struggle for Equality, 1910–1940.* Denver: Arden Press, 1990.

Squier, Susan Merril. *Virginia Woolf and London: The Sexual Politics of the City.* Chapel Hill: University of North Carolina Press, 1985.

Staley, Eugene. "The Myth of the Continents." *Foreign Affairs* 19, no. 3 (1941): 481–94.

Stanislawksi, Bartosz H. "Transnational 'Bads' in the Globalized World: The Case of Transnational Organized Crime." *Public Integrity* 6, no. 2 (2004): 155–70.

Stansell, Christine. *American Moderns: Bohemian New York and the Creation of a New Century.* New York: Henry Holt, 2000.

Stavans, Ilan. *Antiheroes: Mexico and Its Detective Novel.* Translated by Jesse H. Lytle and Jennifer A. Mattson. Madison, NJ: Fairleigh Dickinson University Press, 1997.

Steele, Cynthia. *Politics, Gender, and the Mexican Novel, 1968–1988: Beyond the Pyramid.* Austin: University of Texas Press, 1992.

Sterling, Dorothy. *The Making of an Afro-American: Martin Robison Delany.* New York: Da Capo Press, 1996.

Stowe, Harriet Beecher. *Uncle Tom's Cabin.* New York: Signet, 1981.

Strickland, Barbara. "Rolando Hinojosa-Smith: Crossing Literary Borders." *Austin Chronicle,* August 29, 1997. Accessed December 13, 2007 at http://www.austinchronicle.com/gyrobase/Issue/story?oid=oid%3A529498.

Taibo, Paco Ignacio, II. *An Easy Thing.* Translated by William I. Neuman. Scottsdale, AZ: Poisoned Pen Press, 2002.

———. *Frontera Dreams.* Translated by Bill Verner. El Paso, TX: Cinco Puntos Press, 2002.

———. "Morán y Pancho." In *El juego de la intriga,* edited by Martín Casariego, 185–223. Madrid: Espasa Calpe, 1997.

———. *Return to the Same City.* Translated by Laura Dail. New York: Mysterious Press, 1996.

Taibo, Paco Ignacio, II, and Subcomandante Marcos. *The Uncomfortable Dead (What's Missing Is Missing).* Translated by Carlos Lopez. New York: Akashic Books, 2006.

Taliman, Valerie. "Borders and Native Peoples: Divided, but Not Conquered." *Native Americas* 18, no. 1 (2001): 10.

———. "NAFTA May Clip Native Treaty Rights." *Indian Country* 13, no. 17 (1993): A1.

———. "NAFTA Threatens Native Sovereignty and Threatens Indigenous Economies." *The Circle* 13, no. 1 (1999).

Taylor, Diana. *The Archive and the Repertoire: Performing Cultural Memory in the Americas.* Durham, NC: Duke University Press, 2003.

———. *Disappearing Acts: Spectacles of Gender and Nationalism in Argentina's "Dirty War."* Durham, NC: Duke University Press, 1997.

Taylor, Quintard. *In Search of the Racial Frontier: African Americans in the American West, 1528–1990.* New York: Norton, 1998.

Thacker, Andrew. *Moving through Modernity: Space and Geography in Modernism.* Manchester: Manchester University Press, 2003.

Theado, Matt. *Understanding Jack Kerouac.* Columbia: University of South Carolina Press, 2000.

Thompson, John Herd, and Stephen J. Randall. *Canada and the United States: Ambivalent Allies.* Athens: University of Georgia Press, 2002.

Todd, Jack. *Desertion in the Time of Vietnam.* New York: Houghton Mifflin, 2001.

Traister, Bryce. "Risking Nationalism: NAFTA and the Limits of the New American Studies." *Canadian Review of American Studies/Revue canadienne d'ètudes américaines* 27, no. 3 (1997): 191–204.

Truett, Samuel, and Elliott Young. "Making Transnational History: Nations, Regions, and Borderlands." In *Continental Crossroads: Remapping U.S.-Mexico Borderlands History*, edited by Samuel Truett and Elliott Young, 1–32. Durham, NC: Duke University Press, 2004.

Tuckman, Jo. "Subcomandante Marcos Pens New Twist to Zapatista Struggle." *The Guardian*, December 20, 2004, 11.

Turner, Steve. *Jack Kerouac: Angelheaded Hipster*. New York: Viking, 1996.

Tyler, Ronnie C. "Fugitive Slaves in Mexico." *Journal of Negro History* 57, no. 1 (1972): 1–12.

Tyler, Ronnie, and Laurence R. Murphy. *Slave Narratives of Texas*. Austin: Encino Press, 1974.

Vaughn, Bobby. "Afro-Mexico: Blacks, Indígenas, Politics, and the Greater Diaspora." In *Neither Enemies nor Friends: Latinos, Blacks, Afro-Latinos*, edited by Anani Dzidzienyo and Suzanne Oboler, 117–36. New York: Palgrave, 2005.

———. "Blacks in Mexico: A Brief Overview." Mexico Connect. Accessed February 5, 2007 at http://www.mexconnect.com/mex_/feature/ethnic/bv/brief.htm.

———. "Mexico in the Context of the Transatlantic Slave Trade." *Diálogo* 5 (2001): 1–11.

Vaughn, Bobby, and Ben Vinson III. *Afro-Mexico: El pulso de la población negra en México*. Mexico City: Fonda de Cultura Economica, 2004.

Vázquez, Josefina Zoraida, and Lorenzo Meyer. *The United States and Mexico*. Chicago: University of Chicago Press, 1985.

Venuti, Lawrence. *Scandals of Translation: Toward an Ethics of Difference*. New York: Routledge, 1998.

Verdecchia, Guillermo. *Fronteras Americanas/American Borders*. Toronto: Coach House Press, 1993.

Viotti, Paul R. *International Relations and World Politics: Security, Economy, Identity*. Upper Saddle River, NJ: Prentice Hall, 2001.

Vinson, Ben. *Bearing Arms for His Majesty: The Free-Colored Militia in Colonial Mexico*. Palo Alto, CA: Stanford University Press, 2001.

Walcott, Rinaldo. *Black Like Who? Writing Black Canada*. Toronto: Insomniac Press, 2003.

Walker, Alice. *By the Light of My Father's Smile*. New York: Random House, 1998.

Walker, Brenda. "Mexicans Have Plans for the American Southwest: They Vow to Take It Over." Limits to Growth, June 5, 2006. At http://www.limitstogrowth.org/WEB-text/aztlan.html.

Walker, William O., ed. *Drugs in the Western Hemisphere: An Odyssey of Cultures in Conflict*. Wilmington, DE: Scholarly Resources, 1996.

Walsh, Thomas. *Katherine Anne Porter and Mexico: The Illusion of Eden*. Austin: University of Texas Press, 1992.

Walton, Priscilla L. "Murder Ink: Detective Fiction in Canada." In *Pop Can: Popular Culture in Canada*, edited by Lynne Van Luven and Priscilla L. Walton, 50–55. Scarborough, ON: Prentice Hall Allyn and Bacon Canada, 1999.

Walton, Priscilla, and Manina Jones, eds. *Detective Agency: Women Rewriting the Hard-Boiled Tradition*. Berkeley: University of California Press, 1999.

Warhus, Mark. *Another America: Native American Maps and the History of Our Land*. New York: St. Martin's Press, 1997.

Warrior, Robert. *Tribal Secrets: Recovering American Indian Intellectual Traditions*. Minneapolis: University of Minnesota Press, 1995.

Waters, Malcolm. *Globalization*. London: Routledge, 1995.

Weaver, Jace. *That the People Might Live: Native American Literatures and Native American Community*. New York: Oxford University Press, 1997.

Weaver, Jace, Craig Womack, and Robert Warrior, eds. *American Indian Literary Nationalism*. Albuquerque: University of New Mexico Press, 2006.

Weiss, Jonathan. "Une lecture américaine de *Volkswagen Blues*." *Etudes françaises* 21, no. 3 (1985): 89–96.

———. "Victor-Lèvy Beaulieu: Écrivain américain." *Etudes françaises* 19, no. 1 (1983): 41–57.

Weston, Edward. *The Daybooks of Edward Weston*, vol. 1. Edited by Nancy Newhall. Millerton, NY: Aperture, 1973.

Wetzsteon, Ross. *Republic of Dreams: Greenwich Village, The American Bohemia, 1910–1960*. New York: Simon and Schuster, 2001.

Whitaker, Arthur P. *The Western Hemisphere Idea: Its Rise and Decline*. Ithaca, NY: Cornell University Press, 1954.

Wilkinson, Charles. *Blood Struggle: The Rise of Modern Indian Nations*. New York: W. W. Norton, 2005.

Williams, Phil, and Dimitri Vlassis, eds. *Combating Transnational Crime: Concepts, Activities, and Responses*. London and Portland, OR: Frank Cass, 2001.

Winegarten, Ruthe. *Black Texas Women: 150 Years of Trial and Triumph*. Austin: University of Texas Press, 1995.

Winks, Robin. *The Blacks in Canada: A History*. Montreal and Kingston: McGill-Queen's University Press, 1997.

Wollen, Peter. *Raiding the Icebox: Reflections on Twentieth-Century Culture*. New York and London: Verso, 1993.

Womack, Craig S. *Red on Red: Native American Literary Separatism*. Minneapolis: University of Minnesota Press, 1999.

Woods, Richard D. "Anita Brenner: Cultural Mediator for Mexico." *Studies in Latin American Popular Culture* 9 (1990): 209–22.

Wright, Thomas C. *State Terrorism in Latin America: Chile, Argentina, and International Human Rights*. New York: Rowman and Littlefield, 2007.

Wright, Thomas C., and Rody Oñate. *Flight from Chile: Voices of Exile*. Albuquerque: University of New Mexico Press, 1998.

Youssef, Marcus, and Guillermo Verdecchia. *A Line in the Sand*. Vancouver: Talonbooks, 1997.

Zepeda, Ofelia. "Autobiography." In *Here First: Autobiographical Essays by Native American Writers*, edited by Arnold Krupat and Brian Swann, 405–20. New York: Modern Library, 2000.

Zerubavel, Eviatar. *Terra Cognita: The Mental Discovery of America*. New Brunswick, NJ: Rutgers University Press, 1992.

Zolov, Eric. *Refried Elvis: The Rise of the Mexican Counterculture*. Berkeley: University of California Press, 1999.

INDEX

of the valley and other works) (Hino-
josa), 202
Euro-American modernism, 103
Europe, 8–9, 13–14, 64
European Union (EU), 9, 14, 16
Evans, Rosalie, 122

Farías, Valentin Gómez, 70–71
Farrow, John, 21, 27, 192, 193–99, 215–
16; and *City of Ice*, 193, 196; detective
novels, Canadianicity of, 195; and *Ice
Lake*, 193, 195–97; ratiocinative mode
of, 193; Sherlock Holmes, as succes-
sor to, 193–94; themes of, 198. *See also*
Trevor Ferguson
Faulkner, William, 202
"Fences against Freedom" (Silko), 51
Ferguson, Trevor, 194. *See also* John Farrow
Ferlinghetti, Lawrence, 158, 175
Fernández de Lizardi, José Joaquín: and
El periquillo sarmiento (The itchy par-
rot), 114
Ferron, Jacques, 168
The Fire Line (Ferguson), 194
First Nations, 42
Flight to Canada (Reed), 66, 77
Florida, 61, 71
Ford Motor Company, 178
Forma (magazine), 138
Foster, Frances Smith, 73
Fouché, Luis N., 71
French Canada: and slavery, 68
Fox, Vicente, 53
France, 174
Franco, Jean, 104
Franklin, John Hope, 74
Fronteras Americanas/American Borders (Ver-
decchia), 27, 220–23, 226–32, 234; au-
dience of, 226; Canada, Latinization
of in, 241; Canadianness, challenges to,
226; as collaboration, 229–30; collec-
tive experience, commitment to, 225,
227; as intensely Canadian, 227; as per-
formative, 228; themes in, 238
Front de liberation du Québec (FLQ), 167
Frontera Dreams (Sueños de frontera)
(Taibo), 214
Fuentes, Carlos, 91, 180, 226–27
Fugitive Slave Act, 22, 64–65, 68

fugitive slaves, 61–63, 95, 243; and black
diaspora, 64; in Canada, 65

Gadsden Purchase, 37
Gale, Linn, 108
Gamio, Miguel, 108, 123
García Canclini, Néstor, 183
García Márquez, Gabriel, 91, 202
Gardens in the Dunes (Silko), 257n42
Garnhum, Ken, 226
Garreau, Joel: and *The Nine Nations of
North America*, 1, 3
Gates, Henry Louis Jr., 81
General Motors (GM), 178
Genius of Universal Emancipation (periodi-
cal), 71
genre literature, 26, 216
Georgia, 73
Gibbens, Roger, 21, 222
Gil, Portes, 146
Gila River tribe, 36
Gilroy, Paul: Black Atlantic, concept of,
64, 68
Ginsberg, Allen, 158, 169, 175; and *Yage
Letters*, 170
Glantz, Margo, 269n84
Glissant, Edouard, 18
globalization, 7, 13, 195–96; and
clandestine-transnational actors (CTAs),
190; and nation-state, 23
Glusker, Susannah, 110, 124
Godbout, Jacques, 172
Goitia, Juan Benet, 126
Goldberg, Ella, 124
"The Golden Horseshoe" (Hammett), 199
Gomez, Alberto, 224
Gomez-Peña, Guillermo, 225
Gonzales, Jovita, 18
Good Neighbor Policy, 12
Great Britain, 38; rock music in, 270n106
Green, Mary Jean, 172
Greenblatt, Stephen, 249n3
Greenwich Village, 110; as symbolic geog-
raphy, 184
A Gringo in Mañanaland (Forester), 122
Gruening, Ernest, 108
Guatemala, 33, 51, 223; Mexico, border
with, 48, 50, 53, 57, 239; Venceremos
program of, 53